3rd National Edition

 # TRADEMARK

Legal Care for Your

Business & Product Name

By Attorneys Kate McGrath & Stephen Elias

NOLO PRESS BERKELEY WITHDRAWN

Your Responsibility When Using a Self-Help Law Book

We've done our best to give you useful and accurate information in this book. But laws and procedures change frequently and are subject to differing interpretations. If you want legal advice backed by a guarantee, see a lawyer. If you use this book, it's your responsibility to make sure that the facts and general advice contained in it are applicable to your situation.

Keeping Up-to-Date

To keep its books up to date, Nolo Press issues new printings and new editions periodically. New printings reflect minor legal changes and technical corrections. New editions contain major legal changes, major text additions or major reorganizations. To find out if a later printing or edition of any Nolo book is available, call Nolo Press at 510-549-1976 or check the catalog in the *Nolo News,* our quarterly newspaper. You can also contact us on the Internet at www.nolo.com.

To stay current, follow the "Update" service in the *Nolo News.* You can get a free one-year subscription by sending us the registration card in the back of the book. In another effort to help you use Nolo's latest materials, we offer a 25% discount off the purchase of the new edition your Nolo book when you turn in the cover of an earlier edition. (See the "Special Upgrade Offer" in the back of the book.) This book was last revised in December 1997.

Third Edition	DECEMBER 1997
Editors	RALPH WARNER & PATRICIA GIMA
Cover Design	SUSAN WIGHT
Book Design	TERRI HEARSH
Illustrations for Examples	JOHN MILLER & HEATHER SNYDER
Production	SARAH TOLL
Index	PATRICIA DEMINNA
Proofreading	ROBERT WELLS
Printing	BERTELSMANN INDUSTRY SERVICES, INC.

McGrath, Kate, 1952-
    Trademark : legal care for your business & product name / by Kate McGrath & Stephen Elias. — 3rd ed.
      p.   cm.
    Includes index.
    ISBN 0-87337-396-0
    1. Trademarks—Law and legislation—United States—Popular works.
    2. Business names—United States—Popular works. I. Elias, Stephen. II. Title.
    KF3180.Z9M28 1997
    346.7304'88—DC21   97-28859
                                                  CIP

Quantity sales: For information on bulk purchases or corporate premium sales, please contact the Special Sales department. For academic sales or textbook adoptions, ask for Academic Sales. 800-955-4775, Nolo Press, Inc., 950 Parker St., Berkeley, CA, 94710.

Dedications

Kate McGrath

First, I thank my family for their support and forbearance: my husband, Mike, and daughters, Elena and Alice, who at 8 and 6 have become surprisingly adept at understanding trademarks.

Steve Elias

I dedicate this book to Edna Elias-Johnson and to Stanley and Dorothy Pearson. They don't make 'em like they used to.

Acknowledgments

The authors extend their profound thanks and appreciation to:

Nolo publisher Jake Warner, for the incisive intelligence that he brought to the book as its first editor and Patricia Gima for her fine work on this Third Edition.

Sarah Shena, the predominant author of the chapter on registering trademarks with the PTO;

Terri Hearsh (Second Edition) and Eddie Warner (First Edition), for their dedication to excellence in designing the book's layout and graphics;

Richard Stim, Leslie Norwood and Andrew Bridges (of Wilson Sonsini Goodrich & Rosati in Palo Alto, CA), all of whom made important substantive contributions to the Second Edition;

Patricia Gima for her incisive feedback on how the book works in the real world;

Scott S. Havlick of Holland & Hart in Denver who generously shared his time and expertise and gave encouragement at a time when the book seemed interminable;

R. Lee Hagelshaw of San Francisco, who was kind enough to read and comment on some drafts;

John Miller and Heather Snyder of SignDesign in Montepelier, Vermont, for creatively bringing to life many of the trademarks and service marks we used to illustrate our remarks throughout the book;

The many small business owners in the Bay Area who shared their trademark stories, many of which appear in this book in one form or another;

Susan Wight for the stunning cover;

Ted Beatty, a California entrepreneur who graciously read and commented on the manuscript; and

The entire Nolo staff (especially the production department), a wonderfully uncompromising group that manages to be both perfectionistic and a nice bunch of people (some of whom are even recovering lawyers).

Table of Contents

2 How to Choose a Good Name for Your Business, Product or Service

3 Protecting and Registering Trade Names

4 How to Tell If Two Marks Are Confusingly Similar

5 Preparing for a Trademark Search

6 How to Do a Trademark Search

7 State Trademark Registration

8 Federal Trademark Registration

9 How to Use and Care for Your Mark

10 Evaluating Trademark Strength

11 Sorting Out Trademark Disputes

12 If Someone Infringes Your Mark

13 If Someone Claims That You Infringed Their Trademark

14 International Trademark Protection

15 Help Beyond the Book

Appendix

Index

Important new information on trademark may be obtained from the update section of Nolo's Web site (http://www.nolo.com/). Updates include federal trademark dilution, Internet domain name registrations, registration of European Community marks and informative sites on the World Wide Web.

Introduction

How to Use This Book

What's in a name? To Shakespeare, "a rose by any other name would smell as sweet." But what is true in love can be the opposite in business. *IBM* would not smell half so sweet by another name, nor would *Xerox, Apple Computer, McDonald's* or *Levi-Strauss*. In the business world, the name of a successful product or service contributes greatly to its real worth. Every day, names such as *Allendale Auto Parts* or *Building Blocks Day Care* identify these businesses for their customers, help customers find them and (assuming they provide a good product or service) keep the customers coming back, again and again and again.

And it's not just a clever business or product name that pulls in the customers. Equally important in the vast U.S. consumer marketplace are the logos, packaging, innovative product shapes, cartoon characters, and unique product characteristics (such as the deep rumbling sound of a motorcycle and the smell of an upscale perfume) that businesses are using to hawk their wares. Even the look and feel of a business's site on the Internet—widely known as a Web page—is increasingly becoming important as a means for a business to identify itself and its products in the marketplace.

A. What Are Trademarks?

All of these devices—business and product names, logos, sounds, shapes, smells, colors, packaging—carry one simple message to potential customers—buy me because I come from XYZ Company. To the extent that they are clever enough to distinguish their underlying products and services from those offered by competitors, all of these devices qualify as trademarks. If small business owners were to understand only one point in this book, it is this: The instant a business name is used on a sign, in advertising or in any other way intended to reach out to potential customers, it falls under the spell of trademark law. This of course means that few business owners can afford to disregard what this body of law is and how they can avoid running afoul of it.

B. What Is Trademark Law and Why Do I Need to Know About It?

If every business used a unique name or other mark to identify itself, its products and its services in the marketplace, there would be precious little to write about in this book. In fact, once customers come to associate a name or other type of mark with a particular business or product, would-be competitors frequently copy some or all aspects of the mark—its sound, its appearance, its meaning—in an effort to lure customers away from the original business. Then too, because millions of new businesses get started every year, it is surprisingly easy to pick a new business name, logo or other type of trademark that conflicts in some way with a mark already in use somewhere in this large country of ours.

For these and other reasons, the U.S. marketplace is rife with trademark conflicts. It is the job of trademark law to sort out these conflicts in an equitable and consistent manner. It is this book's job to introduce you, the reader, to how trademark law works so that you will know how to avoid legal trouble when deciding how to identify your business and products in the marketplace, and what to do if despite your best efforts you end up in a trademark conflict anyway.

C. What Are the Basic Principles of Trademark Law?

The basic principles of trademark law are explained in Chapter 1, but a plain English preview here in the introduction might be of interest to many readers. For most purposes, trademark law can be boiled down to these points:

- The first business to actually use a trademark owns it.
- To qualify as a trademark, a name, logo or other device used by a business in its marketing activities must either be unique enough by itself to earn customer recognition or earn customer recognition over time because of its use.
- A trademark owner can sue in federal court to stop another business from using the same or similar trademark if the mark is famous or the use by the other business

would cause potential customers to confuse one business or product with another.

- The more unique or clever a trademark is, the easier it is for its owner to get the court to stop its use by others.
- The usual court remedy in trademark disputes is to order the loser to stop further use of the trademark in question. This can be painful since business good will often is intimately connected with the business name or logo, and expensive because all of the items that carry the mark will have to be destroyed.
- If the court finds that you deliberately used a famous or distinctive mark belonging to another business, you can be ordered to pay large money damages to that business.

This book helps you understand these principles in the contexts you will need them—when you are choosing a trademark and when (or if) you run into conflict with another trademark owner.

D. What Else Do I Need to Know About Trademark Law?

Ideally, just knowing these principles should be enough to answer all your questions and get you started on the road to choosing a clever name for your business or product. Not so fast. The phrases "customer confusion" and "famous mark" need some definition. Unfortunately, Congress has avoided hard definitions and instead opted to let judges decide, on a case by case basis, whether a particular mark is famous or risks confusion with an existing mark. Although we provide some guidelines for you to use when you are faced with interpreting these terms, the rock bottom rules for dealing safely with the ambiguities in trademark law are these:

- Don't choose a business or product name that is the same as that used nationally by a large company. Even if you're in the right on some abstract level, the big company will most likely try to legally terrorize you into dropping the mark.

- Don't choose a trademark that is—in appearance, sound or meaning—the same as a federally registered mark unless the registered mark is definitely used for a product or service that is very different from the ones offered by your business. (We introduce you to federal registration in Chapter 1, Section C6.)
- Don't try to piggyback your marketing efforts on a trademark belonging to another business. For example, don't call your new Web design service Jetscape.

These rules are pretty easy to understand. A fourth rule is not: Stay away from existing marks that resemble yours if there's a likelihood that customers would be confused by use of the two marks. Chapter 1 introduces you to this rule and Chapter 2 helps you apply it when choosing a name or mark for your business or product.

If any of these rules get in your way (you've got a hot name for your business and you want to run with it), a trademark lawyer can help you decide whether your situation is an exception to these rules and what you risk by going ahead with your proposed mark (see Section J below and Chapter 15 for how to find a trademark lawyer).

E. Do Small Startup Businesses Really Have to Deal With All This Trademark Stuff?

Quite possibly. Until several years ago, a local business could reasonably expect its marketing activities to be limited to a neighborhood, town, city, county or even one state. As long as its name (usually its only trademark) didn't conflict with any in use by other local businesses, there was

little likelihood of customer confusion and therefore of any legal conflict. While problems could arise from using a famous mark, there was no federal law on the subject, and state laws protecting famous marks were rarely enforced. So, as long as you checked the Yellow Pages and were able to get your proposed business name registered locally or with your Secretary of State, there was not much else to worry about.

Today, the very concept of local is beginning to disappear for many types of businesses. The most important force for this change is that part of the Internet known as the World Wide Web. For a very low price, any business can establish what's known as a "Web page," which not only allows the business to advertise its goods or services, but also, in many cases, to demonstrate and sell them. Some 600,000 separate commercial Web pages have already been created, and chances are you will no more want to be absent from the World Wide Web than you would from the Yellow Pages.

When you create a Web page, you are entering a realm that is in one stroke local, national and international. Not only can your local customers search you out, but anyone anywhere in the U.S. or the world who has an Internet connection and adequate computer resources can find you as well. Although a number of businesses will never be delivering their primary services outside of their local communities—massage, auto mechanics, construction and hairdressing come to mind—many other businesses will happily take the opportunity to offer their goods or services to anyone willing to pay for them—whether through e-mail (information services), mail order (for tangible products) or both.

Simply doing business on the Web is likely to increase the scope of your business from local to national. You will have to pay attention to how your name or other trademarks fit within the vast sea of trademarks that is the U.S. marketplace. And, as we point out in Chapter 14, you will also have to start paying attention to what businesses call themselves and their products in other parts of the world.

One final note. Even if you think that your business will be too local for you to worry about trademarks, it may succeed beyond your wildest dreams (many of today's most successful entrepreneurs started very small). If that happens, you will surely wish your name was really yours to market on a statewide or even national basis. In short, it makes sense to carefully choose and protect your name so that it is yours to use in any and all contexts.

F. I'm in the Process of Choosing a Name for My New Business. What Parts of the Book Do I Need to Read?

Every reader in this group, whether you do business as a corporation, partnership, or sole proprietor, should read Chapters 1 and 2. In addition, Chapters 3 through 9 take you step-by-step through the process of obtaining maximum protection for your business names and avoiding disputes over them. This process includes:

- clearing your name for use on the Internet as a domain name (the address where people will find your Web page)
- placing your name on a local assumed business name list (or on your state's corporate name list if you incorporate)
- searching to see if others are already using the name as a trademark
- registering the name with the U.S. Patent and Trademark Office, and
- taking follow-up steps necessary to keep your protection fully intact.

Not all readers will use every chapter. Some readers will not be interested in the Internet. Others will see no point in applying for federal registration because their proposed name is so ordinary. Still others will decide that they can forego a trademark search. These readers will not, therefore, need to read the chapters dealing with those subjects.

Not surprisingly, small local service businesses with ordinary names need less protection than do national or regional businesses that have highly clever names. Chapter 1 helps you sort these things out. And each succeeding chapter begins by letting you know whether protecting your business name requires you to study that chapter or skip to the next.

G. I Am Involved With a Dispute Over My Business Name or Other Trademark. What Parts of the Book Should I Read?

After reading Chapter 1 to get a good understanding of trademark law principles, readers in this group may wish to skip Chapters 2 through 9 and go directly to the chapters that address your specific issue. These will usually be:

Chapter 10   Evaluating Trademark Strength
Chapter 11   Sorting Out Trademark Disputes
Chapter 12   If Someone Infringes Your Mark
Chapter 13   If Someone Claims That You Infringed Their Trademark

These chapters will give you a pretty good idea of where you stand legally in a trademark dispute and suggest some strategies for further action. Perhaps surprisingly, even here we strongly favor strategies that you can carry out yourself rather than sending you to a lawyer. The reason for this preference is simple: Very few small business trademarks are worth the expense of litigation, the one option that definitely requires a lawyer.

H. I Have Many Different Types of Questions About Trademarks. How Should I Use This Book?

Some of you will have questions about specific trademark-related issues and you will want to use this book as a reference text. For instance, you may own a federally registered mark and simply want information on how to renew it. (It's in Chapter 9, How to Use and Care for Your Mark.) Or you may want to know what the effect of your corporate name registration is on an out-of-state corporation with the same name. (You'll find the information in Chapter 3, Protecting and Registering Trade Names.) Directly following this introduction we've include a list of 20 Frequently Asked Questions (and answers with references to further discussions in the book). If your question isn't addressed there, consult the book's table of contents and index.

I. What This Book Doesn't Cover

While this book covers the range of trademark issues that may affect a small business owner, some issues are beyond the scope of the book. Thus, we do not tell you how to sue or defend a federal or state court lawsuit for trademark infringement or unfair competition without a lawyer. To do this we could easily fill three volumes. Nor, for this same reason, do we tell you how to:

- register your mark internationally, although we give you some background on the subject in Chapter 14
- handle a case brought in the U.S. Patent and Trademark Office to sort out conflicts between pending applications, oppose the registration of a trademark or cancel a registration that has already occurred, or
- accomplish and record transfers or assignments of trademarks or business names.

To help you get a handle on these and other issues that we don't cover, Chapter 15, Help Beyond the Book, describes several excellent additional resources that are available on the Internet or in a law library, and also suggests some ways to find a good trademark lawyer if you want to pay for professional advice or need legal representation. (See Section J below.)

J. Can I Handle My Own Trademark Work Without a Lawyer?

This question has no definitive answer. Certainly it is possible and customary to choose a business name, logo or other identifier without a lawyer's guidance. Registering business and corporate names is also typically done without lawyers. And trademark searches are most frequently conducted by nonlawyer specialists. But in a number of other situations, a lawyer may be just the ticket, either as a consultant or as your representative. Certainly what you read in this book will help you better take advantage of the lawyer's assistance. In Chapter 15, we tell you how to find a trademark lawyer. Here are some situations where a lawyer's advice may well be worth the price:

1. Deciding Whether the Use of a Proposed Mark Will Get You in Trouble Because of an Existing Mark

Where trademark lawyers typically are brought into the name selection process is when a trademark search discloses the existence of the same or similar mark. The question, then, becomes whether use of the proposed mark will legally run afoul of the owner's rights in the existing mark— possibly leading to an expensive lawsuit and loss of the right to use the proposed mark as well as money damages.

Evaluating whether one mark legally steps on (infringes) another mark is not a science; it is an informed guessing game, an educated stab at how consumers will react to somewhat similar names, and how a judge in the future will rule on the issue. Although this book offers some sound guidelines for dealing with this question, it offers no guarantees. This is because infringement is decided on a case by case basis and clear-cut rules cannot be stated.

For this reason, you may be better off getting a more definite opinion about your situation from a trademark lawyer—who is steeped in the many hundreds of trademark cases decided by our courts each year and who may be better able to fit the whole of trademark law to your precise situation. Still, in the end, the lawyer also will be unable to predict with certainty what would happen in court if a dispute arose.

There is another good reason to consult a lawyer when choosing a mark that might possibly infringe an existing mark. If the lawyer advises you to go ahead, you can later use that advice as a defense if you are accused of deliberately trying to copy the existing mark, which can produce a judgment for money damages if proven. On the other hand, because the lawyer can't say for sure how a judge would rule in the case, lawyers tend to be conservative and may recommend against using a mark which in fact does not place you in much risk of an infringement suit. Since few people are comfortable in disregarding a lawyer's advice, the visit to the lawyer may do you more harm than good. The choice, such as it is, is yours to make.

2. Problematic Federal Trademark Registrations

Thousands of businesses handle their own trademark registrations every year—without incident. The personnel in the Trademark Division of the U.S. Patent and Trademark Office (PTO) are usually quite friendly and willing to help you through the process. There are few traps for the unwary, and in routine cases there is no need for help from a lawyer.

However, not all cases are routine. There may be a dispute over whether your proposed mark qualifies for placement on the Principal Register. Or you may be asked to limit your registration to certain categories. Or you may simply experience one of the many glitches that can arise in any administrative system. If the routine turns into the troublesome, you should definitely consider consulting a trademark lawyer. But beware. Often, pursuing the troublesome is more expensive than what is actually at stake.

If in the course of your registration, the owner of another trademark challenges your right to register the mark, you will probably need a lawyer to meet that challenge in an administrative proceeding conducted by the PTO, assuming you want to fight rather than switch.

3. Disputes With Other Trademark Owners

If you are faced with a dispute over your proposed mark, or over a mark you are already using, you will probably want to consult a trademark lawyer to see what your options are. Although in Chapter 11 we lay out the general principles used by the courts to resolve the major categories of disputes, there is nothing like getting an informed opinion from a knowledgeable human being about the issues involved in your particular dispute.

ICONS USED IN THIS BOOK

Look for these icons to alert you to certain kinds of information.

➡ Fast Track
This icon suggests that you pause and consider whether to skip or skim a section.

⚠ Warning
The caution icon warns you of potential problems.

💡 Tip
This icon highlights helpful hints and considerations for specific situations.

💼 Expert
This icon lets you know when you need the advice of an attorney or other expert.

📖 Resources
When you see this icon, a list of additional resources that can assist you follows.

20 Frequently Asked Trademark Questions

These questions are the ones most often posed to the trademark staff at the Sunnyvale Center for Innovation, Invention and Ideas (Sc[i]3). Brief answers are provided here as well as chapter references for more complete discussions.

1. What does it mean to "trademark" a business or product name or logo?

When people say they plan to "trademark" a name or logo—that is, use the word trademark as a verb—they generally mean they intend to register the name or logo with the U.S. Patent and Trademark Office. While federal registration provides important benefits, trademark ownership is usually determined by who uses the mark first. So, by simply using a name, logo, or other symbol to identify goods or services in the marketplace, a trademark has been created and ownership has been established. [See Chapter 1 (A Trademark Primer).]

2. What is the difference between a trademark and a service mark?

A trademark is any name, logo, symbol or other device used to identify the source of a product. A service mark is any name, logo, symbol or other device used to identify the source of a service. Legally, there is no difference between the two and the terms trademark and mark are often used for all types of marks, including service marks. [See Chapter 1 (A Trademark Primer).]

3. How long does it take to get a trademark registered?

The typical time it takes to get a trademark registered is between 12 and 16 months. However, a trademark search will disclose that the application for registration is pending, and would-be users of the mark are thereby put on notice that you are already claiming ownership. This usually is enough to stop them from using the mark and thus accomplishes the same result as actual registration. [See Chapter 5 (Preparing for a Trademark Search) and Chapter 8 (Federal Trademark Registration).]

4. Suppose I register a trademark for a particular product. What happens when I want to use the same trademark for a different product?

You may go ahead and use the mark and file another application to register the new use of the mark under the appropriate class if the mark is not being used by another business for a similar product. If the same or similar mark is being used by another business for a similar product, then you will need to assess whether the product for which you originally registered the mark is similar enough to your new product to justify extending your trademark registration to it. This type of analysis is best made by an experienced trademark attorney. [See Chapter 8 (Federal Trademark Registration).]

5. Can I apply for my logo, name and slogan all in one application? What happens if I want to use them separately?

A logo, name and slogan are all separate trademarks. Since you may only apply to register one trademark per application, you will need a separate application for each. You may, however, use each of these marks separately or in combination. [See Chapter 8 (Federal Trademark Registration).]

6. What happens if I get a registration but later find out some else had the name first, but never registered it?

This depends on where the name is being used. If the name is being used nationally, then your trademark registration is subject to cancellation, and in any event will not protect you from an infringement suit if the first user can establish that your use of the mark is creating the likelihood of customer confusion. If, on the other hand, the name is only being used locally, you will be entitled to use the name in any region of the country where there would not be a likelihood of customer confusion. In this situation, there would be dual ownership of the mark. [See Chapter 4 (How to Tell If Two Marks Are Confusingly Similar) and Chapter 11 (Sorting Out Trademark Disputes).]

7. Why should I do a search myself if the Trademark Office does one when they get my application?

Good question. Even if you do your own trademark registration, it will cost you at least $245—money down the drain if your registration is denied because of an existing mark. Also, the trademark office search only covers the federal trademark register, not trademarks that are in use but not registered. Since use, rather than registration, determines ownership, the Trademark Office search will not be as complete as your own search of both registered and unregistered marks. [See Chapter 5 (Preparing for a Trademark Search) and Chapter 6 (How to Do a Trademark Search).]

8. What is a "common law" trademark and what rights does it give me?

A common law trademark is any device (name, logo, slogan, etc.) that is being used to identify a business's goods or services in the marketplace and that has not been federally registered. The owner of a common law trademark that is used across state, territorial or international borders is entitled to use the federal courts to enforce its rights. Those rights typically include the right to exclusive use of the mark, the right to recover for harm caused by the infringing use and the right to recover punitive damages and attorneys' fees if it can be shown that the act of copying was deliberate. [See Chapter 1 (A Trademark Primer).]

9. Why should I bother to register a trademark I'm already using on my business or products if I already have rights under the common law?

Simply, federal registration makes it a lot easier to win a federal lawsuit against later users by establishing certain presumptions (meaning facts that you don't have to prove in court). These presumptions include the presumption that you are the mark's owner and that the later user deliberately copied the mark (which makes it easier to collect large damages and attorneys' fees). [See Chapter 11 (Sorting Out Trademark Disputes).]

10. Can I do the application myself or should I hire an attorney?

Most people can handle their own trademark applications without an attorney. The U.S. Patent and Trademark Office (PTO) publishes easy to use instructions and is willing to help you through the process. This book takes these instructions a step further and addresses a number of questions that are likely to come up. If, however, you have questions that this book or the PTO pamphlet don't answer, you should consult with an attorney. Also, if the mark you are planning to register is unusual (a color, sound or scent, for example), or for some reason the PTO doesn't want to accept your application, you definitely will need to consult an attorney. [See Chapter 15 (Help Beyond the Book).]

11. (After finding an exact match or near-exact match in a search) What if I use my trademark anyway? What's the worst that can happen?

In most instances, the worst that can happen is that you will have to pick another mark, which means eating the cost of new stationery, business cards and the like, and expending what sums are necessary to retain any good will that you built up under the first mark. Although the owner of the registered mark is entitled to sue you for punitive as well as actual damages—because use of a registered mark is presumed to be deliberate and thus deserving of punishment—this would not be likely if you were willing to cooperate by stopping use of the mark. [See Chapter 13 (If Someone Claims That You Infringed Their Trademark).]

12. Can I register my domain name/ Internet Web site address as a trademark?

Yes, you may apply to federally register your domain name as a trademark, provided that it is being used to market goods or services on the Internet. If, on the other hand, the domain name is only being used as an address unconnected with goods or services, registration will be denied. [See Chapter 11, Section F.

13. What's the difference between state and federal trademarks?

A state trademark is one that is used within the confines of the state and optionally registered on the state's trademark list. A federal trademark is one that is used across state, territorial or international borders, or that affects commerce across such borders. The term "federal trademark" also is generally taken to mean that the trademark has been federally registered, as opposed to a common law trademark. [See Chapter 1 (A Trademark Primer) and Question #8, above.]

14. If my trademark search finds a mark identical or similar to mine and I find out that the owner is no longer in business (or that the mark is no longer being used by that business), am I free to use it? Can I register it with the PTO?

The answer to both questions is not necessarily. Even if the original owner is no longer in business, the mark itself may have been assigned to another business, which is using it. Similarly, even if the original owner is still in business but no longer using the mark, it may be in use by someone else under an assignment. [See Chapter 11 (Sorting Out Trademark Disputes).]

15. If I add a logo to my business or product name, does that distinguish the name from others that are already registered or in use?

Generally not. If the name accompanying your logo is the same as or very similar to a name that is federally registered or used, you will be precluded from using or registering the name/logo combination. [See Chapter 2 (How to Choose a Good Name for Your Business, Product or Service).]

16. What should I search in order to feel like I've covered enough?

At the very least, the federal trademark register (both principal and supplemental) and state trademark registers should be searched for names or other marks that possibly conflict with yours. In addition, publications that compile business and product names, trade publications that feature advertising and up-to-date announcements about new products and services, and the Internet should all be searched for common law marks. [See Chapter 5 (Preparing for a Trademark Search) and Chapter 6 (How to Do a Trademark Search).]

17. Who exactly reads the Official Gazette published by the Patent and Trademark Office?

Mostly patent and trademark attorneys, patent agents and others whose business involves keeping up with the latest PTO announcements and rules. Also, because new patents and trademark registrations are disclosed in this publication, anyone who wants to stay abreast of new technologies or who is concerned about the possibility of trademark or patent infringements can benefit from reading the Official Gazette. [See Chapter 9 (How to Use and Care for Your Mark).]

18. Does the Trademark Office notify me when the trademark needs to be renewed?

No. You are responsible for keeping track of the required renewal dates. If you miss the deadline, your trademark registration will be canceled. This does not affect your ownership of the mark, but you will have to re-register in order to maintain the benefits of registration. [See Chapter 9 (How to Use and Care for Your Mark).]

19. Can I photocopy the application form or am I required to send in an original?

You may send in the application on any form, original or photocopy, that contains the same information as the official form in the same order. [See Chapter 8 (Federal Trademark Registration).]

20. How do I get an international trademark?

There is no such thing as an international trademark. It is possible to file one application for a group of countries that comprise the European Union, but even if this application is granted, separate procedures are required for protection in the constituent countries. Otherwise, you must seek protection on a country-by-country basis. [See Chapter 14 (International Trademark Protection).] ■

A Trademark Primer

This chapter provides an introduction to trademark law basics. Its purpose is to give you the necessary background to understand your rights and obligations when choosing and using a name, logo or other device to identify your business and products in the marketplace. If you already have a thorough grounding in trademark law, feel free to skip ahead. Otherwise, please read this chapter carefully.

A. An Introduction to Business Names

The most common method adopted by new businesses to identify themselves in the marketplace is their name. For the purposes of trademark law, there are two main types of business names:

- the formal name of the business, called its trade name
- the name the business uses to market its products or services, alternatively referred to as a "trademark," "service mark" or just plain "mark."

Technically, the term trademark refers to any device used to identify a product while the term service mark refers to any device used to identify the services offered by a business. In fact these terms are legally interchangeable, and the even more general term—mark—commonly is used to refer to both. In this book we tilt towards the terms "trademark" and "mark" and seldom use "service mark." But if this makes a difference to you, remember that when we use the term trademark to refer to a business name, or the name given a particular service offered by a business in the marketplace, the technically correct term is service mark.

TRADEMARK, SERVICE MARK AND MARK DEFINED

Trademark

any word, phrase, design, slogan or symbol (including nonfunctional unique packaging) that serves to identify a specific product brand—for instance, *Xerox* (brand of photocopiers), *Kodak* (brand of film and cameras), *Exxon* (brand of gasoline and automotive products), *Nike* (brand of sport shoes), *Apple's* rainbow apple with a bite missing (brand of computers), the red *Coca-Cola* logo (brand of soft drink).

Service mark

any word, phrase, design or symbol that operates to identify a specific brand of service—for instance, *McDonald's* (brand of fast food service), *Kinko's* (brand of photocopying service), *ACLU* (brand of legal service), *Blockbuster* (brand of video rental service), the *UPS* logo (brand of package delivery service), the U.S. Postal Service's eagle in profile (brand of package delivery service), *CBS's* stylized eye in a circle (brand of television network service), the Olympic Games' multicolored interlocking circles (brand of international sporting event).

Almost all legal problems involving business names arise when a business name is used as a trademark—that is, used to build a customer base for the business—and not when the name is used as a trade name simply for billing, banking and tax purposes. The distinction between a trade name and a trademark can be a little confusing at first, since many businesses use at least a part of their trade name as the name they use to market their goods or services. For instance, every time a small business named something like *Pete's Graphic Designs, Elmwood Copymat* or *Good Taste Organic Foods* puts its name on a store sign, window display or brochure, it is using its trade name as a trademark. On the other hand, large businesses often use different names for each type of subsidiary activity. For instance, *Ford Motor Company* puts its name on its cars, but also uses a subsidiary mark for each type of car (for instance, Escort, Probe, Thunderbird) and a different mark entirely for its auto parts division (*Motorcraft*).

While this book is primarily concerned with business names as trademarks, we also devote a chapter to the steps that normally must be taken when a business first adopts and uses a trade name. (See Chapter 3, Protecting and Registering Trade Names.)

> ### CORPORATE AND FICTITIOUS NAMES
>
> A corporate name is simply the name of a corporation as registered at the time of incorporation. It must generally be approved by a state official, such as the secretary of state or corporations commissioner (the names vary from state to state), and followed by a corporate identifier, such as Inc. or Co., like *Time, Inc.,* or *Sony Corp.* A corporate name is a trade name in that it identifies the corporation and not necessarily any product or service the corporation offers.
>
> Another form of trade name is the fictitious business name, which is any assumed business name or alias. When a person or partnership does business under a name not their own (and this also applies to corporations doing business under a name other than their corporate name), that person (partnership) must usually file a fictitious business name statement with the county or state. For example, Laura Smiley uses a fictitious business name when she conducts her sole proprietorship business as *Le Petite Cafe* or *Laura's Bookkeeping*, but not if she operates under the name of *Laura Smiley Enterprises.* Similarly, if the partnership of Renauer, Randolph and Ihara operates the *Reader's Corner Bookshop*, they are using a fictitious business name.

B. An Introduction to Other Types of Trademarks

Although most small businesses rely on their business name as their primary trademark, there are many other ways for a business to inform consumers about it, its services and its products.

1. Logos

Next to a name, the most popular commercial identifier is the logo, a pure graphic or a combination of a graphic and some aspect of the business name. Examples abound. The block-lettered *Ford* set against a blue oval, the distinctive blue lettering used for *IBM*, the gold *McDonald's* arch, the universally recognized swirl used to denote *Nike* products, all demonstrate how powerful a logo can be to garner instant product or business recognition.

2. Slogans

Another popular form of trademark is the marketing slogan. "Obey your thirst" (*Sprite*); "It's everywhere you want to be" (*Visa*); "I love what you do for me" (*Toyota*); "Just do it" (*Nike*); "Life is a sport, drink it up" (*Gatorade*); and "Life is a journey; enjoy the ride" (*Nissan*) all are devices designed to build customer recognition of the underlying businesses and their products, and thus qualify as trademarks which can be protected the same as a business name.

3. Packaging, Decor, Product Shape and Web Pages

In recent years, a type of trademark known as trade dress has become more and more important to businesses trying to build customer recognition. Trade dress includes product packaging, external and internal store decor, product shapes and most recently (according to most observers) the look and feel of a business's Web page. As long as the way a product or its packaging appears to the consumer is intended to operate as a trademark, it will be treated and protected as a trademark, assuming it meets other trademark requirements such as distinctiveness. (See Section C below).

4. Color, Sound and Other Unusual Identifiers

Finally, there is no end to the idiosyncratic types of product or service identifiers that potentially qualify as trademarks. The U.S. Supreme Court has already ruled that a color by itself can be a trademark (the pink used by Corning Insulation products, the chartreuse used by the Qualitex brand of dry cleaning pads). And Harley Davidson has sued Honda for copying the distinctive low rumbling sound of its motorcycles.

By now the point should be clear. Anything used by a business to build customer loyalty and recognition of its products or services can be considered a trademark and subject to the principles of trademark law and the protection offered by federal and state trademark laws.

C. An Introduction to Trademark Law

To recap what we said in the Introduction to this book, trademark law is the body of principles that the courts use to decide disputes about how names or other devices are used to identify goods and services in the marketplace.

Trademark law comes from many sources: federal and state trademark statutes (laws), and federal and state statutes and cases defining and prohibiting "unfair competition" between businesses. While there are subtle differences in all these sources of law dealing with how businesses use commercial identifiers, federal trademark statutes rule most trademark disputes.

Here, briefly, are some basic concepts of federal trademark law that you will need to understand before we go any further. We provide more details as we go along.

1. Trademark Defined

The federal trademark statute defines trademark this way:

> Any word, name symbol, or device, or any combination thereof—(1) used by a person, or (2) which a person has a bona fide intention to use in commerce and applies to register on the principal register established by this chapter, to identify and distinguish his or her goods, including a unique product, from those manufactured or sold by others and to indicate the source or the goods, even if that source is unknown.

As is clear, this language encompasses all devices used to distinguish goods or services in the marketplace, not just names or logos. See the sidebar in Section A above for examples of trademarks.

2. Certification and Collective Marks

In addition to trademarks and service marks, federal trademark law protects two other types of marks—certification marks and collective marks.

Certification marks are only used to certify that products and services that are manufactured or provided by others have certain qualities associated with the mark. For example, *Good Housekeeping Seal of Approval, Roquefort* (a region in France), *Stilton* cheese (a product from the Stilton locale in England), and *Harris Tweeds* (a special weave from a specific area in Scotland) are all certification marks. Among the characteristics that this type of mark may represent are regional origin, method of manufacture, product quality and service accuracy.

A collective mark is a symbol, label, word, phrase or other distinguishing mark that members of a group or organization use to identify the goods they produce or the services they render. For example, the letters "ILGWU " on a shirt is a collective mark identifying the shirt as a product of members of the International Ladies Garment Workers Union. It distinguishes that shirt from those made by non-union shops.

Only members of the group are entitled to use the collective mark in order to indicate, for example, membership in a union, association or other organization. Because a small business's need for these marks is relatively rare, we don't address them further in this book. If you need help in creating and protecting this type of mark, consult a trademark attorney. (See Chapter 15, Help Beyond the Book.)

3. What Trademark Law Protects (Distinctive Marks)

Trademark law has two fundamental goals:

1. To prevent businesses from stealing the goodwill that others have generated by creatively distinguishing their services and products in the marketplace by use of a clever name, symbol or other device.
2. To prevent customers from being misled by the use of confusingly similar marks on products and services originating from different sources.

The degree to which trademark law operates to fulfill these goals depends on how memorable or "distinctive" the marks in question are. Marks are memorable for two reasons:

- They are arbitrary, unusual, unique, evocative, surprising or otherwise effective in setting the product or service off from others (inherent distinctiveness).
- They have become familiar over time and through use—that is, customers have come to associate the name with the business. As mentioned, the legal principle that protects this type of mark is called the "secondary meaning rule." *American Airlines, Burger King* and *General Electric* are examples of marks that were originally bland and undistinctive but became very well known through use over time.

WHAT MAKES A MARK INHERENTLY DISTINCTIVE

The ability of a mark to stand out in a customer's mind—its distinctiveness in the trademark context—can derive from a number of different characteristics related to what they mean in the context of their use, how they sound when pronounced out loud and what they look like.

Inherently distinctive marks include:

- Coined terms—words that are made up and therefore have no meaning at all, such as *Exxon, Kodak* or *Rackafrax*.
- Fanciful or surprising terms—words that are ordinary in one context but distinctive in another. This usually occurs when the meaning of the term is imaginative, unexpected or arbitrary in the context of its use, such as *Apple* computers, *Cherokee* clothes, *Time* Magazine, and *Double Rainbow* Ice Cream.
- Terms that evoke or suggest rather than describe a quality or characteristic of the underlying product or service—marks such as *Greyhound* bus lines, *Suave* shampoo and *Jaguar* cars all fit this category.
- Graphical arrangements of words, letters and/or symbols that are unique in appearance—*Toys R Us* (with the backwards R) is an example.

Distinctive marks have little or no descriptive function but rather operate primarily to set the product or service off from others because of their appearance, sound or meaning in the context of their use. That's why we call them "distinctive." Their uniqueness is what gives them their legal strength. One of the authors' favorite examples of a distinctive mark is the name used by a local bookstore—*Diesel, A Bookstore*. The diesel

part of the name is so surprising in the context that once you see it, you're unlikely to forget it.

Because distinctive marks are memorable, there is a high risk that consumers will associate a product or service carrying a distinctive mark with one business, and therefore become confused if the distinctive mark is used by another business. To prevent this type of confusion, the courts are willing to give distinctive marks the most protection that the law has to offer. For this reason, distinctive marks are also commonly considered to be legally strong marks.

By contrast, marks consisting of common or descriptive words, personal names and geographic terms are considered legally weak marks because they are not memorable, which means it is much less likely that consumers will come to recognize and purchase the underlying goods or services on the basis of the marks themselves—unless, of course, the marks have become distinctive under the secondary meaning rule. (Weak marks are discussed in Section 4, below.)

Chapter 2, How to Choose a Good Name for Your Business, Product or Service, revisits in more detail the subject of what makes an effective trademark, and Chapter 10, Evaluating Trademark Strength, takes this subject a step further. The question of what makes one mark strong and another mark weak often is the key to resolving trademark disputes, and frequently must be understood to handle your own trademark issues.

4. The Role of Customer Confusion in Trademark Law

As mentioned in the Introduction, virtually all trademark disputes that make it to court are resolved on the basis of the answer to this one simple question: Would simultaneous use of the marks in dispute likely cause customer confusion? If there is no customer confusion, then the courts see no reason to intervene. (An exception to the customer confusion rule is sometimes made for famous marks, which by law are entitled to be free from other uses that would dilute their strength or tarnish their reputation for quality. See Chapter 11, Section E for more on the dilution doctrine.)

Section 8 below (What Determines Who Owns a Trademark?) as well as later chapters address various aspects of customer confusion in detail. But one important point needs to be made here at the beginning. Two different marks can be confusingly similar for a number of reasons. Take, for example, the well-known mark *Microsoft*. Could a business avoid the likelihood of customer confusion by using a name that sounds the same as Microsoft but looks different, such as Mikkrowsought or Mike Crow Soft? Or that looks the same but sounds different, such as Macrosoft? Or that looks and sounds different but which means essentially the same thing, such as TinySoft? Or perhaps a fanciful arrangement of the words and letters, such as **M** I **CR**O **S**OFT

The answer to all these questions is no. Why? Whether a mark is similar to another in sound, appearance, or meaning, it is still similar and therefore likely to confuse potential customers. However, the more ordinary the original mark is, the less concerned the courts will be about possible customer confusion and the more acceptable changes in appearance, sound or meaning will be as a way to distinguish one ordinary mark from another.

5. How Trademark Law Protects Trademarks

Now that we've covered what trademarks the law protects, let's turn to how this protection comes about. The most important point to realize is that the trademark system is self-policing. If you don't do anything about your business name or other mark getting ripped off by a competitor, no one else will either. And so, even though the law provides "protections," you will have to step forward and use what tools the law provides.

As a general rule, these tools are very limited. In some situations it is possible to resolve a dispute by filing an administrative petition or complaint with the PTO (see Chapter 8, Federal Trademark Registration), but the vast majority of trademark disputes that can't be settled by negotiations are resolved by filing a federal court lawsuit claiming trademark infringement. Typically the lawsuit asks the court to immediately order a suspected infringer to stop using the mark in question, and, after trial, to award the business bringing the suit large damages on the ground the infringer acted deliberately. Once the judge rules on the request for immediate relief, the case is then typically settled. If the court grants the immediate relief requested by the plaintiff, the case usually is settled on terms favorable to the plaintiff. If the judge denies the relief, the defendant usually comes out better. Few trademark cases make it all the way to trial, and consequently, few cases result in damage awards although money may change hands as part of the settlement.

The unfortunate aspect of this method of dispute resolution is that it can get expensive in a hurry, easily running into tens of thousands of dollars in legal fees. The cost of litigation teaches one very important rule when it comes to trademark disputes: Be flexible and don't get too carried away by the right or wrong of the situation. Always treat the issue as one more business decision that should be resolved in a manner that will most benefit (and least harm) your business. Remember that negotiation is an option and there are many ways to structure a settlement. Using a cease and desist letter if the law is on your side is a first step. How to handle trademark disputes is covered in more detail in Chapters 12 (if you sue someone) and 13 (if you are sued).

6. The Role of Federal Registration in Protecting Trademarks

Under a federal statute known as the Lanham Act, it is possible to register a trademark with the U.S. Patent and Trademark Office (PTO). Registration can increase a trademark owner's ability to win a lawsuit based on infringement of the registered mark, and businesses with marks they consider valuable usually opt for registration.

Although registration increases protection, it's important to understand that registration doesn't create trademark ownership. Instead, ownership is determined by who uses a trademark first in a commercial transaction. See Section 8 below.

Let's take a closer look at how federal registration works. In Chapter 8, we provide detailed instructions on how to get the job done as well as more detailed information on the points covered in this overview.

a. The Principal Register

The PTO keeps two lists of all trademarks that it has decided to register—the Principal Register and the Supplemental Register. In addition to the trademarks themselves, these registers include:

- the owners of the marks
- the dates the marks were registered
- the types of goods or services identified by the marks, and
- other potentially useful information.

Of the two, the Principal Register is by far the most important. It is placement on this list that provides a trademark with the protection that makes it worthwhile to register the mark in the first place.

Registration on the Principal Register provides these protective benefits:

- exclusive nationwide ownership of the mark (except where the mark is already being used by prior users who haven't registered the mark)

- official notice to all would-be later users that the mark is unavailable
- the right to put an ® after the mark, which also puts users on notice that the mark has been registered
- the right to immunize the mark from certain challenges if the mark is kept in continuous use for five years after the registration date
- a legal presumption that the registrant is the owner of the mark (which means the registrant won't have to prove ownership if a dispute over the mark ends up in court).

Taken together, these benefits make it easier to win an infringement lawsuit and make it more likely that large damages can be collected for the infringement (which means there will be money to pay the attorneys and make it worthwhile to bring the lawsuit in the first place). See Chapter 12 for more on infringement lawsuits.

To be placed on the Principal Register:

- The mark must be in actual use in commerce between two or more states or across territorial or international borders. Even if an application has been filed for registration based on intended use, the mark will not actually be registered until it is put into actual use.
- The mark must be sufficiently distinctive (inherently or through use over time) to reasonably operate as a product or service identifier in the marketplace.
- The mark may not be confusingly similar to an existing mark in a context where the confusion of customers would be likely.
- The mark may not fit within one of the categories that Congress has deemed to be off limits for trademarks (such as the U.S. or the name of a living person without his or her consent).
- The mark may not consist primarily of a surname or a geographical name (unless the mark has become well known over time

or the geographical term is clearly arbitrary but not deceptive).

- The mark may not consist of the title of a book, play, recording or movie that is a single issue artistic work (as opposed to a series or serial) unless the title has become well known over time.

b. The Supplemental Register

The Supplemental Register is an option for marks that aren't distinctive enough to qualify for placement on the Principal Register. (See Section 3, above, for a discussion on what makes a mark distinctive.) This lack of distinctiveness means that the courts are unlikely to give the mark much protection in the event of a lawsuit

As a general rule, placement of a mark on the Supplemental Register does not help much if a dispute over the mark ends up in court. However, anyone doing a standard trademark search for the same or similar mark will discover the registration and most likely will decide to choose another mark. Also, placement on the Supplemental Register entitles the mark's owner to use the ® that, to the public, signifies a registered trademark. The bottom line is that the Supplemental Register provides some practical benefits and therefore provides a sensible option if placement on the Principal Register is denied because of the mark's lack of distinctiveness.

State Trademark Registers

All states maintain separate trademark registers. The main function of these is to provide notice to would-be later users that the mark is already in use. Unlike federal trademark registration, placement of a mark on most state registers confers few ownership rights to the mark. Rather, these must be sorted out in court if a dispute arises. Whoever first actually used the mark will usually be determined the owner, regardless of when the

state registration occurred. (See Chapter 7, State Trademark Registration.)

7. What Trademark Law Doesn't Protect (Ordinary Marks)

While trademark law protects distinctive or strong marks, it doesn't protect—that is, it doesn't allow a business to monopolize—ordinary marks (common words or descriptive terms) that competitors might wish to use to accurately identify the types of services or products they provide. For example, most adjectives (soft, fluffy, tasty, accurate, fast, easy, tough, reliable) are available for anyone to use and can't be locked up in a trademark. Indeed, common and descriptive words don't do a good job of distinguishing one product or service from others anyway.

As a general rule, an ordinary (and legally weak) trademark is one that isn't memorable as applied to the product or service it is used on or with. Typically it consists of commonly used—that is, nondistinctive—words or symbols that aren't surprising in the context of their use. Often they either describe the nature of the service or product they apply to (*Unfinished Furniture*, or *A-Z Hardware*); or they describe where the service is located (*Southside Liquors*); or they praise the product or service's quality (*Blue Ribbon Dairy*); or they are just personal names (*Tom's Barber Shop*).

Many businesses try to make ordinary terms distinctive by spelling them in an unusual way or placing them in unusual graphical arrangements. For example, E-Z is used by many businesses in connection with the type of service being offered (*E-Z Car Repairs*). While this name certainly appears different from the word easy, it does not transform the ordinary descriptive term easy into a distinctive mark. Although such marks may become distinctive over time—as their unusual appearance becomes familiar as a unique product or service identifier (the secondary meaning rule)— they are not considered inherently distinctive and will typically be denied trademark status by the PTO and the courts.

If a term is (or becomes) synonymous with the underlying product or service itself, it is generally classified as "generic" and entitled to no protection at all. Sometimes a strong mark is so commonly used to describe the underlying product that the mark merges with the product and no longer serves its function of distinguishing the underlying product from other products. For instance, Aspirin, originally a brand name for a type of analgesic manufactured by Bayer, became so associated with the underlying product (Acetaminophen) that it no longer operated to tell one brand of acetaminophen from another. Presto, it lost its trademark status and now anyone can call its Acetaminophen product aspirin (with a small a).

8. What Determines Who Owns a Trademark?

We saw earlier that trademark law protects a trademark owner against other uses of the trademark that:

- would likely result in customer confusion as to the origins of a given product or service, or
- would detract from the strength of a famous mark or harm the reputation of the mark for quality (the dilution theory).

But how is ownership of a trademark determined in the first place?

In the United States, the first business to use a trademark owns it. There are three ways to qualify as a first user of a trademark:

- by being the first to use the trademark on a product that is distributed in a commercial transaction, or

---

TRADEMARK PROTECTION DOESN'T EXTEND TO COMMON TERMS USED IN THE TRADEMARK

Often a trademark will be completely made up of common words and yet will be memorable because of how the words are combined. For example, the mark *Speedy Turtle Delivery Service* does not use any terribly unusual words but the combination of Speedy and Turtle definitely makes this a clever mark and deserving of protection in its entirety. But if someone else wants to use any of these words in their mark, they are free to do so as long as they don't use speedy turtle for any product or service that might lead to customer confusion. If the owner of Speedy Turtle applies to register this mark with the U.S. Patent and Trademark Office, the trademark examiner would almost certainly require the owner to "disclaim" (agree to give up

any claim to) ownership of all the words in the mark, even though the mark itself would be registered.

A good example of what can go wrong if common words are provided with trademark protection is the current debate over the term "Internet." Many years ago the term Internet was registered as a trademark for a brand of computer network unrelated to today's Internet. Now, when a company whose name includes the term Internet tries to register the name as a trademark, the PTO is rejecting the application because of the previous registration. Most observers believe that the PTO will change its policy regarding the term Internet sometime down the road.

- by being the first to actually use the trademark in connection with advertising or marketing a service genuinely available to the public, or
- by filing an application to register the trademark with the U.S. Patent and Trademark Office on the grounds that the mark qualifies for registration and that you intend to use it in the near future.

Example: In 1998, Jonah creates a new business called *Geezer Sports* and publishes *Geezer Tennis*, the first in a line of sports books for aging participants. In the year 2001, a business competitor sends Jonah a letter stating that it federally registered *Games for Geezers* as a trademark in 2000 and that Jonah is infringing its trademark. Jonah does a little investigating and learns that *Games for Geezers* was first used as a mark in 1999, a full year after Jonah started using the mark. Jonah would be considered the owner of the *Geezer* mark and could in fact require *Games for Geezers* to change its name, since the products of the two businesses compete and would therefore likely lead to customer confusion.

Example: Assume now that in 1998 Games for Geezers had applied for federal trademark registration on an intent to use basis, even though it hadn't actually put the mark in use commercially until 1999. If Jonah started actual use of the *Geezer* mark in March 1998, and Games for Geezers filed its application for registration in April 1998, Jonah would still be considered the owner. However, if the application filing date preceded Jonah's actual use, Games for Geezers would be the ultimate owner, once it put the mark into actual use in 1999.

What constitutes actual use and intended use is discussed in detail in Chapter 8.

Although trademark ownership is determined by first use as we've defined it here, it's possible for a mark to be "owned" by two or more separate businesses as long no customer confusion will likely result. If the underlying products or services of two businesses are quite different and

don't compete, then customer confusion is unlikely. Similarly, if the underlying products or services are distributed and marketed in different channels or parts of the country, then again there is little likelihood of customer confusion. But as we pointed out earlier, the more famous and/or distinctive a mark is, the more likely it is that customer confusion will result (and the less likely it is there will be more than one owner).

What happens if a mark is owned by more than one business because of different geographical markets, and one of the businesses decides to move into the other business's territory? Or suppose that dual ownership has been possible because one business used the mark on sportswear and another on lawn mowers, and both businesses decide to move into gardening clothes? In these situations, some rules kick in that help a court decide the respective rights of the owners. The rules revolve around such facts as:

- Did the second business to actually use the mark know of the first business's previous use?
- Is the first user's mark federally registered, and if so did the second use begin before or after the registration?
- Is the second user's mark federally registered?
- How broad were the first user's marketing efforts when the second use began?

Chapter 11 deals with all these issues and tells you how the courts are likely to resolve them in specific fact situations.

⚠ The World Wide Web May Render Dual Ownership Obsolete

As more and more businesses use the World Wide Web to market their goods and services, it will be harder and harder for two marks to coexist, since they will be sharing the same marketing channel, which happens to be national and even international. The risk of confusing customers who are using the Web to shop will be high.

D. An Overview of Internet Trademark Issues

Most small retail or service-oriented business owners well know the mantra for success: location, location, location. The idea is that if your business is situated where your potential customers can find you, you will do well as long as you adhere to the other sound business principles such as offering marketable products or services, keeping accurate account of your finances and maintaining excellent customer service.

As the Internet took hold in the early 1990s, the concept of location, while still central to business success, took on a whole new meaning. Instead of being rooted in physical space, businesses were now being required to jockey for locations in the virtual or electronic space (also termed cyberspace) known as the Internet.

The Internet is a computer network that allows near-instantaneous communication between computers anywhere in the world. Unlike the telephone, or fax, the Internet allows the transmission of digital files which can be read by computers to produce text, photographs, graphics, sounds, videos and movies.

The World Wide Web (a part of the Internet) adds to the Internet by providing an appealing graphical interface that makes it much easier to get around and that, for businesses and consumers, has become a powerful new type of "yellow pages" extending to all parts of the country and many parts of the world. As more and more consumers turn to the Web to shop for goods and services, most businesses will find it necessary to create and maintain a Web presence. This means creating what's known as a "Web page," which ideally can be located under the name the business chooses to use as its trademark.

Today there are more than 600,000 business-related sites on the Web. Most national businesses have a Web site, as do a huge number of small and medium-sized businesses. Even Nolo Press, which in size would be classified as a small business, has been operating a Web site for a couple of years. By all accounts the Web will be the marketing channel of the future, and anyone who wants to do business, whether local, national or international, will have to join up. And so, the location mantra remains the same, but this time it's about how customers can find you "out there" on the Web.

1. The Importance of Domain Names

How do customers find businesses on the Web? Every business on the Web has what's called a domain name. The domain name is a unique "address" that computers understand, and so if you enter a particular domain name in a Web browser, the computer will know what to do: It links your computer with the Web site (business location) connected with the domain name you entered. If you watch television you no doubt are familiar with the little message that appears at the end of virtually every advertisement ("You can find us on the World Wide Web at 'www dot homepage dot com' ")

Because each domain name must be unique—so that all the computers attached to the Internet can find it—it is impossible for two different businesses to have the same domain name. If when Nolo applied for its Web address another business had already grabbed Nolo as its second level domain name, Nolo would have had to come up with something at least a little different.

2. Issues of Concern for New and Established Businesses

Any business that wants to do business on the Web will necessarily be concerned with these issues:

- If the business is in the process of choosing a name, is the name available as a domain name on the Web or has it already been taken by another business?

- If the business already has an established name, what happens if its name has already been taken as a domain name by another business?
- When does a domain name qualify as a trademark?
- What happens if two similar domain names are likely to confuse customers?
- What happens if a domain name owned by one business is the same as a famous trademark owned by another business?
- How do you get a domain name?

These and other Web-related trademark issues have not yet been fully explored by the courts and so there are no firm answers to many of them. Still, some courts have ruled on some questions and some tentative answers are possible. How to register a domain name is covered in Chapter 3 and resolving disputes between domain names and trademarks is addressed in Chapter 11, Section F.

E. The Difference Between Trademark and Copyright

The terms trademark and copyright are often used interchangeably by the general public. However, Trademark and copyright protect different aspects of creative expression. Trademark protects expression that is used to identify and distinguish a product or service in the marketplace. Copyright protects all creative expression except for slogans, names, titles and short phrases, the very things that are protected by trademark. Let's take a closer look at what copyright does protect because when it comes to trade dress and graphics used on Web pages, trademark and copyright both may apply.

Copyright provides writers, artists, photographers, musicians, software programmers and other creators of expressive works the exclusive right to control how their works are used. But it is important to understand that only the expression itself is protected—not the ideas being expressed.

For example, assume that Lloyd Sagal, a self-identified but unknown philosopher, writes a book exploring the religious implications of life on other planets. Under copyright law other philosophers are free to use any or all of Lloyd's ideas in their own books (and don't even have to give him credit, although most would because of professional scruples). However, each of these other authors will have to do their own writing. They can't just copy verbatim how Lloyd has expressed the ideas.

(For a thorough exploration of this dichotomy between expression and ideas, see The *Copyright Handbook* by Stephen Fishman (Nolo Press).)

A copyright develops in a work of expression as soon as the work takes a tangible form—for instance, on paper, tape, disk, CD, film or canvas. It is common to give notice of the copyright by placing a © and the year the work is published next to the author's name. The creator can optionally register the work with the U.S. Copyright Office to gain some additional protections. Whether or not registered, the copyright lasts for the life of the creator plus fifty years, with some exceptions.

Copyright covers the following types of works: advertising copy, catalogs, directories, price lists and other compilations of information, fiction, interviews, lectures, speeches, jokes, etc., that are put into a tangible medium of expression, leaflets and pamphlets, letters and diaries, magazines, newspapers, newsletters, periodicals, journals and other serial publications, nonfiction, plays, poetry, reference books and technical writings, screenplays, song lyrics, textbooks, music, art, graphic designs, motion pictures, sculptures, videos, software of all types, architectural designs and blueprints, choreographic works, pantomimes, photographs and slides.

Copyright law and trademark law most commonly intersect in advertising copy. The trademark laws protect the name of the product or service, any distinctive slogans used in the advertising, and the distinctive features associated with the name or logo, such as its color or lettering style. The copyright laws protect any additional literal expression that the ad contains, such as the artwork and overall composition of the ad. This means that a similar design can't be used as a trademark by anyone else when customer confusion would result (trademark law) and even absent customer confusion the identical design can't be used without the design owner's permission (copyright law).

This same dual protection probably also exists for the graphical content of Web pages, although the courts have yet to deal with this issue. See Chapter 11, Section F.

F. The Difference Between Trademark and Patent

By filing for and obtaining a patent from the U.S. Patent and Trademark Office, an inventor is granted a monopoly on the use and commercial exploitation of the invention described in the patent for a limited time. There are several types of patents. The most common is what's called a utility patent, which lasts for 20 years from the date of filing the patent application. A utility patent protects the functional features of a machine, process, manufactured item, composition of matter or new use for any such items. To qualify for a utility patent, an invention must be novel and surprising (nonobvious) to somebody who is familiar with the field of technology into which the invention falls. There is almost no intersection between this type of patent and trademark.

It is also possible to obtain a patent on an innovative design of a manufactured item if the design serves an ornamental rather than functional purpose. Because trademark protects a product shape that is intended to operate as a trademark, it is sometimes possible that a product design/shape can be protected under both patent and

trademark law, although this point is currently the subject of much debate in the courts.

For complete information on patents and how to apply for them, see *Patent It Yourself,* by David Pressman (Nolo Press).

G. A Sensible Strategy for Choosing and Protecting Your Business or Product Name or Logo

Until very recently, there were two strategies for choosing and protecting business and product identifiers, a more complex one for a business that intended to operate on a large scale with a clever name or logo, and a simpler one for a business that by nature expected to offer services to a primarily local consumer market. Because of new computer-based technologies and networks—the World Wide Web in particular—all this is changing very rapidly and the keep-it-simple and local approach will seldom be the best approach.

Assuming that you or your business will want to become part of the vast commercial community taking shape on the Web, your concern about what names or logos are already being used will be of much wider scope. See, for example, the list of new issues raised by the Internet in Section D above. Whether your business is small or large, local or national, retail or wholesale, you will be well advised to look beyond your immediate geographic community when choosing your business name, assuming you want (or may want in the future) to use that name to market your goods or services on the Web. We tell you in Chapter 6 how to search the Web in order to clear your proposed name for use and to find out whether your proposed name or logo is being used as a trademark anywhere in the country.

1. Steps to Take When Choosing Your Business Name

Here are the steps that every business—local or national—should take before finally deciding on a business name or logo.

Step 1: Search for potential conflicts among local businesses. Your first step is to find out whether your proposed name or logo is being used by any other local or regional businesses for goods or services that are similar to the ones your business will be selling. If Bob's Beastie Bagels shows up in the Yellow Pages that serves your marketing area, and you want to call your shop Beastie Boy Bagels, you'd best hunt for another name, since Bob would have a pretty good argument that you're just trying to confuse his customers.

Step 2: Assuming you haven't yet encountered a name or logo that would prevent you from using yours, the next step depends on the form of your business. If you are planning to incorporate, you will want to check with the Secretary of State for your state to see whether your name is already taken by another corporation. If you are planning to operate your business as a sole proprietorship or partnership, then you will need to register your name with your local county clerk's office (or with the Secretary of State in a few states). We tell you how to register corporate and noncorporate business names with local agencies in Chapter 3.

Step 3: If your name is still free of conflict, then the next step involves finding out whether your name or logo is being used as a mark or domain name on the World Wide Web. We tell you how to do this in Chapter 6. If the results of this search indicate that you would be precluded from using the name to identify your own Web site, you should seriously consider coming up with another name that you can use for that purpose.

⚠ Exceptions to the National Protection Approach

There are two exceptions to our advice that all businesses take a national perspective when choosing a mark for their business:

- If your proposed mark is ordinary—for instance, Steve's Trademark Services—it is less important to search for conflicts because the law generally does not afford much protection to ordinary marks and you therefore don't need to be as concerned about the possibility of another "Steve's Trademark Services" coming after you for trademark infringement. (See Chapter 10 for more on trademark rules regarding weak marks.)

- If you are certain that you won't be on the Web anytime soon, and your business is very local and unlikely to expand to other areas of the country, then you can probably focus more on the local scene and not worry so much about what names are being used in other parts of the country. But by taking this more casual approach, you risk having a large company that actually used the name first expand into your market area—directly or through franchising—and force you to stop using the name. The more cautious approach is to take the additional steps outlined here.

Step 4: The next step is see whether the name conflicts with a name on your state's trademark register or a name or logo on the principal trademark register maintained by the U.S. Patent and Trademark Office.

> ### CLEARANCE OF YOUR BUSINESS NAME BY THE SECRETARY OF STATE OR COUNTY CLERK DOESN'T MEAN YOU CAN USE IT AS YOUR MARK
>
> You may wonder why you need to do this additional searching if your name has been approved by your state's Secretary of State or your local county clerk. The answer is, those agencies are only concerned with whether your business name conflicts with another business name in your state or locality, not with whether it conflicts with a business name that is being used as a trademark. For instance, it's possible you could get your county clerk or Secretary of State to register the business name "Block Financial Services" if there is no prior registrant using that name. But the instant you went out into the world and used that name to market your goods and services, the chances are great H&R Block would force you to change it.

While you can do a trademark search yourself for free if you visit a Patent and Trademark Depository Library (there's at least one in every state except Vermont), the more common approach is to pay a trademark search service to do the search for you (at this stage it costs about $50). Trademark searching is explained in depth in Chapters 5 and 6. As we also point out in Chapter 2, if your name is the same or very similar to a name on the federal or state trademark register, and the registered name is used for goods or services that are similar to those offered by your business, you should probably come up with a different name.

Step 5: One final step. It's always a good idea to make sure your proposed business name isn't being used by another business as an unregistered trademark. Even if a business hasn't gotten around to registering its name as a trademark, it still has the right to go to court to prevent others from using it if customers might be confused by the dual use. Trademark search firms will also conduct this type of trademark search (called a common-law search). If you are doing it yourself, the best approach to searching for unregistered marks is to browse through the magazines or other trade literature that are targeted toward your type of business. A targeted search on the World Wide Web will also be helpful. See Chapters 5 and 6.

2. Avoiding Conflicts When Choosing a Product Name

If your primary concern is how to choose a clever name for a product you plan to produce or distribute, your main concern will be to find out whether your proposed name is already in use on the same or similar products. You can do this by searching:

- state and federal trademark registers
- product-specific magazines
- the World Wide Web
- the Thomas Product Registry (available on the Web at http://www.thomasregister.com).

See Section 1 above.

3. How to Protect Your Business or Product Name From Use by Others

Once you have gone through the arduous process of choosing a business or product name that doesn't conflict with an existing name, your very next task will be to make sure that only you can use the name in relation to the types of goods or services offered by your business, and that everyone else will know to not trample on your rights as a trademark owner. If you are in a position to start using your business name as a mark in commerce right away, and the use is across state, territorial or international lines (which is automatic if you are on the Web) you can apply for a federal trademark registration on the basis of that use. (See Section C.6 above.)

If there is likely to be a time lag between when you choose your business or product name and when you put it into actual use in commerce, you can still immediately apply for federal registration, but your application will be based on your "intent to use" the mark. In this type of application, your application date will be considered the date you first used the mark, but your mark won't attain registration status until you actually use it. Because the date of first use is the primary factor in deciding who owns a mark in case of a dispute, either putting the mark into use immediately or filing an intent-to-use application immediately accomplish pretty much the same goal—establishing ownership of the mark. How to prepare and file a trademark application of either type—actual use or intended use—is described in detail in Chapter 8.

In addition to registering your business name with the PTO, you may also want to create a web page for your business and register your name as your domain name with the appropriate registrar. See Chapter 3 for how to do this.

4. What Happens If a Rival Crowds Your Name?

If you have already been using your name as a mark for some time and you find a rival using a mark that you think is too close to yours, you may be able to do something about it, if you were the first user or the first to register the mark. The more distinctive your mark is, the easier this will be. But if your mark is ordinary you will face two additional hurdles:

- the other mark must be very similar to yours in order to make it likely that customers would be confused, and
- your mark must be familiar enough in your marketing area for customers to recognize it as clearly identifying your business or product.

Practically speaking, it is at best expensive and difficult for a small local business using an ordinary mark to prove this second requirement in court. But if your competitor's use of the mark appears to be an obvious attempt to mislead the public into believing the competitor's products or services are related to yours (trading on your reputation), you may get some relief. (See Chapter 11.)

Now that you have some general guidelines to work with, let's further orient you to real-world concerns by looking at several scenarios illustrating common questions about business names. Following each is a brief analysis and some cross-references to sections of the book where the issue is discussed in more detail.

Reading this section should give you a better picture of how trademark law works to protect commercial names in situations that commonly occur. However, if you are in the process of choosing a name for your business product or service, and simply want to complete that process while achieving the maximum protection possible for the name, skip to Chapter 2, How to Choose a Good Name for Your Business, Product or Service.

THE UNCERTAINTIES OF TRADEMARK LAW

Throughout the book we stress that because answers to trademark questions depend so heavily on the facts of each situation, advice about trademark issues must often be equivocal. Here are a couple of real-life stories to illustrate this point.

A local bookstore in Oakland, California, calls itself *Diesel, A Bookstore*. Intrigued by this name, one of the all-time distinctive names for a bookstore, we asked the store's owner what he had done to protect it. "Protect it?" the owner asked back in astonishment. The owner's casual attitude toward "protection" is certainly understandable. After all, how likely is it that someone else would attempt to use that name or anything close to it for a bookstore? Just being the first to use such a distinctive name in that context would appear to secure the owner all the protection the name/service mark was likely to need.

We also spoke with the manager of a small retail outlet and mail order company that formerly had been known by the distinctive service mark *The Body Shop*, specializing in natural soaps, perfumes and cosmetics. That company had been persuaded to sell its name to a large British company which had tied up the mark for identical products in the European market. The U.S. company regretted not having taken all possible steps to protect its trademark from the beginning and adamantly advises new businesses to always seek maximum protection (including international registration) for distinctive marks. In that case, they had registered their mark federally but not internationally.

Why take additional steps to protect *The Body Shop* but not *Diesel, A Bookstore*? There is no definitive answer. One could argue that the term *Diesel* when applied to bookstores is so improbable that no one (other than the current user) would ever want to use it, whereas *The Body Shop* is a "natural" for the type of business with which it was being used and so more susceptible to being copied. Or you could argue that *Diesel* should protect the trademark because one day it might be a chain organization with lots of outlets, like *Waldenbooks*.

The point is, if you want to be as certain as possible of keeping the right to use your name, get as much protection for it as you can. If you are willing to gamble a little on your common sense, however, then you may choose to forego some available protection.

Scenario 1

A local business with a garden-variety name.
John decides to start a small local business called
Carry-It-All Hauling Service. He detests computers
and has no intention of getting caught up with
the Internet hype. He's heard that you need to
register a business name before using it and
wants to know what steps a sole proprietor
should take before using a business name.

Analysis

**Register the business name locally, but don't
worry about trademark protection.** Since
John's business is a small, local unincorporated
business, all John is required to do is to comply
with state fictitious business name laws. In most
areas these require anyone who does business
using a name other than their own to register it
by placing the name on a county or (in some
states) a state "fictitious" or "assumed name" list.
By doing this, John has the right to sue others in
court to collect on unpaid bills owed to the business, and in some states this will also serve to
keep local competitors from using his name. To
find out more about this registration requirement
John should read Chapter 3, Protecting and Registering Trade Names.

Should John also attempt to register the name
as a trademark? Since he will not be operating
across state, territorial or international lines (or
catering to travelers) the name is not eligible for
federal registration. Even if John did operate on a
larger scale, the name is too descriptive to qualify
for placement on the Principal Register, which
provides most of the benefits of federal registration.

What about state registration? Probably not.
Again, the name is so descriptive of what John's service is that it might not even qualify for state registration. Even if the state trademark office accepts it
for registration, the courts might well refuse to protect it unless and until it has become distinctive by
becoming well known in the community.

Chapter 2, How to Choose a Good Name
for Your Business, Product or Service, tells
John about what he could do to pick a more
legally strong name. This would be important for
John to consider if he has plans to expand his
business and particularly important if he changes
his mind about the Internet or will eventually
operate in other parts of his region or state in the
future.

Chapter 11, Sorting Out Trademark
Disputes, Section C, explains what legal
protection John may have under the legal doctrine
of unfair competition should he decide to stick
with *Carry-It-All Hauling.*

Scenario 2

Corporation with a small market niche. Terry
and Ellen have formed a corporation to operate
their new enterprise designing direct-access consumer databases for small publishers. The name
they chose—Access For All, Inc.—is approved by
the corporations Department of the Secretary of
State for their state. Ellen and Terry want to use
their corporate trade name as a trademark to market their services. Because theirs is a very small
market niche, Ellen and Terry wonder if they can
safely use the name to market their services without worrying about conflicting with others and
possibly having to change it later.

Analysis

**Do a thorough trademark search before using
or registering the trademark.** Terry and Ellen
get no trademark rights just by virtue of their corporate registration. When a state accepts a corporate name, it simply means that the name does
not identically or closely duplicate the name of
another corporation registered in that state. It
does not mean that the name has been cleared for
use as a mark. Assuming Terry and Ellen want to
market their goods or services under their business name (that is, their trade name and service

mark will be the same), it is important that they find out whether *Access For All* is already being used as a mark by someone else (which would preclude Terry and Ellen from using it as their mark). Once the mark has been cleared, they can register it with the state or the PTO.

To conduct their search, Ellen and Terry should definitely check state and federal trademark lists. And because the legal rights to a mark also depend on who used it first (whether or not it was ever registered), Ellen and Terry should also check to see if other businesses are using the mark without registering it by searching the Yellow Pages and lists of trade name uses.

Finally, assuming that Ellen and Terry plan to market their business on the World Wide Web, they will want to make sure the name can be used as their domain name (Web address) and if so take the appropriate steps to secure the right to use it for those purposes.

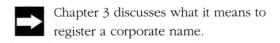 Chapter 6 tells Ellen and Terry how to search for their name on the World Wide Web and Chapter 3 tells how to register their name as a domain name for their Web site.

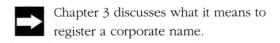 Chapters 5 and 6 tell Ellen and Terry how to search among existing marks and other commercial trade names for potential conflicts. Once their name is cleared for use (that is, no conflicts have been found), they should try to register it as a service mark. See Scenario 7 for more about this.

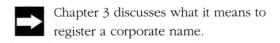 Chapter 3 discusses what it means to register a corporate name.

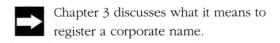 Chapter 11 discusses priorities among conflicting marks.

Scenario 3

A small business wants to use initials that are the same as those used by another local business. Barbara Kate, who is known to her friends as BK, wants to call her new exotic shoe boutique *B-K's*. Five blocks away is another store named *B-K Merchandise* that sells a variety of discount goods, including shoes. Barbara Kate wants to know if it's legally risky to use *B-K* as part of her name.

Analysis

Pick a different name or modify the name to make it different. A store's name (its trade name) usually also acts as its trademark (the name that identifies the services the store offers the public). In this case Barbara Kate wants to use her trade name *B-K's* as her mark. The risk is high that *B-K Merchandise* will try to force Barbara Kate to change the *B-K's* name sometime soon. This is because, even among businesses that don't have interstate sales or registered marks, if two businesses are direct competitors and the names are similar enough to confuse customers, the second user must modify her name to sufficiently distinguish the two businesses.

How much must Barbara Kate modify her name to avoid potential infringement? Generally, the answer to this type of questions depends on how distinctive (memorable) the first user's name is. Initials usually are not considered particularly distinctive unless they are an unusual combination or until they have become well known to the consumer over a long period of time. Therefore, Barbara Kate might only have to add "Fashion Boutique" or something similar to her name to distinguish it from *B-K Merchandise*.

But if *B-K Merchandise* has been in business for a long time and is very well known (if, for example, "Did you buy that at B-K?" is a common local refrain), the *B-K* mark may well have acquired a secondary meaning (distinctiveness through use) sufficient to lock Barbara Kate out of using her own initials, even with "Boutique" or something similar in the name. (See Chapter 10, Evaluating Trademark Strength, for more on secondary meaning.)

One strong argument in Barbara Kate's favor is that the graphical appearance of the two logos is quite different. It's possible that if the dispute ever reached the courts and the judge found that the original *B-K* mark had not acquired distinctiveness through secondary meaning, the judge also would probably decide not to intervene, due to the fact that the two ordinary marks were not similar enough to warrant such action.

Practical Suggestion
A start-up business can rarely afford a lawsuit, regardless of the strength of the defense. So Barbara Kate should avoid any risk of infringement by calling her business *Barbara Kate's*, or some other name that isn't so similar to a local competitor's trademark.

Scenario 3 1/2
Small local business owner wants to use her own name on her business. Barbara Kate takes our suggestion and calls her business *Barbara Kate's Shoe Boutique*, but now wonders if there is something else she should do to be sure her new name (trademark) is legally safe to use. Since shoe and other retail stores are often chain or franchise operations, she should definitely check the state and federal trademark registers and the appropriate trade magazines to be sure that the *Barbara Kate* mark has not already been taken by another company selling shoes or related goods such as hosiery (or even outdoor sports equipment). If it has, even though the other company operates in a distant area and competition is currently not a foreseeable problem, the fact that they have used (and/or registered) the name first as a mark means that they own the rights to the name and may be able to stop Barbara Kate from using it if they later decide to expand their marketing activities into Barbara Kate's market territory.

See Chapter 11 for the effect of prior use of a name. See Chapter 8, Federal Trademark Registration, for the rights of a federally registered trademark owner.

CONFLICTS WITH WELL-KNOWN MARKS—DILUTION

In some cases the owner of a well-known mark can prevent anyone else from using the mark on any type of product or service, even if there is no actual likelihood of customer confusion. The theory for this is that the famous mark is so distinctive that to allow its use on unrelated products or services would diminish or dilute its strength by being placed in common use. In this example, Barbara Kate might be out of luck if her proposed mark was the same or very similar to one that qualified for protection under the federal or state antidilution statutes. See Scenario 6. Also, dilution is discussed in more detail in Chapter 11, Section E.

Scenario 4

Small local businesses that use similar descriptive names. Fred owns a model shop—*Remote Control Garage*—specializing in selling and fixing remote control cars and planes. A cross-town competitor opens a shop named *Remote Control Hangar*. Fred thinks that the new local competitor's business name is unfairly and confusingly close to his. What are his legal rights?

Analysis

Second user can't intentionally copy name. Both Fred's name and his rival's are descriptive service marks, that is, they describe the services advertised and they are not particularly distinctive, or memorable. Chapter 2, How to Choose a Good Name for Your Business, Product or Service, tells Fred that under federal and state trademark principles, unregistered marks that simply describe the product or service being sold—such as "remote control"—can freely be used by a competitor. For this reason, Fred is not in a very strong position to stop his competitor's use of the name, at least under trademark law.

However, Fred may be entitled to some legal protection under a legal doctrine known as "unfair competition" if he can establish that customers are confused and the second user refuses to distinguish his business from Fred's in some way. Fred's legal position will depend on whether he can show that he owns the name (was the first to use it) and whether customers will be confused by the two marks. The emphasis here is on "likelihood of confusion." Other important issues will be whether the businesses are marketed in the same area and how well known each is. In addition, in some states, civil damages or even criminal penalties may apply if Fred can show that the rival adopted his name in an intentional attempt to imply a connection between the two businesses and so to steal some of Fred's customers.

 See Chapter 11, Section C, for more information on unfair competition, and priorities among users, including those whose marks are not registered on any lists.

 Chapters 12 and 13 discuss strategies for handling conflicts.

Scenario 5

Small service business using the owner's personal name that's also the name of a famous national business. Howie has always made mixed drinks that his friends rave about. Now he decides to open a bar and call it *Howard Johnson's*, which is his real name. Can he do this without infringing on the more famous hotel and restaurant chain's mark?

Analysis

No. It's risky to use a famous personal name, even if it's your own. Although most personal names can be freely used by anyone, an exception is made for personal names that have developed substantial recognition over the years as the mark for a particular business, like *Howard Johnson's*. The owner of a famous mark such as *Howard Johnson's* can use the dilution approach to prevent others from using the mark without having to show that customers would likely be confused by the use. See Scenario 6.

Even if the case was not brought under a dilution theory, a bar is so closely related—in a commercial sense—to a hotel/restaurant that Howie will be either enjoined from using his name at all—under the theory that customers would be confused—or at best he might be permitted to use a modified version, if it were different enough not to mislead customers. For example, even *Howie Johnson's*, for example, or *Howard C. Johnson's* might be too close to *Howard Johnson's* to pass muster, but *H.C. Johnson's* might be okay.

One important question would be whether Howie's trademark evokes the more famous trademark in the public's mind. In this inquiry it would matter what the graphical presentation of the name, or the establishment itself looked like; that is, does Howie's mark use the same font and colors as the more famous mark, or does the decor mimic *HoJo's* orange motif? In all likelihood, he probably would have to put "not associated with *Howard Johnson's* restaurant and hotel chain," etc., on all his uses of the name. Further, it might help if there were no *HoJo* facilities anywhere near where Howie plans to open his bar.

 See Chapter 2 on using personal names as marks.

💡 Practical Suggestion
It's rarely worth trying to use your own name as a mark if a large business already uses it, and the name has become well known. They are almost sure to object to your use if they find out about it. Once in court, it's very hard to refute the inference that you are attempting to gain free publicity or at least to trade on the more famous use of your name, which makes it a tough case to win and puts you at risk for damages as well as having to stop using the mark. And even if you do prevail, the cost and stress of the legal battle is likely to make your victory not worth the fight. A recent study by the American Intellectual Property Law Association showed that the median national cost of trademark litigation through trial was $110,000, regardless of outcome. Under such conditions, even if you win, you lose.

Revlon

YARD DESIGNS

▲▲▲▲▲▲▲▲▲

Scenario 6
Using a famous mark on a small unrelated business. Frieda is a landscape architect. She decides to call her business *Revlon Yard Designs*. She receives a letter from the *Revlon Cosmetics* company demanding that she stop using the name *Revlon*. Her question is, can you use a well-known mark for your products or services if they are completely different from those to which the well-known mark is attached?

Analysis
Probably not. Avoid famous marks. As alluded to in previous scenarios, under a legal theory known as dilution, the owner of a nationally well-known mark has a right to keep others from using the mark if the use could be said to diminish the strength of the mark as a distinctive product or service identifier or if the use would detract from (tarnish) the mark's reputation for quality. Frieda learns from Chapter 11, Sorting Out Trademark Disputes, Section D, that even though her business is unrelated to cosmetics, a court would probably enforce *Revlon's* demand on the ground that Frieda is cashing in on *Revlon's* name recognition and that her use of the name dilutes its market strength.

Scenario 6 1/2
Using a not-so-famous trademark on a small unrelated business. Now suppose Frieda chooses another name, *Sochi*, which turns out to be the registered trademark of a tofu-manufacturing company, but one that is not particularly well known. She can probably use it because her use will be so different that no one is likely to be confused by the concurrent uses. In creating her mark, Frieda can also employ design elements and type styles that minimize the likelihood of confusion with the other mark.

Scenario 7

How to protect a new distinctive mark.
Marnine names her new jewelry consulting business *Pearls Before Wine*. She plans to market her services nationwide under that name, and wants to make sure no one else in the U.S. can use it. She wants to know the best way to keep competitors from using her mark.

Analysis

Search for conflicts and register mark. First Marnine must do a thorough search to eliminate potential conflicts with existing trademarks and make sure the proposed mark can be used on the Internet. (See Scenario 2.) Next, Marnine should register the mark with the U.S. Patent and Trademark Office if she is using the mark across state (or territorial or international) lines—as in operating a Web page. Marnine must, of course, also comply with the state and local corporate filing and/or fictitious business name rules if she is also using the mark as a trade name or corporate name.

Chapter 8, Federal Trademark Registration, tells Marnine how to apply to have the name placed on the federal trademark register. Once this is done, she can keep everyone from using the name, unless someone was already using it before she registered.

Scenario 8

How to protect the name of a new local restaurant to be marketed nationally. Rebecca plans to open an expensive nuovo-Italian restaurant named *Ospettini*, in Boulder, Colorado, a university town visited by academic travelers, tourists and outdoor enthusiasts. She wants to market the restaurant nationally and internationally through reviews in food magazines, guide books, travel and sports magazines, and in food columns in newspapers, such as the *N.Y. Times*, *Washington Post*, *Chicago Tribune*, and *L.A. Times*. Can she protect this name from use outside of Colorado?

Analysis

Yes. Register it federally on an intent to use basis. Assuming it is not already in use in Colorado, she can easily protect the name within that state simply by using it as a mark. If she also registers the name with the state trademark office once she actually begins to use it, would-be users will be informed that the name is already in use as a mark. In some states the registration might also entitle Rebecca to some extra benefits if the matter ends up in court.

Assuming *Ospettini* will do a substantial business with patrons from outside Colorado, can Rebecca register the name as a federal trademark even before she begins using it? Yes. She can file a federal registration application on an intent to use basis, which under federal law means that Rebecca will be considered to have first used the mark on the date of her application, even if she doesn't actually use the mark until later. If Rebecca doesn't put the mark into actual use within six months (she can apply for several additional six-month reservation periods at $100 a crack), her first use date will disappear. But if she does begin actually using the mark, it can be formally registered. Meanwhile, just by applying for a registration on an intended use basis, Rebecca has put anyone who does a trademark search on notice that the mark is reserved.

Rebecca's rights against other users of the *Ospettini* mark will be determined according to the principles set out in Chapter 11, Sorting Out Trademark Disputes.

BUILD-RIGHT

Scenario 9

The first user of a mark doesn't register it. Later a second user of the identical mark does register it. For twenty years Charlie has conducted his furniture assembly kit business under the trade name *Build-Right*. Charlie has a large shop and sells building kits and unfinished furniture to customers in wide areas of Minnesota, Iowa and Wisconsin under the *Build-Right* name (that is, he uses his trade name as a trademark and as a service mark). One day Charlie receives a stiff letter from a New York attorney informing him that five years ago the attorney's client placed the mark *Buildright* on the federal trademark register as the name of a computerized block game, and that Charlie must cease and desist from further use of the name. Does Charlie, as the first user of a mark, have to stop using his mark just because someone else got it on the federal register first?

Analysis

No. The first user retains the scope of his existing use; the second (registered) user gets the rest of the country.

Charlie's use of the name is protected for two reasons. As the first user of the mark, he is entitled to keep using it in the way (and in the same market territory) he has established over the years. Remember, first use, not registration, dictates who has the right to use a trademark.

But what about the computer company? Do they have to change their name? Probably not. Since computer games are not even vaguely re-lated to furniture, there is no competition between them. And Charlie's business is small enough that he hasn't established *Build-Right* as a well-known name except perhaps in a few households in the three states where he does business. In short, the potential for customer confusion—which is the primary harm that trademark law seeks to avoid—is very small. And Charlie's mark is not well known enough to warrant protection based on the dilution doctrine—which can apply regardless of customer confusion.

On the other hand, the second *Buildright's* federal registration may prevent Charlie from expanding his business into product areas (as opposed to geographic areas) where the computer software is being marketed. For example, Charlie might not be able to sell computerized sets of plans for his furniture.

In Chapter 11 we discuss in detail why Charlie has priority to use *Build-Right* in his existing market territory over the federally registered name. In Chapter 13, we discuss negotiation strategies that Charlie might use in responding to the letter, including how to approach coming to an agreement about the separate ways in which each will have marketing rights. If Charlie has marketed nationally, he might even threaten to bring a trademark cancellation proceeding against *Buildright*.

Scenario 10

International business venture with mark to be used nationally. Tom and Henry, whose corporate name is *Attitudes For Adventure, Inc.*, want to market their new U.S.-based international adventure trip service under *AFA International*. They decide to register this service mark on the federal trademark register, but before paying the $245 application fee, they want to be sure that someone else in a similar business isn't already using the name without registering it. Tom and Henry are concerned because they have heard that the owner of a federally registered mark does not have exclusive rights if another person has been using the mark beforehand. How do they find out whether that name is already in use by someone else?

Analysis

Do a thorough conflict search before registering. Tom and Henry are right—first use, not registration, bestows ownership rights. (But remember, an application to federally register a mark on an intent to use basis serves as the first use date for the applicant.)

To find potential conflicts, Tom and Henry should first search the Internet and the federal trademark register for similar trademarks, since Tom and Henry will be marketing their service nationwide. They should also check all other major resources where actual but unregistered uses of the name are likely to appear, such as:

- the Yellow Pages for their area and surrounding areas
- the Yellow Pages for other major metropolitan cities
- the state trademark register for their state
- trade magazines and compilations of names of related businesses and products—many of which are available in most large public libraries.

If their proposed name is shown to be clear of all potential conflicts with identical and similar marks through this searching process, they can then proceed to register it on the federal trademark register with confidence.

Chapters 5 and 6 tell you how to search the Internet, These chapters also inform you how to conduct thorough searches of both state and federal trademark registers, as well as all major resources for nonregistered names.

Chapter 10 tells you how to analyze the results of a search.

Chapter 8 tells you how to fill out and file an application to register your mark on the federal register with line-by-line instructions and troubleshooting tips.

Scenario 10 1/2

National business wants to go international. Tom and Henry plan that, once launched, *Attitudes For Adventure, Inc.*, will attract some international clients and will operate in foreign countries on a number of treks. So after they clear their name for use in the United States, Tom and Henry turn their attention to whether they can get international trademark rights to the name. They learn from Chapter 14, International Trademark Protection, that each country has its own trademark laws and procedures, and that they will have to register their trademark separately in each, although in some countries, U.S. trademarks are entitled to certain reciprocal rights. They also learn that they will first have to search for other uses of their name in each of those countries. Chapter 14 gives them enough of an overview of the process of registering a trademark internationally to convince them to try to get international trademarks in at least some countries, but that they should hire an experienced trademark attorney to do it for them. ■

How to Choose a Good Name for Your Business, Product or Service

Now that you have absorbed some trademark basics in Chapter 1, it's time to set about choosing a trademark for your business and/or its services and products. Because most developed trademark principles apply to names rather than other types of business and product identifiers, we focus on names in this chapter.

➡ If you want to know about choosing logos, trade dress, Web pages, slogans and other items that also can qualify for trademark status, skip to Section G below.

If you are not choosing a commercial name but rather are reading this book because you are involved in a dispute, skip directly to Chapter 11. That chapter covers much of the material in this chapter but in significantly more detail, the kind of detail you'll need to handle your dispute in an informed manner.

If you think you understand the basics about what makes a trademark legally strong or weak, skip ahead to Section E, Guidelines for Making a Mark Distinctive.

Finally, please keep in mind the steps outlined in Chapter 1, Section G1, Steps to Take When Choosing Your Business Name, when reading through this chapter and naming your business or product.

The goal of this chapter is to help you choose a name that will:

- do a good job of identifying your products and services in the marketplace, and
- have enough legal strength to give you the exclusive right to use it.

Not all readers will care about these goals. For instance, the name *Rob's Pastry Center* may be just the ticket for the bakery Rob Johnson plans to open, but the name certainly won't leap out and grab the average consumer's attention. Nor would the law give such a name much protection because of its ordinary and descriptive nature. Nevertheless, Rob likes the name and so he should

use it despite what the lawyers say (yes, both authors are lawyers).

What follows, then, is the type of information you'll need if you do agree with our goals or at least want more information before you decide whether to pursue them.

A. Anatomy of a Product or Service Name Trademark

To understand when a product or service name trademark will qualify for legal protection, a review of what does and does not qualify for trademark status is in order.

1. A Name Trademark Always Has Two Parts

As mentioned, the most common type of trademark is the name assigned to a product or service to uniquely identify it in the marketplace. In fact, name trademarks always have two different parts. The first part is the name itself. It is the part that is intended to identify the product or service. Sometimes the first part is just one or two words, as in *Cadillac* or *Kaiser Permanente*. Other times the first part includes not only a unique name but also the type of product or service the name refers to. For instance, the business name *Wildside Pet Shop* is a trademark identifying the service of selling pets and pet supplies. As we'll see below, while this name might qualify for trademark protection as a whole (because of the distinctive term *Wildside*), the words "pet shop" would not be protected and could be used by anyone in combination with terms other than the term "wildside."

The second part of a name trademark is the type of service or product to which the name applies. In the case of *Cadillac*, this second part would be the generic description for the underlying product—that is, automobile. In the case of *Wildside Pet Shop*, the second part would be something like "pets and pet supplies sales and services." Because the first part of the name—the trademark part—is intended as a unique identifier, the name's owner (and, properly, anyone else who uses it) should always capitalize it as a proper adjective. Because the second part of the name—the description of the underlying type of product or service—is not unique, neither the owner nor anyone else should ever capitalize it.

2. A Name Is Not a Trademark If It's the Generic Term for the Underlying Products or Services Offered by the Business

As we have mentioned, for a name or other symbol to qualify as a mark, it must be unique enough to distinguish the underlying product or service from others in the marketplace. Sometimes, however, a mark assigned to a product or service is very close or identical to the generic name for the underlying type of product or service being marketed. For example, assume that a business names its new soft drink product *Diet Cola*. As it turns out, "diet cola" describes a group of carbonated soft drinks with cola flavoring and some form of sugar substitute. That fact makes the would-be *Diet Cola* mark generic and not a trademark at all because it could refer to any of several brands of the underlying diet cola product. But add *Shasta* to diet cola, and *Shasta* qualifies as a trademark because it specifies one particular brand of the several diet colas available on the market. Other examples of terms that have always been generic are lite beer, superglue, soft soap, matchbox cars and supermarket.

The upshot of all this is that the courts will not provide protection for a mark that essentially is the generic name for the underlying product or service—nor will the U.S. Patent and Trademark Office accept such a mark for federal registration.

B. Distinctive Names Make Legally Strong Trademarks

As we stress throughout the book, the more unique a business, product or service name is, the easier it is to protect the name from use by others. Because distinctive names make legally strong trademarks, it behooves you to choose a unique name. A product or service name can be unique for a number of reasons, including:

- The name may be coined (made up), as in *Exxon* petroleum products
- The combination of words and letters in the name may be so creative that no one else has come up with it, as in *Trader Joe's* food market chain)
- The name may carry a clever double meaning, as in *Peas in a Pod* maternity stores
- The name may have a clever appearance, as in *Toys R Us*
- Certain words in the name may be completely arbitrary in the context and therefore highly original, as in *Diesel, A Bookstore.*

Whatever the reason, a unique name is by nature considered to be a distinctive name, and a distinctive name is by law entitled to protection as a trademark. We explain how to make your mark distinctive in Section E below.

C. How Trademark Law Treats Marks With Common Terms

If unique trademarks are deserving of the most protection, then common or ordinary trademarks are entitled to little or no protection. But when deciding whether a trademark is legally strong or legally weak, you have to look to the whole mark. For example, many marks that the law will protect are completely made up of ordinary words. Consider the example of *Peas in a Pod* as a name for a maternity store. There is nothing terribly unusual about any of the words, but the phrase is terribly clever—because of its double meaning suggestive of a uterus (the pod) and an embryo (the pea) and would definitely qualify as a distinctive mark.

While this subject is taken up in detail in Chapter 10, the basic rules that apply to marks containing ordinary terms are these:

- If the overall mark is distinctive, it will be protected no matter how many ordinary terms are used.
- The owner of a trademark using ordinary terms cannot claim ownership to the terms themselves, but only to the overall mark.
- If the ordinary terms in a mark do not create a distinctive or clever whole, the mark will not be given protection unless a) the terms are distinctive in the context of the product or service (for instance the ordinary word apple becomes distinctive in the context of computers) or b) over time consumers come to associate the mark with the underlying product or service, as in *Best Buy* (retail electronic products).

Let's examine these rules in a little more detail.

1. Most Ordinary Words Are Not Protected

So far, you should know that on a protection scale of 1 to 10, generic terms rate a zero while distinctive marks are near the 10 end. Now let's lump all the rest of the terms that businesses frequently like to use as names of services or products into a category we will call "ordinary names."

Into this category are consigned all the sorts of words that aren't usually distinctive by themselves, but that aren't generic either:

- place names (*Downtown Barber*)
- personal names (*Harris Sales, Rubin's Assembly Service*)
- words that describe the product or service (*Slim-Fast Diet Food*), and
- laudatory words or words of praise (*Tip-Top Pet Shop*).

Misspellings or alternative spellings (like "lite") cannot make an ordinary term (like light) distinctive. Nor do common foreign language equivalents, like "le" for "the" and "casa" for "house."

Because marks that use ordinary terms in ordinary ways are, by definition, not distinctive—that is, the terms aren't unusual or surprising in the context—they receive little legal protection at the outset of their use. That means that under the principles of trademark law, it's more difficult to keep others from using them or something similar.

For example, the mark *Dependable Dry Cleaners* merely describes the business, without distinguishing it from its rivals. In fact, some of the rivals might also need to advertise their services as reliable or efficient. If trademark law prevented such ordinary uses of common terms, our language would be seriously depleted. As a result, *Dependable Dry Cleaners* gets little protection as a mark from the courts. Does this mean you can't protect the trademark of a dry cleaner? Of course not. A fanciful name like *Cinderella Dry Cleaners* (if it's not already used by someone else) is a distinctive and therefore fully protectible trademark.

2. Even Undistinctive Marks May Be Entitled to Protection Once They Become Widely Recognized as Marks

As mentioned in earlier chapters, there is an important exception to the general rule that weak marks are difficult to protect. It's this: Consumer familiarity with an ordinary mark can make the mark distinctive and therefore legally protectible. This is called the "secondary meaning" rule. Many of the most famous and effective marks, like *McDonald's* or *The Yellow Pages*, originally consisted of ordinary terms that over time became widely recognized as product and service identifiers and thus were transformed into strong marks (*McDonald's* is probably one of the strongest marks in the world).

Using a mark that can't be protected until it has acquired secondary meaning can be a serious drawback to the small business owner. Either the business owner must accept the fact that the mark will be weak, and therefore subject to use by others, until the mark's reputation has been built up over time, or the owner must be prepared to spend a lot of money to promote the mark when it is first used, so that the public recognizes it sooner. Unless money is no object, it may be better to start out with an unusual word, phrase or design that is protectible from the outset as a mark.

As with other topics touched on in this chapter, we discuss secondary meaning in detail in Chapter 10, Evaluating Trademark Strength.

REAL RAY'S BEST FAMOUS ORIGINAL PIZZA

Here's a Big Apple anecdote that illustrates the problem with trying to protect a name that's not distinctive. In New York City, which many view as pizza heaven (along with Chicago), there has been a proliferation of *Ray's Pizzas*, some of which are known for great pizza. There now are more than two dozen in the city, most of them under separate ownership. They call themselves *Ray's Original Pizza, Real Ray's, Famous and Original Ray's,* and variations on that theme. From a pizza lover's point of view, when two people set a date to meet at Ray's, no one knows which pizzeria anyone means. (*Ray's* on 7th Ave.? *Ray's* on Christopher St.? Which *Ray's* on 2nd Ave.? Or is it *Ray's* on Houston?) Consumers never know what quality to expect because they don't know which *Ray's* are related. The pizza parlors get each other's mail and complaints, and none of the owners can sort it out. Resorting to the courts has failed because, with so many *Ray's*, no owner can prove that consumers associate the name *Ray's* with any one pizzeria. So none is distinctive enough to be protected as a trademark.

D. What Makes a Distinctive Trademark a Legally Strong Trademark?

Let's take our earlier discussion of distinctiveness a little farther to explore why distinctive marks make legally stronger marks. A distinctive mark has a greater ability to ward off copiers than does a common name, for three reasons.

1. The more distinctive a mark is, like *Kodak*, the greater an impression it makes on the

customer's memory, and the more likely it is that a similar mark, say *Kodec*, will remind the customer of the original mark. That can lead to confusion. The customer may think *Kodak* and *Kodec* are the same brand, or that they are related. They may buy one instead of the other, or they may be misled into thinking the reputation of one applies to the other. In either case the customer is confused, and the rightful owner of the *Kodak* mark will have probably lost profits.

2. The more distinctive a mark is, the more likely it is that potential customers will assume that all products and services carrying the mark originate from one source. This is the opposite of what consumers are likely to think when confronted with ordinary marks that are similar to each other. For instance, it's reasonable to assume that *Double Rainbow Ice Cream* is manufactured by one company whereas you wouldn't make that same assumption for several ice cream outlets that use some combination of *Tastee* in their marks. The greater the likelihood that customers will associate a product or service carrying a particular mark with a particular source, the greater the need to protect them against the confusion that would likely result if the same or similar mark was adopted and used by another business.

3. The more time, money and creativity that goes into making a mark distinctive, the more sense it makes to provide the mark with adequate protection. And if the distinctiveness comes from widespread customer recognition over time (the secondary meaning rule) it also makes sense to protect the business good will that has been built up under the mark. Although the main reason for the trademark laws is to prevent customer confusion, the dilution principle (discussed in Chapter 11) recognizes that the

value of a well-known mark should be protected in its own right, whether or not customers are confused.

STATE AND FEDERAL UNFAIR COMPETITION LAWS CAN PROVIDE LIMITED PROTECTION TO WEAK TRADEMARKS

There's one more important point to understand about descriptive and ordinary words or phrases used as trademarks. While they are not effective as trademarks without secondary meaning, ordinary names can receive certain kinds of limited protection from confusing use by other businesses under state statutes or cases barring activities that amount to "unfair competition."

Protection from unfair competition is most useful where the second user of your trade name or mark is trying to create the impression that their business is affiliated with your business. In other words, unfair competition laws can help you if someone isn't making it clear through a variety of ways that they are not connected to your business.

We discuss unfair competition more fully in Chapter 11, Sorting Out Trademark Disputes, Section C.

E. Guidelines for Making a Mark Distinctive

Short of words that have been coined for the precise purpose of operating as trademarks, such as *Exxon*, the quality of distinctiveness in a mark is most likely to arise from downright cleverness. For a name mark to be clever and therefore distinctive, it need not use words that are unusual or even weird. For example, distinctive trademarks often consist of ordinary words used creatively in an unusual context (example: *Camel* for cigarettes, *Apple* for computers), or several ordinary words combined in an interesting way (*Thistle Dew Inn*) or with an innovative design (*SC[i]3*), and words that evoke fanciful associations (*Double Rainbow Ice Cream*).

Also commonly used for distinctive marks are ordinary words that indirectly suggest what the underlying product or service is all about without describing it outright. Examples of these suggestive marks are: *Verbatim* (for computer disks), *Banana Republic* (for a store that specializes in stylish rugged-wear clothes), or *Bloomers* (for a flower shop).

Clearly, whether a trademark is distinctive will depend on both its components and the context in which these components are used. Here we describe the sorts of marks that are routinely considered by the courts to be inherently distinctive and therefore legally strong. (We go into much greater detail on this in Chapter 10, Evaluating Trademark Strength.) These, therefore, are the kinds of marks we advise you to use, taking into account the marketing considerations outlined in Section F below.

1. Marks Using Coined Terms—Such as *Kodak*, *Exxon* and *Rackafrax*— and Terms Made Up of Parts of Different Words, Such as *Unisys*

These are wholly new, made-up words with no meaning and probably not even any connotation other than the one you will create for it with your advertising and other marketing activities. The key to a coined mark is making it pronounceable and appealing to both eye and ear, or at least suitable to the image you want to project for your product or service. To avoid coined terms that evoke unintended images, run your choices by a variety of people and note their responses to the sound and appearance of the mark. (Sample surveys of customers should be saved for marks that have passed the legal availability test.) As men-

tioned in Chapter 1, the best way to make a mark distinctive is to make it up.

Despite their legal strength, most coined words require extensive marketing efforts—and the attendant costs—to get established as product or service identifiers in the first place. More than any other kind of mark, coined words require lots of initial advertising, because coined words don't mean anything to the general public without it. That's a major drawback for a small business with limited start-up capital.

Opting for a coined term as your trademark has a second drawback. With over 70,000 new trade names and marks being registered each year, the well of coinable words is fast being drained. Despite our rich Celtic, Anglo-Saxon, Norman and Latin linguistic heritage, new combinations that sound good and look appropriate— that is, ones that are marketable and not already in use—are becoming harder to develop.

2. Marks That Suggest but Don't Outright Describe the Product or Service, or Some Aspect of It (Such as *Obsession* Perfume, *Sharp's* Nonalcoholic Beer, *Intuit* Software)

A mark is usually considered suggestive when you need to take at least one more mental step to figure out what is being suggested. Suggestive marks are favored by marketing folks because they operate to evoke an image or idea they want customers to associate with the product or service being marketed. *Obsession*, for example, creates the aura of irresistibility, certainly a desirable attribute for a perfume. This kind of mark is especially effective for the sorts of services or products that sell by affecting one's self-image, like beauty services, clothing, jewelry, sports businesses or even cars. Again, test your ideas out on a number of people to see if they perceive the suggestion you hope to send.

While suggestive marks may also require marketing to become broadly identified with a product, they are usually easier to promote than coined ones, because they connote something about the product or service. Some name consultants argue that suggestive names are the most useful, because of their comparative legal strength (customers remember them), and because the images they evoke make them very effective marketing tools. On the other hand, it takes lots of thought to come up with one that's appropriately evocative, suits your customer base and hasn't been taken.

3. Marks That Use Fanciful Terms in the Context of Their Use (*Such as Bugle Boy* Clothes, *Double Rainbow Ice Cream, !Excite* Internet Search Service and *Penguin* Books)

These types of marks are fun to invent, because you can use any term or combination of terms that does not in fact describe your service or product in any way. The trick is to think up a term that is interesting, memorable and somehow appropriate without literally describing some aspect of your service or product. For example, *Guess?* works for youthful sportswear—it carries the idea of a company/products that are innovative, unusual and related to adventure. Of course clothes by themselves have none of these attributes, but that doesn't matter. Also, being the first to use such an original mark (a verb with a question mark) makes the company seem innovative. A company that comes along later and names its products *Why?* would only seem imitative.

Clearly consumer responses to these types of marks are subjective and intuitive, and the creator of a fanciful or arbitrary mark must therefore try to consider all the possible evocations that a mark may have and make the most of them.

4. Marks That Use Arbitrary Terms in the Context of Their Use

Words that are descriptive or ordinary when associated with one product or service (and thus weak marks or unprotectible altogether) can be very strong for another. For example, the trademark *Apple Computer* is distinctive and therefore strong because apples have nothing to do with computers, whereas the trademark *Green Apple Applesauce* is weak because it literally describes the product. Similarly, the word *Cherokee* works well as a trademark on a 4-wheel drive utility vehicle and on women's apparel, because in each case the word is arbitrary in the context—that is, it doesn't describe any aspect of the underlying products. But *Cherokee* wouldn't work well as a trademark on Native American crafts, because in that context it simply describes the expected origin of the goods. Finally, *Jellibeans* is a distinctive name for a skating rink, but is mundane (and probably generic) as the name of a line of oval, colored, chewy candies.

5. Common Terms in Uncommon Arrangements

As mentioned earlier the individual terms that make up strong marks need not themselves be inherently distinctive. So far we have focused primarily on what are essentially one-word trademarks—such as *!Excite, Exxon* and *Apple*. However, the distinctiveness of a trademark can also reside in a phrase, or in several words put together in an unusual way. Their common characteristic is that taken together they are somehow different from everyday words and names. For example, *Taco John's* has weak components—

taco is a common food item and there are millions of John's in the world—but the way the two words combine make the whole trademark distinctive and therefore protectible.

When evaluating a phrase to see if it's a strong or weak trademark, it is the overall impression that counts. If the phrase as a whole has an original ring to it, the fact that some of its elements are ordinary won't matter. For example, *Speedy Turtle Delivery Service* is memorable for the contrast of speed and turtle. This makes it distinctive, despite the fact that *Speedy Delivery Service* without the "Turtle" would be purely descriptive and therefore weak.

6. Ordinary Terms Combined With Novel Designs

Distinctive design elements can add distinctiveness to an otherwise trite name. *Toys R Us* is one example of a trademark where the words themselves incorporate a design that lends the name originality. More often, the words have a conventional design, but they are portrayed as part of a distinct design or type style that accompanies them. One example is the bell inside a circle that indicates one of the *Baby Bell* telephone companies. Others are the profiled eagle with red and blue bands signifying the *U.S. Postal Service*, the script letters "G" and "E" inside a circle indicating *General Electric*, the red *Texaco* star or the face of an Eskimo on the tail of *Alaska Airlines* planes.

Again, remember that what counts in evaluating a trademark's strength is the overall impression that the trademark creates in the mind of the consumer, rather than the impact of any single word or design element.

SOURCES OF MARKS THAT YOU MIGHT NOT THINK OF

While it may seem that all the good marks have been taken, there is in fact a virtually inexhaustible supply. But like diamonds, they usually aren't just lying on the ground for the taking; a little mining must take place and like the diamond in the rough, some cutting and polishing may be required to make them shine. Some of the sources for finding a distinctive name for a trademark are:

- new combinations of existing words (*Palmolive, Diehard*)
- combinations of word roots (*Navistar, Soloflex*)
- distinctive foreign words (*Scirocco* car, Soleil watches)
- abandoned marks that are no longer in use but which were once famous can make strong marks. They may bring a certain cachet to your product or service, if their former image corresponds to the one you now want to project.

If you do discover a mark you know has been in use at one time, you should find out if it is now available for your use by doing the sort of searches we describe in Chapter 5.

7. Names to Avoid

Now that we've suggested what types of words make distinctive marks, it will help to describe the types of words that cut against distinctiveness (unless they obtain secondary meaning through use over time).

a. Personal Names, Including Nicknames, First Names, Surnames and Initials

Probably the most common type of name trademark used for a business is one that carries the owner's first or last name. *Mary's Pizza* (yes, it is owned by Mary), *Thurlow's Web Designs* and *Brian Loman Electronics* are examples. For the most part these personal name trademarks are legally weak and not much good for customer recognition outside the business's locale. But combined with a non-name term, such as *Taco Johns* or *Trader Joe's*, a mark built around a personal name can be quite distinctive. And if you have a name like *Orville Redenbacher's*, you have no distinctiveness worries at all.

WHEN CAN YOU USE YOUR OWN NAME AS A TRADEMARK?

One of the reasons that personal names are not protectible is the idea that no one should have a monopoly on a personal name. Unless the name has already come to mean a particular service or product through the secondary meaning rule, it isn't fair for one Jones to prevent all the other Joneses from using their family name. For this reason, the courts used to say that anyone had an absolute right to use his or her own name to identify a product or service.

That's been qualified over the years. Now individuals still have the right to use their own names, but not if it will confuse consumers or smack of an unfair attempt to ride on the coattails of their famous namesakes. Generally that means you can use your own name, but not in the same line of work as a trademark owner of the same name. So, for example, Prosper Champion (unrelated to the original sparkplug Champion) was not allowed to make and market spark plugs under his name. Nor would anyone named Marriott be permitted to open a hotel under that name. For the same reasons, a person who sells his name as the mark for a business can't later go into the same field using his own name again. Finally, you won't be able to use your own name as an Internet domain name if somebody else has beat you to it. For information about domain names and trademark law, see Chapter 11, Section F.

b. Practical Pointers on the Use of Personal Names as Trademarks

Now that you have a general idea of how personal names fit into the general rules regarding strong and weak marks, here are some pointers on using specific types of personal names.

Surnames. Using your surname (last name) as a trademark has a few drawbacks you might want to consider. You may want to sell the business someday, and it will be necessary, as a practical matter, to sell the name with it. This means a stranger will be operating under your name. And perhaps worst of all, the sale of your business may prevent your children or other relatives from capitalizing on the family expertise by opening their own similar business under their own name. Finally, as we saw, marks that are "primarily surnames" do not qualify for federal registration, absent a showing of secondary meaning or perhaps an association with another term that makes the combination inherently distinctive as a whole, such as *Warner's World* for a line of stores specializing in 100% cotton products.

First Names and Nicknames. First names are generally even weaker as trademarks than surnames, because most are so much more common. But, for the same reasons, they have fewer of the disadvantages that go with selling the business.

And, as we have seen, they can also become unusual simply with the addition of an unusual modifier, like *Trader Vic's* or *Aca Joe*.

As with surnames, anyone can use their first name or nickname on a business unless it's too close to a famous one. For example, "Sony" Florendo can't call her restaurant Sony's, and Mayo Priebe can't call her drugstore Mayo's Drugs. Sony Corp. and the Mayo Clinic objected to these uses and won, even though there was little likelihood of confusion between the local businesses and their more famous namesakes. Perhaps the judge felt that these were really attempts to capitalize on the more famous trademarks or that the second uses diluted the original marks. (See Chapter 11, Sorting Out Trademark Disputes.) But one is tempted to conclude that the size and wealth of the complaining parties was a significant factor.

Initials. Use of initials won't change the strength or weakness of the trademark if they are part of what is essentially a first or last name. For example, the owners of *P.T. Dann's* (as a trademark for a national clothing chain) won't infringe on the rights of others using the Dann name. On the other hand, until the company develops a lot of public awareness of the name as a mark (that is, it acquires a secondary meaning), they probably can't stop anyone else from using the same or similar trademark, except in the retail apparel business. But if another Dann opened up competing clothing stores, even without secondary meaning, P. T. Dann could probably stop them under unfair competition laws, as well as under trademark laws, once secondary meaning is shown.

A trademark consisting completely of letters that aren't a person's initials is not inherently weak. Rather, its trademark strength depends on the strength of the words the initials represent. If the initials do not stand for anything and are an uncommon arrangement of letters, the mark can be distinctive from the outset. For instance, *ABC* is not considered distinctive because this combination of letters is in such common use as a mark (except, of course, in the media world, where the network initials have secondary meaning). However, a mark consisting of *XQE* may be.

c. Marks That Describe Attributes of the Service or Product or Its Geographic Location

The main reason to avoid these marks is that they are legally weak and therefore not extensively protectible until they have been in use long enough that they have become easily recognized by your customers. However, many business owners believe that if they use some words in

---

BE CAREFUL ABOUT DECEPTION WHEN USING GEOGRAPHIC MARKS

Earlier we warned about using deceptive or misleading marks. This warning is especially appropriate for geographic terms that are used fancifully. There are really two types of possible deception in the use of geographic marks:

- actual deception in which the customer is induced to buy a product in the belief that the item comes from the region on the label
- deceptive misdescription in which the public might make a false geographic connection, but wouldn't particularly rely on the geographic factor in buying the service or product.

For instance, a deceptive trademark would be the mark *Limoges* for china that was neither made in France nor of French clay; or *American System*, for clothing made in Italy. A deceptive trademark is not protectible and can never become so even if it acquires secondary meaning. Further, using a deceptive mark may subject you to legal liability for false advertising.

On the other hand, using a mark like *Neapolitan* (especially with an Italian flag on the label) for Italian sausages made in Florida is seen as merely "deceptively mis-descriptive." That is, some people might be confused into thinking the sausages come from Naples, but that's either unlikely or not the main reason they would buy the sausages. Another example is calling a chewing tobacco *Durango* even though it is not from the noted tobacco growing region of Durango, Mexico. Such marks are not protectible until they have developed secondary meaning. Once the mark has secondary meaning, the potential for confusing the public is lessened, because presumably the public knows the product for what it is, and doesn't care where it comes from.

Obviously, the trademark implications of geographic terms can get a little muddy. We suggest this general rule: Don't use a geographical term, even if the place named has nothing to do with the origin of the product, as long as a reasonable consumer might think it does. If you decide that you absolutely have to use a geographic trademark, either make sure your mark has only a vague suggestive connection to your product or service (like *Sedona*, for a Portland, Maine, restaurant) or try combining it with other more inherently distinctive terms that make the trademark protectible from the outset, like *The Abilene Albatross* for a bar.

their trademark that either describe the type of business or some positive characteristic of the business, they will benefit far more by the marketing payoff than they risk from would-be copiers. (See Chapter 10, Evaluating Trademark Strength, for more on why these marks have such limited legal protectability.)

d. Names With Bad Translations, or Unfortunate Homonyms (Sound-alikes) or Unintended Connotations

These you should avoid because they can easily backfire as advertising tools. A famous example is the French soft drink called *Pschitt*, which had to be renamed for sale in this country. Also, the Chevy *Nova* is an unwise trademark for a car in Spanish-speaking countries (including perhaps our own because of the high proportion of Spanish speakers) because the mark means "it does not run" in Spanish.

e. Names That Closely Resemble Well-known Marks

If you definitely want to avoid being sued for trademark infringement, avoid using famous marks or obvious variations of them. Whether they succeed or not, claims of trademark infringement and dilution (a type of protection for well-known marks) are commonly brought by owners of famous marks in order to clear the field. McDonald's regularly sues companies that use the "Mc" prefix or yellow arches. Often they succeed—preventing the use of "McSleep" for motels and yellow arches for a computer company. (See Chapter 11, Section E for a more complete discussion.)

F. Marketing Considerations When Choosing a Name Mark

Now that we have dissected what makes a mark distinctive, here are a few practical pointers that combine the legal information just discussed with some marketing savvy that is part of picking the "right" name for your business, service or product.

1. General Advice

George Eastman, founder of Kodak, and a man with an eye for a good trademark, suggested that trademarks should
- be short
- be vigorous
- be easily spelled, and
- mean nothing.

While this advice certainly worked for him, it may not apply to your situation. If not, heed the advice of other trademark experts who recommend that name marks be:
- pronounceable
- memorable
- graphically attractive (for instance, no hyphens), and
- legally available.

Chapters 5 and 6 explain how to find out whether your mark is legally available. Whether your mark meets the other criteria discussed in this section is a more subjective decision that you will have to make yourself. However, these lists of desirable trademark characteristics omit an important point—your mark must also be tailored to meet the needs of your business and your customers.

2. How to Come Up With a Good Name

Like most business decisions, your choice of how to select a good name mark will reflect your own personal style of decision-making. Here are some alternative methods:
- Delegate the job to a committee.
- Throw a naming-brainstorming party and ask all your friends.
- Make lists yourself.

- Use a computer to generate lists of names. (There is software available for this purpose; see Section 5, below.)
- Devise a contest to generate a name.
- Use all of the above methods.
- Hire a professional name consultant. (See Section 4, below, for more on this method.)

An excellent book to aid you in the naming process is *The Name's the Thing*, by Henri Charmasson, published by Dow Jones-Irwin, Homewood, IL 60430. It's a thorough and beautifully written analysis of the art and science of creating effective commercial names.

Whatever method you use, you will probably want to develop a long list and a short list. The long list would consist of likely possibilities that meet the criteria we discuss in Section 3, below, for tailoring your mark to your needs. Then you can use any of the above methods again to narrow the list to five or ten of the most likely.

When you have your short list, you must next go to Chapter 3 to find out how to tell which of your trademark possibilities can also be used as an Internet domain name, and to Chapters 5 and 6 to discover which possibilities meet the all-important criterion of legal availability. Only when you have searched and cleared each name for possible conflicts with existing marks and Internet domain names (if you plan to use the Internet for marketing purposes) can you make a final decision based on aesthetics or marketability or whatever you decide is your ultimate criterion.

3. Useful Concepts in Creating a Name Mark for Your Product or Service

The most useful concepts in creating a name mark are the same ones you or your advertising consultant would think about in devising a marketing scheme. Your mark is, after all, the most important aspect of your advertising plan. What will help you invent your mark are basic common-sense conclusions about what kinds of advertising will work best with your product or service, based on what you know about your customers.

Use the following questions to develop criteria that are specific to your needs and that you can then use, along with the suggestions in Section F1, to develop a list of potential marks. If you already have developed these criteria, this section tells you how to apply them to trademarks. And if you haven't, you might as well figure this stuff out now.

- What is your (projected) customer base? Is it a broad economic group, within a small region? Or is it a select group of professionals scattered nationwide? (This is the most important factor, as it affects all of the other criteria below.)
- What are your customers' demographics and income/educational level? (This will tell you the tone and style of your advertising, as well as what sort of words to use in your mark—for example, whether to use words that are young and hip or older and more traditional, funny or serious, highly literate or simple.)
- What are your customers' buying habits? Are they typically made in a hurry or more carefully considered? If they tend to buy in a rushed manner, then your trademark needs to be simple with a high visual impact. If your customers tend to buy in a more considered manner, then your mark can be more subtle and complex.)
- What aspect of your service/product will appeal to your potential customer base? This affects the image you want to project —if the main appeal of your service is convenience, then the trademark should somehow evoke that idea.
- Can you distill the essence of your product or service into a word or phrase? If there is a dominant idea connected with your service or product, then a mark that incorporates or reflects that idea will be easier for

you to promote and for your customers to remember.

- What image do you want to associate with your service or product? If the image you have is not exactly the one you want, you can try to develop a mark that reflects better your vision of your service or product. (A mark incorporating symbols popular with teenagers may not help you if you seek to appeal to stable young families.)

- How is your service or product different from the competition's? Perhaps the main thing about your service or product is that it is unique—the mark should help identify that characteristic, or that it's cheaper, or fancier, or whatever sets you apart in the marketplace.

- How will the mark be advertised—in what media and with what level of visibility? This affects whether you need both a logo and a name, whether a short word is essential or a longer phrase will do, or whether you want to focus on trade dress (creative packaging, etc.). Also, how broadly and where you will advertise your mark—on business cards, letterhead, pamphlets, a storefront, signs, packaging, radio ads—affects what sort of mark to use. That's because a complicated logo may translate well to business cards but you may not be able to see it clearly on a storefront.

The answers to some of these questions will also help you figure out what sources to use to create your mark, and what attributes the mark should have. For example, if your customer base is gourmet coffee drinkers, you could consider using foreign words, mythological names or literary references in creating a mark that evokes sophistication/good taste. But if your customers comprise a broad section of the population whose main concerns are value and convenience, you might want a more straightforward simple name using American roots or references.

4. Using a Professional Name Consultant

Most name consulting firms cater to large corporations and are not likely to meet the needs or the budgets of small businesses. To find one that will help you on a smaller scale, take the advice of Ira Bachrach of Namelab, a corporate name consulting firm in San Francisco. He recommends calling a small- to medium-sized ad agency and asking them to help you create a name as a discrete time-limited project for a fixed fee.

He advises you to specify what they are expected to produce for that fee, and to propose paying when you get the result, or paying half in advance, half at the end. Often, at ad agencies, creative people will have little gaps of free time in which they could work on your project. If you explain that you are not a potential client, they will treat you as a one-time project. Bachrach also says that he is often surprised at how many established agencies will sometimes help small businesses in naming their product or service.

A few well-established naming firms do routinely consult for smaller companies. One such is Alias, which provides both search services and naming assistance, as well as trademark legal advice. Henri Charmasson, who is a principal in the firm, is a trademark lawyer and the author of *The Name's the Thing*, described above.

Alias Product and Corporate
Name Laboratory
1545 Hotel Circle So., Suite 150
San Diego, CA 92108
619-294-2924

Another name consulting service known as Name-It may be contacted at any of the following locations:

4546 El Camino Real, Suite D
Los Altos, CA 94022
800-776-0530

2706 Harbor Blvd., Suite 212
Costa Mesa, CA 92626
800-550-1520

2025 Pennsylvania Ave. NW, Suite 1004
Washington, DC, 20006
800-340-2010

5. Computer Software

Some computer software programs that may also be helpful when brainstorming possible business, product or service names, although they may cost too much for a one-time naming process. Below we list a couple. Call the companies for the current price and other details.

The NameStormers
4347 W. N.W. Highway
Suite 1040
Dallas, TX 75220-3864

They provide a comprehensive name consultation service, called NameStorming, and sell two name-generating computer programs that help you name products, services or corporations in a variety of ways. Namer® (DOS platform) costs $195 and NamePro (Windows) costs $495. The service, which is individually tailored, costs $5,500.

IdeaFisher Systems Inc.
2222 Martin St., #110
Irvine, CA 92715
800-289-4332

This software company produces IdeaFisher, a "concept thesaurus" in a database that can generate ideas, associations or connotations for use in naming businesses, marketing products and any other creative activity that uses free-associated ideas. You can follow an initial concept through a hierarchy of linked ideas and images to arrive at a list of related names. It also allows you to walk through a set of questions and answers that deal specifically with naming businesses, products or services. The product costs between $39.95 and $89.95, depending on your needs and the type or size of business.

G. Beyond Names: Graphics, Packaging, Color and Product Designs as Trademarks

Most businesses use their name in combination with graphic images, colors, packaging and other symbols or devices. As we will see, there are many devices other than names that can distinguish your products or services in the marketplace. In this section we discuss how these devices relate to your name mark and how they can function separately as marks in their own right.

1. Graphics

The term logo (short for logotype) is often used to connote graphic combinations of lettering and imagery. A logo can be a name used with stylized lettering (*Rolling Stone Magazine*), geometric shapes (the *Chevrolet* logo, the *Nike* swirl) or iconographic imagery (the multicolored *Apple* computer logo). These combinations are discussed below.

a. Typefaces and Stylized Words

You may wish to use your product or service mark with a specific typeface or stylized form of lettering. For example, the computer service *America Online* uses a stylized script for the word "Online." The publisher of this book, *Nolo Press*, has a distinctive script style featuring a "tail" for first and last letter (see back cover of this book). A unique form of lettering draws attention to a name mark. It may also add some distinction to an otherwise nondistinctive term, as does, for example, the distinctive typeface used in *The New Yorker* magazine name. If the words in the mark are distinctive in their own right and you want to register only one mark, register the mark without the typeface. (See Chapter 8.) But most businesses always use the typeface with the word mark to achieve protection if the words are not distinctive on their own.

b. Graphic Designs and Words

The combination of words and a graphic image can have a powerful impact on consumers. For example, preceding a motion picture you may see the word *TriStar* featured with a galloping stallion, *Columbia* superimposed behind Lady Liberty, or *Universal* surrounding the globe. See Chapter 8, Federal Trademark Registration, Section B7, for an explanation of the registration options for these types of marks.

c. Graphic Designs Without Names

A graphic image can serve as a separate trademark if it creates its own commercial impression. The cross-shaped *Chevrolet* logo and the upside down "peace sign" graphic for the *Mercedes Benz* need no words for product identification. The public recognizes these as a unique source of origin apart from the words or name. A graphic image can be inherently distinctive (the image of the girl with the umbrella for *Morton's* salt) or it can acquire distinctiveness through extensive sales and advertising (the "triple A" logo for the Automobile Association of America services.) The less distinctive the graphic design, the less likely it will function as a trademark. Simple graphic shapes such as oval frames, horizontal bands or parallelogram borders are difficult to claim as marks. A bakery could only claim its checkered gingham design as a trademark after demonstrating that the public recognized the graphic image apart from the bakery's name (that is, it had acquired secondary meaning). In order to

"strengthen" a graphic image, the image should be used often, and the company should draw attention to it in advertising. ("Look for the Windows 95 logo.")

For information on how to federally register graphic designs, see Chapter 8, Federal Trademark Registration, Section D.

2. Trade Dress

Trade dress refers to the total image of a product or service created with a combination of such features as size, shape, color or color combinations, texture, graphics, or even particular sales techniques. To the extent that the decor of a business, the packaging of a product or the shape of a product are both distinctive and intended to operate as marks, they will be treated as marks and can even be registered as marks with the PTO.

A complete discussion of trade dress is beyond the scope of this book, but basic legal principles that apply to trade dress are presented below and may be helpful, particularly in relation to the use of product and service names with trade dress elements.

Visitors to a Hard Rock Cafe can identify various features that distinguish this chain of restaurants from competitors. In a liquor store, you can distinguish the bottles of *Absolut* vodka from those of its competitors. Most schoolchildren know the colors of Superman's uniform and the *Coca-Cola* logo. These are all examples of trade dress.

Whether or not a particular trade dress qualifies as a trademark depends on the same general concepts as those used with word marks. For example, a Mexican restaurant chain uses Mexican artifacts and murals in its interior decor. These are common elements of Mexican culture and no restaurant could claim them exclusively as a trademark (in the same way that you can't monopolize common words). However, if a restaurant chain uses murals and artifacts but also uses a specific indoor and outdoor decor based upon neon colored border stripes (primarily pink), distinctive outdoor umbrellas and a novel buffet style of service, then that unique combination of trade dress elements functions like a trademark. On this basis, the U.S. Supreme Court ruled that one Mexican restaurant chain could prevent another from copying its overall decor. (The official cite for this case is: *Two Pesos, Inc. v. Taco Cabana, Inc.* (112 S.Ct. 2753, 120 L.Ed.2d 615 (1992).)

Like the decor of the restaurant, the design or elements of your product packaging, or the features of your ads or promotion may combine to form trade dress that will qualify for trademark protection whether or not the trade dress is federally registered. But as with word marks, federal registration enhances the protection. See Chapter 8, Section C for how to register some elements of trade dress.

Despite the importance of trade dress and the need to protect it against copying by others, the law on the subject of trade dress is still not predictable. For example, a federal court found that there was no trade dress infringement in the case of two skin care products with similar lettering, colors, and graphic design. The court determined that the prominent use of each company's name on its own product would prevent consumers from being confused by the similar trade dress. And, as with word trademarks, without the likelihood of customer confusion there is no trademark infringement. So, despite distinctive trade dress, the issue in those cases still came down to whether the name mark was copied. For this reason, prominent use of your name or logo is recommended in combination with all trade dress.

Trade dress, whether it is decor, color, product shape or packaging, requires three elements for protection.

1) The trade dress feature for which protection is sought cannot have a functional purpose other than to distinguish the product or service in the marketplace. This may seem confusing, because all trade dress features have at least some utilitarian function. For instance, packaging protects products against wear and tear and a uniquely

shaped bottle holds the bottle's contents. But if the design elements are not essential for the underlying product's purpose (for instance, the curved shape of the *Coca-Cola* bottle isn't a necessary part of the cola product), then the trade dress is considered not functional in a legal sense. On the other hand, the blue dot on *Sylvania* flashcubes was considered too functional to qualify for separate trademark status, because it served the utilitarian purpose of indicating when a bulb was used (when the blue dot turns black).

2) The trade dress feature must be distinctive (either inherently distinctive or acquired distinctiveness.) For example, the egg-shaped *L'eggs* pantyhose container is inherently distinctive because it has a unique visual impact on customers. If the trade dress is not inherently distinctive, distinctiveness can still be acquired through extensive sales and advertising. A red star may not be inherently distinctive but when it is used extensively in advertising for gasoline sales and automotive services ("Look for the Big Red Star") then it will have acquired secondary meaning.

3) In the case of the actual shape of the product itself, the trade dress feature sought to be protected must be intended to operate as a mark—that is, as a means of designating the product's origin or distinguishing the product from others in the marketplace.

a. Colors Used in Combination With a Name or Graphic

Colors help to distinguish products and services. A box of film that is gold and black connotes a *Kodak* product. A yellow arch indicates *McDonald's* food services. When color is used with a name or graphic design of a trademark (such as the red lettering and blue star of *Con-*

verse footwear) it is registered as an element of the trademark. Federal registration ensures that you can stop competitors from using a combination of similar elements (that is, a similar name and similar colors). However, this form of registration does not ensure that you can stop competitors from using similar colors with a different word mark. For more on registering marks that contain specific colors, see Chapter 8, Federal Trademark Registration, Section C2.

b. Color as a Separately Registrable Trademark

For many years, color by itself was not considered to be registrable as a trademark. For instance, Campbell's Soup was unable to register the colors red and white for its products. However, the law on this subject has slowly evolved. In the 1980s, Owens-Corning registered the color pink for its fiberglass insulation and in 1995, the Supreme Court ruled that a manufacturer of dry cleaning press pads could claim registration for a green-gold color. *Qualitex v. Jacobson Products*, 115 S.Ct. 1300; 131 L.Ed.2d 248; 63 U.S.L.W. 4227 (1995). Also, in 1995, a federal appeals court in New York ruled that a color combination (signifying different tensions in an exercise band) could be protected. *Fabrication Enterprises v. The Hygenic Corporation*, 64 F.3d 53; 1995 (2d Cir. 1995). For information about federally registering a color, see Chapter 8, Section C2.

CHOOSING A COLOR AS A TRADEMARK

There are several rules to keep in mind when choosing a color as a trademark:

1. A color that serves a purpose or suggests characteristics (white for life preservers, red for chili) cannot function as a trademark.
2. Color combinations or shades of colors are better than primary colors like red, blue, etc.
3. The strength of your color trademark (and its ability to be registered) increases as a result of sales, promotion and advertising (e.g., "Look for the Yellow Arches"). When possible, use the color in combination with your name.
4. Do not choose colors commonly associated with your product class (for instance, black for marine engines).
5. Avoid using color combinations that are unique to competitors (especially competitors who have invested time and money in the promotion of those colors).

---

c. Product Designs

The rules surrounding protection for product design (also known as product configuration) are extremely complex and a full explanation is beyond the scope of this book. However, the following information may assist you in deciding whether your product design qualifies as a trademark. (Details on federally registering a product design are contained in Chapter 8, Federal Trademark Registration, Section C2.)

Your product may be distinguished by a uniquely designed element, shape or container. For example, scotch buyers can easily identify the products of Haig & Haig by its pinched decanter. This unique shape or design can be registered and protected under trademark law. Similarly, the unique placement of a brass button on jeans may signify the Levi Strauss company. As with colors, the Trademark Office will permit registration of product configurations or designs (1) if the configuration is not functional; (2) if the design is distinctive; and (3) if the configuration was intended to operate as a trademark.

One way to determine whether a design is functional is to consider the alternative designs available. For example, a bottle for *Mrs. Butterworth* maple syrup is sculpted in the form of a three-dimensional female figurine. A competitor selling maple syrup could think of many alternative ways to bottle syrup other than in a Mrs. Butterworth shaped bottle. Therefore, that design would be considered ornamental rather than functional and qualify for registration as a trademark.

Another way to examine if a design is functional is to determine whether it would be costly or difficult for a competitor to do without it. For example, it would not be costly or difficult for a competitor to do without the distinctive geometric lines of the Mogen David wine bottle, nor would treating the Mogen David wine bottle shape as a trademark deprive competitors of essential design features. However, it would be unfair and costly to deprive a company from using the convenient and historically common jug-shaped container for liquid bleach—a container that has no ornamental qualities.

Distinctiveness in product design is a separate issue from function. Distinctiveness is determined by the same standards discussed earlier in the chapter. Some designs are highly original and by their nature, inherently distinctive. Some designs, though not functional, are not inherently distinctive and require proof of sales or promotion. For example, a plastic planter designed to look like a Grecian urn was considered not inherently distinctive and required proof of consumer recognition through sufficient advertising and sales (that is, secondary meaning).

Product designs can be federally registered as trademarks. See Chapter 8, Federal Trademark Registration, Section C2.

WHERE TO FIND MORE ON TRADEMARK STRENGTH

Now that we have taken a closer look at what makes an effective trademark, you may want to go on to Chapter 10, Evaluating Trademark Strength. That chapter teaches you how to classify your (or another's) mark in terms of its legal strength. It discusses in much greater detail the varieties of distinctive and ordinary trademarks, including coined, fanciful and suggestive categories of distinctive marks, and descriptive, geographic, personal name and initial types of ordinary marks.

IF YOUR DESIGN IS FUNCTIONAL AND NOVEL

If your design is functional and novel you should research whether it can be protected as a utility patent. For example, let's say you have created a unique method of packaging compact disc recordings. If it is functional and unprotectable under trademark law, it may still be protectable under patent laws. For more information, review Nolo's *Patent It Yourself*.

Protecting and Registering Trade Names

In Chapter 1, we explained the basics of trademark law and how it applies to business names. We emphasized that business names become trademarks when they are used to identify a product or service in the marketplace. This happens, for instance, when a small business puts its name on its storefront, or features the name in a Yellow Pages advertisement to draw customers, or puts the name on products they produce, as Ford Motor Co. does on its automobiles and Nolo Press, Inc., does on its living trust software (Nolo's Living TrustMaker).

But business names also serve a nontrademark function. They serve as trade names to identify the business for such purposes as opening bank accounts, securing credit, ordering supplies, paying taxes and suing or being sued. Every business has a trade name. And, with a few exceptions, every business is required by state law to take certain legal steps to list its name with a public agency. These vary somewhat depending on the form of the business—for instance, corporations must follow a different procedure than partnerships. In addition to providing a registry where members of the public can check on a business ownership, these name registration procedures are designed to screen out the use of identical or very similar names within the state or county where the business is based. However, as we will see, they don't do a perfect job in accomplishing this.

⚠ An overview of state and county name registration requirements is set out in Section A. If you already have a business name and have taken the appropriate steps to register it, you

can skip that section. But be sure to read Section B, which deals with the most common misunderstanding in the field of business names—the belief that compliance with state corporate and assumed name registration requirements is all you need to do to assure you the right to use the name. As you'll see, nothing could be further from the truth. Section D deals with how to register a business name as an Internet domain name.

A. Mandatory Registration Requirements for Trade Names

All names that identify business entities—corporate names, fictitious business names, assumed names, partnership names, the names of nonprofit, charitable, religious and educational institutions and the names of sole proprietorships—are trade names. Each state has business license requirements which involve registering these names with city, county or state offices. Corporations usually must register with their state's secretary of state or corporation commissioner's office. Unincorporated businesses must usually register with an agency that keeps track of "fictitious or assumed names." Rather than describe the specific requirements of all fifty states, we will explain generally the requirements for most of the states and give you enough information to easily find out the rest on your own.

1. Corporate Name Registration

Corporations are creatures of state law. By a legal fiction, they are considered persons—artificial persons. When they are created, we say they are incorporated (literally translated—given a body).

This process involves filing articles of incorporation, paying a fee (and possibly an advance on corporate taxes), picking a board of directors and, most important for our purposes, registering the corporate name with the secretary of state, state department of corporations or corporations commissioner. Each state's laws on this are a little different. Registering a corporate name involves three steps.

Step 1. Selecting a permissible name

All but three states (Maine, Nevada and Wyoming) require you to include a word or its abbreviation indicating corporate status, like "corporation," "incorporated," "company," "limited." Several states also require that the name be in English or Roman characters.

In addition, most states forbid including in your corporate name words that imply a purpose different from the one stated in the articles of incorporation, or that mislead or deceive the public. For example, if you are forming a corporation that will help people fill out their medical insurance forms, you probably shouldn't call it Oil Drillers, Inc.

Step 2. Clearing your name

Next you will need to make sure that your corporate name is distinguishable from any corporate name already registered in that state. The reason is simple—your state won't register a corporate name that too closely mimics a name already on file. To ease your task, the secretary of state or other corporate filing agency will do a search for you prior to authorizing the use of your name. In about half the states, you may phone to check on the availability of a name in advance. In the others you must write to request a search. Often you may request a search of more than one name at a time. Those who are fairly confident that their name is unique may simply submit their articles of incorporation without a search, and risk rejection if the name is, in fact, already taken.

How thorough the search is varies from state to state. Generally the state agency will compare your name with registered and reserved names of other corporations incorporated in your state and with those incorporated elsewhere that have registered to do business in your state. In some states, the search encompasses other trade names, such as limited partnerships and assumed (fictitious) names. Some states—but not most—also search the state trademark and service mark lists before registering a corporate name.

Each state's rules vary on how different your name must be from an existing name. Some will accept names that sound the same as long as they are spelled or punctuated differently. Others require that corporate names differ more than just in variations in spelling, punctuation, articles or corporate indicator (like "Inc."). All require a proposed user to make enough changes in a confusingly or deceptively similar name to make it distinguishable from an existing name, even if the two corporations are in very different fields. What "distinguishable" means varies from state to state, and the office that oversees corporate registrations generally has complete discretion over such decisions.

⚠ Don't Choose a Too-Similar Name

Should your choice of a corporate name be rejected, you may be tempted to change a letter or two or punctuate it differently. This is usually a lousy idea. Even if the slightly amended name is accepted for registration, you will still have the real-world problem of distinguishing your name from the other one if you both use your names as trademarks or service marks. It is far better to select a new name—one that is different from all existing names—if you wish to use it as a mark without fear of a trademark infringement dispute.

Nearly all states make exceptions to this general prohibition against registering deceptively similar corporate names. The most common one is that states will usually register a name that's deceptively similar to an existing name if the owner of the existing name gives written permission to use it. Most states make this exception because they are more concerned about existing rights of corporate name owners than about possible confusion in the marketplace.

OUT-OF-STATE CORPORATIONS

When a corporation that is incorporated in one state decides to expand its operations into another state, it is required to register in that state as "doing business" there. The purpose of this requirement is to give consumers, law enforcement officials and the secretary of state enough information about the corporation to bring it into court, should a dispute make it necessary. But sometimes a foreign corporation (that is, a corporation from another state) tries to register in a new state and discovers that its name is already in use there. Then it has to select another corporate name that is acceptable and not already in use. Even so, the corporation may be able to use its original name as a trademark or service mark in the state, if it does not conflict with a trademark in use in the state. Whether or not there's a trademark conflict—even with a corporate name—is decided under trademark law discussed in Chapter 11, Sorting Out Trademark Disputes.

Step 3. Reserving your corporate name

A corporation can usually reserve a name prior to actual incorporation if the name otherwise qualifies for registration. This freezes out other would-be registrants of that name (or one deceptively similar) during the period of reservation, usually 120 days. Most, but not all, states permit you to extend the reservation for one or more additional 120-day periods for additional fees. Some states even allow corporations to register their names only, without doing business in the state, and even to renew that name registration annually, which provides the equivalent of a long-term name reservation for out-of-state corporations. Check with the secretary of state to discover more about these options if you wish to use them.

The reservation process involves sending an application for reservation to the secretary of state, or the equivalent, with a fee. (Of course it's wise to check the name's availability first. See Step 2 above.) Some states even permit you to reserve a corporate name by telephone. You can find out the exact information by calling the secretary of state or corporate commissioner in your state.

Registering your corporate name may give you far fewer legal rights than you think it does. As discussed in Section B, below, it does not give you the legal right to use that name to identify your products or services, only the corporation.

2. Fictitious Business Names or Assumed Names

In all states, any person who uses a trade name other than his or her surname, or any organization that goes by a name other than the last names of the owners, must register the name with the state or county as a fictitious or assumed name.

This process, which is analogous to a corporate filing with the state, usually means filing a certificate with a fee with the county clerk stating who is doing business under that trade name. In many states, it is usual for the statement, often called a DBA (doing business as) to be published several times in a local newspaper, saying something like, "Clark Kent is registered with the county (or state) doing business as Superman." Such a statement allows creditors to find the people behind the business.

Some states require, instead of or in addition to publication, that you file the statement with the department of revenue or with some other state agency.

Not every type of business must file a fictitious business name—it varies with the state. In almost all states, fictitious business name laws apply principally to individuals (sole proprietorships) and general partnerships. Because corporations have their own regulations, fictitious business name laws do not apply to corporations, except in the fairly rare situation in which a corporation does business under a name different from its corporate name. In most states, fictitious business name laws also do not apply to limited partnerships because other laws govern their registration. In some states the law also covers nonprofit organizations and corporations, including churches, labor unions, hospitals, etc.

Contrary to the effect of registering a corporate name, registration of an assumed or fictitious business name does not necessarily prevent others from registering the same name. Because many states do not maintain a central register of fictitious business names, few states "clear" a fictitious business name by checking it against any other lists before registering it. As a result, several businesses might use the same trade name in the same state.

This means that if you want to be sure (for your own reasons) that no one else in your state is using the name as a trade name, you'll need to check any proposed fictitious business name against the records of every county, not just yours, if your state has no central fictitious name registration. But as we discuss below, whether

someone else is using the same trade name as yours is of less practical importance than if they were using the same trademark, or using the same trade name as a trademark as well. For this reason, we aren't suggesting you check every county list if all you are concerned about is use of a trade name.

B. The Legal Effect of Corporate and Fictitious (Assumed) Business Name Registrations

As mentioned, people often think that once they have complied with all the registration requirements for their trade name, they have the right to use it for all purposes. Because this point is so important, let us again emphasize that this isn't so. As we have seen, there are two very different contexts in which a business's name may be used:

- the formal name of the business for purposes of bank accounts, creditors and potential lawsuits (trade name)
- the name that the business uses to market its goods or services (trademark or service mark).

The registration requirements address the first context only. They don't address the second. That is, Backyard Fantasies, Inc., may be properly registered as a corporate name (trade name) but, because of the previous use of that name by someone else as a trademark, be totally unusable as the name the business puts on its signs, displays, advertising and products (trademarks, service marks). So, for every business that is considering adopting a name, there are two considerations:

- Can the name be registered as a trade name?
- Can the name be used as a mark?

In Section A we have discussed some of the considerations for registering trade names. Let's now get a quick overview of what's involved in using the same name as a mark.

WHEN IS A TRADE NAME A TRADEMARK?

A trade name acts like a trademark when it is used in such a way that it creates a separate commercial impression. Or put more directly—when it acts to identify a product or service. This can sometimes be a tricky determination, especially comparing trade names and service marks, because they often both appear in similar places—on letterheads, advertising copy, signs and displays. But some general principles apply:

- If the trade name is used with its full name, address and phone, it's probably a trade name. For instance, consider "The Goodnight Meat Company." When it appears with an address, the eye scans it, registering it as information only. This impression is intensified if an obvious trademark that also belongs to the company ("Sunrise Sausage") is used alongside it. *Sunrise Sausage* serves as the identifier of goods, while the Goodnight Meat Company only identifies the company.

- If a shortened version of the trade name is used (for instance, "Goodnight Meats"), especially with a design or logo beside or incorporating it, the trade name becomes a mark. Large companies often use a shortened version of their trade name such as *ConAgra*, alongside marks for specific goods that it produces, including *Swift Meats, Hunt-Wesson Oils, Peter Pan Peanut Butter*, and *Banquet Frozen Dinners*. Used this way, the name *ConAgra* acts like a mark because it has a design surrounding it and it is sufficiently different from the full corporate name, which is Consolidated Agriculture.

1. Effect of Registering a Corporate Name

Simply put, if the corporate name you have registered was already in use or federally registered as a trademark or service mark, you will have to limit your use of the corporate name to your checkbook and bank account. The minute you try to use the name in connection with marketing your goods or services, you risk infringing the existing trademark or service mark.

There are several key factors in determining whether your corporate name is likely to run afoul of an existing mark:

- Was the same or similar name previously in use as a mark by another business prior to your actual use of the name? If it was, then any actual conflict between the names in the marketplace probably will be resolved in favor of the previous user.

- Was the same or similar name placed on the federal trademark register as a mark prior to your first use? If so, you will be considered a deliberate trademark infringer to the extent the two names come into actual conflict.

Here is the point: If your corporate name figures in your future marketing plans, you must search for use of the name as a trademark in addition to complying with the corporate name registration requirements. (In Chapter 5, Preparing for a Trademark Search, and Chapter 6, How to Do a Trademark Search, we teach you how to look for such uses.) If you plan to market your goods or services on the World Wide Web, then you'll also want to check to see whether someone else has already taken your proposed name as their domain name, which would mean, at the least, that you'd have to use a slightly modified name (since every domain name is unique). See Section D for how to register a domain name.

2. Effect of Registering a Fictitious or Assumed Business Name

As mentioned, the rules about registering or filing fictitious business names are chiefly designed to enable the public, creditors and the state taxation department to identify and locate who operates a business under an assumed name. It gives the registrant no ownership rights in the name in the sense of preventing others from using it, although as a practical matter, in some states, later users may be prevented from registering a name that is the same or very similar to one already on the list. To repeat, in most states, registering a fictitious business name or an assumed name only indicates the person or entity behind the facade, not who owns the name. Whether a name can be used as a trademark or service mark is determined by the basic principles outlined in Section 1, above, and, in case of a dispute, the principles discussed in Chapter 11, Sorting Out Trademark Disputes.

To be sure that no one is already using the name as a trademark, you'll need to familiarize yourself with the trademark search material in Chapter 5, Preparing for a Trademark Search and Chapter 6, How to Do a Trademark Search. Remember this important point: If someone else is the first to use your name as a mark, it doesn't make any difference whether you or they have previously registered it as a fictitious or assumed business name. They will still have the right to exclusive use of the name in the marketplace.

CENTRALIZED STATE TRADE NAME REGISTRATION SYSTEMS

We have mentioned that in some states, fictitious business names are registered with the state. Such names are generally checked against a state list of fictitious business names before registration. A few states even check fictitious business names against the names of corporations and limited partnerships as well. But even in those states, registering an assumed name creates no trademark ownership rights. The right to use a particular trade name as a mark can only develop through being the first to use it (or to federally register it on an intent to use basis).

C. Legal Protection for Trade Names

It is important to understand that conflicts between trade names almost always occur when the trade names are being used as marks to identify goods or services. As a practical matter, there is no conflict unless the duplicate use of two trade names creates the possibility of customer confusion—that is, one business doesn't want its name pirated by another business because of the fear that customers will be lost as a result. The use of a trade name just to identify a business, and not as a trademark, rarely creates the sort of customer confusion that must be present to get any legal relief. Simply put, you need not worry much about protecting a trade name unless you also are trying to protect its function as a mark.

But assuming you decide to use your trade name as a mark, what rights do you have against the use of the same name by others? If you are using the name as a mark in more than one state, you have all the rights that are granted trademark owners by the federal trademark act and federal law. (See Chapter 1, A Trademark Primer, for a listing of these rights and Chapter 11, Sorting Out Trademark Disputes, for what happens in the case of conflicts between marks.) If you are using the name as a mark within your state's borders, you have the rights granted a mark owner by your state's laws and cases on trademarks. Generally this means that the first to use the mark will be given priority over later users in case of a conflict that creates the likelihood of customer confusion. (See Chapter 7, State Trademark Registration.)

Even though most name disputes involve the use of the names as marks, it is possible to have disputes over who owns a trade name. For example, take Fred's Remote Control Garage from Chapter 1, Section G4. Fred's competitor, who opens with a nearly identical name and business, might not actually be infringing Fred's trademark, since the mark is descriptive (and therefore legally weak). But the competitor's name could still be too close for Fred's comfort, and unfortunately it's fairly common for one local small business to choose a name that's confusingly similar to that of another.

Fred may be entitled to relief under laws against unfair competition, the legal beach umbrella under which disputes involving local trade names used as weak trademarks are usually resolved. Simply put, if a competitor engages in any conduct (which can range from identical trade names to imitative interior decor) that might cause someone to confuse its business with yours, you have a potential unfair competition claim. We don't cover here what you have to prove in court to enforce such a claim. But consult Chapter 11, Sorting Out Trademark Disputes, Section C3, for help in analyzing priorities among trade names, or other aspects of unfair business competition, and Chapters 12 and 13 for strategies for handling business name disputes.

D. How to Clear and Register Domain Names

In Chapter 1, Section D, we introduced you to Internet domain names and explained how they tell people your location on the World Wide Web. Before adopting a name for your business or product, you will want to find out whether your proposed name can be used as your domain name.

1. How to Clear Your Name for Use as a Domain Name

There are two ways to find out whether you will be able to use your proposed mark as a domain name. One is to buy a domain name search from Thompson and Thompson [http://ttdomino.thomson-thomson.com/]. The other is to do it yourself by visiting Tabnet on the World Wide Web [http://www.tabnet.com]. Tabnet not only lets you search to see whether your name is available, but also provides information about the registrant if it turns out that someone got there ahead of you. Selling domain names is a cottage industry; they go for about $2000. So if you are set on a particular name but find that you are blocked, you may want to try to negotiate a sale.

2. Registering a Domain Name

Domain names are reserved for your use alone by registering the name with a domain name clearinghouse organization called Network Solutions, Inc. (NSI). Once a domain name is registered with NSI, no one else can use it for the same purpose.

Domain names are like trade names in that they identify business entities. And like trade names, they can also function as trademarks or service marks by identifying the source of goods or products. (See Chapter 11, Section F for more on conflicts between domain names and trademarks.) Like trade names, domain names are registered. And, like trade names, a domain name registration does not guarantee trademark status. For instance, even if you are first to register the domain name Ixas (as in Ixas.com), which gives you the exclusive right to that domain name on the Internet, you can't necessarily use it as a trademark or service mark, either on or off the Internet. That will depend on a different set of principles and facts—basically, whether someone else has used Ixas first as a mark and whether your use of that term as a mark in reference to your products or services would likely create customer confusion.

There are two ways to register your name:
- use Tabnet (http://www.tabnet.com) to do it for you (for $50 plus the registration fees),
- get help from your Internet service provider, or
- do it yourself.

If you choose to do it yourself, the first step in registering a domain name is to acquire "operational name service." This is usually done by signing on with an Internet service provider (ISP). These providers are companies that connect to the Internet and can be located in the Yellow Pages or in computer magazines. An Internet provider can also help with the registration of your domain name with NSI.

The domain name application can be obtained electronically. However, you will have to be familiar with the Internet in order to connect and locate it at ftp://rs.internic.net. You will find the application file (domain-template.txt) located in the template library. The file includes instructions on completing the application. Registration used to be free, but the explosive volume of domain registrations (over 100,000) has resulted in a registration fee of $100.00. This charge covers the $50.00 maintenance fee for two years. After the two-year period, an invoice will be sent on an annual basis.

The NSI application requires you to certify that:
- the information you provide in the application is true.
- you intend to use the domain name, and
- your use of your domain name will not infringe an existing trademark or violate any other law.

NSI makes it clear that registering a domain name does not confer any legal rights to that name and any disputes between parties over the rights to use a particular name are to be settled between the contending parties using normal legal methods. Equally important, the applicant agrees to be bound by the terms of NSI's current domain name policy ("Policy Statement"), which is located at ftp://rs.internic.net/policy/internic/internic-domain-1.txt.

3. Disputes Regarding Domain Names

In the past few years, over 300 disputes have arisen over the use of domain names. For example, the MTV network battled with a former employee about the right to use the domain name, "mtv.com." An electronic company, Fry's Electronics, sued another business (Frenchy Frys) over the right to use the domain name "frys.com." The rules for resolving domain disputes are complicated and are increasingly getting more so. See Chapter 11, Section F for a complete discussion of domain name disputes and the relationship between domain names and trademarks. ■

CHAPTER

4

How to Tell If Two Marks Are Confusingly Similar

In Chapter 3, we outlined the requirements for registering a trade name. There we suggested that if you think the name might also be used as a mark—as is often the case—it is important to conduct a trademark search to find out whether anyone else is already using the name in a context that might lead to customer confusion. This advice applies equally to other types of proposed marks, such as logos, slogans and trade dress.

There are two good and obvious reasons to search for potentially conflicting marks:

1. If someone else began using a mark that is similar or identical to yours before you did, it probably belongs to them. If so, you may have to change your mark and, in some cases, possibly pay damages to the first user if a judge concludes that your use of the mark creates a likelihood of customer confusion.

2. If you are planning to apply for federal registration of the mark, you will save time and money by discovering that your proposed mark is already taken and therefore not registrable by you.

The process of finding out whether your proposed business, product or service name or mark is confusingly similar to an existing mark is called "clearing" the mark. Here's how it's done:

- First, search lists of marks and trade names for existing uses of the same or similar trademark.
- Second, analyze the information you obtain from the search to determine whether customer confusion would be likely if you put your proposed mark into use, and whether your mark will have legal priority if you do proceed to use it.

This and the following two chapters (Chapters 5 and 6) explain this process. We start in this chapter by teaching you how to compare marks for possible customer confusion. Then, in Chapters 5 and 6, we teach you how to do the necessary trademark search itself and also suggest a good resource if you want someone to do it for you. In Chapter 11, we explain the rules for deciding which mark has priority if a real-world conflict arises after you begin using a name as a mark for your product or service.

A. What Is Customer Confusion and How Can You Predict It?

You will most likely first encounter the issue of customer confusion if and when you do a trademark search and the results indicate that the same or similar mark is already being used by another business. Whether or not you should go ahead with your mark depends on whether your use would create a likelihood of customer confusion.

Being able to assess whether customer confusion is likely in a particular situation is a skill that depends as much on experience and intuition as it does on any hard and fast principles. While we can and do explain how the courts generally go about assessing the likelihood of confusion, each case is inevitably unique in some particular. Predicting the future outcome of any given case is definitely an art rather than a science. As we suggest in the book's introduction, if you are uncertain about the correct course of action after applying our guidelines to your situation, you will be wise to consult with an experienced trademark lawyer (see Chapter 15, Help Beyond the Book.)

1. Understanding the Likelihood of Confusion Test

The phrase "likelihood of confusion" is the key to most trademark conflicts; famous marks are protected regardless of possible confusion.

A likelihood means that confusion is probable—not necessarily that it has happened, or that it will happen, but that it is more likely than not that a reasonable customer will be confused.

Confusion in this context can mean two different things. Most commonly, it means that the goods or services a customer buys are different from what the customer intended to buy. For instance, if a consumer wants to purchase the services of ABC Emergency Care on the basis of a friend's recommendation, but ends up going to ABD Emergency Room by mistake because of the similarity of the two names, you have an example of customer confusion between the two services.

The other situation that creates customer confusion is where a misleading mark causes the customer to believe—wrongly—that a product or service is sponsored by, approved of or somehow connected with a business she already frequents or knows about. In other words, the customer is confused about the source of the product or service. This would be the case, for example, if a customer took his or her TV to a repair shop called IBM Electronics because they thought that IBM somehow sponsored the business.

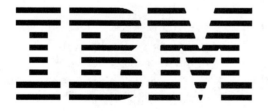

Just to see how judges apply this likelihood-of-confusion standard, let's examine a hypothetical conflict between two uses of very similar trademarks.

EXAMPLE 1: Ethereal Fragrance Company produces a line of products, including perfume, carrying the distinctive and therefore strong registered trademark *Ekbara Scents.* These products are marketed primarily to middle- and upper-income women in boutiques throughout California and several other western states. The *Ekbara* mark has been used in this manner by Ethereal for two years when Rubin Santiago of Oakland, California

opens a small printing company specializing in business cards, which he calls *Ekbara Cards.* The cards are marketed to small businesses in the San Francisco Bay area. Ethereal claims infringement and demands that Rubin stop using the *Ekbara* mark on his cards. When Rubin refuses, Ethereal files a trademark infringement lawsuit and seeks a preliminary injunction (an order to bar Rubin from further using the *Ekbara* name). The key point for the judge to decide is whether there is a likelihood of customer confusion created by Rubin's use of the *Ekbara* mark. In deciding this question the judge will probably engage in something like the following analysis:

"It is not likely that purchasers of business cards will think a fragrance company is involved in the printing business. Neither business is likely to go into competition with the other. The purchasers of the two products as well as the distribution channels are likely to be quite different. There is no similarity between the two goods in terms of what they accomplish. Ethereal's customers are unlikely to care who manufactures or distributes business cards. There is no indication Rubin Santiago intended to get a free marketing ride on Ethereal's mark. By contrast, the only factor supporting Ethereal's claim of infringement is the strength of the word Ekbara as a mark (it suggests the Middle East which itself is suggestive of fragrances). This is simply not enough to overcome all the other factors that lean against the likelihood of customer confusion."

EXAMPLE 2: If Rubin Santiago creates a line of enamel earrings, calls them *Ekbara Designs,* and franchises them for sale in shopping malls containing the boutiques that carry Ethereal's products, the judge's decision would be very different because the likelihood of confusion is much higher due to the fact that the two marks are used on related goods (explained more below) and because the same consumers are exposed to both marks.

See Section B, below, for more on the factors courts use to determine whether two marks create the likelihood of customer confusion.

2. Do the Confused Customers Have to Be Reasonable Customers?

Before we go on to discuss all the factors that can help you assess a likelihood of confusion, let's take a moment to examine who these hypothetically confused customers really are. The law imagines a "reasonable" customer who exercises ordinary care to distinguish among the products or services being purchased. This reasonable customer is neither someone who confuses two products as a result of bizarre reasoning, nor someone who obsessively checks all references before buying a product or service, but rather someone in between.

Courts recognize that a reasonable consumer will often make a snap judgment. If, after only a hurried glance, Mrs. Serrano is confused between *Heartbeat* and *Heartlite* cooking oils, then the marks are too similar. However, the law would surely not find it reasonable if a customer confused *Heartbeat* cooking oil with *Esther's Cooking Oil* because her Aunt Esther had recently died of a heart attack. Nor would a customer be reasonable in confusing *Heartbeat* with *Esther's* because of similar packaging, so long as the very different names are prominently displayed on the packaging.

The law says that in cases of conflicting trademarks, the challenger must show that a reasonable customer might be confused. How is this done? Typically the challenger must somehow prove that a significant percentage of customers would likely be confused—anywhere between 5% and 50% depending on the situation. A more exact number can't be given, because the number varies from one court decision to the next.

B. How to Evaluate a Competing Mark for Potential Customer Confusion

Court decisions have produced a number of criteria to determine when there's a likelihood of confusion between two marks. As would a judge, you will want to ask the following questions:

Factor 1: Are the goods and services represented by the marks related—that is, are they sold in the same marketing channels to the same general group of customers?

Factor 2: Do the goods or services compete—that is, will the decision by customers to buy one business's product or service be made at the expense of the other business?

Factor 3: How similar are the marks in sound, appearance and meaning?

Factor 4: How strong is each mark? (Is the mark in question very distinctive when compared to a competing mark?)

Factor 5: How much do the underlying goods or services cost? (How carefully does the public usually decide whether to buy the goods or services offered by the two businesses?)

Factor 6: Do the two marks share the same customer base?

Factor 7: Does one owner use the mark on several different products or services, or is she likely to do so in the future?

Whether use of a trademark is likely to cause customer confusion depends on the exact facts of the case, how the criteria listed above are weighed in light of the facts, and the subjective perceptions of the judge, based on the evidence.

The three most important factors to examine in deciding how likely it is that the use of a mark will cause customer confusion are the first three on our list above:

Factor 1. How closely related are the goods/services?

Two services or products with the same or similar names that are distributed in the same markets are far more likely to confuse the public than if very similar names were to grace dissimilar products. In this case the confusion is more likely to come from confusion about the source of the products than from confusing one product with another.

Factor 2. Do the goods or services compete?

If the underlying goods or services directly compete with each other, then the use of the same or similar marks on both is likely to cause the type of confusion that will lead to the customer purchasing the wrong product.

Factor 3. How similar are the marks in terms of their appearance, meaning or sound?

The more alike two marks are, the more likely it is that someone will be confused by them. This is known as the "sight, sound, and meaning" test for customer confusion.

You should apply these three factors first to your situation. If none indicates a likelihood of confusion, you can probably stop there. In a borderline case, you will want to consider the four additional factors which we discuss in Section 3, below. Or you can pick which of these seven factors seem relevant to your mark and use them selectively to determine if your mark may cause a likelihood of confusion with another. But before you conclude that you are safe in going ahead with your chosen mark, look at the final three factors in Section 4, below. They do not predict a likelihood of confusion so much as a likelihood of success in a lawsuit, which may be a more practical determination anyway.

1. How Closely Related Are the Goods/Services?

A good place to start in determining if one mark conflicts with another is to ask if the goods and services that the two marks promote are related—in a commercial sense. That's because when products or services are considered to be totally unrelated, the courts will generally find that use of the same or similar mark does not constitute infringement.

If the products or services are found to be related, infringement may be found to exist, assuming the other requirements for infringement are also present. However, even where goods are not related, if the mark claiming infringement is very strong or well known, infringement can also sometimes be found under a concept called "dilution." (See Chapter 11, Section E.)

When similar marks are used on related marks, the risk of consumer confusion is high. You can determine whether the potentially conflicting marks are used on related goods by asking either of two questions:

- Do the goods or services belong to the same "classes" of goods or services?
- Do the goods or services pass through related marketing channels?

We discuss these two questions in further detail below.

a. An Overview of the Trademark Classification System

Trademark "classes" are descriptive categories of goods or services used by the U.S. Patent and Trademark Office to help keep track of the many thousands of new marks that they register every year. There are 42 classes in all, 34 for products and 8 for services. The Appendix contains a complete list of the international classes and Chapter 8 explains how to classify a mark when filing an application for a federal registration.

If and when you search the list of registered trademarks (see Chapters 5 and 6) to see whether someone else got to your mark ahead of you, the search report will indicate to what class any similar mark has been assigned. If your mark belongs in the same class, this is a pretty good indication that the underlying products or services will be considered related. Here are some examples to help familiarize you with how this classification system works.

Class 1   Chemicals, including those used in industry, science and agriculture (such as neon), but not those used in medical science (see Class 5).

Class 3   Cosmetics and cleaning preparations, including soaps, substances used for laundry and cosmetics, but not degreasing preparations used in manufacturing (see Class 1).

Class 5   Pharmaceuticals (and other substances used for medical purposes), but not deodorants for personal use (see Class 3).

Class 14 Jewelry, including precious metals and their alloys, clocks and watches, but not gold used by dentists (see Class 5) or gold writing pens (see Class 16).

Class 16 Paper goods and printed matter, including writing instruments and other office tools, but not artists' tools.

Class 35 Advertising and business, including, for
(services)   example, advertising agency services, but not commercial enterprise services primarily involving the sale of merchandise.

Class 38 Communication, including distribution
(services)   of television and radio programs, but not radio advertising services (see Class 35).

b. Fitting Your Goods and Services Into the Appropriate Class

It may take a little study to determine the class to which a product or service fits best. For instance, does a belt made of woven cord belong under Class 22, which includes cordage and fibers? As it turns out the answer is "no," because the cord is made into clothing, which belongs in Class 25.

Similarly, if a mark represents a new type of service or product it may be difficult to decide how to categorize it. For example, about thirty years ago the service mark *Synanon* was registered for use in connection with drug rehabilitation services. At the time, drug rehabilitation was a novel service and placed in the miscellaneous category, Class 42. But today the same service might be assigned to Class 41, education services.

Because goods or services in the same class are usually considered related or competing, the use of the same or similar marks within the same class has a high potential for customer confusion. For example, the owner of *Titan* brand cigarettes was able to stop a cigar maker from using the *Titan* mark. Cigars and cigarettes are in the same PTO class, Class 34, which also encompasses "tobacco, raw or manufactured, smoker's articles, and matches."

On the other hand, the owner of *Titan* cigarettes probably couldn't stop a maker of biodegradable soap, which is in Class 3, from using the same mark. That is because cigarettes and soap do not compete in any way; they are not considered related goods; and the *Titan* mark could be used on both without creating the likelihood of customer confusion.

It's important to understand that by itself the fact that two products or services are in the same or different classes does not conclusively establish whether two marks are legally in conflict. For example, because the international classification system has packed all goods and services into only 42 classes, combining for example, abrasive cleansers and cosmetics, products within the same class may be marketed in totally different ways so as to avoid customer confusion. So, in evaluating a conflict, you may at least argue that a trademark for a scouring powder that is similar to a trademark for lipstick won't confuse customers.

To place a product or service within its appropriate classification, follow these steps:

Step 1: Study the list of classifications in the Appendix. See whether the goods or services for which the mark is being used naturally fits into one of the groupings.

Step 2: If you are unsure, study the list in the appendix that provides examples of goods and services for each class. Does that help?

Step 3: If you are still not sure, pick the three most likely classes and use these as possibilities.

If you are using these instructions as part of the federal registration process, remember that you can obtain help in classifying a mark from the U.S. Patent and Trademark Office—in the manner we describe in Chapter 8.

c.   Marketing Channels

In addition to using the classification system for determining whether two marks might confuse customers in the marketplace, it is also useful to look at the marketing channels through which the goods or services reach the public.

The fundamental question here is how closely the products or services compete in the marketplace. Goods and services are considered related when they are sold in similar outlets, marketed in similar media, placed near each other in stores, and generally considered alike by the consumer. If they are marketed quite differently, then no likelihood of confusion can exist, regardless of what class they are in for registration purposes.

For example, you should determine if the same sorts of information sources (billboards, newspapers, magazines, radio) carry ads bearing both marks. Would both marks appear in ads in the same trade journals? Might the products or services be displayed or sold in the same store/catalog, or under the same heading in a trade directory? Will they both target the same customer base? Do both marks appear in advertising on the World Wide Web? If so, then they most definitely are being used in the same marketing channel. If the answer to most of these questions is yes, the marks are used in the same marketing channels. That increases the likelihood of customer confusion. In that case, what classification the two marks are in won't make much difference.

Especially because of the way people search out information on the World Wide Web (by using a search tool to locate sites containing a set of words chosen by the user), it is likely that the use of two marks on the Web will cause customer confusion and therefore legally conflict.

Even if your proposed mark falls into a different class from another mark, we recommend that you not use your mark if it is very similar to the other mark and would appear in the same marketing channels. Keep in mind that the prohibitive cost of litigation usually makes all borderline decisions too risky.

2. How Similar Are the Marks?

The second factor in determining whether using similar marks will cause a likelihood of confusion is how similar the marks are. Do they sound or look alike, and if so, how much? Do they convey the same meaning? The closer two marks are in sight, sound, and meaning, the more likely it is that a legal problem will arise.

In comparing marks, remember that variations in spelling or punctuation do not make marks different if they sound the same. Thus, *Phanseepants* is the same as *Fancy Pants*, and *Duncan Doughnuts* duplicates *Dunkin Donuts*. Even using foreign language equivalents can't make a mark different enough, if most of the public could tell they mean the same. So *La Petite Boulangerie* would infringe on *The Little Bakery*, and *El Sombrero Blanco* probably infringes on *The White Hat*.

Even marks with more definitive differences may be confusingly similar, in the same market. So courts have found *Quirst* is too close to *Squirt*, *Sarnoff* too much like *Smirnoff*, *Lorraine* too reminiscent of *La Touraine*. Each of these pairs of marks were used on nearly identical goods. Probably the use of such duplicate marks would have passed legal muster if they had been on very different kinds of products. Again that's because the more competitive marks are in a class or market channels, the less similar the marks have to be to cause confusion.

> ### ARE TWO MARKS CONFUSING? USE THE GOLDEN RULE AND GET SOME FEEDBACK!
>
> Telling whether the simultaneous use of two marks risks customer confusion can be a very subjective exercise, heavily influenced by the experience and mind set of the person doing the analyzing. Nevertheless, there are two ways to get a handle on the question of potential confusion. First, ask yourself how you would feel if you were out there using your proposed mark and the other business came along with theirs. If you think you'd become energized to take some action, you have your answer. Second, if you are able to arrange for several objective friends or relatives to eyeball the two marks and give their honest impression of how they would react as customers, you'll probably have a pretty good idea of how a judge would react. If even one of your friends or relatives think they might be confused by the marks, then chances are a judge would reach the same conclusion as to hypothetical customers and rule that the two marks are confusingly similar. Since this is a risk you don't want to take, chances are you should pick another name.

3. Additional Factors

The next four factors from our list also affect whether the likelihood of customer confusion exists between any given pair of marks.

Factor 4. How strong is each mark?

A strong mark is generally given a wider range of protection than a weak one. Remember from Chapter 2 that a mark is considered strong either because:

- the words, phrases, or symbols it consists of are distinctive (arbitrary, coined or suggestive), or
- long and continuous use has made the public recognize it as the symbol of a particular product or service (the secondary meaning rule).

The point is, the stronger the original mark, the more likely it is that the second mark will be found to be confusingly similar if it has any similarities to the original mark at all. Conversely, the weaker a mark is, the less legal protection it is given and the more likely it is that a second mark will be found not to be confusingly similar, even if it has many similarities. This means you are safer in using a mark that is similar to an existing weak mark than a mark that is similar to an existing strong mark. For more information on what makes a mark strong or weak, see Chapter 10.

Factor 5. How much do the goods or services cost?

Cost will also affect the likelihood of customer confusion. Since customers tend to take their time and consider carefully when buying an expensive item, the more expensive the item the less chance of confusing customers. Conversely, an item that is cheap or subject to impulse buying is more likely to result in customer confusion if sold with a mark that is similar to another on goods that are even slightly related.

Factor 6. Are the two marks directed toward the same customers?

Two businesses that use similar marks to sell to the same customers are highly likely to cause customer confusion. Conversely, if businesses have separate customer bases, then the use of similar marks is unlikely to confuse anyone. For example, the market for replacement wood windows is likely to be limited to contractors and homeowners with spare cash. As a result, a window manufacturer who uses the mark *Walls of Light* in its advertising probably won't confuse the customers of a magician who calls his show the *Wall of Lights*, because the two groups of customers won't often overlap.

It's useful to look at how large a sector of the market uses your product or service. If a small sector of the market knows and purchases a service, a similar mark used by a different small group is unlikely to confuse the two sets of consumers. But if a large segment of the public knows one mark, use of a similar mark is more likely to cause customer confusion, even if aimed at a slightly different market, because of the greater potential for overlap between the two groups.

Factor 7. Does one owner use the mark on several different products or services?

A red flag should go up when you see a potentially conflicting mark that has already been used on a variety of products or services by the same mark owner, even if you wish to use it on a product that is unrelated to any of these uses. The problem is that since the first mark owner has already begun to use its mark on several products or services, it has asserted what is called in legal lingo the "right of expansion." Some examples of businesses that do this are Calvin Klein or Pierre Cardin (although the "dilution" rule would also keep anyone from using an identical mark or marks—see Chapter 11, Section E.).

Once this right of expansion is asserted (by using the mark on a number of different products), the courts will assume that the first user may wish to expand its use further and protect this right of expansion by permitting very few other uses of the same mark. So a second user seeking to use such a mark even on greatly dissimilar products will have less luck than if the mark were being used in a more limited fashion. By the same token, the public, having seen the mark on a variety of goods by the same owner, is more likely to assume that any new uses also belong to that owner, and thus is likely to be con-

DILUTION

Even if there is no likelihood of customer confusion, you may still run into problems if your mark has an adverse effect on a well-known mark. Under a trademark principle known as dilution, you can be prevented from using a mark that diminishes the impact or tarnishes the effect of a well-known mark. These laws (sometimes known as antidilution laws) can be applied even if your mark is used on different products and appeals to different consumers than the well-known mark. There are antidilution laws in at least 31 states and a federal anti-dilution statute has been proposed but not yet adopted by Congress. (The new provision would entitle owners of famous trademarks to obtain injunctive relief against unauthorized commercial use of those marks, if that use causes dilution of the distinctive quality of the mark.)

There are two common types of dilution. One type, known as "blurring," occurs when the public's perception of a famous mark is blurred or altered so that the famous mark seems to lose some of its distinctiveness. This is often the case when a distinctive mark is weakened by non-related uses. For example, the owners of the *Playboy* mark stopped an auto body shop from using the same name because it diluted the distinctive quality of the mark. *The Greatest Used Car Show on Earth,* was determined to dilute the mark, *The Greatest Show on Earth,* used for circus productions. Similarly, the Hyatt Hotel company claimed that the use of "Hyatt" for legal services blurred the consumer's perception of the hotel chain. As a result, Hyatt legal services agreed to carry a disclaimer.

When a mark damages the reputation of a famous mark, a second type of dilution occurs— "tarnishment." For example the Anheuser-Busch company argued that use of *Where There's Life, There's Bugs* (for a combination floor cleaner and insecticide) tarnished their mark, *Where There's Life, There's Bud.* Courts also found that the *Gucci* fashion mark was tarnished by *Gucci Goo*

diaper bags and that *Garbage Pail Kids* sullied the wholesome mark for *Cabbage Patch Kids.*

Not all uses of well-known marks create dilution. The Hormel Company, owners of *Spam,* were unable to prove that use of the name *Spa'am* for a Muppet character diluted their mark. The judge in that case determined that given the history of negative *Spam* comments in newspaper articles, cartoons and TV shows, Hormel should consider it fortunate to be associated with a Muppet version of a wild boar.

A new type of dilution appeared in 1995, when a tractor company modified a rival's logo (the John Deere "leaping deer" logo) in a comparative advertisement. Although it is permissible to use rival logos in comparative ads, the tractor company had animated the Deere logo and gradually diminished its proportional size in the ad. By modifying the John Deere mark, the courts held that the tractor company had diluted it.

If you parody a famous mark and use it to sell products, there is a good chance the mark's owner will sue you. Although you may win in court (there is substantial case law protecting the rights of parodists), it will cost you dearly.

Claims brought under the dilution theory are generally successful when the well-known mark is used in an unwholesome manner. Subjecting the Pillsbury Doughboy to pornographic poses, using the *Enjoy Coca-Cola* style logo for *Enjoy Cocaine* t-shirts, or using a cheerleader logo in an adult film ("Debbie Does Dallas") have all been enjoined because of their tarnishing effect.

Even if the states where you do business do have a dilution statute, you should still stay away from this type of activity. Some states apply dilution principles without a statute. Other states permit related claims under product disparagement or trade libel laws. If your product or service is provided or advertised in a state that has such a statute you can be sued there (New York is one of the more popular states in which to bring antidilution claims).

fused. Thus the public would expect the mark *Yamaha*, which already appears on motorcycles, lawnmowers and guitars, to represent the same company if it also appeared on computers or musical recordings.

4. Final Factors

After you have determined whether there is a likelihood of customer confusion between the marks you are evaluating, look at the following additional factors. They will help you determine the likelihood of getting into a lawsuit or of prevailing if you are mired in one. Then you will have a very clear idea of whether it's wise to use a particular mark.

- What is the owner of the other mark's history of suing potentially infringing mark owners?
- How long has the allegedly infringing business been using the mark?
- What did the alleged infringer intend in adopting and using the mark in question?

Additional   History of trademark
Factor 1.   infringement lawsuits.

This is the most practical factor in predicting the likelihood of a lawsuit. It makes great sense to be wary of using a mark if the owner of a similar mark has a history of bringing trademark infringement suits. This generally means that the other mark owner will vigorously challenge any uses that are potentially confusing, and perhaps even some that are clearly not. Even if you eventually win such a suit, the cost, averaging $100,000, is rarely worth it in the long run.

For example, anyone who follows these matters knows that *McDonald's* vigorously protects its golden arches and the prefix "Mc" when it comes to any type of fast, efficient and low-cost service business. For this reason, you should stay away from using anything that might get *McDonald's* ire up.

One way to discover a company's litigation history is to look up some of the secondary sources of trademark law listed in Chapter 15, Help Beyond the Book. Those books have tables in the back which list cases by the names of the litigants (parties to a lawsuit). If you don't find the name of the business with which you may have a conflict there, the records of the county and federal courthouses nearest their corporate headquarters will probably list cases in which they have been litigants (not all of which will be trademark cases). Or, you can consult an attorney who will search for the company name on one of several comprehensive legal databases that list all cases in a given field. Consulting an attorney is likely to be the most expensive, but also the most effective method.

Additional   How long has the allegedly
Factor 2.   infringing business used the mark?

If an alleged infringer has used a mark for a long time without complaint from the owner, that may establish two things:

1. It makes it look as though the alleged infringement has not harmed the true owner very much. This is known in legalese as "sleeping on your rights," and a court is less likely to give the owner any relief if it has not taken action to protect its rights despite another's use of the same mark for a long time.

2. The alleged infringer has established some rights in the mark that may be superior to the true owner's rights, if only in the geographic area in which it has been used. (See Chapter 11 for more on priorities of use in such situations.)

Additional Factor 3. **What did the alleged infringer intend in adopting and using the mark in question?**

The intent of the alleged infringer also affects the question of whether one mark infringes on another. If it appears probable to the court that a business could only have chosen its mark in order to take advantage of its similarity to another mark, then the court is very likely to find an infringement to exist. If, for example, a successful and well-known marketer of French bread uses *Staff of Life* as a trademark, and a new rival calls its product *Stuff of Life*, the court will be very suspicious about the intent of the rival—and it may be hard to persuade the judge or jury that the owner of the Stuff of Life mark did not intentionally copy the first mark. ■

Preparing for a Trademark Search

Now that you have learned from Chapter 4 how to recognize the possibility of customer confusion between two marks, you are ready to clear your name or other commercial identifier for use as a trademark or service mark. You do this by conducting what is known as a trademark search. (If you are still not sure you want to conduct a trademark search, see Chapter 1, Section G.)

In this chapter we:

- explain what a trademark search is,
- introduce you to the materials generally used for trademark searching,
- describe the different types or levels of trademark searches,
- give you a framework for deciding what level of search you should undertake, and
- describe the main tools and methods available for trademark searching.

In Chapter 6 we tell you how to hire and use a trademark search service, or, in the alternative, how to do your own search using the major available tools, materials and methods introduced in this chapter.

A. What Is a Trademark Search?

A trademark search is a systematic hunt for the existence of any registered or unregistered trademark or service mark that:

- is the same or similar to a mark proposed for use by the searcher,
- is being used anywhere in the country (or world if the proposed mark is to be used internationally), and
- is being used in a context that would likely result in customer confusion if the proposed mark is also put into use.

B. What Resources Are Used in a Trademark Search?

A trademark search may involve some or all of these resources, depending on the scope of the search:

- **The federal trademark register:** a list of all trademarks and service marks that have been authorized for federal trademark registration.
- **Pending trademark applications:** a list of all trademarks and service marks for which a federal registration application has been filed.
- **State trademark registrations:** a list of all trademarks and service marks that have been registered at the state level (usually with a state's Secretary of State).
- **Publications containing relevant product and service names:** trade magazines, print directories of commercial names, Yellow Pages and electronic databases containing product and service names that are in use in the U.S. generally, or in respect to specific fields such as computers, biotechnology and bicycles.
- **The Internet:** domain names, World Wide Web sites and goods and services being offered on the World Wide Web.

C. Where Can Trademark Search Resources Be Found?

Many of the resources used in a typical trademark search are available online—by computer— including some free or low-cost Internet sites and some more expensive electronic databases that can be accessed directly or over the Internet by any member of the public who is willing to pay for the privilege. It is also possible to do a free, reasonably competent trademark search by using workstations and print collections found in special public libraries known as Patent and Trademark Depository Libraries, or PTDLs. (See Section F2 for more on doing a trademark search in a PTDL).

1. Trademarks on the Federal Trademark Register and Described in Pending Applications

The most important resource for a trademark search is the list of federally registered trademarks—called the federal trademark register—and a list of pending applications for federal trademark registration (applications are typically pending for a year or more before registration is actually accomplished). While the federal trademark register obviously doesn't include nonregistered trademarks—which may cause trouble down the road if you don't know about them in advance—a search of the federal trademark register and pending applications is a necessary first step.

There are three different ways that the public can search for trademarks that have been placed on the federal trademark register or whose registration application is pending:

- Use DIALOG (an online service owned by Knight-Ridder) to access a proprietary database, called TrademarkScan, which is owned by Thompson and Thompson.
- Use CompuServe (another online service) to access the TrademarkScan database.
- Use a public domain database called CASSIS, distributed by the U.S. Patent and Trademark Office on CD-ROM and available for free in every Patent and Trademark Depository Library.
- Use the Internet to access the equivalent of the CASSIS database for a reasonable fee.
- Use X-search, the same electronic database as that used by the Patent and Trademark Office's trademark examiners (not generally available to the public).

Each of these approaches to searching the federal trademark register has its strengths and weaknesses, which are explored in greater detail in Section F below. However, as a general rule:

- TrademarkScan through DIALOG is the most flexible database in terms of the types of searches that can be performed, and the ability of the database to produce relevant terms that sound like, look like or mean the same thing as the mark being searched. However, for users doing their own searches, this easily can turn out to be the most expensive option and involve the steepest learning curve.
- TrademarkScan through CompuServe is less flexible than DIALOG (because the DIALOG interface to TrademarkScan adds considerably to the flexibility in question) but is likely to be cheaper and involves less of a learning curve.
- CASSIS is the easiest database to use and, as mentioned, is available for free in every Patent and Trademark Depository Library. However, it is the least flexible of the databases and is often two to three months behind the TrademarkScan database in terms of the most recent registrations and trademark applications.
- The CASSIS-derived database on the Internet (offered by a company called Micropatent) is a reasonable alternative to visiting a PTDL, but costs $20 for a 24-hour period of searching.
- X-Search is perhaps the most powerful database of all but is not generally available to anyone other than the PTO trademark examiners, visitors to the PTO public search room in Virginia, and two special Patent and Trademark Depository Libraries in Sunnyvale, California and Detroit, Michigan.

Chapter 6 explains how to search each of these resources.

2. Trademarks Registered with State Agencies

Many trademark owners who use their trademark solely within a particular state register the mark with that state's trademark agency. Because such a registration might block the use of a later proposed mark within that state, the owner of the proposed mark will often search for instances of state registration. You can do this by:

- Using the TrademarkScan State Database, available through DIALOG and CompuServe. As with the federal trademark database, this can get expensive and involves a learning curve.
- Calling the Secretary of State's offices for the states you are interested in. (See Chapter 7 and the Appendix for a list of State Trademark Agencies and Statutes.)

3. Unregistered Trademarks and Service Marks

Because trademark ownership is based on who uses the mark first (see Chapter 1, Section C8), it is important to search for unregistered marks in actual use if you wish to avoid a conflict somewhere down the line. To do this, you must hunt for the use of your proposed mark (or something very similar) on products and services that are similar to the products or services you plan to use with the mark.

There are several approaches to performing this type of search (called a "common law search" because the importance of unregistered marks stems from court decisions, which are called the common law):

- Use DIALOG to access a number of databases listing product and service names in use around the country (again, this can be costly and a learning curve is involved).
- Use one of the Internet search engines to search for use of your proposed mark on the Internet and as an Internet domain name.
- Use the Thomas Register of Products and Services, available for free on the Internet at http://www.thomasregister.com.
- Use print resources in a PTDL or a large public library that contain listings of product and service names.

Chapter 6 explains how to conduct a common law trademark search.

D. Different Levels of Trademark Searches—What They Are; When They're Appropriate

In Section A we defined a trademark search in its broadest sense. In fact, there are three different levels of trademark searching:

- **A direct hit federal trademark register search.** This search compares your mark with identical or very similar federally registered (and pending) marks in one or more of the classes set up by the U.S. Patent and Trademark Office. (We discussed the international class system in Chapter 4.) This type of search is the quickest, cheapest and most minimal ("shallowest" in trademark-speak) search you can do.
- **An analytical search of federal and state registered and pending marks.** This type of search compares your mark with all registered and pending marks (both federal and state) that sound or look like your mark, plus all marks that mean the same or in some other way might lead to customer confusion between them and your mark. This type of search is more thorough, or "deeper," than a direct hit search, and consequently more expensive and time-consuming.

- **A comprehensive trademark search.**
  This type of search hunts for all possibly relevant unregistered marks (the common law search) as well as for federal and state registered (and pending) trademarks.

Because you may want to undertake all three types of searches in the course of adopting a new mark, or only parts of each, you should understand in more detail what each type of search covers and what benefits each offers.

1. A Direct Hit Federal Trademark Register Search

This type of search—for identical or very similar federally registered and pending marks—is appropriate for any business in the process of choosing a name that the business is likely to use as a trademark. The reasons most readers will want to conduct this level of search are:

- If you adopt and use a mark that clearly conflicts with one already on the federal register, whether or not you actually know of it, you will be considered a willful infringer of that mark and may be sued for large damages. The obviousness of your infringement will greatly reduce your ability to negotiate an acceptable settlement with the existing mark's owner.
- A direct hit search tells you whether it's worthwhile applying for a federal trademark registration. Your trademark won't qualify for placement on the federal register if the Patent and Trademark Office thinks customers are likely to confuse it with a mark already on the register. (See Chapter 8.) This means that a direct hit search can potentially expose marks that may conflict with yours and tell you whether or not an examiner is likely to approve your application.
- A direct hit search will also tell you if your proposed mark has been registered for so many goods or services that it is considered legally weak and therefore not very

protectible. You may want to use the mark anyway, but at least you'll have a better idea of its legal status. (See Chapter 10, Section C2 for what makes a mark legally weak.)

- Practically speaking, a direct hit search is especially helpful when you have several choices of potential trademarks and you wish to narrow the field by eliminating obviously unavailable marks.

For many businesses, especially those that plan to operate regionally or nationally, direct hit searching is only the first step to clearing a name. Especially if the proposed name is distinctive, a more thorough search—at the very least, an analytical search of federal and state registered and pending marks—will be in order. However, if your proposed name is weak, or your business is small and local and you can tolerate some risk that an undiscovered prior user will pop up at a later time, the direct hit search is really all the searching for registered marks that you'll need to do.

Direct hit searches are quick and easy to do because the information is directly available to you through the CASSIS database, either for a reasonable fee on the Internet (see Section F3 below) or for free at a PTDL (see Section F2 below). You may also hire a search firm to do a direct hit search for you, often for a very reasonable fee. Chapter 6, How to Do a Trademark Search, gives you detailed instructions about how to hire someone to do direct hit searches for you and how to do them yourself.

2. Analytical Search of Federal and State Registered and Pending Marks

This is a more thorough search that includes searching for homonyms, synonyms, phonetic equivalents, alternative spellings, anagrams (words with the same letters rearranged), marks with similar components, and marks that start or end the same, or that have any other similarity you can think of. It is a much more thorough ("deeper") search than a direct hit search, and permits you to uncover more potential conflicts.

For example, doing an analytical search for the mark Bioscan, you would look first at all the marks that immediately surround Bioscan alphabetically, and then look up all Bio marks, then all -scan marks, then all marks with the sounds -io or -osc in the middle. Next you would search for all synonyms you could think of. Then you might want to check for anagrams (scaniob) and alternative spellings (bayou-, -skan).

This deeper search is essential for any business that wants to make sure its proposed mark isn't likely to be challenged on the ground it is confusingly similar to, or evocative of, an existing mark. For instance, assume the manufacturer of certain gas barbecue components wants to use the mark *Flamethrower.* Because the components will all be stamped with this mark, the manufacturer wants to make sure that no existing mark has priority. To do this, an analytical search would look for all marks with the word "flame," all marks with the word "thrower," and all marks with words that sound like or mean the same thing as either of these.

It is especially wise to do this level of search if your prospective mark is distinctive. Since distinctive marks can be protected to a much greater degree than those that lack distinctiveness, it's worth making sure they are completely clear of all possible conflicts. For instance, the maker of *Raintree Shampoos* would want to do an analytical search before marketing their product regionally, as would the operator of an 800-number information service that had a distinctive name.

For companies that expect to expand their use of a particular mark in the future, an analytical search reduces the likelihood of eventual problems due to customer confusion caused by marks that are not identical but are reminiscent of each other.

3. Comprehensive Trademark Search

This type of search involves not only an analytical registered trademark search but also an examination of telephone directories (Yellow Pages), trade directories, the Internet, product catalogues, business ratings services and so on. The goal is to discover any actual use of your proposed mark, whether or not it is officially registered. As mentioned, the reason for this is that most disputes between marks are resolved in favor of the first actual user. All businesses should do this type of search before finally deciding on a name that is likely to be used as a trademark or service mark.

For local businesses the search should, at a minimum, consist of checking the relevant Yellow Pages, newspapers, trade and product journals, and any other resource that might show a possibly conflicting locally used mark. For businesses that need to find out whether the mark is in use anywhere in the U.S., this type of search can become more complex and costly. Several large computer databases available through CompuServe and DIALOG most likely contain the materials that you need for this type of search, but you may also need to visit a large public library with business-related resources. (See Section F2 below.)

E. Planning Your Trademark Search

Now that you have a pretty good idea of what is involved in a trademark search, you need to decide what is the appropriate search for you and your particular situation.

⚠ Let us start by saying that if all other things were equal (notably time and money), you would be well advised to do a comprehensive trademark search for every mark you plan to use. You can only gain from being as careful and conscientious about clearing your mark as possible. But two warnings apply here:

1. No search is going to uncover every possible conflict in the whole U.S. and certainly not internationally. It's just too difficult to know if there's a prior unregistered user of a similar mark in North Noluk when you are in South Sunstroke. The best you can do is to make sure that your proposed mark doesn't obviously conflict either with registered marks or with any unregistered marks you can find by systematically examining pertinent sources of trademarks, service marks or trade names.

   This means no matter how thoroughly you search, you will have to live with a small degree of uncertainty that someone else began using your mark first. What does it mean, legally, if they did? Nothing, if the other user doesn't object. Even if they do object, and sue you in court to force you to stop using the mark, you probably would be allowed to continue to use the mark in your present marketing territory (unless both marks are used to market related or competing goods or services on the World Wide Web). However, you may be prevented from acquiring the nationwide exclusive rights to your mark that otherwise would be available to you by being the first to register it. (See Chapter 11, Sorting Out Trademark Disputes, for a discussion of priorities among trademark users.)

2. As you are undoubtedly tired of hearing by now, there are no absolute answers in trademark law. Even the most extensive search will probably not end your uncertainty, because it will likely uncover at least some somewhat similar marks used on products that are at least vaguely related to yours. Whether such a trademark definitively infringes on another is a decision that only a judge or jury can make when the dispute is brought before them. In many real world situations, you can be pretty sure that the other user is unlikely to sue. But a thorough search will give you as much assurance as possible under the circumstances.

Since the best you can do is weigh factors and estimate probabilities, it's important for you to decide what level of risk is acceptable to you now, when you are clearing and evaluating your mark. Then you can tailor your search to minimize the risk in line with your decision. Below we set out some general rules to follow when planning the scope of your trademark search.

WILL ADVICE FROM A LAWYER PROVIDE MORE CERTAINTY?

Some people believe that they are protected against infringement claims if they get a practicing trademark lawyer to give them an opinion that no legal conflicts exist between their proposed mark and existing marks. Not so. Trademark lawyers are subject to the same limitation as are the authors of this book—that is, there is no firm way to predict the outcome of a trademark dispute. All a trademark lawyer can do is give his or her professional opinion. But if that opinion turns out to be wrong, it is you and not the lawyer who will face the consequences, with one important exception. A lawyer's opinion that your mark doesn't conflict with a mark on the federal trademark register may save you from a stiff damage award if you go ahead and use the mark and are later sued for infringement.

Knowing that they aren't likely to get in trouble if they act conservatively, most lawyers won't give you the go ahead if there is much of a chance of a trademark dispute in the future. In short, the lawyer's advice may be both a disservice in that it may be overly cautious and an important service in that you will feel more confident about your choice if it passes the lawyer test.

There are six basic rules that apply to all trademark searches:

Rule 1: Always check the federal register for a direct hit.

All searches should check the federal trademark register first for the same or very similar mark as the one you propose to use. It is relatively easy and inexpensive to do, and it is the best way to uncover federal conflicts. That's important for everyone, because businesses that have federally registered their marks may own rights in a region in which their name is not yet obviously in use. (See Chapter 11, Sorting Out Trademark Disputes.) It also avoids the risk of incurring the substantial penalties that infringement of a federally registered mark can incur.

Rule 2: A big advertising budget warrants a more extensive search.

Because comprehensive searches—full analytical and common law searches—can cost time and money, it may not make sense for a small business to check for every possible conflict. Whether or not you should depends on the size of your business, your future goals, your mark and how you plan to use it. A good general rule is that if you plan to spend a fair proportion of your budget on promoting your mark, you should first spend whatever it takes (perhaps hundreds of dollars) making sure the name is safe for you to use. Otherwise you risk wasting your advertising dollars if you have to change the mark later. On the other hand, if your advertising budget is tiny, it may make more sense to accept a more limited search as sufficient.

Rule 3: A strong mark requires a thorough search.

How extensive a search is appropriate for you will also depend on how much protection you need or can get for your mark. With a strong mark, there is more to protect, and a thorough search process is a better investment than in the case of a weak mark, where the extent of your rights is likely to be more limited anyway. Also, the more distinctive, and therefore the stronger, the mark, the greater degree of assurance you need that no one else is using a similar mark elsewhere. If you have a strong mark and your goal is to be able to use your mark exclusively regionally, nationwide or even worldwide, that will entail thorough direct hit, analytical and common law searches.

One important reason you need a comprehensive search to protect a proposed strong mark is that the existence of similar marks may prove that your chosen mark is not as strong as you originally thought. Remember that marks are distinctive either because they are inherently memorable (fanciful, suggestive or coined), or because they become well known to the public through widespread use over time. If existing marks sound or mean the same thing as your proposed mark, or look like it while sounding different, or have elements in common with it, your proposed mark may not be as legally strong as you had hoped.

You also want to be sure not to evoke unintended connotations because of a likeness to another mark in an unrelated field. For example, a sports fishing manufacturer would want to avoid the mark National Harpoon, because it evokes National Lampoon, the mark of a business specializing in satire. You can't avoid such unintended effects unless you uncover them through a deep search.

Owners of proposed marks that are weak (ordinary, descriptive, laudatory, geographically descriptive or a personal name) generally won't want to do a deep search. That's because such marks can only be protected from identical marks used on related goods anyway, and these are easy to discover with a more shallow search.

But you may need an extensive search to clear a weak mark in some circumstances. For example, if you plan to do vigorous marketing on the World Wide Web, or you expect your mark to someday become distinctive by acquiring a secondary meaning, in the interim you may want to keep your eye on other existing marks that are potential conflicts. In addition, if your mark is descriptive, you may want to know of an arbitrary or fanciful use of the same mark, because the owner of that stronger mark might object to your use, even on unrelated products or services. For instance, if you plan to adopt the mark *Guess Who?* for your new board game, you would need to know about the *Guess?* clothing mark. If the owners of the existing mark are very aggressive about protecting it, or have applied it to a wide variety of products, such information would tell you to choose another mark for your product or service.

Rule 4: Think long-term.

In determining your trademark search goals, consider the future. For example, if your local engineering consulting service is limited to one city now, but there is a possibility you'll want to expand later, perhaps through the World Wide Web or franchising, you'll want to conduct a more extensive search than might otherwise be appropriate for a firm of your current size. Rather than facing the possibility of having to change your mark later, you should conduct your trademark searches with those long-term goals in mind. This involves doing both direct hit and analytical trademark searches, as well as thorough common law searches. By contrast, if you run a local hobby or kitchenware shop and plan to stay small, a direct hit search coupled with a local or statewide common law search should prove sufficient (unless, again, you plan to market on the Web).

Rule 5: Geographic scope of the use affects the size of the search.

As we said before, where you will use your mark will determine what kind of a search you need to perform. This makes each case a fact-specific determination. Nevertheless, the following general guides are reliable:

- For a mark used only in one region of one state, and for which there is no expectation of expansion: Generally speaking, the smaller the geographic area in which you market your goods or services, the less extensive the search needs to be. If you check federal and state registered trademarks for direct hits and then do a thorough common law search for your area and type of business, you should be relatively well protected. That's because if another similar mark is not registered federally or with the state, and is not in use in your geographic area or line of business, you will not likely cause customer confusion. The only potential concern you may have is dilution, and if the other mark is not famous enough for you to run across it through these searches, then it is not famous enough to get relief under the theory of dilution.

- For a mark in use in two or more states: Suppose you are clearing a mark for your new computer program, gardening supply catalog, or 800-number phone service. You can only clear such a mark with a comprehensive search. That ideally should include federal and state analytical searches and a thorough common law search. This more extensive search is necessary because other businesses may have rights through registration in marks that are not yet being used in your particular region. In addition, because such marks are marketed nationally, they will face a greater array of potentially conflicting marks and thus the greater potential for infringement claims. Thus, a more thorough search is necessary to clear them.

Remember that the Internet is rapidly eliminating the very concept of local marketing territories, and if you expect to do business on the Web some day, you'll want to do your search just as if you planned to do business on a national level.

Rule 6: Marketing channels affect the size of the search.

- For a mark used in a narrow niche of the market: It may be cleared with a search that is limited to direct hits on similar names used on related and competing goods. That's because with a narrow circle of competitors and limited marketing avenues, you can minimize the chances of a confusingly similar mark hurting your sales by looking only at similar marks in the same market. For example, a mark used only on industrial ball bearings probably need only clear conflicts within industries related to machinery and steel, along with the recommended direct hit search of the federal trademark register.

- For a mark used by a wide variety of businesses: Such a mark is weak, and so you need not be careful to find all other similar marks as used on a whole wide range of products. That's because the potential for confusing the public is much less if the mark is already in wide use. Its use on any one product or service will mean less to the public than if it were rarely used.

- For a mark used by one owner on a wide variety of goods or services: If you plan to use one mark on several of your own different services or products, then you must be extremely careful to find all other marks that are even vaguely similar. That's because your investment in such a mark will be high, and because you will need to be sure it evokes no other images than your own business's. For example, if you were intending to develop a mark for eventual use on clothes, shoes, luggage, jewelry and cosmetics, you would conduct the most thorough searches you could.

F. Who Will Do the Trademark Search

There are three ways to conduct a trademark search:

1. Hire someone to do it for you (a search service or an attorney).
2. Do it yourself.
3. Do some of it yourself and hire someone to do the rest.

Here we summarize the costs, drawbacks and advantages of these various search approaches. In Chapter 6 we provide the nuts and bolts involved in using each one.

Before you decide whether to do your own searching or farm it out, let us suggest that a combination of approaches may give you the best legal protection for your time and money. For example, using your own computer to access the CASSIS-derived database on the Internet (Micropatent at http://www.micropatent.com) can be quick, easy and provide good preliminary information. But unless you have the opportunity to practice, you probably should not attempt an analytical or thorough common law search on your own. For that you should pay someone who knows what they're doing. Fortunately, at least one service offers quality searching at fees that will probably compare favorably with what you would spend getting up to speed. See Chapter 6, Section A1 on Using Sc[i]3 to Do Your Trademark Search.

1. Using a Search Service

Traditionally, most trademark searches were conducted by specialized trademark search firms at the behest of trademark attorneys who were handling the trademark registration process. Even today, some of the largest trademark search firms refuse to conduct searches for anyone but a lawyer. But most search firms aren't so choosy and will conduct a search for anyone willing to pay them.

THE ROLE OF ATTORNEYS IN TRADEMARK SEARCHES

If you decide to hire a trademark attorney to advise you on the choice and registration of a trademark or service mark, the attorney will be able to arrange for the trademark search. Some attorneys do it themselves but most farm the search out to a search firm, the same as they've always done. Once the report comes back from the search firm, the attorney will interpret it for you and advise you on whether to go ahead with your proposed mark. Although you are getting considerably more in this attorney package than you'll get from a search service, it will cost you.

The services provided by various trademark search firms, and the fees they charge for different types of searches, vary considerably. Often the cost of the service will depend on how much massaging of the information is done before it is delivered to you. Generally, the more raw the data you receive, the cheaper it will be. Only attorneys are allowed to offer opinions about potential trademark conflicts, and as a result, trademark search services offered by attorneys tend to cost the most because they come with legal advice.

Next to hiring a trademark attorney, paying a trademark search firm is the most expensive means of clearing your mark. However, except for a direct hit search—which you can reliably do yourself—a search service is likely to provide more reliable results than you will produce on your own. There are several reasons for this. Most importantly, analytical and common law searches come with a considerable learning curve, regardless of which database or resources are being used. Searching for possible conflicts is a kind of art form that involves a lot more than typing in a word or phrase and asking whether it appears on

the source being searched. In Chapter 6, we provide several examples of what can be involved in an analytical or common law search.

What do search services charge? Firms that search (but do not give legal advice) generally charge as follows:

- direct hit search (for identical marks)—from $30 to $100 per mark searched.
- analytical federally registered trademark search (for similar or related marks)—from $85 to $300 per trademark.
- common law search only—from $100 to $200 per mark searched.
- comprehensive search (combining analytical federal, state and common law)—between $185 and $500 per mark searched.

The difference in rates may reflect variations in the coverage of the search, the sort of report you get, the experience of the searchers or simply economies of scale. On the other hand, some firms may advertise an unusually low price to draw in customers, but then add on charges that end up exceeding another firm's total price (a professional version of bait-and-switch). For example, does one fee cover the whole cost, or is there also a per-page charge for the report? Obviously, to shop sensibly you need to know the total cost of each service.

See Chapter 6 for more on hiring a search service.

2. Using a Patent and Trademark Depository Library to Do Your Own Search

Using a Patent and Trademark Depository Library (PTDL) to do your own federal trademark search involves the least cash outlay, but will cost you in time and transportation expenses unless you live or work close to one. Most PTDLs offer free access to the CASSIS CD-ROM (see Section 3 below and the Appendix for a list of PTDLs). The CASSIS trademark list is a good way to search for a direct hit. It is also possible to use CASSIS to do an analytical trademark search, but the results are not likely to be as reliable as would be the case if the TrademarkScan or X-Search databases were used. See Sections 3 and 4 below for why.

If you are computer-challenged, or the wait to use the PTDL CASSIS workstation is too long for comfort, every PTDL has print materials (described in Chapter 6 Section C6) that also let you search the federal registered trademark database. Whether or not the use of a PTDL is cost-effective for you will depend on such factors as:

- how many potential marks you wish to search for
- how far you are from the nearest PTDL
- whether you can free the time to visit a PTDL during regular working hours, and
- the time it takes you to learn the CASSIS system (library staff will provide help).

If you only want to search for one mark, it may be that the cost in terms of time alone will favor using a trademark search service. Or if you want to search a lot of marks and are connected to the Internet, you may be better off paying a daily fee ($20 for 24 hours of access) to use the Micropatent online trademark search service (see Section F3 below)—which offers pretty much the same access to federally registered trademarks as does CASSIS. On the other hand, if you live near the Sunnyvale (Sc[i]3) or Detroit PTDLs, you may wish to pay an hourly fee to use their X-Search terminal to do a higher level search than is available from either CASSIS or Micropatent.

For those of you who opt to visit a PTDL, see Chapter 6, Section C6 on how to conduct a PTDL trademark search.

3. Using the Internet to Do Your Own Trademark Search

The Internet now offers access to a database derived from CASSIS (see Section C1 above) for a reasonable fee. Owned by a company called Micropatent [http://www.micropatent.com], this database offers unlimited online searching of the federal trademark register for a 24-hour period for $20. If you are adequately prepared, you can get an awful lot accomplished in 24 hours. This is potentially the cheapest way to search, especially if you wish to conduct a direct hit search for two or more prospective marks. You can best prepare by downloading the help file and studying it before starting your search. Micropatent's online help tells you how to save the help file and your search results to your hard disk.

The Micropatent database contains all active trademark registrations and pending applications filed with the United States Patent and Trademark Office, as well as inactive registrations and applications for recent years. The database is updated weekly. For each federal trademark it provides:

- the mark owner's name and address
- the mark's class and goods and services
- dates of first use, filing, and publication (if any) in the Official Gazette
- status of application or registration, and
- related information, such as assignments, serial number, etc.

You can:

- search according to Boolean operators (the familiar method of key word searching that uses the words And, Or, and Not to target the exact phrase you're looking for),
- search trademark designs, and
- use wildcards (symbols that can stand for any letter or number, or for any group of letters and numbers).

The Micropatent interface is very user-friendly and the help is written in plain English. You should be up to speed in less than 15 minutes, a small bite out of your 24-hour window of opportunity. See Chapter 6, Section C1 for how to use Micropatent to do a patent search.

You may also use the Internet to search for unregistered marks. You can use a variety of search engines to find out whether your proposed mark appears anywhere on the Internet and if so in what context. Probably the best way to get started is to use the Alta Vista [http://www.altavista.digital.com]

or Excite [http://www.excite.com] search engines. Run your mark through the Yellow Pages and through the general-purpose search boxes that these services provide. If the list you get back is too long, pare it down by adding some additional search terms to limit the search.

Another useful Internet search tool is the Commercial Sites Index, a central index for Web sites representing commercial businesses. You may access this index by typing http://www.directory.net. Simply enter the name of the product or service that you're looking for and you will obtain a list of sites that have such products or services. This may give you an indication of some names or marks in use that are the same or similar to the one you propose to use.

If you are interested in finding out whether your proposed mark is already in use as an Internet domain name, you can access the InterNIC Directory, which, as explained in Chapter 3, Section D, is the site where domain names are determined. If you are using a Web browser, type http://www.internic.net. The InterNIC directory can be used to find domain names (which may assist in searching for trade names or common law service marks). From the home page, select the link to Network Solutions, Inc., Registration Services. In the search field, enter the trade name (usually followed by ".com") such as sony.com.

Finally, the Thomas Register of goods and services is now available on the Internet at http://www.thomasregister.com.

MORE ABOUT THE INTERNET AND THE WORLD WIDE WEB

Basically, the Internet is a collection of computers connected by phone lines around the world, and the World Wide Web provides a graphical interface to information stored in those computers. The World Wide Web is helpful in trademark searching because it provides instant access to vast amounts of information. Searching (or surfing) the Web is an art that is still evolving. The challenge for computer users is to search for and locate the appropriate information without wasting time. The basic requirements for searching are a computer, a modem, software that navigates the World Wide Web (a Web browser) and a connection to the Internet through an Internet service provider (CompuServe and America Online provide Web access, as do many independent service providers).

4. Using CompuServe to Do a Trademark Search

As a member of CompuServe, you have access to TrademarkScan, which includes eight trademark databases:

- United States (federal registrations)
- United States (state registrations)
- Canada
- France
- Germany
- Italy
- the United Kingdom, and
- an International Register covering trademarks worldwide.

The two TrademarkScan databases that assist in U.S. trademark searching are:

U.S. FEDERAL—a database that contains all active trademark registrations and pending applications filed with the United States Patent and Trademark Office, as well as inactive registrations and applications from 1984 forward. The database is updated twice weekly. For each federal trademark it provides:

- the mark owner's name and address
- the mark's class and goods and services
- dates of first use, filing, and publication (if any) in the Official Gazette
- status of application or registration, and
- related information such as assignments, serial number, etc.

U.S. STATE—a separate database that contains trademark registration information obtained from the Secretary of States' offices in all 50 U.S. states and Puerto Rico. Trade names, assumed names and fictitious names are generally not included, but may be identified for some states. Corporate name records are not covered.

You may also use CompuServe to access the Thomas Register, a worldwide listing of brands and their companies. You can search for common law names, product names and trade names. Also available through CompuServe is a database known as Dun & Bradstreet's Electronic Business Directory (also known as the Biz*File). This database helps to identify existing common law service marks and trade names.

As with Micropatent, CompuServe is best suited to a direct hit search. However, because it uses the TrademarkScan database, CompuServe can also produce a reliable analytical search of registered trademarks, assuming you conquer the trademark search learning curve. The cost of doing your own search is likely to be higher than the lowest cost trademark search services (see, for example, the sidebar in Chapter 6 about Sc[i]3, which offers an analytical search for $85), but less than an analytical search using TrademarkScan through DIALOG (which typically runs well over $100 for novices). Also, as mentioned, CompuServe provides fee-based access to several large databases that can be used to search for unregistered marks.

See Chapter 6, Section C2 for more on using Compuserve to do a trademark search.

5. Using DIALOG to Do a Trademark Search

If price is no object and you are willing to study the DIALOG search techniques, this approach is likely to produce the most thorough search of the federal and state registered and pending trademark database. That is true for two reasons:

- The TrademarkScan database has powerful built-in enhancements that produce not only the words or phrases you search for, but also words and phrases that sound or appear the same or that have the same meaning.
- The DIALOG interface to the TrademarkScan database allows you to search for the distinctive parts of your mark as they might appear at the beginning, middle or end of other marks on the federal register (called a rotated search), an important feature if your proposed mark has some unusual component.

Dialog is a subscriber service costing $75 per year plus per-minute and per-result charges for using the service.

Updated several times a week, for each federally registered trademark it provides:

- the mark owner's name and address
- the mark's class
- the date the mark was first used (as listed by the mark owner on the registration application)
- the date the mark was placed on the register
- the identities of past owners of the mark, if any, and
- other less pertinent information.

    Each entry for a state registered trademark contains significantly less information.

In addition to the federal and state trademark registers, DIALOG also offers numerous general information databases such as:

- a national index of trade names,
- an electronic national version of the telephone book white and Yellow Pages for businesses, and
- several directories of information about U.S. businesses and products.

It also provides a variety of databases applicable to specific industries, such as the Software Products Database, the Business Software Database, the Fine Chemicals Database and the Health Devices Sourcebook, as well as trademark databases for Canada and the United Kingdom.

DIALOG works pretty much the same as other electronic databases, such as America Online, CompuServe and GEnie. You use your computer and modem to connect with Dialog over the telephone. Once you connect, you type in your user number and password, both of which the service assigns you when you subscribe. You then are free to search any of the individual databases. You are billed for:

- the length of time you are connected to the database—currently $2.30 a minute for TrademarkScan; less for other databases, and
- the number of times you display the results of your search on the screen or send them to your printer.

A direct hit trademark search for one mark might cost as little as $5–$15. But doing a broad enough analytical search to thoroughly clear a mark can easily run well over $100 in a short span of time, an amount that is still less than an equivalent search by a search firm (except, perhaps for Sc[i]3; see Chapter 6, Section A).

See Chapter 6, Section __ for how to use DIALOG to do a trademark search.

6. Purchasing CD-ROMs to Search

CD-ROMs look like standard audio compact discs; however, they contain information that must be "read" by a computer, not a compact disc player. Vast amounts of information can be stored on one disk but you must have a CD-ROM drive in your computer.

Federal & State Trademark Registration

The PTO offers two CD-ROMS good for trademark searching: one for pending applications and one for registered marks. These are the same CD-ROMS as are available in the PTDLs described in Section 2 above. Each costs $300, which includes bi-monthly updates for one year. If you have a fair amount of trademark searching to do, it may be worth your while to purchase these products. For more information on how to order them, call 1-800-PTO-9199.

The TrademarkScan database of federal and state trademarks is also available on CD-ROMs from the Thompson & Thompson company. A subscriber to a CD-ROM service receives periodic updates to the database. There are two disadvantages to using CD-ROMs. Unless you are doing large numbers of searches, the cost is prohibitive. Second, the discs are not updated as regularly as the online services. The advantage of using a CD-ROM is that there is no cost per search.

Only if you are doing large numbers of federal trademark searches, should you acquire CD-ROMs.

Service Marks and Trade Names (Yellow Pages on CD-ROM)

If you are trying to locate common law service mark and trade name information, there is a new breed of CD-ROM products that contain the names and phone numbers of millions of U.S. businesses. Priced between $40 and $50, these directories are compilations of business phone book listings and are easier to search and often more comprehensive than printed white pages or Yellow Pages. You can limit searches to a geographic area (even by zip code). The most popular versions are Select Phone (from Pro CD) and Phone Disc (from Digital Director Assistance). Both Select Phone and Phone Disc contain over 10 million business listings. More expensive versions of these products include residential and fax phone listings. These CD-ROMs are available from software stores and mail order companies.

You will find many uses for these CD-ROM phone books, but be sure that the CD-ROM works with your system (Windows or Macintosh) and meets your system's requirements.

By now you should have a pretty good idea of what is involved in a trademark search, and have made some decisions about what sort of search you want to undertake, what source of information you want to use, and whether you want to do the search yourself or have someone do it for you. If so, you are ready to go on to Chapter 6, How to Do a Trademark Search. ■

How to Do a Trademark Search

n this chapter we give you the information you need to either:

- hire a search service and understand the report they give you, or
- do your own search using one or more of the databases available to the public (see Chapter 5, Sections C and F for more on these databases).

Cost, convenience and your practical trademark situation will tend to dictate your choice.

Before you can sensibly undertake a trademark search, you'll need the information in Chapter 5. Please don't skip it.

If you are not comfortable using your computer for this purpose but live close to a Patent and Trademark Depository Library (a list is in the Appendix), you can use the PTDL's CASSIS workstation to cull obvious conflicts from a list of proposed names, and then pay someone to do a more comprehensive search on the best of the names that survive your preliminary search.

Whatever method you use, make sure that it is as thorough as practicable before you begin using your new mark, or you will have little assurance that your mark is protectible or that you are not inadvertently infringing on another's mark.

If you need trademark answers right away and can pay for them, you can skip most of this chapter. Read the information in Section A, contact the search firm of your choice and request their immediate turnaround service.

A. How to Find and Use a Trademark Search Service

There are many trademark search services in the country. Because trademark searching is a purely information-based business, you don't have to worry about where a particular service is located. Telephone, fax and e-mail make it possible for a customer in Bangor, Maine to comfortably deal with a service in California, Texas or Virginia. With this in mind, we feature only two trademark search services in this section—the Sunnyvale Center for Innovation, Invention and Ideas (Sc[i]3), and Trademark Express. We don't mean to guarantee their results or even vouch for the quality of their services. Rather, we intend them as examples of what search services cost and the types of services they provide. And both are completely accessible by fax or phone.

If you don't like doing business over the telephone or fax, you can find trademark search services in your area by looking in the Yellow Pages of the nearest good-sized city under trademark consultants or information brokers. If that yields nothing, consult a legal journal or magazine for your area. You'll find the ads of a number of trademark search firms—these are aimed at lawyers, but many of these search companies will also do searches for individuals and businesses.

Beware Aggressive Marketing Techniques.

Some trademark search services will try to convince you that you are stupid if you don't search every corner of the globe for possible conflicts. Before taking the bait, review our remarks in Chapter 5 about the different levels of searching and make an independent decision about what scope of search is appropriate for you. Also, some search services (including Trademark Express) provide additional services—such as the preparation of applications for federal and state trademark registrations. As with trademark lawyers, these businesses have a vested interest in convincing you that you will be better served by paying them to handle the tasks in question than by doing them yourself. If you feel that this point of view—which may be perfectly reasonable—is being too aggressively pushed in your situation, get a firm hold on your wallet and consider finding another service.

1. Using Sc[i]3 to Do Your Trademark Search

The Sunnyvale Center for Innovation, Invention and Ideas (Sc[i]3—pronounced "Sigh Cubed") is one of two Patent and Trademark Depository Libraries (the other being in Detroit) that have formed partnerships with the U.S. Patent and Trademark Office. Under this partnership, Sc[i]3 is encouraged to offer a variety of information services—including trademark searches—for very reasonable fees.

As a PTO partner, Sc[i]3 has been given direct access to the PTO's trademark database, called X-search. (See Chapter 5, Section C1.) Although X-search can be used for an hourly fee by members of the public who visit the Sc[i]3 library, X-search also is available for Sc[i]3 staff to conduct analytical searches of the federal trademark register. In addition to name marks, X-search provides easy access to registered logos and designs. As an extra service, which is included in the base price, Sc[i]3 also uses the Trademarkscan database (see Chapter 5, Section F4) to cross-check the search results obtained from X-Search.

As a general rule, you can get a Sc[i]3 analytical or comprehensive trademark search for less than it would cost you to do your own search, unless you have already gone through the learning curve necessary to carry out efficient trademark searches. Sc[i]3's direct hit search is also competitive with other search services, although you can do it cheaper yourself if you are connected to the World Wide Web or visit a PTDL.

As of October 1997, Sc[i]3's fees are:

- $30 for a direct hit federal trademark search using the PTO CD-ROM called CASSIS (they call it a "jiffy search"),
- $85 for an analytical search of the federal trademark register,
- $185 for a complete trademark search, including state trademark registers and common-law marks.

As with most trademark search firms, Sc[i]3 doesn't interpret its results; it leaves that to you. In Section B of this chapter, we take you step-by-step through a Sc[i]3 search report to help you with the interpretation task should you decide to use that search service.

A Sc[i]3 trademark search may be ordered by calling 408-730-7290. Visit Sc[i]3 on the World Wide Web at http://www.sci3.com.

⚠ We Make No Guarantees.

We have singled out Sc[i]3 here because of its competitive pricing, its relationship with the PTO, and the positive experience we've enjoyed when using it. However, we do not intend to guarantee the quality of its search in any given case.

2. Trademark Express

Trademark Express is a private company that in addition to other trademark-related services offers a full choice of trademark searches. Here is the Trademark Express price list as of October 1997:

- $159 U.S. Federal and State Trademark Research,
- $100 per country International Trademark Research (if a U.S. search is also ordered),
- $150 per country International Trademark Research (without a U.S. search),
- $169 National Common Law Research (United States),
- $39–$79, one state, State Common Law Research,
- $169 world region International Common Law Research.

Trademark Express also will check on Internet domain name availability ($20) and do a common law search of the Internet for $100.

Here is a general description of the search services offered by Trademark Express, taken from their World Wide Web site:

"To determine whether your proposed name is available for trademarking in the United States, we research pending and registered federal marks

and registered state marks using the online data-base provider Lexis. Because we break your name down into smaller segments (truncation) and search for combinations of these segments (ro-tated), we find conflicting marks as well as those similar in sound, appearance or meaning. Similar marks are important to find, as trademark law protects against any name that could be confused in commerce with an existing trademark.

"The fee includes same day or next business day service, analysis of the research, free legal re-ferral, free trademark application review and a fully documented search. Results are faxed and mailed, and we will call you to discuss the results and your options, and provide free legal referral as needed."

More information about Trademark Express and the services it offers is available on its World Wide Web site at http://www.tmexpress.com. You can reach it by e-mail at info@tmexpress.com or at any of the following telephone numbers:

    800-776-0530 (Los Altos, CA)

    800-550-1520 (Costa Mesa, CA)

    800-340-2010 (Washington, DC).

We Make No Guarantees.
We are listing Trademark Express only for the purpose of using its trademark search service as an example. We do not intend to guarantee the results of any particular search or make any rep-resentation as to the quality of its services. Fur-ther, as we are only concerned with trademark searching in this chapter, we make no representa-tions—and provide no information—about any additional services offered by Trademark Express.

B. How to Read a Trademark Search Report From Sc[i]3

In Section A1 above, we suggested that the Sunnyvale Center for Innovation, Invention and Design (Sc[i]3) might be a good choice for obtain-ing a quality trademark search at a reasonable

price. In this section we take you step-by-step through a sample Sc[i]3 trademark search report so that you'll have a better understanding of what such a report looks like and what it means. If you use another service, this information should help you understand their report as well.

As it happens, the sample report was for a search commissioned by Nolo Press for the term SharkTalk. SharkTalk is the name of an interactive online game that teaches legal vocabulary in a very amusing fashion and that is operated by Nolo on its Web site.

Because the mark will be used nationally (as necessarily happens with everything on the Web), Nolo requested that Sc[i]3 undertake a compre-hensive search for both registered and unregis-tered marks in all classes. This is the broadest possible search. Also, because Nolo needed the information right away, it paid a 50% surcharge for a 48-hour turnaround time (the usual turn-around time is 10 days). The report was faxed to Nolo within the 48-hour period, and Nolo pro-ceeded to put the SharkTalk game up on its Web site. (If you want to play SharkTalk, visit Nolo's Web site at http://www.nolo.com.)

Because Sc[i]3 is constantly reevaluating and improving its services, some aspects of its search report may change by the time this book goes to print. If some of what you find here doesn't match the report you get from Sc[i]3, and the report itself doesn't contain adequate informa-tion to fill in the gap, ask the searcher indicated in your cover letter for an explanation of the change.

1. The Cover Letter

With each report, Sc[i]3 includes a cover letter:
- explaining that the report may point out existing trademarks, trade names and busi-ness and product names that might legally conflict with your proposed mark

- reminding you that the decision as to whether to attempt a trademark registration is up to you and your attorney (if you have one)
- stating that it is not responsible for inaccuracies in the databases accessed in the course of the search
- disclaiming responsibility for any potentially confusing marks or names it may have missed in its search (standard for all search services)
- suggesting that it can't analyze and interpret the results of the search for you, and referring you either to this book or to a trademark attorney
- thanking your for your business, and
- summarizing the costs of the search.

Here is a sample cover letter for the SharkTalk search report.

Sunnyvale Center for Innovation, Invention and Ideas	465 South Mathilda Avenue Suite 300 Sunnyvale, California 94086	phone: 408.730.7290 or 408.730.7289 fax: 408.735.8762 deaf access: call TDD/TTY 408.730.7501

Sunnyvale Center for Innovation, Invention and Ideas
Trademark Search Report

Sc i³

Enclosed please find your Sc[i]³ report on the trademark search you requested.   The report may include trademarks, trade names, and product and business names which may be likely to cause confusion with your proposed trademark.

The marks listed in this report must be reviewed by you and your legal counsel. Securing a trademark registration depends on whether there are other similar marks on similar types of goods and services in the marketplace, the strength or weakness of the mark, and the decision you and your attorney make to go forward with an application to the U.S. PTO or a Secretary of State's Office in a particular state where you will conduct trade.

The enclosed list is generated from a variety of computer databases, depending on what level of search you requested. You will find a detailed description of database coverage, along with the search results attached. The accuracy of the data is limited to the methods used by database creators to collect the information and the accuracy by which the information is input. Sc[i]³ disclaims all responsibility for any inaccuracies in the search results.

Sc[i]³ has generated a list of exact marks and near exact marks by searching the database for marks that look like yours or are similar to yours. Truncated searching, when possible, also may be used to achieve a broader search. Every effort has been made for accuracy and completeness. However, because of the complex and subjective nature of trademark searching, we cannot guarantee that the search identified all potential sources of conflict.

Sc[i]³ staff is not qualified to analyze and interpret your search for you. If you find you need more detailed information, we suggest you purchase a copy of *Trademark: How to Name Your Business & Product* at our Center for $32.42 In addition, you may wish to consult an intellectual property attorney in your area.

Thank you for taking advantage of the unique partnership between the City of Sunnyvale and the United States Patent and Trademark Office. Please inquire about our many other intellectual property services and best of luck with your mark!

Sincerely yours,
[signature of staff librarian]

Staff Librarian

Date: 7/3/97

Cost:	$185.00	+	$92.50	+	$6.00	=	$283.50
	cost of search		other charges		shipping/handling		TOTAL

2. Federal Registration Search

In this introductory page, you are told that the following section of the report deals with trademarks that are registered and pending (still in the application process) in the U.S. Patent and Trademark Office. You are also alerted to the fact that a mark may still be in use even though its registration status is inactive, canceled or "dead."

> ### WHY THIS ALERT IS IMPORTANT
>
> The reason this alert is important is that if a mark shows up as canceled on the report, the natural assumption is to think that it's available for use by another business. Nothing could be further from the truth. Often the registration for a mark that is still being used is canceled without prior notice from the PTO because the registrant failed to submit certain required papers within 6 years after the original registration date. Although the registration is canceled, as long as the mark is still in use, no one else can use it (in a way that would create the likelihood of customer confusion) without infringing it.

You are then introduced to the databases for this section of the report. These will either be the CASSIS CD-ROM database for what Sc[i]3 calls its jiffy search ($30), or the X-Search (maintained by the PTO) and Trademarkscan (Knight-Ridder) databases for the complete federal trademark search. (See Chapter 5, Sections C and F for more on these databases.)

This page also alerts you to the fact that the search strategy is explained at the beginning of each section of the report and that some or all trademark classes may have been searched, depending on the search's scope. Finally, the codes that are used to do both the X-Search and Trademarkscan searches are set out in boxes for your reference. As we go through the sample search report, we'll be referring back to these codes.

Here is a copy of the Federal Registration Search Introduction Page

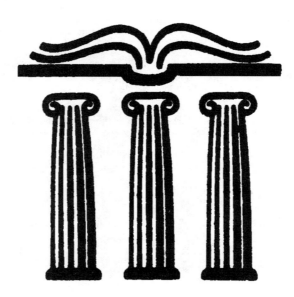

Federal Registration Search

This section of your report includes a list of trademarks registered and pending with the U.S. Patent and Trademark Office. This list is generated from X-Search (the Trademark Office database) and Trademarkscan®, a commercial database. Each trademark has a status: live or dead. All active and inactive marks are covered through the dates specified in the body of the attached search report. You may need to research inactive marks with diligence as they may still be "in use" in the marketplace and simply have lost their "live" status temporarily. Consult your attorney for more information.

About the Databases Used for a Federal Search:
X-Search makes it possible to search for federally registered and pending trademarks which are phonetically or syllabically similar to your proposed trademark. This advanced method of searching is used to search for trademarks which sound similar to your mark although the actual spelling may vary considerably. X-Search may also used for design (logo) searching since it includes trademark images. Trademarkscan® may also be used to search for federal trademark information.
X-Search is updated on a daily basis. This search covers **complete** trademark records through the following dates:
Active marks: 1884-present date listed. Exact dates of coverage are provided at the beginning of attached search.
Inactive marks: January 1, 1984-present date listed. See attached search for exact dates.

Classes Searched and Search Strategy
The U.S. Patent and Trademark Office uses a classification system (class numbers 1-42) which categorizes goods and services by type. If no class numbers appear in the search strategy, all classes were searched. Classification numbers may be used to narrow a search.

The search strategy used to search your mark appears at the beginning of each section of the search report, starting on the following page. The search strategy itself may be complex, and the following list of "character codes" are provided to help you understand the search process.

X-Search Codes

no code	basic index search
PHRASCH/	phrase search
PHONSCH/	phonetic search
EXSYLSCH/	syllable search
SYLSCH/	phonetic syllable search
/GS	goods and services description
/IC	international class search
/LD	live/dead indicator
/OW	owner name and address
/DC	design code
&	Boolean operator for "and"
^	Boolean operator for "or"
~	Boolean operator for "not"
:	truncation symbol which tells the computer to search a word "stem" and any words that contain it. For example, a search for **comput**: would find **compute, computing, computers**, etc.

Trademarkscan® Codes

no code	trademark keyword index
tr	rotated trademark index
et	exact trademark index
ic	International Class number
gs	goods and services description
s	set number (S1, S2, etc.). A number the computer assigns to a set of search results.
?	truncation symbol which tells the computer to search a word "stem" and any words that contain it. For example, a search for **comput?** would find **compute, computing, computers**, etc.
t	type formats—"t s1/8/all" is asking the computer to type set 1 in format 8 (short format), for all records retrieved. Format 5 is the full format.
/active	limit to only active (live) trademarks.

3. Trademarkscan

The next page in the SharkTalk sample report shows us the results from Sc[i]3's Trademarkscan search, conducted through DIALOG. (For more information on Trademarkscan through DIALOG, see Chapter 5, Section F5.) We learn that the Trademarkscan database includes marks listed in official applications through May 28, 1997. As the search was conducted on July 3, 1997, the search was only about one month behind the most recent application date.

```
File 226:TRADEMARKSCAN(R)-US FED  OG970624/AP970528
    (c) 1997 Thomson & Thomson
*File 226: Preliminary Records through 5/30 * * *


DIALOG(R)File 226:TRADEMARKSCAN(R)-US FED
(c) 1997 Thomson & Thomson. All rts. reserv.

            OFFICIAL GAZETTE PUBLISHED
                  JUNE 24, 1997

       OFFICIAL APPLICATIONS FILED THROUGH
                  MAY 28, 1997

      PRELIMINARY APPLICATIONS FILED THROUGH
                  MAY 30, 1997
?s tr=(shark? and talk?)
        584  TR=SHARK?
       2830  TR=TALK?
    S1    1  TR=(SHARK? AND TALK?)
?s shark?()talk? or sharktalk?
        566  SHARK?
       2423  TALK?
          0  SHARK?(W)TALK?
          0  SHARKTALK?
    S2    0  SHARK?()TALK? OR SHARKTALK?
?t 1/tx

  1/TX/1
DIALOG(R)File 226:(c) 1997 Thomson & Thomson. All rts. reserv.

    05129049
SHARK STALKER
```

Trademarkscan Search Request #1

Let's start with the first search request (called a "query") that Sc[i]3 made to the Trademarkscan database: **[?s tr=(shark? and talk?)]**. This means that a search was made for any federally registered trademark that contains both the word "shark" and the word "talk," either as stand-alone words or as parts of other words. We know this because:

- the term "tr" tells the computer to search not only for stand-alone occurrences of the words but also for other words that have these words within them (for example, as we see at the bottom of the page, the search produced a mark with the word "stalker" in it), and
- the search term "and," when placed between two words, tells the computer to list only marks that have both words.

The question mark at the end of each word listed in the search request extends the search to marks with words containing shark plus any other letters (sharky, sharks) and words containing talk plus any other letters (talky, talks).

THE ROLE OF CLASSES IN TRADEMARK SEARCHES

Note that by not specifying a particular class (for instance, cl=028, or Class 28) in the report, the searcher is searching all registration classes for the mark, as requested by Nolo Press. If this all-inclusive search had produced a long list of marks, then the searcher would have had to narrow the search by specifying two or three of the most probable classes for the SharkTalk service—according to Nolo's description of how the mark was to be used.

The report for the first search query (S1) tells us that of all the registered marks, 584 contain the word shark (or sharks or sharky) and 2830 contain the word talk (or talky or talks), but only one mark contains both words **[s1 1 tr= (shark? and talk?)]**.

Trademarkscan Search Query #2

The second search query, **[?s shark()talk? or sharktalk?]**, is a variation on the first search query. Here the computer will be searching for any mark that:

- has the literal term shark (not as part of another word) directly in front of talk (or talks or talking), separated only by punctuation (which is what the () means), or
- consists literally of "sharktalk."

The report for this second search query (S2) is that no marks are registered with this configuration. At the very least this means that Nolo can use SharkTalk without fear of using an exact copy of somebody else's federally registered mark. But what about federally registered marks that may be similar in look, sound or meaning? It's now time to go back and see what the first search query (S1) turned up:

The 1/TX/1 command tells the computer to display the results of the first search query in the most simple format. The results of that search turn out to be "Shark Stalker." (Later, we'll explain what impact Shark Stalker had on Nolo's decision to use SharkTalk.)

THE EXACT TRADEMARK INDEX

It is possible to use Trademarkscan to call up an alphabetical list of marks exactly as they have been placed on the federal trademark register. This list is called the Exact Trademark Index. The portion of the index that is shown will be a handful of the marks that alphabetically come before and after the proposed mark. In the Sc[i]3 search report being discussed here, this technique was used for the state registrations maintained by Trademarkscan. See Section B5 below.

---

4. X-Search

The X-Search database is the same database used by the PTO trademark examiners. This database can be used to search for images as well as words. However, since the proposed mark SharkTalk didn't contain any images—as submitted to Sc[i]3 by Nolo for searching—this report only features a search for words.

```
*** User: PTDLSV1  ***




===========X-SEARCH DATA BASE=====JUNE 24, 1997===========




==================FILING DATE========SERIAL NO====X-SEARCH LOAD
TEXT DATA============05/27/97=========75-298399=======06/23/97
DESIGNS==============05/27/97=========75-298379=======06/23/97




Information contained in X-SEARCH NEWS regarding highest serial number and
filing date for text and images is an approximation and is not intended as
a declaration of availablity of all new application data up through the
serial number or filing date reflected.
```

The first page of the X-Search report provides the approximate dates for the last database update. The page tells us that the last updates for text and images (Designs) was made 6/23/97. The page also warns us that these dates are approxi- mate. To the extent that these dates are accurate, the X-Search database is less than 2 weeks behind the date of the search, while the Trademarkscan database is more than a month behind (5/30/97).

The second page of the X-Search report contains five search results.

```
    *** User: PTDLSV1  ***


    STMT    TOTAL   LIVE    DEAD
    NUMBER  MARKS   VIEWED  VIEWED   SEARCH

    01         0       0       0     PHRASCH shark:&talk:

    02         0       0       0     PHONSCH  shark&talk

    03         0       0       0     PHONSCH  sharktalk

    04         0       0       0     SYLSCH   sharktalk

    05         1       0       0     75-129049/sn

    TERMINAL SESSION STARTED 07/03/97 7:25 P.M.  (EASTERN TIME)
    TERMINAL SESSION FINISHED 07/03/97 7:26 P.M.  (EASTERN TIME)
    ELAPSED TIME THIS SESSION 0 HRS AND 1 MIN
```

This page contains the results for five search requests. The numbers running down the left side of the page under the title "STMT NUMBER" denote the number of the search (01-05). The titles running across the top of the page mean the following:

- **Total Marks** = number of marks turned up under the type of search conducted.
- **Live Viewed** = the number of marks that are currently federally registered.
- **Dead Viewed** = the number of marks that were once on the federal register, but which are no longer currently registered. (This may only mean that registration renewal formalities have not been complied with. See Section B2 above.)
- **Search** = type of search and word or words searched for.

The first search query (01) searched for any phrase (PHRASCH) that contained the words Shark and Talk. The result? No marks turned up. The second search query (02) was a phonetic search (PHONSCH) for any mark that contains words that sound like Shark and Talk. This search also turned up no marks. The third search query (03) was another phonetic search for any mark that sounds like SharkTalk. This query also turned up no marks. The fourth query (04) was for any mark that contains the same or similar phonetic syllables (SYLSCH). This search also turned up no marks. Finally the fifth search query (05) turned up one mark with the serial number (sn) 75-129049.

The X-Search report then shows the mark with the serial number 75-129049: Shark Stalker (the same mark discovered in the search of the Trademarkscan database, in Section 3 above) on the next page. This time the search report displays more information about the Shark Stalker mark:

```
*** User: PTDLSV1  *** Serial Number: 75129049 ***

Word Mark
     SHARK STALKER

Goods/Services
     IC 028; US 022 023 038 050; G & S: toy vehicles

Mark Drawing Code
     (1) TYPED DRAWING

Serial Number
     75-129049

Filing Date
     1996.07.01

Owner Name/Address
     (APPLICANT) Empire Industries, Inc. CORPORATION NORTH CAROLINA 5150 Linton
     Blvd. Delray Beach FLORIDA 33484

Type of Mark
     TRADEMARK

Register
     PRINCIPAL

*** Search: 5 *** Document Number: 1 ***
```

- Under the Goods/Services heading we learn that the Shark Stalker mark has been registered in international class (IC) 028 under the goods and services (G&S) category toy vehicles. (The U.S. classes are no longer used by the PTO.)
- Under the Mark Drawing Code heading we learn that Shark Stalker is a typed drawing, which means it doesn't come with a logo or graphic design.
- Under the Serial Number heading, we find the serial number for the mark.
- The Filing Date heading shows that the mark was registered on July 1, 1996 (year, month, day).

- The Owner Name/Address heading provides information about the mark's owner. The report will also reflect changes in ownership that occurred since the original registration (under the assignment section).
- The Type of Mark heading shows that the mark is a trademark, which means it was used as a label on some type of product.
- The Register heading shows that the Shark Stalker mark is registered on the Principal trademark register. (See Chapter 1, Section C6, for more information on the Principal and Supplemental trademark registers.)

State Registration Search

This section of your report includes a list of trademarks registered with the Secretary of State's offices in each of the 50 states and Puerto Rico. These marks each have a status, active or inactive. All active and inactive marks are covered through the dates specified in the body of the attached report. You may need to research inactive marks with diligence as they may still be "in use" and simply have lost their "active" status temporarily. Please consult your attorney for more information.

Period of coverage:
This search covers state registered marks as far back as each individual state has provided records. Dates of coverage are listed on the provided chart (see following page).

Search Strategy and Classes Searched
The U.S. Patent and Trademark Office uses a classification system (class numbers 1-42) which categorizes goods and services by type. If no class numbers appear in the search strategy, all classes were searched. Classification numbers may be used to narrow a search.

The search strategy used to search your mark appears at the beginning of each section of the search report, starting on the following page. The search strategy itself may appear complicated, and the following list of "character codes" may help you understand the search process.

no code =	trademark keyword index
tr =	rotated trademark index
et =	exact trademark index
ic =	International Class number
gs =	goods and services description
s =	set number (S1, S2, etc.). A number the computer assigns to a search results set.
? =	symbol for truncation. It tells the computer to search that word "stem" and any words that contain it. For example, the truncated term **comput?** would retrieve **compute, computing, computer, computers**, etc.
t =	type formats--"t s1/8/all" is asking the computer to type set 1 in format 8, which is a short format, for all the records retrieved. Format 5 is the full format.

**Every effort has been made to provide you an accurate and complete search.
However, because of the complex and subjective nature of trademark searching,
we cannot guarantee that the search identified all potential sources of conflict.**

5. State Registration Search

If you are having a trademark search done for you, it's always a good idea to have the search firm include a search of the state trademark registration database. (See Chapter 5.) In this introductory page, you are told that the following section of the report deals with state trademark registrations. As with the introduction to federal trademark registrations, you are also alerted to the fact that a mark may still be in use even though its registration status is inactive, canceled or "dead." The introduction also explains that:

- the period of coverage for each state is set forth in a chart that the report provides (see below),

- all classes are searched unless the search strategy shows that particular classes were searched, and

- no guarantee is made that all possible conflicting marks will be produced by the search.

The introduction page also contains a list of codes that appear in the State Registration Search results.

a. State Updates

This page contains a chart which shows when each state's trademark registration database was last updated. The page also notes that the dates only apply to trademarks, which means that service marks may not be registered at all or that service marks are being entered into the database after trademarks. (See Chapter 7 for more on state trademark registrations.)

```
File 246:TRADEMARKSCAN(R)-U.S. STATE  1997/JUN 25
       (c) 1997 Thomson & Thomson

DIALOG(R)File 246:TRADEMARKSCAN(R)-U.S. STATE
(c) 1997 Thomson & Thomson. All rts. reserv.

                    STATE UPDATES
        (THESE DATES APPLY TO TRADEMARKS ONLY)

          EFFECTIVE DATE - 06-24-97


    STATE NAME       LAST UPDATE        STATE NAME       LAST UPDATE
  ------------------------------------------------------------------
 |ALABAMA         NEW  01-31-97|      |MONTANA         NEW  05-15-97|
 |ALASKA          NEW  03-24-97|      |NEBRASKA        NEW  04-09-97|
 |AMER. SAMOA     NEW  06-30-95|      |NEVADA          NEW  05-29-97|
 |ARIZONA         NEW  01-29-97|      |NEW HAMPSHIRE   NEW  02-26-97|
 |ARKANSAS             11-28-95|      |NEW JERSEY           05-29-97|*
 |CALIFORNIA      NEW  04-28-96|      |NEW MEXICO      NEW  12-31-96|
 |COLORADO        NEW  03-31-97|      |NEW YORK        NEW  03-31-97|
 |CONNECTICUT     NEW  03-12-97|      |NORTH CAROLINA  NEW  04-30-97|
 |DELAWARE        NEW  12-12-96|      |NORTH DAKOTA    NEW  02-27-97|
 |FLORIDA         NEW  03-14-97|      |OHIO                 03-26-97|
 |GEORGIA         NEW  05-16-97|      |OKLAHOMA             04-30-97|
 |HAWAII          NEW  04-11-97|      |OREGON          NEW  04-30-97|
 |IDAHO           NEW  05-28-97|      |PENNSYLVANIA         05-16-97|
 |ILLINOIS             04-29-97|      |PUERTO RICO          02-28-97|
 |INDIANA         NEW  05-30-97|      |RHODE ISLAND    NEW  02-28-97|
 |IOWA            NEW  04-29-97|      |SOUTH CAROLINA  NEW  04-30-97|
 |KANSAS          NEW  05-21-97|      |SOUTH DAKOTA    NEW  05-30-97|
 |KENTUCKY        NEW  03-19-97|      |TENNESSEE            05-30-97|
 |LOUISIANA       NEW  05-30-97|      |TEXAS           NEW  02-13-97|
 |MAINE           NEW  05-27-97|      |UTAH            NEW  05-27-97|
 |MARYLAND        NEW  03-28-97|      |VERMONT         NEW  03-26-97|
 |MASSACHUSETTS   NEW  03-31-97|      |VIRGINIA             03-31-97|
 |MICHIGAN             04-18-97|      |WASHINGTON      NEW  03-31-97|
 |MINNESOTA       NEW  03-31-97|      |WEST VIRGINIA   NEW  03-20-97|
 |MISSISSIPPI     NEW  04-25-97|      |WISCONSIN       NEW  02-12-97|
 |MISSOURI        NEW  05-29-97|      |WYOMING         NEW  03-26-97|
  ------------------------------------------------------------------


*Due to a filing error within the office of the New Jersey Secretary
of State an undetermined number of records registered in 1987 are
irretrievable. Any questions should be referred to that office at
(609)-530-6422.
```

b. State Search Report

At the beginning of the report, the same search strategy is shown as appeared on the Trademarkscan search of the federal registration database. (Section B2 above). Both reports (S1 and S2) show that no marks were found.

c. The Exact Index Search

The searcher then changes her strategy by searching the exact trademark index for state-registered marks maintained as part of the Trademarkscan state database. This same technique may be used when searching federal trademark registrations. See the Sidebar in Section B3 above.

By typing in et=(mark), the searcher can produce an index of all state registered marks that are alphabetically close to the proposed mark. This type of search accomplishes two things:

- it shows you marks that may be similar to your proposed mark in how they sound or appear (two criteria that may cause customer confusion), and

- assuming that your proposed mark is the only one exactly like it in the index, it reassures you that, to some extent, your choice for a mark is unique among registered marks.

In our sample report, three different exact index searches were made: sharktalk, shark-talk and shark talk. Each search showed that there were no occurrences of the proposed mark (the one marked with an asterisk in the search) on any state registration list.

File 246:TRADEMARKSCAN(R)-U.S. STATE 1997/JUN 25
  (c) 1997 Thomson & Thomson

```
Set  Items  Description
---  -----  -----------
      182  TR=SHARK?
     1105  TR=TALK?
S1     0  TR=(SHARK? AND TALK?)
      180  SHARK?
     1015  TALK?
        0  SHARK?(W)TALK?
        0  SHARKTALK?
S2     0  SHARK?()TALK? OR SHARKTALK?
```

```
?e et=sharktalk
Ref  Items  Index-term
E1     1  ET=SHARKSKINS
E2     1  ET=SHARKSTREAMS
E3     0 *ET=SHARKTALK
E4     1  ET=SHARKWARE
E5     2  ET=SHARKY
E6     6  ET=SHARKY'S
E7     1  ET=SHARKY'S BAJA BROILER
E8     1  ET=SHARKY'S BREWERY & GRILL
E9     1  ET=SHARKY'S DIVE CENTER
E10    2  ET=SHARKY'S FISH MARKET KAUAI
E11    2  ET=SHARKY'S PIZZA
E12    1  ET=SHARKY'S RAW BAR & SEAFOOD RESTAURANT MOM
```

```
?e et=shark-talk
Ref  Items  Index-term
E1     2  ET=SHARK-OFF!
E2     1  ET=SHARK-SHAD
E3     0 *ET=SHARK-TALK
E4     1  ET=SHARK'S
E5     1  ET=SHARK'S BAY HAWAII
E6     1  ET=SHARK'S COVE CLOTHING COMPANY
E7     1  ET=SHARKBITE
E8     1  ET=SHARKBUSTER
E9     1  ET=SHARKBYTE
E10    1  ET=SHARKDOG
E11    1  ET=SHARKDOG DESIGNS HAWAII
E12    1  ET=SHARKEES ISLAND PIZZA
```

```
?e et=shark talk
Ref  Items  Index-term
E1     2  ET=SHARK SHIRTS HAWAII
E2     1  ET=SHARK SKINZ
E3     0 *ET=SHARK TALK
E4     1  ET=SHARK TANK
E5     1  ET=SHARK TEETH EXCAVATION SUPPLY
E6     1  ET=SHARK TOOTH THE ANCHOR WITH A BITE
E7     1  ET=SHARK-ENER PRODUCTS
E8     2  ET=SHARK-OFF!
E9     1  ET=SHARK-SHAD
E10    1  ET=SHARK'S
E11    1  ET=SHARK'S BAY HAWAII
E12    1  ET=SHARK'S COVE CLOTHING COMPANY
```

6. Report on Company and Product Names

As with other sections of the report, this introduction explains the dates covered by the search, what databases were covered in the search and a code box for the abbreviations that show up in the search strategy and report.

REPORT ON COMPANY and PRODUCT NAMES

This section of your report includes a list of company names which may be in conflict with your mark. This list was compiled from databases which include over 30 million company names, many of which are not registered as trademarks. However, because company names are often used as trademarks, and because trademark rights in the United States may be conferred by usage alone (common-law marks), any match in this section may indicate potential areas of conflict. Files consulted may vary according to the nature of your product or service.

We have provided a list of company names which may be in conflict with your mark. We can provide additional information on any of these companies at your request.

A. **Dates Covered through:**
    1997

B. **Databases Covered:**

    •   **American Business Directory** - Offers information on over 10 million companies large and small. The American Business Directory is compiled by American Business Information from nationwide yellow pages, annual reports, news releases, and other public records.

    •   **DIALOG® Company Name Finder** - a search aid database designed to locate company information in other DIALOG® databases.

    •   **Thomas Register Online®** - Corresponds to the Thomas Register of American Manufacturers, a premier source of product information for North American manufacturing companies. Covers over 180,000 U.S. and Canadian public and private companies and over 115,000 brand names.

    •   **Brands and Their Companies** - A worldwide directory of over 282,000 consumer brand names and their owners.

    •   **New Product Announcements/Plus®** - Full-text of product-related press releases from all industries, with a focus on product and service industries.

    •   **Other databases searched as needed.**

C. **Search Strategy**
    The exact search strategy used to search your mark appears at the beginning of the Company Names section on the following page. The search strategy itself may appear complicated, and the following list of "character codes" may help you understand the search process.

no code =	trademark keyword index
co =	company name index
tn =	trade name index
gs =	goods and services description
s =	set number (S1, S2, etc.). A number the computer assigns to a search results set.
? =	symbol for truncation. It tells the computer to search that word "stem" and any words that contain it. For example, the truncated term **comput**? would retrieve **compute, computing, computer, computers**, etc.
t =	type formats–"t s1/3,k/all" is asking the computer to type (display) set 1 in format 3, which is a short format, and to display all keywords (search terms) for all the records retrieved.

**Every effort has been made to provide you an accurate and complete search.
However, because of the complex and subjective nature of trademark searching,
we cannot guarantee that the search identified all potential sources of conflict.**

As with the state trademark registration search, these searches each start with a search for SharkTalk and any possible variations and then move to a search of the exact trademark index. The final database, a listing of new product an-

nouncements, is searched according to the words in the announcement. This search uncovered several occurrences of announcements that contained both shark and talk, but none that indicated the use of these terms as a trademark.

File 531:Amer. Bus. Directory 1997/Apr
    (c) 1997 American Business Information

```
Set  Items  Description
---  -----  -----------
S1     0   (SHARK? AND TALK?)
S2     0   SHARK?(3N)TALK?
S3     0   SHARK?()TALK? OR SHARKTALK?
?e co=sharktalk
Ref  Items  Index-term
E1     1   CO=SHARKSKINS INC
E2     1   CO=SHARKSTOOTH RECORDS
E3     0  *CO=SHARKTALK
E4     1   CO=SHARKTEL INC
E5     1   CO=SHARKWOOD ADVERTISING SPEC
E6     1   CO=SHARKY ELECTRIC INC
E7    27   CO=SHARKY'S
E8     1   CO=SHARKY'S AT FIVE POINTS
E9     2   CO=SHARKY'S BAR & BILLIARDS
E10    2   CO=SHARKY'S BAR & GRILL
E11    1   CO=SHARKY'S BEACH BAR & EATERY
E12    1   CO=SHARKY'S BEACH CLUB

?e co=shark-talk
Ref  Items  Index-term
E1     1   CO=SHARK WRECKING CORP
E2     1   CO=SHARK-FIN PRODUCTS INC
E3     0  *CO=SHARK-TALK
E4     1   CO=SHARK-TRON
E5     1   CO=SHARK-TV
E6     1   CO=SHARK'S BEACHWEAR
E7     1   CO=SHARK'S CLUB BILLIARD BAR
E8     1   CO=SHARK'S COVE
E9     1   CO=SHARK'S COVE MARINA RESTAURANT
E10    1   CO=SHARK'S DELI
E11    2   CO=SHARK'S INC
E12    1   CO=SHARK'S SHOES

?e co=shark talk
Ref  Items  Index-term
E1     1   CO=SHARK SYSTEM INC
E2     1   CO=SHARK TALES
E3     0  *CO=SHARK TALK
E4     1   CO=SHARK TEES SCREEN PRINTING
E5     1   CO=SHARK TEETH JEWELERS
E6     1   CO=SHARK TESTED PRODUCTS
E7     1   CO=SHARK VALLEY TRAM TOURS
E8     1   CO=SHARK WRECKING CORP
E9     1   CO=SHARK-FIN PRODUCTS INC
E10    1   CO=SHARK-TRON
E11    1   CO=SHARK-TV
E12    1   CO=SHARK'S BEACHWEAR

?e tn=sharktalk
Ref  Items  Index-term
E1     7   TN=SENTRY/DAIRYLAND
E2   121   TN=SHAKEY'S PIZZA
```

```
E3     0  *TN=SHARKTALK
E4  1768   TN=SHARP
E5  5314   TN=SHELL
E6  1390   TN=SHELTER INS
E7   196   TN=SHERATON
E8  2116   TN=SHERWIN WILLIAMS
E9   167   TN=SHOE CITY
E10  130   TN=SHOPKO
E11   87   TN=SHRINERS (TANGIER TEMPLE)
E12   72   TN=SILVER REED

?e tn=shark-talk
Ref  Items  Index-term
E1     7   TN=SENTRY/DAIRYLAND
E2   121   TN=SHAKEY'S PIZZA
E3     0  *TN=SHARK-TALK
E4  1768   TN=SHARP
E5  5314   TN=SHELL
E6  1390   TN=SHELTER INS
E7   196   TN=SHERATON
E8  2116   TN=SHERWIN WILLIAMS
E9   167   TN=SHOE CITY
E10  130   TN=SHOPKO
E11   87   TN=SHRINERS (TANGIER TEMPLE)
E12   72   TN=SILVER REED

?e tn=shark talk
Ref  Items  Index-term
E1     7   TN=SENTRY/DAIRYLAND
E2   121   TN=SHAKEY'S PIZZA
E3     0  *TN=SHARK TALK
E4  1768   TN=SHARP
E5  5314   TN=SHELL
E6  1390   TN=SHELTER INS
E7   196   TN=SHERATON
E8  2116   TN=SHERWIN WILLIAMS
E9   167   TN=SHOE CITY
E10  130   TN=SHOPKO
E11   87   TN=SHRINERS (TANGIER TEMPLE)
E12   72   TN=SILVER REED
```

File 416:DIALOG COMPANY NAME FINDER(TM) 1997/MAR
  (c) 1997 Dialog Info.Svcs.

Set Items Description
--- ----- -----------
S1   0 (SHARK? AND TALK?)
S2   0 SHARK?(3N)TALK?
S3   0 SHARK?()TALK? OR SHARKTALK?
?e co=sharktalk
Ref Items Index-term
E1   1 CO=SHARKSTOOTH RECORDS INC
E2   1 CO=SHARKSTREAMS
E3   0 *CO=SHARKTALK
E4   5 CO=SHARKTEL INC
E5   1 CO=SHARKTOOTH LIMITED
E6   2 CO=SHARKTOOTH STEAKHOUSE
E7   1 CO=SHARKTREE LIMITED
E8   1 CO=SHARKUR KHALID ABDUL
E9   2 CO=SHARKUS DONNA
E10   2 CO=SHARKUTIS JOINT STOCK COMPANY
E11   1 CO=SHARKVALE LIMITED
E12   3 CO=SHARKWARE

?e co=shark-talk
Ref Items Index-term
E1   1 CO=SHARK-MICRO SARL // C H P
E2   1 CO=SHARK-OFF INC // GAG ME WITH A
E3   0 *CO=SHARK-TALK
E4   3 CO=SHARK-TRON
E5   1 CO=SHARK-TV
E6   1 CO=SHARK/TITO EL TIBURON/EVA KRANTZ/WARR // TITO
E7   1 CO=SHARKA
E8   1 CO=SHARKA DESIGN // JOSEPH
E9   1 CO=SHARKA IND
E10   1 CO=SHARKA INVESTMENTS LIMITED
E11   1 CO=SHARKA MARIE 1958- // PROKES
E12   1 CO=SHARKADELIC MUSIC

?e co=shark talk
Ref Items Index-term
E1   1 CO=SHARK TABOO
E2   2 CO=SHARK TALES
E3   0 *CO=SHARK TALK
E4   2 CO=SHARK TANK INC
E5   1 CO=SHARK TANNERY-KALASH & CO
E6   1 CO=SHARK TEA & SUGAR PACKAGING CENTER
E7   1 CO=SHARK TECHNOLOGIES
E8   1 CO=SHARK TECHNOLOGIES INC
E9   1 CO=SHARK TECHNOLOGIES LIMITED // RED
E10   1 CO=SHARK TECHNOLOGY
E11   6 CO=SHARK TECHNOLOGY // RED
E12   3 CO=SHARK TECHNOLOGY CORP

?s (shark? and talk?)
    3864 SHARK?
    7582 TALK?
S4   0 (SHARK? AND TALK?)

SYSTEM:OS - DIALOG OneSearch
  File 116:Brands & Their Companies 1996/Oct
    (c) 1996 Gale Research
  File 535:Thomas Register Online(R) 1997/Q1
    (c) 1997 Thomas Publishing Co.

  Set Items Description
  --- ----- -----------
S1   0 (SHARK? AND TALK?)
S2   0 SHARK?(3N)TALK?
S3   0 SHARK?()TALK? OR SHARKTALK?
?e co=sharktalk
Ref Items Index-term
E1   1 CO=SHARK-FIN PRODUCTS INC.
E2   1 CO=SHARKSTREAMS
E3   0 *CO=SHARKTALK
E4   2 CO=SHARKY'S CLOTHING CO.
E5   1 CO=SHARLIN LITE CORP.
E6   1 CO=SHARMARK LAS VEGAS, INC.
E7   1 CO=SHARN ENTERPRISE, INC.
E8   1 CO=SHARNEY CONTAINER CO., INC.
E9   2 CO=SHARNOA CORP.
E10   1 CO=SHARON AERO MACHINE CO.
E11   1 CO=SHARON B. WILSON
E12   1 CO=SHARON BURCH INC.

?e co=shark-talk
Ref Items Index-term
E1   1 CO=SHARK PRODUCTS
E2   1 CO=SHARK-FIN PRODUCTS INC.
E3   0 *CO=SHARK-TALK
E4   1 CO=SHARKSTREAMS
E5   2 CO=SHARKY'S CLOTHING CO.
E6   1 CO=SHARLIN LITE CORP.
E7   1 CO=SHARMARK LAS VEGAS, INC.
E8   1 CO=SHARN ENTERPRISE, INC.
E9   1 CO=SHARNEY CONTAINER CO., INC.
E10   2 CO=SHARNOA CORP.
E11   1 CO=SHARON AERO MACHINE CO.
E12   1 CO=SHARON B. WILSON

?e co=shark talk
Ref Items Index-term
E1   1 CO=SHARIN' FOODSERVICE SALES, INC.
E2   1 CO=SHARK PRODUCTS
E3   0 *CO=SHARK TALK
E4   1 CO=SHARK-FIN PRODUCTS INC.
E5   1 CO=SHARKSTREAMS
E6   2 CO=SHARKY'S CLOTHING CO.
E7   1 CO=SHARLIN LITE CORP.
E8   1 CO=SHARMARK LAS VEGAS, INC.
E9   1 CO=SHARN ENTERPRISE, INC.
E10   1 CO=SHARNEY CONTAINER CO., INC.
E11   2 CO=SHARNOA CORP.
E12   1 CO=SHARON AERO MACHINE CO.

?e tn=sharktalk

```
Ref  Items  Index-term
E1     1  TN=SHARKSKIN // AEROHEAD
E2     1  TN=SHARKSTREAMS
E3     0 *TN=SHARKTALK
E4     1  TN=SHARKTOOTH
E5     1  TN=SHARKWEAR
E6     1  TN=SHARKY
E7     1  TN=SHARKY SKUL-SQUIRT
E8     1  TN=SHARKY'S
E9     1  TN=SHARLIN
E10    1  TN=SHARMARK
E11    1  TN=SHARME // DU
E12    1  TN=SHARNOA
```

```
?e tn=shark-talk
Ref  Items  Index-term
E1     2  TN=SHARK TOOTH
E2     1  TN=SHARK-FIN
E3     0 *TN=SHARK-TALK
E4     1  TN=SHARK-WISE
E5     1  TN=SHARKILAGE
E6     1  TN=SHARKRUISER
E7     2  TN=SHARKS
E8     1  TN=SHARKS // CARD
E9     1  TN=SHARKS // CHEF BOYARDEE
E10    1  TN=SHARKS // EMPIRE II: INTERSTELLAR
E11    1  TN=SHARKS // RAZZBERRY
E12    1  TN=SHARKS // SUPER
```

```
?e tn=shark talk
Ref  Items  Index-term
E1     1  TN=SHARK REPELLENT // CAPT'N PAT'S
E2     1  TN=SHARK SHIFTER
E3     0 *TN=SHARK TALK
E4     2  TN=SHARK TOOTH
E5     1  TN=SHARK-FIN
E6     1  TN=SHARK-WISE
E7     1  TN=SHARKILAGE
E8     1  TN=SHARKRUISER
E9     2  TN=SHARKS
E10    1  TN=SHARKS // CARD
E11    1  TN=SHARKS // CHEF BOYARDEE
E12    1  TN=SHARKS // EMPIRE II: INTERSTELLAR
```

```
File 621:IAC New Prod.Annou.(R)  1985-1997/Jul 03
        (c) 1997 Information Access Co
>>>CURRENT started

     Set  Items  Description
     ---  -----  -----------
     S2     0    SHARK?()TALK? OR SHARKTALK?
     S3     7    (SHARK? AND TALK?)
     S4     1    S3/CO,TN
?t 4/ti,co,tn,k
```

4/TI,CO,TN,K/1
DIALOG(R)File 621:(c) 1997 Information Access Co. All rts. reserv.

SeeQuest Video Conferencing Introduced; Real-Time Video Conferencing on a Single Telephone Line.

COMPANY: **SHARK** Multimedia

```
     S6     6    S3 NOT S4
?t 6/ti,co,tn,k/all
```

6/TI,CO,TN,K/1
DIALOG(R)File 621:(c) 1997 Information Access Co. All rts. reserv.

Hilton Hotels Corp. issues copy of letter sent to ITT board of directors.

COMPANY: ITT Corp.; Hilton Hotels Corp.

...of control penalty
provisions into its management contracts with FelCor, but has
already placed these **shark** repellent provisions into numerous other
management contracts signed since announcement of Hilton's offer for...

...core assets also raises the more
fundamental question of why ITT continues to refuse to **talk** to us.
The benefits of combining our two companies remains compelling. We
are more committed...

6/TI,CO,TN,K/2
DIALOG(R)File 621:(c) 1997 Information Access Co. All rts. reserv.

MCI Provides Telecommunications Facilities For Nickelodeon's Third Annual Big Help-A-Thon

COMPANY: MCI Intnl; Nickelodeon

...Students will
be controlling an underwater robot by telemetry via MCI Global ISDN
in a **shark** tank at Mote Marine Aquarium in Sarasota, Florida and
talking via ISDN Video to a marine biologist. MCI earlier used this
popular demonstration of MCI...

6/TI,CO,TN,K/3
DIALOG(R)File 621:(c) 1997 Information Access Co. All rts. reserv.

Humongous Entertainment Ships a New World of Animated Fun in Freddi Fish 2: The Case of the Haunted Schoolhouse; Free Limited-Edition Sing Along with Freddi Fish and her Friends Book and Audiotape to be Available with CD-ROM at Launch.

COMPANY: Humongous Entertainment

...ROM Today Children's Entertainment
Title of the Year and Rommie Award.

Everyone's favorite **talking** fish is back with an ocean full of fun
in Freddi Fish 2: The Case...

...lead programmer and co-designer of
Freddi Fish 2.

 Lovable Characters

Players will want to **talk** with all of the characters they meet,
since they may provide clues to help them solve the case. Eddie the
Eel with an electric personality, Ray the fast-**talking** Manta Ray,
the bungling **sharks** Boss and Spongehead, and the Squidfather are all
back in Freddi Fish 2. Colorful new...

 6/TI,CO,TN,K/4
DIALOG(R)File 621:(c) 1997 Information Access Co. All rts. reserv.

Humongous Entertainment Handcrafts Another Junior Adventure(tm), Freddi Fish 2: The Case of the Haunted Schoolhouse(tm); Freddi Fish 2 to Be Previewed at Electronic Entertainment Expo May 16-18.

COMPANY: Humongous Entertainment
TRADE NAME: Freddi Fish 2

...Co-Designer Mark Peyser added, "People's favorite
characters Eddie the Eel, Ray the fast-**talking** Manta Ray, the
bungling **sharks** Boss and Spongehead, and the Squidfather are back in
Freddi Fish 2. The diverse cast...

...experience of
directing the story as they make decisions about where to go, whom
to **talk** to, and what to do next to achieve the goals they set for
themselves. Each...

 6/TI,CO,TN,K/5
DIALOG(R)File 621:(c) 1997 Information Access Co. All rts. reserv.

Opening in Time for "Snoopy's Joe Cool Summer"; Knott's New "Boardwalk" Themed Area to Re-energize Roaring 20s with Ocean-Oriented Thrills.

COMPANY: Knott's Berry Farm

...r) to
survive the area-wide renovation.

Hosted by HammerHead Hank(tm), a frisky hammerhead **shark** character,
The Boardwalk(tm) will be anchored by a high-intensity,
water-oriented thrill ride...

...new ride will spin riders from the
surface of a grotto inhabited by magnificently sculpted **sharks** ,
mermaids and other sea creatures to a height of 80 feet, at times
holding passengers...

...opportunity to try out the latest in arcade games, see
themselves on giant video screens, **talk** to each other on
table-to-table AirPhonz(tm), listen to the park's new...

6/TI,CO,TN,K/6
DIALOG(R)File 621:(c) 1997 Information Access Co. All rts. reserv.

Another strong year for games and puzzles from Milton Bradley.

COMPANY: Milton Bradley

...electronic light and sound puzzler that features
plenty of fun and challenge.

 Bike Max -- the **talking** computer control center for your bicycle
that tells you speed, distance and even serves as...

...Bradley also has a great track record for extending
successful products in new ways. Electronic **Talking** Magic Works
combines electronics and voices with no-fail magic in three great
tricks. Space...

...year with Spitfire Space Shooter featuring two 20 disc clips
for fast action and Thunder **Shark** Space Shooter featuring mega-sized
discs that travel over 35 feet.

Always on the cutting...

7. CASSIS Search for Federal Trademark Registrations

The searcher decided to use the trademark database published by the PTO as part of its CASSIS series as a final check on the previous results. As mentioned in Chapter 5, this CASSIS database is available for free searching by users of any Patent and Trademark Depository Library (and for a reasonable fee over the Internet) and is also used by Sc[i]3 searchers when conducting its low-cost "jiffy" trademark search. (See Section A1 above.) The CASSIS search is only done as part of a comprehensive search when the other methods fail to turn up enough hits—as happened in this case.

This search—which separately combined the terms Shark and Talk with terms related to the underlying service (game, Internet, Web, computer, interactive)—produced several pages of registered and pending marks using Shark and Talk, but none using both words together. Here is a list of marks that were uncovered by this search that the searcher felt Nolo should know about:

SHARK BITE
SHARK STALKER
SHARKWARE
SHARETALK

8. How Nolo Interpreted the Sc[i]3 Trademark Search Report

Nolo learned several important things from this search:

- Lots of marks use the word shark.
- Lots of marks use the word talk.
- Lots of games use the word shark.
- No federal or state registered mark contained the exact term SharkTalk.
- No federal or state registered mark contained the two words shark and talk.
- No federal or state registered mark carried the same meaning as SharkTalk.

- No federal or state registered mark looked or sounded like SharkTalk except for Shark Stalker (discussed below).
- No business or product name contained SharkTalk or the two words shark and talk.

The only mark to give Nolo pause was the term Shark Stalker, a mark used for a children's game product. Because Nolo proposes to use SharkTalk for an online computer adult game that teaches legal jargon, Nolo felt that there was little likelihood that its use of SharkTalk would confuse its own customers or those of the company that produces the Shark Stalker product. On that basis, Nolo decided to adopt the mark and apply for a federal registration. That process is still ongoing as this book goes to print.

C. How to Do Your Own Search

In this section, we discuss how to do a search on your own by using various approaches. We first describe how to use Micropatent, CompuServe and DIALOG in some detail. Then we profile the other systems. Manual methods of clearing a mark come last. At the end of this chapter, we also list alternative resources that contain more help with how to search.

1. Using Micropatent to Do a Direct Hit Search

To sign up for a Micropatent search, visit the Micropatent homepage [http://www.micropatent.com] and click on the trademark button. This will take you to a page that sorts the registered users from the new users. Click on new user and you will be asked to enter some basic information, including a login name, a password and your e-mail address. Micropatent will then send a confirmation code to your e-mail address. Next, you call an 800 number to set up your billing account. If you only want the 24-hour access deal, you will be asked for a credit card number and your confirmation code. By the time you get off the phone and back to the Micropatent site, your service will be activated.

As suggested earlier, Micropatent is best used for direct hit searching. (See Chapter 5, Section C for a review of the three types of searches.) This is because the other two major databases—Trademarkscan and X-Search—have more "intelligence" built into them which allows you to search for more potentially confusing marks. Here are some tips for how to use Micropatent to do a typical direct hit search (based on material in Micropatent's excellent online help file).

a. Enter the word or words into the Word Mark field and click the Search button. Example: flexiline.

b. If this search produces one or more identical registered marks that are used on goods or services somewhat related to yours, and the registration status shows that the mark is currently registered, choose another mark.

c. If your first search results don't knock you out of the water, re-run the search, each time truncating back one character and using in its place the asterisk as a wildcard. For example, try "flexilin*", then "flexili*", and then "flexil*". The asterisk represents any one character or group of characters. So a search on "flexil*" will find "flexiline", "flexilube", etc. By truncating back a character at a time and using wildcards, you can broaden the search as little or as much as you like and may uncover some surprisingly similar marks.

d. If words have punctuation in them, for example, "T.J. Tibbs", try leaving out the punctuation: TJ Tibbs.

e. If your mark involves several words, try another search with the words joined together into one: for instance, "TJTibbs".

f. Try phonetic equivalents. For example, replace the letter "y" with "i" in "lynx" ("linx"), and vice versa. Other common phonetic equivalents are:

"s" for "z"

"f" for "ph"

"g" for "j"

"j" for "h"

"c" for "k"

"x" for "ks"

You can use the wild card character "?" to search for both equivalents at once: for instance, "l?nx" will find both "linx" and "lynx".

You can also use Micropatent to search by one or more additional fields.

EXAMPLE 1: (owner and class): You want to find all marks that belong in International class 002 (paint-related products) and that belong to Sears. You would enter "002" in the Int'l class field and Sears in the Owner field. The result would list all marks that fit your search parameters.

EXAMPLE 2: You want to find all marks applied for by Dow Chemicals on an intent-to-use basis. You would enter Dow in the owner field and the word "all" in the Sec 1B ITU field. The result would give you some idea of what Dow has in mind for future products.

EXAMPLE 3: You want to find all marks dealing with wine and cheese. You would enter wine and cheese in the Goods and Services field. This search would list every registered or pending mark whose application for registration contains the words wine and cheese to describe the goods and services on which the mark would be used.

When you register and log on to Micropatent the search input screen will show you all the different ways you can search for a mark.

2. Using CompuServe

To become a member of CompuServe, you must pay a monthly fee of $9.95 for five hours of online use per month and $2.95 for each additional hour. Interface software is provided free. CompuServe's extended services, such as Trademarkscan and Biz*File, are an additional charge (usually $.15 or $.25 per minute). In addition to these costs, there is a $20 trademark search fee (for the first five matches), and a $1 charge for the search if there is no match. For example, if you search for the word Virtuosity and you are told that there are no marks containing that word in the Trademarkscan database, you will only be charged $1. However, if you search for the word Virtual and are told that there are 200 matches, you will be billed $20 to examine the first five records and $20 for each additional group of 5 records that meet your search criteria.

EXAMPLE OF TOTAL COSTS: You spend ten minutes to search for a federal trademark. In addition to your monthly CompuServe fee, you would pay:

	No Matches Found	5 Matches Found	10 matches Found
10 Minute Search			
@ .15 per minute	$1.50	$1.50	$1.50
Trademarkscan charge	$1.00	$20.00	$40.00
Total	$2.50	$21.50	$41.50

Once you have logged on to CompuServe, use the GO feature and type in **trademark, traderc** or **iquest** (all of them take you to the Trademarkscan database).

TERMINAL MODE TIPS

Those of you who have become dependent on the graphical user interface approach—used in most Windows and Macintosh application programs as well as by online services such as CompuServe—prepare yourself for a semi-rude shock. Once you enter the Trademarkscan database, the service will turn from pretty to ugly. Perhaps most upsetting, you cannot click on items with your mouse. And there are no colorful graphics to guide you. This is what is sometimes known as "terminal mode" in which the user interacts by choosing numbers or text. Fortunately, this system (though old-fashioned) is simple to use.

The biggest problem with terminal mode is moving around. For example, you may find yourself unable to return to the first menu. The following commands work in all terminal mode applications. After each command you must press the key marked "RETURN" or "ENTER" on your keyboard.

C shows a list of all terminal mode commands.

H offers you help.

M takes you to the top (or main) menu.

B takes you back one screen.

L or **Exit/** or **Bye/** returns you to CompuServe and exits the current service (Trademarkscan or IQuest).

a. Trademarkscan (Federal & State Registrations)

Your first activity will be to choose the proper database. As mentioned, Trademarkscan offers eight databases. Once you enter the Trademarkscan service area, you will see a list like the following:

NORTH AMERICA
1   Trademarkscan—Canada
2   Trademarkscan—U.S. Federal
3   Trademarkscan—U.S. State
EUROPE
4   Trademarkscan—France
5   Trademarkscan—Germany
6   Trademarkscan—Italy
7   Trademarkscan—U.K.
WORLDWIDE (WIPO—World Intellectual Property Organization)
8   Trademarkscan—International Register

You are going to use the U.S. Federal database. You will type:

2   (and press RETURN)

Next you will see a list of choices as follows:

PRESS TO SELECT
1   by trademark
2   by International Class code
3   by goods/services description
4   by serial number
5   by registration number
6   by owner name
7   by trademark status
8   by year

If you are a novice trademark searcher, your best choice here is "1 by trademark." This choice will retrieve all registered marks that meet your search criteria (discussed below). People with more experience in searching for trademarks and analyzing the results of the search may prefer choices 2 or 3. These choices narrow your search to only those marks that fit within the classifica-

tions you identify or that are attached to the goods and services you describe. The reason why we recommend that novice searchers perform the broader search is that we think you will be best served by knowing about all registered marks that meet your search criteria, not just the ones that fit within a particular set of classifications or descriptions of goods and services. Once you have the complete picture, you will be in the best possible position to assess whether you want to continue with your proposed mark or choose another.

If you prefer to search by goods/services descriptions, choice 3 offers the following suggestions for product and service searches:

- Enter words that describe your goods or service product.
- Omit punctuation and common, small words (examples: for, of, to, a).
- To ensure a more comprehensive search, include synonyms, using OR.
- Use the wild letter slash (/) to search plural and singular endings.

SEARCH EXAMPLES: If you sell a camera product, enter Camera/

If you sell jewelry, enter Jewelry OR Jewelry OR Pin/ OR Brooch/

If you sell a wood stain, enter Paint/ or Lacquer/ or Varnish/

If you prefer to search by International Class code, first assign the most appropriate classification to your proposed mark. (See Appendix, International Schedule of Classes of Goods and Services and Descriptions of Goods and Services (From USTA—International Classes).) The International Schedule of Classes of Goods and Services is used by the U.S. Patent and Trademark Office to differentiate categories of goods or services. For that reason, using the class may be more comprehensive in searching than describing the product or service. If you choose the class code option, you will see a screen like this:

Intn'l Class	Related Classes
3	5
5	3,10
6	40
7	40
10	5
12	39
19	37
23	26
24	23
28	41
29	30, 41
30	29,31
31	29,30
32	33
33	32
37	19
39	12
40	6,7

International Class Code Menu
1   explanation of Class Code searching
2   search by International Class code
3   list of International Class codes
4   previous menu

The Compuserve interface to Trademarkscan also provides a listing of related product classes. For example, Classes 30 and 31 are related (Staple Foods, Natural Agricultural Products) and should be searched at the same time. To search more than one class, enter each class separated by a space (30 31). After you have entered your class(es), you will see a screen as follows:

PRESS TO SELECT
1   Add a field
2   Change terms in a field
3   Remove one or all fields
4   Start the Search ... $20.00
5   Database Description and Pricing Information
6   Consult with a Search Specialist
7   Cancel Search (Return to Main Menu)

Since you still have not entered the terms for your mark, you must add another field. You

would type: 1 (and press RETURN) and see the following menu:

1   perform broad trademark screening
2   search by key words in trademark
3   help in choosing between above options
4   rules for searching options 1 or 2
5   previous menu

Broad Screening v. Key Word Searching

In Chapter 5 we spoke of two fundamentally different types of searches—the direct hit search and the analytical search. The key word searching option is equivalent to the direct hit search. Your goal is to locate exact matches and marks that are substantially similar. You must search for any close variations to your mark. If you want to use the Trademarkscan database to do an analytical search, then you can use the broad screening option after you have performed your direct hit search. In broad screening, you search a word or word fragment that may appear anywhere within the trademark name (a search for "can" would uncover both Canada Dry and American International). Key word searching only searches complete words in a trademark (a search for "can" would uncover National Can Company).

As mentioned, the broad screening option is more comprehensive than the key word approach. It usually retrieves a larger set of results than key word searching. However you should use key word searching (and avoid using broad screen searching) when searching phrases that are common to many words, such as the phrase "ABLE," or one to three-letter words, such as the "C" in "C Plus." These word fragments will retrieve too many irrelevant marks in broad screen style.

For example, let's say you wanted to name your business Telequick-Faxomatic. You want to search all marks that used "tele" and "fax" and submitted the search request as Tele/ and Fax/. ("/" marks after each word will uncover plural, singular and similar word endings.)

SEARCHING

by Broad Screen	by Key Word
Telex by Fax	Telex by Fax
U.S. Fax & Telex	U.S. Fax & Telex
Aaron's Tele-Fax Directory	
Hotelecopy Fax Mail	
Intelefax	
Omnitelefax	
Telefax	
Telefax 1000	
Tele-Fax	

After you have selected the type of search and typed in the appropriate number, you must enter your search terms. Searching for a trademark is not simply a matter of typing in the name of your mark. Trademarkscan uses a system known as "fuzzy logic" that will uncover sound-alike marks, as well as marks with alternative spellings (cola or kola). Trademarkscan offers various tips for entering search terms:

- Use the wild letter slash (/) to search variable word endings, including plural and possessive forms of words.
  EXAMPLE: Child/ (to find *Child, Child's, Children, Children's,* etc.).

Note however, that the "/" will not function with irregular possessives (don't type "mouse/", instead type "mice OR mouse."

- Use the "AND" connector if you have two search terms and want to locate marks with both terms.
  EXAMPLE: Cool/ AND Cola

- Use the "OR" connector if you have two search terms and want to locate marks with *either* term. You can also use OR if you want to search two trademarks at one time.
  EXAMPLE: Cool/ OR Chill/

- Use "AND" and "OR" with parentheses if you have a mixture of terms.
  EXAMPLE: Cool/ OR Chill/ AND Cola

- Omit punctuation and compress resulting spaces. Search both full and shortened forms of contracted words.
  EXAMPLE: OsCal (for *Os-Cal*)
  What Is Cooking OR Whats Cooking
  Thats Life OR That is Life

- Search all variations in spacing, especially for marks containing compound words; combine using OR.
  EXAMPLE: Peekaboo Pals OR Peek A Boo Pals

- Use common, American spelling of words to find variant spellings and some foreign spellings. Search all variations of names using OR.
  EXAMPLE: Color (to find *Color, Colour, Kolor, Colors,* etc.)
  Sue/ OR Susan/ OR Suzy/ OR Suzanne/ (to find *Suebee, Lazy Susan, Suzy's Stables, Suzanne's Muffins,* etc.)

- Search both the abbreviation and the full term using OR.
  EXAMPLE: CNN OR Cable News Network

- Small common words (the, an, a, of, to, for) are searchable, but use these with caution if you are doing a broad trademark search.
  EXAMPLE: All The News That Is Fit to Print

- If the words "and," "or," or "not" appear in the mark you want to search, enter those words within double quotation marks; use them only when they are essential to retrieving the mark.
  EXAMPLE: To Be "Or" "Not" to Be

- If the trademark includes a Roman or Arabic numeral, enter it along with the word equivalent.
  EXAMPLE: 9 Lives OR Nine Lives

- If the trademark includes a special character ($ % + - = #), enter the word equivalent for it. **EXAMPLE:** A Plus Mini Market (for *A+ Mini Market*)

- When performing broad trademark screening enter a word or word fragment from anywhere within the trademark followed by the wild letter slash (/) at the end of each term.

- When performing broad trademark screening do not enter overly short or common word fragments, because they will retrieve large numbers of irrelevant results.

    After you submit your search and press RETURN, you will be notified if there are any matches.

    EXAMPLE 1: You have a pet food product you want to call *Woof Woof.* You search in Class 31 (Natural Agricultural Products). You enter the search term "woof/" and retrieve the name "*Woofies*" as a registered trademark for pet food.

WOOFIES
INTL CLASS: 31 (Natural Agricultural Products)
U.S. CLASS: 46 (Foods & Ingredients of Foods)
STATUS: Registered; Section 8 & 15 -Accepted & Acknowledged
GOODS/SERVICES: DOG FOOD
SERIAL NO.: 73-053,426
REG. NO.: 1,064,601
REGISTERED: April 26, 1977
FIRST USE: March 18, 1975 (Intl Class 31)
FIRST COMMERCE: March 18, 1975 (Intl Class 31)
FILED: May 27, 1975
PUBLISHED: February 1, 1977
AFFIDAVIT SEC.: 8-15; June 28, 1982
LAST LISTED OWNER: MORTON PET FOOD COMPANY, HOPKINS, MINN.
ASSIGNEE(S): HUBBARD MILLING COMPANY (Minnesota Corporation), 424 NORTH FRONT ST., MANKATO, MN (Minnesota), 56001, USA (United States of America)
ASSIGNOR(S): MORTON PET FOOD COMPANY (Minnesota Corporation)
REEL/FRAME: 0485/0090
ACKNOWLEDGED: December 12, 1984
RECORDED: December 24, 1984
BRIEF: ASSIGNS THE ENTIRE INTEREST AND THE GOOD WILL EFFECTIVE AS OF MARCH 1, 1984
ASSIGNEE(S): TERRA ACQUISITION, INC. (Delaware Corporation), 582 GREAT ROAD, FORESTDALE, RI (Rhode Island), 02824, USA (United States of America)
ASSIGNOR(S): TERRAGRAFICS, INC. (California Corporation), 7000 MARINA BOULEVARD, BRISBANE, CA (California), 94005, USA (United States of America)
REEL/FRAME: 0738/0553
RECORDED: September 14, 1990
BRIEF: ASSIGNS THE ENTIRE INTEREST AND THE GOODWILL AS OF SEPT. 7, 1990

EXAMPLE 2: You have a doll that looks like a large lollipop. You want to call it *Lollipop Dolly.* You search in International Class 48 (Toys and Sporting Goods) and related Class 41 (Education and Entertainment Services). A search of "loll/ AND doll/" retrieves a match for a mark that was abandoned prior to registration.

04556130
DOLLY LOLLY
INTL CLASS: *28* (Toys & Sporting Goods)
U.S. CLASS: 22 (Games, Toys, & Sporting Goods)
STATUS: Abandoned - Failure to Respond; Intent to Use -
Application; Intent to Use - Current
GOODS/SERVICES: NOVELTY LOLLIPOP IN THE SHAPE OF A HEAD

SERIAL NO.: 74-556,130
FILED: August 1, 1994
ABANDONED: August 15, 1995
ORIGINAL APPLICANT: CAP TOYS, INC. (Ohio
Corporation), 26201
RICHMOND ROAD, BEDFORD HEIGHTS, OH
(Ohio), 44146, USA (United States of America)
FILING CORRESPONDENT: ARNOLD S.
BLOOM, CAP TOYS INC., 26201
RICHMOND ROAD, BEDFORD HTS, OH
44146-1439

Summing Up Trademarkscan Through Compuserve

The eight databases offered by Trademarkscan operate in a similar method and you can easily search for state registrations or international marks. Some helpful tips to remember when using Trademarkscan through Compuserve:

- Prepare your search before connecting. Know your class and description of goods and determine if you want to do broad screen or key word searching. Have your search terms ready.
- Save your work. At the bottom of your screen in terminal emulation you can click on a button which will create a log. Clicking on a different button will create a printout (which prints after disconnecting). This will enable you to review your data off-line.
- When in doubt, type "SOS" and seek the assistance of an online advisor.

b. The Thomas Register—Product Names

The Thomas Register is a database of products and manufacturers. It is commonly used by people looking for the manufacturer of a product (for example, you want to replace a part on your toaster but don't know the company). The Thomas Register does not include service industries and it does not use fuzzy logic (the ability to find sound-alikes), but if you have a product name, it is an inexpensive first step in the trademark

search. For example, if you wanted to find out if anyone was using *Buckeye* as a mark for animal food, you would learn that Proctor & Gamble makes a stock feed using cottonseed oil known as *Buckeye Cowlike*. This would eliminate your need to use more expensive searching techniques such as Trademarkscan. You can access the Thomas Register by typing "iquest" at the GO prompt on CompuServe. Thomas Register is also available on the Internet at http://www.thomasregister.com. You will see the following menu:

1. Companies
2. Business & Industry
3. Markets & Products
4. Intellectual Property
5. Computers & Telecommunications
6. Medicine, Science & Engineering

Select either "Markets & Products" or "Intellectual Property," and then select "Thomas Register." The searching principles are the same as in Trademarkscan. The cost is $1 per search and $7.50 if you locate any matches.

c. The Biz*File—Service Marks and Trade Names

The Biz*File is Dun & Bradstreet's Electronic Business Directory. It is similar to an electronic Yellow Pages and contains more than 10 million U.S. and Canadian business listings. Company names can be searched by type of business, name or geographic location. It is a first step for searching trade names or common law service marks. It does not use fuzzy logic. You access the Biz*File by typing "biz*file" at the GO prompt on CompuServe. The searching principles are the same as in Trademarkscan except you must name the category of the services according to Yellow Page listings. These categories are available online. For example, if you type in music as the category, you will get more than 40 choices such as computer music products, motion picture film music scoring, music boxes, music colleges & music teachers, and music copyists. After you choose a category, you type in the name and search. The cost is $1 per search.

As noted earlier in this chapter, similar information in the form of national business telephone directories is now available on CD-ROMs for a cost of between $40 and $50.

d. Searching News Libraries

Another method of performing a common law search on CompuServe is to find an applicable business or trade magazine and search the contents of that magazine for any references with similar names. For example, if you wanted to name your product Medley, you would learn from the computer magazine database that International makes a printer by that name. This type of search may eliminate the need for more expensive searching. The IQuest Service on CompuServe includes a vast database of publications. At the GO prompt, type **iquest**; you will then see a list of selections as follows:

1. Companies
2. Business & Industry
3. Markets & Products
4. Intellectual Property
5. Computers & Telecommunications
6. U.S. & World News
8. Humanities, Social Sciences & General Reference
9. Consult with an IQuest specialist (SOS)

If one of the specialized categories is sufficient, select that. Otherwise, select (9) and consult with a specialist on the proper business or industry database. Searching principles are provided online and are similar to those in Trademarkscan.

Summing Up CompuServe

Because it is designed for business users, CompuServe is good for trademark screening and searching. It is best to plot out your search before you begin, including a definition of your search

terms and product categories. Some suggested searching methods are listed below. Each methodology begins with the least expensive search.

CompuServe Searching Techniques

Product Name
1. Search Thomas Register for matches.
2. Search IQuest News Libraries for matches.
3. Search Trademarkscan Federal for registered marks.
4. Search Trademarkscan State for registered marks.

Service Mark
1. Search the Biz*File for similar matches (or if you own a CD-ROM drive consider a CD-ROM phone disk).
2. Search IQuest News Libraries for matches.
3. Search Trademarkscan Federal for registered marks.
4. Search Trademarkscan State for registered marks.

Trade Name
1. Search the Biz*File for similar matches (or use phone disk CD-ROM).
2. Search IQuest News Libraries for matches.
3. Search Trademarkscan Federal for registered marks.
4. Search Trademarkscan State for registered marks.

As noted earlier in this chapter, national telephone directories are now available on CD-ROMs for a cost of between $40 and $50.

3. Using DIALOG

Anyone who has a computer and a modem can subscribe to DIALOG. To order an information packet or a starter package, call 800-334-2564, or write DIALOG Information Services, 3460 Hillview Ave., Palo Alto, CA 93404.

DIALOG gives you training materials and a couple of hours of free time online to help you master search techniques. In addition, several times a year DIALOG offers training seminars in most major cities at $140 a session. Taking one will shorten your learning curve and give you greater confidence in your search results.

Once you have subscribed, you log on to the system through one of three electronic networks (your choice) using the instructions and passwords that DIALOG provides. DIALOG explains all this clearly, and we won't repeat it here.

Once you are online (that is, connected to DIALOG), you choose which database to use. Each of the several databases that are useful in trademark searches has a number assigned to it, and each offers different sorts of information. You will notice that Trademarkscan is also available with DIALOG as well as with CompuServe. The most useful databases are:

- Federal Trademarkscan (226)—lists all federally registered trademarks, including each mark owner, its class, a description of the goods and services, the date of registration (or application, if it is pending).
- State Trademarkscan (246)—provides state trademark lists for all 50 states.
- Brands and Their Companies (116)—a comprehensive list of trade and brand names used throughout the world.
- Dun & Bradstreet's Electronic Business Directory (515)—a type of electronic business Yellow Pages put together by Dun & Bradstreet.
- Thomas Register Online (535)—a directory of product and business names, including a company name, address, phone and officers, along with descriptions of its products/services and the main trade names for each.
- DIALOG Product Name Finder (413)—locates product names and other information in all DIALOG databases.
- DIALOG Company Name Finder (416)—locates company names in DIALOG databases.

DIALOG provides details about its databases in separate "Blue Sheets" for each database. When you sign up, make sure you order the ones specific to each database that you will be using. Or if you plan to use DIALOG for additional purposes, consider buying a complete set.

The Blue Sheets describe the information in each database and explain the formats of each. They also explain how you can ask for specific segments of the record, as well as providing general database details, such as access codes and abbreviations. The Blue Sheets are updated monthly in a magazine for subscribers called Chronolog.

We'll show you how DIALOG works by starting with the federal database Trademarkscan.

You begin, logically enough, by typing **begin** (or **B**) and the number of the database (for example, **begin 226** for Trademarkscan—Federal).

 DIALOG doesn't care whether you use upper case or lowercase.

DIALOG responds with a "**?**", which invites you to tell the database what you want.

In response you type **select** (or **S**) and whatever name or names you want the database to retrieve for you. Let's say you want to do a direct hit search for the name *Zaruma* without regard to any specific trademark class. (Unless you specify the class to search, DIALOG automatically searches in all classes.) You would type **Select zaruma**. The screen would respond:

s1 0 ZARUMA

This tells you that DIALOG searched for the mark Zaruma, and it put the answers into set 1 (s1). But since set 1 has 0 entries, you quickly learn that DIALOG could find no federally registered trademarks or pending applications containing the word Zaruma. Since Zaruma is a pretty unique word, and that's all you wanted to know, you have completed your direct hit search and can leave DIALOG by typing **logoff** or go on to do an analytical search for *Zaruma*.

THE IMPORTANCE OF DOING AN ANALYTICAL SEARCH FOR ZARUMA

As a general rule, the more unique the word you are searching, the more important it is to also search for existing marks with words that have elements in common with the word being searched. (We discuss this concept in more detail in Chapter 5.) This is because the unique word would tend to evoke other words with common elements. For example, the word *Zaruma* is evocative of such words as *ZarZuma*, *Umazar* and *Rumazar*, and would most likely be considered confusingly similar to those words, if used in a similar context. Thus, an analytical search for *Zaruma* might include a search in the same class for all marks containing *uma*, *Zar* and *ruma*, as well as the many possible phonetic equivalents to the word *Zaruma*.

Let's try another example, *Armchair Theater*, as a trademark for a video rental service.

s (for select) **armchair(w)theater**

Here you have typed a (w) without spaces between Armchair and Theater to ask the database to link the two words in that order.

DIALOG responds,

23 ARMCHAIR

130 THEATER

S1   1 ARMCHAIR(W)THEATER

Here S1 means that you have a set, numbered "one," which contains all registered trademarks that contain both Armchair and Theater. "Set" in this context is just a term for the group of marks that meet the descriptive criteria you asked the computer to search for.

Now we know that there are 23 marks with Armchair and 130 with Theater, but only one with both Armchair and Theater in that order. The "1" next to "ARMCHAIR(W)THEATER" tells us how many matches the computer found. Now let's look at what that mark is. The way you do this is to enter:

TYPE (or T) s1/tx/1

You have asked the computer to list for you information from set 1 (s1). Specifically, you want to see a list of the trademarks only (tx), for the first (and only) item in set 1 (1). (Don't worry about these codes—the Trademarkscan Blue Sheets explain what the codes mean.)

DIALOG responds:

1/tx/1

ARMCHAIR THEATRE.

Bad news. Now we know that an identical trademark is already registered, but we don't know how the mark is used, on what products or services. So next we'll ask for a full format report on Armchair Theatre by typing:

t 1/5/1

t = type; 1 = set 1; 5 = full format, meaning the whole record on that trademark; and 1 = the number within set 1 for the particular trademark we want to see. (Again we got the format code from the Blue Sheets.) Now DIALOG prints for us:

03438352

ARMCHAIR THEATRE

US CLASS: 107 (Education and Entertainment)

INTL CLASS: 41 (Education and Entertainment)

STATUS: Registered REG. NO. : 1293392

REG. DATE: September 04, 1984

PUBLISHED: June 12, 1984

GOODS/SERVICES: RENTAL OF VIDEO SYSTEMS AND VIDEO TAPES SERIES CODE: 73 SERIAL NO.: 438352

FILED: August 08, 1983

DATE OF FIRST USE: June 07, 1983

ORIGINAL OWNER: TRIPLE T VIDEO, INC., WINTER HAVEN, FLA

DIALOG
Information Services, Inc.

This information tells us to forget the use of Armchair Theater as a video rental trademark—it's already been registered for exactly that use.

You may have noticed that this trademark is spelled differently from our descriptive parameter "theater," and yet DIALOG delivered it anyway. That's because DIALOG picks up phonetic equivalents, or words that sound the same even if they are spelled differently.

But some words won't get picked up automatically. For example, a very unusual spelling of a word (like psyleaux for silo) may not have been entered into the database as a phonetic equivalent. Fortunately, DIALOG makes it easy to account for many variations in spelling. You can use a wild card character (?) to include all possible letter combinations, by typing theater as **theat?**, or silo as **s?l?**. By doing this we ask DIALOG for all marks with "theat" plus any ending, or "S" plus any letters followed by "L" plus any ending.

We can see another example of why using wild card characters is a good way to find unexpected trademark permutations. Searching for a trademark that includes the word "pictures," you could type **s pictures** and get 129 possibilities. Or you could use **s pictur?** and get 433 choices. The more you get the better, because then you have a better chance of uncovering conflicts.

Now let's say we are looking for *Popcorn Pictures* as another trademark for a video rental service. We start with **pictur?**. And we might as well use **popcorn** because that's the distinctive feature of the phrase. But out of 433 possibilities that DIALOG finds for **pictur?** (s2) and 183 for **popcorn** (s3), we get no direct hits, or hits for combinations of the two. Does that take care of our search? No, because we also need to check for synonyms for pictures.

THE WORD "TYPE" IS EXPENSIVE

Beware—until now you have only been charged for connect time on the database at a basic charge of $2.00 a minute or $120 per hour. As soon as you enter the magic word "type," you will be charged per trademark at varying rates from the minimum of $.20 per name in the trademark only format (tx), to $1.20 per name reported in the full list format (which we just saw). If we had requested a report of all the items in a larger set, say the Armchair set with 23 marks in it, it would be expensive ($1.00 times 23 adds up fast). So stick with the tx format until you find a name you need to know more about. Then ask for a fuller report.

How to Check for Synonyms

Whether your mark is *Popcorn Video* or *Popcorn Pictures* does not make much difference to the owner of Popcorn Movies—either would probably infringe on his mark. So to check for synonyms we type: **s pictur? or movie? or video**. By using "or," we've asked for any marks with either picture, pictures, movie, movies or video in it. Now our universe of choices is much bigger: DIALOG responds,

s4 2584 PICTURE? OR MOVIE? OR VIDEO

S4 is the name of our new set. S3, remember, was the set for popcorn.

Using "or" in this way illustrates one approach to combining searches. Doing so asks for any mark that uses any of the words listed in the entry. You can also use "and" to ask for all marks that have both your first and second (or third or fourth, as many as you wish) words in them. We already did this with **Popcorn** and **Pictur?**. In addition, the word "not" can be used to ask for a subset of marks within a larger one. For example, if you are searching for Homespun and you want to see all marks with home+ but you want to omit marks with homes as a single word, you would ask for **home? not homes**.

How to Combine Search Terms With Sets

You can also use "and," "or" and "not" with sets. For example, we can combine popcorn (set 3) and our larger set 4 using "and" in this way:

> s s3 and s4

DIALOG responds, giving the answer a new set number,

> S5 7 S3 and S4

Success! DIALOG has found seven hits that combine popcorn and either pictures, movies or video. To see what they are, we type:

> t s5/tx/all

Again, s5 is the new set number; tx asks for the simplest listing format (names only); and "all" requests all items in the set. DIALOG responds:

> 7/tx/1
>
> MOVIE POPCORN
>
> 7/tx/2
>
> MOVIE QUIK POPCORN
>
> 7/tx/3
>
> POPCORN VIDEO
>
> etc.

Bingo. In our list of all seven items in set 5, one proves to be very close: Popcorn Video. So we ask for a full printout by typing: t s5/5/3. (Remember, t = type; s5 = set 5; 5 asks for a full report on the mark; and 3 indicates Popcorn Video, because it is the 3rd item of set 5.)

When we get the full report, we discover that it is owned by a California company renting video hardware and tapes. This would also not be a good mark to use on a video rental service, since the name's been federally registered. We'll have to pick another mark.

Summing Up DIALOG

Now you know the basics of direct hit searching for federal trademarks on DIALOG. When you are ready to use the other DIALOG databases, you can apply these same principles—they have very similar commands. Again, the main variations are detailed in the Blue Sheet lists of information specific to each database.

When using an interactive database such as DIALOG that charges by the minute, it is very important to plan your search—on paper—ahead of time. Nothing wastes your money as fast as thinking about what terms you want to search for while the meter is ticking at $2.00 a minute. DIALOG does provide a way for you to temporarily disconnect from the expensive Trademarkscan database if you need to reformulate your search on the basis of the results your first attempt produces. But even then, you will be paying some charges while you think.

DESIGN SEARCHING BY COMPUTER

All the trademark databases, save the CASSIS CD-ROM (see Chapter 5), offer the capability of searching for marks with logos or designs online. DIALOG requires special software at $99. In addition you will need to obtain a separate directory listing the codes that computer databases use to categorize design trademarks. Consult DIALOG's customer service department for exactly what you need. Be aware that it is expensive ($2.00 per visual trademark image and $1.00 per written description or code listing of the design trademark) to display the results of your search, so use their training and manuals to narrow your search results as much as possible to minimize the need to display expensive records. (See the description of how to use DIALOG in Section C3, above.)

---

4. Using a Patent and Trademark Depository Library to Do a Trademark Search

There are approximately 80 specialized libraries known as Patent and Trademark Depository Libraries (PDTLs). A list of these libraries is set out in the Appendix. Each of these libraries offers hardcopy materials and a CD-ROM database known as CASSIS to help you do a search of registered trademarks. Also, the PTDLs in Sunnyvale California (Sc[i]3) and Detroit offer direct access to the PTO database (X-Search) for a fee.

Using a PTDL may not be as convenient as using your home computer to carry out your trademark search, but it may end up being a lot cheaper. And, for people who don't want to use a subscription service, the PTDL offers both hard copy resources and a CD-ROM database to carry out a direct hit trademark search that is reasonably up to date (see also Section C1 above for a discussion of using Micropatent to do a direct hit search from your home computer). If, on the other hand, you want to make a thorough analytical trademark search, you will be better off with the Trademarkscan database available through CompuServe or DIALOG, or ordering an analytical trademark search from Sc[i]3 or another trademark search service.

a. Starting With Non-Computer Sources

It may be tempting to start your trademark search with CASSIS, the free CD-ROM database that allows you to perform a computerized search of the federally registered trademark database. However, you may find that a lot of people have already signed up ahead of you and that you will have to wait. If so, consider getting on the waiting list and then starting your search by using the hardcopy resources available in most PTDLs. Later, if you wish, you may use CASSIS to obtain descriptions of marks you find listed in the hardcopy resources. Of course, if you can get on CASSIS without much waiting and aren't computer phobic, start there. (See Section b below.)

Assuming that you want to start with the hardcopy resources, the first step is to use the Acceptable Identification of Goods and Services Manual. That resource helps you assign an international class number to your product or service. You should search this material alphabetically under the kind of product or service that the mark is or will be attached to. Your mark may fit in more than one class. As an alternative to using the *Acceptable Identification of Goods and Services Manual*, the materials in the Appendix to this book may be all that are necessary for you to confidently classify your mark. (See Appendix, International Schedule of Classes of Goods and Services and Descriptions of Goods and Services (From USTA—International Classes).)

Once you have properly classified the mark, the next step is to search alphabetically for the proposed mark in the *Directory of U.S. Trademarks—All Classes*. If you find a mark that is the same or similar to yours, look for that same mark in the *Directory of U.S. Trademarks—All Classes* under its appropriate classification. This will provide the date the mark was published by the U.S. Patent and Trademark Office in the *Official Gazette*. You will then want to search the *Official Gazette* for that date to find out more about the mark you have found—such as who owns it and when it was first used.

If you do not find your proposed mark in the *Directory of U.S. Trademarks—All Classes*, look for it in the *Updates to the Directory of U.S. Trademarks—All Classes*. If you find the mark in that resource, note the date that accompanies it and search the *Official Gazette* for that date to find out more about the mark—such as who owns it and when it was first used.

If you do not find the mark in either the *Directory of U.S. Trademarks—All Classes* or the *Updates to the Directory of U.S. Trademarks—Classes*, your next step is to search all Official Gazettes that have been published since the date of publication for the Updates to the Directory of U.S. Trademarks—All Classes. (See sidebar, Searching the Official Gazette.)

SEARCHING THE OFFICIAL GAZETTE (OG)

If your search in the hardcopy resources fails to turn up a relevant mark, or you have completed your work on CASSIS, you must now search each individual OG dated after the publication date of the hardcopy resource or CASSIS CD-ROM. To search an individual OG, look first in Section 2 (edged in red) under the class number for your mark. The marks in the OG are not in alphabetical order, so you will have to search all marks coming under the relevant class. In addition to carefully searching Section 2, you also should scan for your mark on all other pages before and after Section 2.

b. CASSIS

CASSIS at a PTDL is not a database linked to an information source by telephone, but rather a CD-ROM (compact disk—read-only medium) source of information. Because the computer is scanning a compact disk when it performs its searches, the information is dated to some degree. The PTO issues updates for CASSIS every two months. You can tell when the CD was issued by ejecting it from the drive (the machine that plays the CD) and reading the date printed on it. Your search will therefore not be accurate for any marks registered or applied for after that date. You will need to use the *Official Gazette* (see the sidebar, Searching the *Official Gazette*) to check for conflicting marks more recent than the date of the CD.

The librarian will most likely be happy to connect you to the CD-ROM and show you a little about how to get around. But in case he or she doesn't, here's what to do.

You will be asked to type in your mark. If you type in one that is not in the database (*Zaruma*, for instance), it tells you so and asks if you want to proceed or cancel.

If you search for a more common mark, like *Cherokee*, CASSIS tells you there are 44 entries. You then follow the instructions on the screen to get a basic display of these 44 entries complete with registration/application dates. You also can get a full format report, including owner, date of registration or application, serial number or registration number, goods and services, date of first use, whether it's on the Principal Register or Supplemental Register, the status of the registration, the type of mark, and the mark drawing code.

CASSIS does not make it easy for you to narrow a field when you get many responses (for example, sorting by class). You just have to go through the list, entry by entry, to see how the marks are used.

CASSIS does let you use wild card terms to draw in more possible conflicts. So if you type *olar, you would get all words ending in "olar," like Solar, Molar, Scholar, and Antiolar. Likewise, B?ll retrieves Bell, Ball, Bull, Bill, Boll, etc. The difficulty, again, lies in narrowing down a field if you get too many responses.

There should be a printer attached allowing you to get a hard copy of your results, either for free or for around ten cents per sheet.

To get a better handle on what a CASSIS search produces, see the Sc[i]3 search report in Section B above.

c. Searching for Design Marks

You will find a workable system for searching for designs at Patent and Trademark Depository Libraries. If one is not available to you (consult Appendix for their locations), do not consider this option.

CASSIS does describe registered design marks in words and by logo category, but does not show you a picture of them. However, you can take the reference number from CASSIS (or any other system that gives you a description of a design mark) and look up that mark in the *Official Gazette*. The *Official Gazette* lists design marks as well as word marks, and shows you the exact design that is being registered. The main drawback of this method is that CASSIS may be a few months out-of-date, which means you may need to manually check *Official Gazettes* for each week after the publication date of the CASSIS CD.

Many Patent and Trademark Depository Libraries will have a PTO manual categorizing all designs into specific codes, which you will need to do computer searches for design conflicts. Elicit the help of the librarian in finding the manual and in using it.

5. Searching State Registered Trademarks in Non-Computer Sources

To search for trademarks on state trademark registers, you must check the registers for each state. How many state registers you will sensibly decide to search depends on the goals you set out in Chapter 5, Preparing for a Trademark Search. Usually you will only search in your own state. But if you plan to operate in several states, you would want to check each. If you decide to search in more than a few states, you would be smarter to have your trademark search done by a professional, or to search state trademark databases by computer.

The method for doing a search for state registered trademarks varies from state to state. Many states will do a pre-application search for you by phone, either for free or for a small charge. In other states, request a search by mail. In still others, the trademark office will not search for you but will let you peruse the microfiche or looseleaf lists of registered trademarks in person. The state agency in charge of trademarks is generally within the department of state, the department of corporations or the department of revenue. (See the Appendix for the phone and address of a pertinent agency in each state, and Chapter 7 for trademark laws in different states.)

Regardless of who does it or how the search is performed, state trademark agencies provide limited types of search services—most commonly marks can only be searched in alphabetical order. Sometimes they are broken down by class of goods or services. (Remember from Chapter 4, How to Tell If Two Marks Are Confusingly Similar, that all trademarks are assigned a class when registered.) If so, you will need to specify which class to search.

The main drawback to state searches is that state laws vary somewhat about what constitutes a conflict with a registered trademark. This means the criteria the state uses to conduct its search may not be the same as federal or common law criteria. As a result, while attaining a state clearance probably means there are no directly identical marks in your class, it may not give you any assurance that your trademark does not legally conflict with other marks in that state.

If you will be personally searching state trademarks, apply the principles we discussed in searching for federal trademarks in Section C2 of this chapter—look for synonyms, homonyms, phonetic equivalents, etc., both in your class and in as many other classes as might be relevant. Unfortunately a phone or written request only permits checking a few permutations, so you will have to pick first the ones most likely to cover the largest sample of marks.

Paying a search firm to do this or doing it yourself through DIALOG will produce better results because all state trademarks are on the Trademarkscan state computer database, and you or the search firm can do either a direct hit or analytical search tailored to your own specifications.

6. Searching Non-Computer Sources for Trade Names

The goal here is to make sure your mark won't conflict with a trade name or corporate name in use in your state. While trade names, used solely to identify businesses, do not have all the same kinds of rights attached to trademarks (for instance, unlike trademarks, they cannot be registered), they can be protected by unfair competition law. For example, someone can sue you if you use their trade name as a mark in a way that causes the public (or suppliers) to confuse you with them. Also, if the trade name is being used as a mark but is not registered as such, a search of one of the trade name indexes we describe below may result in discovering a mark that no other search method would have brought to your attention. In short, you will need to make sure your mark is not going to conflict with a registered corporate name or unregistered trade name by searching all sources of trade names that you can reasonably find.

One good way to search for a trade name conflict is to make sure no corporation registered in your state already uses the name. You can do this via a phone call or letter to the agency in charge of corporations, usually the department of corporations or the secretary of state. See Chapter 3 for more about different state laws regarding corporate names.

 Registering a Corporate Name Does Not Give You Trademark Protection

The fact that you have already incorporated and wish to use your corporate name as your mark does not mean you should skip a trade name search. When you incorporated, your proposed corporate name was checked against other corporate names, not against trademarks or any other trade names. So you still need to check how it compares to marks, other trade names and perhaps even corporate names in other states if your mark will have a presence in those states.

If you need to search for corporate names in more than one state, it is much easier to pay someone or to use Dun & Bradstreet's Electronic Business Directory, which is not a state-by-state corporate register, but is extremely thorough and includes noncorporate business names as well.

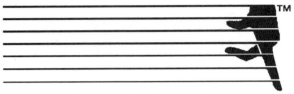

Let your fingers do the walking

a. Searching Telephone Directories

The purpose of this search is to find unregistered service marks and trade names acting as service marks that are currently in use. Telephone directories are excellent sources for these. Most of the major Internet search engines provide access to a database known as the national Yellow Pages (for instance, Excite! at http://www.excite.com). Most large city public libraries also have a complete selection of white and Yellow Pages for all the major cities in the country and for all the areas in your state. If yours doesn't, enlist the aid of the librarian in finding a library that does. (In that case, you will also need his or her help in locating the other books you'll need for a trademark search.)

At a minimum, you should consult all the phone books for your marketing area. You may also want to do the directories for each major city in your state. If you live in a populous state, you may end up perusing a lot of directories. In addition, many search services also check the phone books for the 30 largest cities in the country, especially when they are dealing with a product or service that will be marketed nationally. This is a big task, recommended mostly for those who want the greatest degree of certainty possible that no conflicts exist, so decide if you really need to do it before starting, or hire a helper.

When searching telephone directories, you are looking by subject in the Yellow Pages and by name in the white pages. To do this efficiently, it's helpful to make a list of each name permutation you want to check (white pages), and each heading (Yellow Pages) and check them off as you go, using a different column for each set of phone books. Depending on how many permutations you are looking for, it could take 15–30 minutes per directory.

GET HELP SEARCHING TRADE DIRECTORIES AND PHONE BOOKS

This sort of searching is time-consuming and tedious. It can take several hours just to do a minimal search. It's a perfect job for a reliable paralegal, secretary, clerk, summer intern, college student or even high school student, as long as the person is thorough and conscientious. Choosing the right person and providing good instructions will help you get more reliable results.

---

b. Trade Associations/Directories

Trade associations are usually limited to a particular field. Find the association for the field you plan to use your mark in (your library's reference section will have a guide to associations), and examine its directory. This should provide you with a pretty good idea of whether the mark is already in use. You may already be familiar with relevant trade associations or directories in your fields, or you may have to go to the library card catalog or

computer index and look under several relevant subject headings to find them. Most types of businesses, from anchovy fishermen to zoo suppliers, will have them, but a few small or new endeavors won't. Contact the Chamber of Commerce or your librarian for further help in tracking them down. For example, the trade journals Candy Industry or Candy Marketer would help you find trademarks and names in use among candy manufacturers.

c. Business Directories

Several publishers compile business directories that cover all businesses. They contain lists of as many business names and marks as the authors can find. One example is *Brands and Their Companies* (formerly the *Trade Name Dictionary*), published by Gale Research Co., a guide to over 220,000 consumer-oriented trade names, brands, and marks with the names and addresses of the companies to which they belong, compiled from trade journals and direct contact research. Another is the *Trade Name Index—Standard Directory of Advertisers*, published by the National Register Publishing Company, which contains over 62,000 of the better known trade names and trademarks currently in use by national advertisers. A third is *Thomas Register of American Manufacturers*, which has names and brands listed by business category, also available online via DIALOG.

You will want to examine these in your class or field, for direct conflicts as well as similar sounding or looking names, applying the same criteria we discussed for online federal trademark searching. Since here you are working in alphabetical order, you will have to remember to make separate checks on synonyms, variations in spelling and punctuation, and other differences. (See Chapter 15, Help Beyond the Book, for other resources.) ■

State Trademark Registration

S tate trademark registration normally provides only one significant benefit: it places your mark on your state's list of registered marks and thereby lets the world know that you claim ownership to the mark. Since federal registration offers this same benefit, state registration usually only makes sense for marks that don't qualify for federal registration. (See sidebar.)

In a few states, state registration also provides several rights and remedies that are helpful in lawsuits over the right to use a trademark. But again, this usually only benefits those who don't qualify for federal registration.

DOES YOUR MARK QUALIFY FOR FEDERAL REGISTRATION?

There are two main qualifications for placement of a mark on the federal trademark register:

1. It must be distinctive enough to really operate as a trademark or service mark.
2. It must be in use in commerce across state, territorial or international lines.

As a general rule, using your mark in this type of commerce means that your mark must:

- accompany a product
- be used to market services, or
- be used in a way that affects the commerce (as most hotels or restaurants that serve travelers from other states do).

By contrast, if your mark is used solely on a local service business—for instance, retail, food, manufacturing, crafts, professional, automotive—it probably doesn't qualify for federal registration, unless you cater to a significant number of interstate or international travellers.

⚠ If it appears after reading the sidebar that your mark qualifies for federal registration, skip ahead to Chapter 8. But if you anticipate a period of time in which your mark will be used solely within a state, continue reading.

A. What State Registration Accomplishes

Begin by understanding that state registration of a trademark in no way diminishes any existing trademark ownership rights others have acquired through using their mark (common law rights). If no new rights are created by registering a trademark with the state, then what is the point?

1. In every state, registration puts others on notice that you claim ownership of your mark. In a few states, registration may also be strong evidence in a court of law that you own and are entitled to exclusive use of the mark. Although these "benefits" may sound similar, there are practical differences between the two, which we explain below.

2. In addition, each state issues a certificate of trademark registration which serves as competent proof in any court of law that the mark was registered on a certain date. If you later end up in a lawsuit over infringement of the mark, this can help establish your date of first use, which may well determine whether you win or lose. (See sidebar below.) But whether the certificate can help prove the truth of the facts in the registration application depends on the law of each state.

3. You will be entitled to any remedies that the state trademark law provides by virtue of that registration, unless the validity of the registration is in dispute. Such remedies include injunctive relief and profits or damages, and occasionally attorneys' fees or penalties for fraud or willful use of a conflicting mark. (For more on remedies, see Section B9 at the end of this chapter.)

HOW STATE REGISTRATION HELPS PROVE FIRST USE

Even if your certificate shows that you have registered your mark, your opponent in court may still prove that the facts you asserted in that registration (date of first use, or your ownership of the mark, for example) are not true. However, if you are challenged several years later, the fact of your registration helps demonstrate that you were probably using the mark as of the registration date, assuming you have no other, stronger evidence of earlier use. If the other user claims a later date of first use, this may help prove you used the mark earlier.

The following chart divides the states into two categories:

- states in which registration provides no important benefits other than notice to would-be copiers
- states in which registration does provide some important benefits in addition to notice.

Look up your state and then read the explanation of that category set out below. Armed with this information, you should have a pretty good idea of what registering your mark will accomplish. But as we stated, just the fact that registration notifies the world that your trademark is in use justifies state registration, whether or not other benefits are obtained.

BENEFIT OF STATE TRADEMARK REGISTRATION

Weak Benefits	Strong Benefits
Alabama	California
Alaska	Connecticut
Arizona	Florida
Arkansas	Illinois
Colorado	Iowa
Delaware	Massachusetts
Georgia	Michigan
Hawaii	Minnesota
Idaho	Nevada
Indiana	Oregon
Kansas	Puerto Rico
Kentucky	Rhode Island
Louisiana	South Dakota
Maine	Texas
Maryland	Utah
Mississippi	Washington
Missouri	West Virginia
Montana	Wisconsin
Nebraska	
New Hampshire	
New Jersey	
New Mexico	
New York	
North Carolina	
North Dakota	
Ohio	
Oklahoma	
Pennsylvania	
South Carolina	
Tennessee	
Vermont	
Virginia	
Wyoming	

Category 1: States with weak trademark registration benefits.

In these states, the main benefit of registration is that your mark appears on the list of state registered trademarks. Being on the list essentially makes it easier for anyone who is thinking of adopting a similar mark to find out that you are already using it. Not only is this a significant practical advantage, it also signals to others that you intend to protect your trademark.

Once again, giving others notice that you claim a mark by registering it is of great practical importance, but it does not change your legal rights or the rights of anyone who used that mark before you.

Category 2: States where registration offers strong trademark benefits.

These states grant significant additional rights that make it even more worth your while to register. Basically the registration eliminates or lessens the need for the registrant to prove a number of facts in court in case of a lawsuit. That is, some or all of the information in the registration application is presumed by the court to be true unless disproven by the other user. States in this category can be further divided into two groups. The first group, Connecticut, Florida, Massachusetts, Oregon, Rhode Island, South Dakota, Texas and Washington, provides the most protection through registration. By contrast, registration in California, Iowa, Illinois, Michigan, Puerto Rico, Utah, Wisconsin and West Virginia provides somewhat fewer benefits. For a quick overview of what these presumptions mean, see the sidebar.

B. How to Register Your State Trademark

In most states, registering a trademark is easy. Compared to federal trademark examiners, state

HOW PRESUMPTIONS WORK IN TRADEMARK LITIGATION

When a fact is presumed to be true it means that the judge will consider it true unless and until evidence is introduced to refute it. In the states with stronger benefits from registration, the presumption must be actively overcome with strong evidence. In the states with weaker benefits, the presumption that the facts in the application are true will cease to exist if *any* evidence to disprove it is introduced. But whether the presumption is of the strong or weak variety, it still provides an advantage in litigation, since overcoming it is a bit like starting a battle by having to charge uphill.

EXAMPLE: Assume a San Angelo, Texas, ranch harvests and sells mesquite wood for barbecues under the state-registered mark *Mess o' Mesquite*. If the rancher goes into court against an identical or confusingly similar mark, the judge will view the fact that the mark was registered in Texas as strong evidence that the ranch owner owns and has the exclusive right to use the mark, and that the registration is valid. The alleged infringer can try to show that in fact he used the mark first, but he will need strong evidence to rebut the facts regarding first use set out in the registration application. If the same case arose in one of the weaker presumption states, the amount and type of evidence the alleged infringer would have to introduce to overcome (rebut) the presumption would be much less.

trademark officials tend to be much more lenient in accepting borderline trademarks.

1. The Basic Process

In a nutshell, you just file a trademark application with the relevant state agency. The agency then conducts a search to compare your mark with those of other existing state-registered trademarks, and, in some states, with registered corporate names, trade names and assumed names. If your mark meets the agency's statutory criteria for registration, it is registered. That's it.

2. The Basic Trademark Law in Most States—Registrability

Almost all states base their trademark statutes on a model statute prepared by experts in the field (known as the Model State Trademark Bill). Hawaii, New Mexico, West Virginia and Wisconsin are exceptions. We will go through the Model Bill briefly, noting where individual states differ from it. If your state is not mentioned, you can assume it follows the Model Bill in most respects.

In New Hampshire and Georgia, even five years' continuous use will not automatically make a descriptive mark distinctive enough to register, although both states register somewhat descriptive marks.

3. Prohibitions on Registration

Most states forbid the registration of certain types of trademarks. For the most part these are the same types that can't be federally registered. (For further explanation of what these terms mean, see Chapter 8, Section A2.) Trademarks that usually can't be placed on a state register are those that:

- are so similar to another mark registered in this state or a mark or trade name previously used in the state (and not aban-

TRADEMARK DEFINED

For purposes of state registration, the term "trademark" generally means trademarks and service marks. But some states will not register service marks, including Alaska, North Dakota, Vermont, West Virginia. Others will do so only on a special form. These are: Arizona, Kentucky, Massachusetts, New York, Puerto Rico. These states will register trade names: Alabama, Hawaii, Louisiana, New Mexico, Wyoming. Some states will also register collective marks or certification marks: Colorado, Connecticut, Florida, Georgia, Iowa, Illinois, Maine, Minnesota, Mississippi, North Carolina, New Hampshire, South Carolina, Wisconsin, Wyoming. A trademark may be registered with the state if it is:

1. in use (see subsection e, below, on the use requirement), and
2. distinctive.

Trademarks which are specifically not distinctive fall into these categories (discussed in more detail in Chapter 10, Evaluating Trademark Strength):

- merely descriptive (or falsely descriptive in a deceptive way) of the goods or services of the applicant
- primarily geographically descriptive (or falsely descriptive in a deceptive way) of the goods or services of the applicant
- primarily a surname.

Even if a trademark falls into one of these categories, in most states it can still be registered if it has become distinctive through long and continuous use for (usually) five years or more. (This is the state equivalent of the secondary meaning rule, discussed in Chapter 1B3.) Also, many state trademark offices do not rigorously enforce these "exclusions," which means you may want to try to register your trademark anyway and see what happens.

doned) that it is likely to confuse, mislead or deceive customers when applied to the goods or services of the applicant (see Chapter 4 on the "likely to confuse" standard, and subsection 4f, below, on what kinds of searches different states perform to determine whether a mark meets this criterion)

- consist of immoral, deceptive or scandalous matter
- may disparage or bring into contempt or disrepute, or falsely suggest a connection with persons living or dead, institutions, beliefs or national symbols (persons includes corporations, associations and other organizations)
- consist of or comprise the flag or insignia of the United States or any state, city or foreign nation, or an imitation of such flag or insignia, or
- consist of the name, signature or portrait of any living individual without written consent.

Some states have not adopted all these provisions, and others have added their own. Check the laws of your state before proceeding if your mark falls into one of these categories.

⚠ Georgia, Kansas and Ohio add a requirement that they will not register marks that are similar or identical to marks that are already federally registered.

4. Application Procedure

All states have a trademark registration form. In a few, it's not mandatory (they will accept a letter), but it's always better to use the form they are used to. To obtain the necessary form, call or write your state trademark agency listed in the Appendix. (Some states have different forms for trademarks and service marks.)

CODY·S BOOKS

a. State Pre-Application Trademark Search

Many states will perform a pre-application search to help you discover if others within the state are using a similar mark before you begin using yours and before you even apply to register it. Some state agencies view the pre-application search as an informal courtesy provided upon request. In those states, even a search that doesn't turn up any conflicts is no assurance of your mark's availability at the time you move to register it. Other states take the pre-application search more seriously, and view it as a reliable indicator of registrability, although not a guarantee.

Call your state trademark office for information on how to initiate this search.

b. The Trademark Registration Form

Here is a brief overview of what most state trademark registration forms cover:

- name and address of the person applying for the registration, and if a corporation, the state of incorporation
- the goods or services on which the mark is used
- the manner in which the mark is used on those goods or services

- the class in which such goods or services fall (see Chapter 4, How to Tell If Two Marks Are Confusingly Similar, to remind you about "classes"; the U.S. and international classification systems are included in the Appendix)
- the date the mark was first used anywhere and the date when it was first used in the state by the applicant or his predecessor in business
- a statement that the applicant is the owner of the mark and that no other person has the right to use such mark in that state.

STATE CLASSIFICATION SYSTEMS

The majority of states use the U.S. scheme of trademark classification (see Appendix). There are many exceptions, however:

- Hawaii and Nevada have no classification system.
- Kansas, Indiana, Oklahoma, Wisconsin and Puerto Rico have their own systems.
- Alabama, California, Delaware, Florida, Louisiana, Maine, Massachusetts, Minnesota, Ohio, Oregon, Pennsylvania, Rhode Island, Texas and Washington use the international classification system (set out in the Appendix).

---

c. Signing the Form

The application must be signed and verified by the applicant or by a lawyer representing the business. If it's a sole proprietorship, the signer is the owner; if it's a partnership, the signer is one of the partners; if it's a corporation, it must be signed by an officer of the corporation; if it's an association, then one of the directors or chief office holders must sign it.

d. Number of Copies, Specimens and Fees

Each state's rules differ on the number and type of specimens required, the number of copies and the fees for filing your application. For example, some require three copies of an example of the mark as used or photocopies of it. But some insist on original examples of the mark or a photograph of it, and will refuse photocopies. To find out the rules in your state, we suggest you call the agency to verify the requirements before filing the application.

e. Use Requirement

Almost all states require that a mark be in actual use at the time of application for registration. (In 1989 Congress adopted a provision allowing federal registration of marks not yet in use, but most state trademark laws have not yet made a similar change.)

A few states do allow the reservation of a trademark before use, provided that use of the mark begins shortly, usually within six months. Florida permits a 120-day reservation; Louisiana and West Virginia will give you 60 days with possible 30-day extensions. In Vermont you can reserve a trademark for ten days only, and in Wisconsin the term of reservation is unclear.

f. Search at Time of Registration

Most state trademark agencies conduct searches of existing trademarks at the time of application, even if they have earlier conducted a pre-application search upon the request of the applicant. The registration search is generally done as part of the registration process and requires no separate fee or request.

One state, Wisconsin, does not search for conflicts, and apparently will register almost any trademark.

As outlined in the pre-application search discussion in the section just above, the sort of search each state conducts varies in scope. Because these searches are often done by computer, the results are sometimes arbitrary. In addition, most state searches for conflicting marks are not as thorough as the federal search, which includes phonetic equivalents and ignores punctuation differences. As a result, people attempting to register marks have reported success in resubmitting a mark that was initially rejected, with a minor change, sometimes even as small a one as a comma or a minor spelling change.

⚠ Don't Choose a Too-Similar Name

Should your choice of a mark be rejected, you may be tempted to change a letter or two or punctuate it differently. This is usually a lousy idea. Even if the slightly amended name is accepted for registration, you will still have the real-world problem of distinguishing your mark from the other one. It is far better to select a new mark—one that is different from all existing marks—so you can use it without fear of a trademark infringement dispute.

5. Renewal

State registration generally lasts for ten years, after which all states permit renewal for a similar term. The procedure for renewal is generally the same as for registration, although the fee may be less and the number of specimens may differ. (Call the agency to be sure.) Generally renewal must occur within the last six months of the registration term. Some states will notify you within six months of the end of the term that you need to renew your trademark registration. That practice may change, however, so don't rely on it as the sole means of remembering to renew.

In most states, a statement that the mark has been in continuous use since the original registration is required for renewal.

6. Assignment

A mark owner can assign a mark to a new owner, along with the goodwill of the business with which it is used. This transfers all trademark rights owned by the previous owner to the new owner. The assignment must be in writing (no special form is required in most states) and recorded with the secretary of state (or the equivalent). That agency then issues a new certificate of registration for the remaining term of the registration.

This assignment of trademark should be a separate form from the purchase agreement, even if that agreement contains a statement that one of the assets purchased is the trademark and trade name. It should state that the previous owner has assigned to the new owner a particular trademark and/or service mark, along with the goodwill of the business, and that the state registration shall be maintained in the name of the new owner, reciting the registration number. The assignment should also state that consideration (money) was paid for the assignment, although it need not reveal how much.

The assignment of registration is not valid notice of the change in ownership unless it is promptly recorded with the secretary of state (generally within three months). That means someone who later buys the trademark in good faith without knowing about the previous assignment would legally own the mark unless the assignment had been recorded first.

7. Cancellation

The state trademark agency can cancel a trademark that has not been renewed as required by law or upon the voluntary request of the registrant. In addition, any person who believes a trademark has been registered improperly can bring a court action to have the state trademark agency cancel the registration for the following reasons:

- abandonment (when a mark is no longer being used as a trademark, another potential registrant may request a court to declare that it has been abandoned).
- fraudulent or improper basis for registration. Fraudulent registration occurs when the registrant knowingly makes any false representation, verbally, in writing or in any other way, to obtain the registration of a mark. A person who does so is also liable for any damages another may suffer because of that false information.
- the registrant is not the true owner of the mark.
- the state mark is confusingly or deceptively similar to a mark that has been registered with the U.S. Patent and Trademark Office (PTO) before the date of state registration. (See Chapter 4 for what "confusingly similar" means.) However, South Dakota and Texas specifically bar cancellations based only on the fact that a state trademark is similar to a mark registered with the PTO.

8. Infringement

In most states, infringement of a trademark occurs when another person or business

- uses that trademark, or a close approximation of it (often called a "colorable imitation" in legal lingo), without consent, on goods or services, and in a way that is likely to confuse, mislead or deceive another about the source of origin of the goods or services; or
- copies or imitates any mark for use on or advertising of goods or services for sale or distribution within the state.

Since infringement of a state trademark generally follows the same criteria as does the infringement of a federal trademark, we will not duplicate that discussion here. (See Chapter 4, How to Tell If Two Marks Are Confusingly Similar and Chapter 11, Sorting Out Trademark Disputes.)

Having a state registered mark does not shield you from an infringement suit. As we discussed above, ownership rights in trademarks derive from use, and state registration merely makes it easier to prove your rights, but does not create rights you don't have in the first place as would be the case if someone else in your state was using the same mark before your use and registration.

9. Remedies

As noted at the beginning of this chapter, the remedies you can get for state trademark infringement on the basis of registration are less extensive than those available under federal trademark law. In fact, in many states, the remedies are not significantly different from those available for the infringement of an unregistered mark.

The Model State Trademark Bill provides the remedies described below, some of which are available to unregistered mark owners as well. Many states provide that the person or business who owns a mark registered under state law that has been infringed may seek:

- an injunction restraining the manufacture, use, display or sale of goods or services with an infringing mark
- profits that the infringer has gained from the infringement
- damages that the owner of the infringed mark has suffered, which may or may not include lost profits
- seizure and destruction of goods with the infringing trademark.

So much for the generalizations. When it comes to the details of what remedies are available, the states differ considerably. For instance, a winning plaintiff does not always receive an award other than an order preventing the infringer's future use of the mark. Profits or damages may depend on a showing that the infringement was intentional. Hawaii, Texas and

Wisconsin provide for awards of damages but not profits; and many states offer the possibility of either damages or profits, but not both. Some states make it clear that profits and/or damages are available only if the infringer knew or intended that the mark would confuse or deceive as used; these include Arizona, Georgia, Idaho, Indiana, Maine, Maryland, Montana, New Jersey, South Dakota, Texas, Virginia and Wyoming. An additional 11 states offer profits and/or damages as a matter of course, except where a defendant innocently contributes to the infringement (such as a printer): Illinois, Kansas, Massachusetts, Michigan, New Mexico, Nevada, New York, North Dakota, Oklahoma, Pennsylvania and Tennessee. Likewise a few states offer triple (3X) damages or extra (punitive) damages designed to punish the infringer where fraud, malice or bad faith is shown (New Jersey, North Carolina, North Dakota, Oregon, Texas and Wisconsin).

All but the following six states offer the option to seize and destroy the goods bearing an infringing mark: Alabama, California, Hawaii, Minnesota, Oregon, Puerto Rico.

Some states also provide:

- attorneys' fees (usually in exceptional cases or ones where intentional or bad faith infringement is shown: Alaska, Colorado, Illinois, Iowa, Maine, Minnesota, Mississippi, North Carolina, Oklahoma, Puerto Rico, Texas, Washington, Wisconsin).
- costs of suit (Alabama, Arizona, Florida, Indiana, Maine, Mississippi, Puerto Rico, Wisconsin).
- criminal penalties (Connecticut, Indiana, Nevada, New Jersey, North Dakota, Oklahoma, Pennsylvania, Tennessee, Vermont, Wisconsin).
- fines (Hawaii, Maryland, North Carolina, Tennessee, Vermont).

We have tried to give you the broad outlines and most significant details of each state's trademark registration law; if you need more detail, look up the statute in your local law library. The statute number is listed in the Appendix along with the address and phone number of the agency in charge of administering your state's trademark statute. Any law librarian should be happy to help you find that particular statute, once you know the number you are looking for. Make sure you copy it down exactly, as dashes and periods often make a difference. And see Chapter 15, Help Beyond the Book, for a discussion of how to do legal research in the trademark context. ■

Federal Trademark Registration

This chapter provides the nuts and bolts for registering a trademark or service mark with the United State Patent and Trademark Office (PTO). You are reading this chapter because you wish to apply to have your mark placed on the federal trademark register.

⚠ Before you go further, it is very important to understand the information presented in previous chapters. That is, you should know :

- how trademark law works (Chapter 1)
- what makes a legally strong trademark (Chapter 2)
- the state law requirements for registering business names (Chapter 3)
- how to tell whether your mark is confusingly similar to another (Chapter 4)
- how to find out whether other marks exist that might conflict with yours (Chapters 5 and 6) and
- whether state or federal registration is most appropriate for your mark (Chapter 7).

If you aren't up to speed on these topics, go back and read the appropriate material. Then return here.

Also be aware that once you decide to register your mark, it is wise to do so as quickly as possible. Life is full of coincidences, and if someone else is in a hurry to register a mark that is the same or similar to yours, you will usually benefit by getting your application in first.

You will be happy to learn that attorneys are seldom needed to successfully accomplish a federal registration. Usually there are three simple steps:

- You fill in one very simple form and file it with the U.S. Patent and Trademark Office, along with some samples of how your mark is being used. To give you an idea of just how simple this part of the process is, the form itself says it shouldn't take more than 1 hour to complete, including the time it takes to read and understand the instructions, gather the necessary information and enter the information in the form.

THE FEDERAL SUPPLEMENTAL TRADEMARK REGISTER

There are two federal trademark registers—the Principal Register and the Supplemental Register. This chapter is about getting a mark on the Principal Register.

However, if a mark doesn't qualify for the Principal Register because it lacks distinctiveness, it can be placed on the Supplemental Register. Marks in this category usually are descriptive marks and geographic marks that are used descriptively and do not yet have secondary meaning.

While providing far fewer benefits than the Principal Register, placement on the Supplemental Register does accomplish the following:

- Your mark will appear on all the lists of registered trademarks that others search for conflicts. This provides notice to others that your mark is already in use, but doesn't give you any additional rights.
- The PTO will refuse to register another mark that is identical and used on closely related services or goods.
- You can use the ® after your mark instead of the familiar TM. This may make your mark appear stronger than it really is. (See Chapter 9, Section A, for a discussion of the trademark symbols.)
- You will have an easier time registering your mark in other countries.
- Keeping the mark on the Supplemental Register for five years will help you establish secondary meaning for the mark, which qualifies it for the Principal Register.

You should always first apply for placement on the Principal Register. If your application is rejected on distinctiveness grounds, you can simply amend your application to apply for the Supplemental Register and keep your original filing date. For this reason, and because of its few benefits other than notice, we do not discuss the Supplemental Register in any greater detail elsewhere in this book.

- You make some changes in your application based on specific suggestions by the trademark examiner.
- You pay the trademark registration fee of $245 (as of September 1997).

If you want to apply to register your mark before you actually use it (this is called an "intent to use" application), you will pay an additional $100 and file an extra form when you actually start using the mark. More fees and forms are required if you delay getting the mark into use past an initial six-month period.

PTO HELP PHONE NUMBER

The number for general information on patents or trademarks is 703-308-HELP. The automated trademark information line is 703-557-4636.

Now that you have an overview of the trademark registration process, let's start by examining the basic qualifications for placement of a mark on the federal trademark register. There are, in fact, two trademark registers—the principal register and the supplemental register. Your goal is to get your mark placed on the principal register, as it is that register that provides most of the benefits of federal registration. However, if your mark doesn't qualify for the principal register because it is considered too weak, you may have it placed on the supplemental register—which does provide a few benefits (See Chapter 1, Section C6 for more on the supplemental register.)

From this point on, when we speak of federal registration, we are referring to registration on the principal register.

HOW TRADEMARK REGISTRATION WORKS

- You complete an application form and send it to the PTO.
- When the PTO receives your application, they give it a number and check to make sure you included all the necessary parts (such as specimens, filing fee and drawing, as described in this chapter).
- The application is then sorted—according to the goods or services involved. For example, any application for a mark used on computer software would be reviewed in one of the three offices that inspect Class 9 applications (electrical and scientific apparatus).
- The PTO sends you a filing receipt explaining that the PTO received the application but that you shouldn't expect to hear from them again for three months.
- During that time, a trademark examiner decides whether your application is complete and consistent; whether your mark qualifies for registration; and whether your mark contains common words to which you have no particular claim.
- Once the examiner is satisfied that the mark is clear for registration and that you have adequately corrected any technical problems in the application, the PTO publishes the mark in the *Official Gazette* (an official PTO publication) to give others a chance to object to your application being registered.
- If after publication nobody objects to your registration—which is usually the case—your mark will be registered if you are already using it. If you filed an intent to use application the mark will be registered when you establish actual use.
- If someone does object (opposes your registration)—perhaps because your mark is too close to theirs or because they believe your mark is misleading—you'll need to hire an attorney to continue pushing for registration. (See Chapter 15, Help Beyond the Book.)

A. Is Your Mark Eligible for Federal Trademark Registration?

In Chapter 1 we spoke about qualifications for federal trademark registration. To review, a mark qualifies for federal trademark registration if:

- the mark is considered distinctive, inherently or because it has obtained a secondary meaning (Chapter 2)
- the mark does not conflict with an existing registered or unregistered mark (Chapter 4)
- the product or service is used in commerce (that is, it moves across state, territorial or international borders, or affects commerce across these borders), and
- the mark is not scandalous, immoral or deceptive.

The first two qualifications have been covered in the indicated chapters. Now it is time to find out what the last two mean.

1. Will You Be Using a Trademark in Commerce?

Federal registration is only allowed for marks that are in use in "commerce." Commerce is defined in this context as business or trade which the federal government, through the U.S. Congress, may control. Technically, Congress may control interstate commerce, territorial commerce and international commerce. In practice, this means that to use a mark in commerce—for the purpose of qualifying for federal trademark registration—your business must do one or more of the following:

- Ship a product across state lines, as do most manufacturers, wholesalers and mail order businesses.
- Ship a product between a state and a territory or a territory and another territory (for instance, between New York and Puerto Rico or between Puerto Rico and the Virgin Islands).
- Ship a product between a state or territory and another country (for instance between California and Hong Kong or between Puerto Rico and Cuba).

- Advertise services offered by your business outside of your state, as does Disneyland and many businesses that have sites on the World Wide Web.
- Conduct a service business across state lines, as do most trucking operations, many 900 numbers, and, increasingly, businesses that offer services over the Internet.
- Conduct a service business in more than one state (*McDonald's, Holiday Inn, Hilton Hotels*) or across international or territorial borders.
- Operate a business that caters to interstate or international travelers, such as a hotel, restaurant, tour guide service or ski resort.

The basic reason for the commerce requirement is that the federal government has no constitutional authority to regulate marks that are used only within one state's borders.

Here are examples of marks that are being used in commerce that Congress may regulate:

Goods

Alan's mousetrap is already being sold in three states under the mark *Mice-Free*, and the mark appears on the packaging.

Rosebud, Inc., distributes a computer program called *ROSECARE* to nurseries throughout the country.

Ruth lives in White River Junction, Vermont, a town just across the river from Hanover, New Hampshire, where Dartmouth University is located. She sells a brand of baked goods in both towns—under the label *Ruth's Bakery Delights*.

Travelers come to Berkeley, California from around the world to buy *Peet's Coffee*. Peet's doesn't advertise but it draws a national and international trade under the service mark *Peet's* and the trademark *Peet's Coffee*. Peet's also operates a brisk international mail-order business.

Services

Etta's computer consulting services are marketed by telephone and direct mail to potential customers in Canada, California and Nevada under the mark *Quick-Bytes*.

Toby Drysdale's 900-number for sports trivia, *Sports R Us*, is marketed through ads on national radio and television networks and is also available to purchasers in Puerto Rico and Mexico.

Rose's newspaper advice column is syndicated in three northeastern states under the name *Rosie to the Rescue*.

Doug's mail-order shoe repair service is marketed under the name *Sole Security* via ads in national magazines and newspapers.

Nolo Press uses its site on the World Wide Web to distribute products and provide free legal information through its on-line legal encyclopedia.

Ninth Wave Surfing provides lessons in Hawaii to vacationers from all over the world.

⚠ This last example shows an "effect" that a business can have on interstate commerce. While the "effect" may also qualify a mark for federal registration, it is not as clear-cut a case as when the mark actually appears in more than one state—for instance, in advertising or mail-order catalogs.

⚠ As a general rule, the PTO trademark examiners do not investigate the statement made in an application that a particular mark is being used in "commerce that Congress may regulate." Nor is there any place in the application to describe exactly where, geographically, the mark is being used. So, applications are seldom rejected because the commerce requirement hasn't been satisfied. However, if you ever have to defend your registration—in court or before the PTO—

ARE YOU—OR WILL YOU BE—USING YOUR MARK?

"Use" has a special meaning when it comes to the trademark registration requirement. As a general rule, "use" means that the mark has been, is being or will be actually utilized in the marketplace to identify your goods and services. This doesn't mean that the product or service has to actually be sold, as long as they are distributed under the mark in question for eventual resale.

Goods: Your mark is "used" for goods if the mark was on the goods—on labels or tags attached to them—and the goods were shipped to a store for resale or use as a sample. However, sales made only for the purpose of getting your mark "in use" don't count. The use has to be a bona fide attempt to identify and distinguish your goods or services in the marketplace.

EXAMPLES:

1. The day Ben sent his first samples of pants to a department store potentially interested in selling them was the date of first use anywhere of his mark *No-Knees*.
2. When Emily's earrings were shipped in a box carrying the label *All Ears*, for the legitimate purpose of resale by a local street vendor, that was the date of first use of her mark.

Services: Your mark is being used for services if the services have been marketed using the mark and you can legitimately deliver them.

EXAMPLES:

1. Toby purchased a 900 line for providing sports trivia under the name *Sports R Us*. The date he began his advertising was the date he first used the mark, as long as the line was up and running (it doesn't matter how long he waits for the first call).
2. Helen decided to call her California/Nevada housecleaning service *Mrs. Clean*. When she first advertised her services under that name on a bulletin board at a local market, that was the date of first use of her mark.

you may be required to prove that the mark was in fact being used in commerce at the time you filed your registration application.

2. Is Your Mark Immoral, Deceptive or Scandalous?

You may not register a mark if the mark:

- Contains "immoral," "deceptive" or "scandalous" matter. For example, a mark resembling a sex organ would be considered immoral; a mark suggesting miracle properties in a product that are not substantiated would be deceptive; and a mark showing a mutilated corpse would be scandalous.
- Disparages or falsely suggests a connection with persons (living or dead), institutions, beliefs or national symbols.
- Includes the flag or coat of arms or other insignia of the United States, or of any state or municipality, or of any foreign nation, or any simulation thereof.
- Consists of or contains a name, portrait or signature identifying a particular living individual (except with his or her written consent), or the name, signature or portrait of a deceased president of the United States during the life of his widow, if any, except with the written consent of the widow.
- Is already taken by an organization that has been granted the exclusive right by statute to use the marks or symbol. The Boy Scouts and the U.S. Olympic Committee are examples. Similarly, the use of the character/ name *Smokey the Bear* is reserved to the Department of the Interior.

- Is misleading or just plain false. For example, a trademark that suggests chocolate in a product that contains no chocolate is not registrable.
- Is primarily a geographic name or a surname. (See Chapter 10, Evaluating Trademark Strength, for a discussion of these types of names and when they are and are not considered distinctive.)

EXAMPLES OF DISPARAGING OR UNAUTHORIZED MARKS

A mark showing a picture of the United States president standing on the American flag would constitute a disparagement of a person, of an institution (the presidency) and of a national symbol. A baseball-related mark suggesting a connection with Babe Ruth also would not qualify, unless authorization were given by Babe Ruth's heirs. Another very recent example of a mark denied registration under this section was a condom resembling the American flag.

B. Gather Information for Your Trademark Application

In this section we describe what information you will need to complete your trademark application. This will vary depending on whether you are filing:

- an application for a mark that is already being used in commerce (actual use) or
- an application for a mark that you intend to put into use in commerce in the future (intent to use).

If after reading the "use" definitions and examples in Section A, above, you believe you have not yet used your mark, but you intend to use it within the next six months, you will be checking the box on your application form that makes it an intent to use application. We will alert you to skip certain portions of these instructions that apply only to actual use applications.

1. Deciding Whether to File an Intent to Use Application

When you file an application for registration based on an intent to use the mark in commerce, you must state that you have a bona fide intention to use it within six months of the date your application is approved by the PTO. If you are unable to put the mark into use within that period, you can purchase additional six-month extensions, one at a time until three years have passed, assuming you are able to convince the PTO that the reasons for the delays are legitimate. As a practical matter, then, the initial requirement that you put your mark into use in commerce within six months is expandable to a total period of three years.

The advantage to filing an intent to use application is that your filing date will serve as the date of your first use of the mark—assuming you go on to

put the mark in actual use and take the other steps necessary to get the mark placed on the federal trademark register. This first use date can be very important in the event a conflict develops with another mark—in the PTO or in the marketplace. (See Chapter 11 for the importance of the date of first use.) Clearly, once you decide to file on this basis, you should do so as quickly as possible, to obtain the earliest possible date of first use.

As mentioned, the intent to use approach is more expensive than simply filing an actual use application—at least $100 more expensive, plus $100 for each additional six-month extension that is needed. Therefore, it is most appropriate to use the Intent to Use application when you have come up with a truly distinctive name (see Chapter 10) or you plan to spend big bucks "tooling up" to use the mark and you don't want to lay out the cash until you know that the mark will be yours and yours only. On the other hand, if your mark is legally weak—for instance, it uses common words in a common way or is descriptive of the products or services—you may be better off waiting until your actual use begins and then submit an application at that time. You may forfeit the advantage of the early use date, but since your mark is legally weak, that date is not as important.

2. Questions to Be Addressed in Your Application

In the course of preparing your application you will need to address the following questions:
1. Does (will) the mark be used to identify goods or services, or both?
2. If the mark is in use, when was it first used in a commercial context?
3. If the mark is in use, what examples of your mark's usage (specimens) will you choose to submit with your application?
4. Which trademark class does (will) your mark fit under?

Let's look at each question in some detail.

3. Does the Mark Describe Goods or Services, or Both?

Goods are tangible products, items you can touch—for example, cans of soup, pens, cookies, cars, oxygen canisters, calendars, computers and clothing. Even creative works such as software, music and inventions are also goods, since they are marketed in a tangible form (floppy disks, tapes, CDs). For policy reasons, the PTO also considers software that is distributed via telephone line from a World Wide Web site or bulletin board to be a product.

Services are activities directed to customers. Examples of services are: professional advice or consultation; physical maintenance and/or repair (for instance, the fixing of washing machines and typewriters or caring for gardens); performances (such as those by actors, rent-a-clowns and singing telegram services); delivery (such as overnight mail services, trucking and bus companies and airlines); financial services (such as banking, lending, real estate or credit); and selling items, whether food, products or services.

It is important to understand that many businesses provide both a service and a product under the same mark. For instance, Nolo Press provides:

- a service to its authors (of publishing their books),
- a service to its readers of helping them understand the law and get through court procedures without a lawyer, and
- products known as *Nolo Press* books and software.

Similarly, *Weight Watchers* and *Jenny Craig* are used as marks both for diet foods (goods) and for weight-loss counseling services. And *Xerox* and *IBM* are used as marks both for office machines (products) and for machine repairs and maintenance (services).

On the other hand, it's also common for businesses to use one mark for their service and another mark for their product. For instance, Sears Roebuck & Co. uses *Sears* as a service mark for its department store services and *Craftsman* as a trademark on its line of tools (products).

4. When Was the Mark First Used?

➡️ If you are not yet using your mark and intend to file an intent to use application, skip to Section B6.

You'll need these two dates to complete your trademark application:

- when you first used your mark anywhere (The term "anywhere" does not include use within a company. The use must be external—out in the marketplace.)
- when you first used your mark in "commerce that Congress can regulate." (Commerce that crosses state, territorial or international boundaries.)

The date of first use anywhere obviously can be a different date than when you first used the mark "in commerce that Congress can regulate." For instance, you may have used the mark just in your neighborhood for years and then decided to expand. The date the mark was first used in your neighborhood would be the date of first use. The date you marketed your product or service in a second state (or territory or outside the country) would be the first use in commerce that Congress can regulate.

⚠️ **The Importance of the Date of First Use**
The first date on which you used your mark anywhere establishes the beginning of your legal rights to the mark. It is important to know and be able to prove this date because the business that has been using the mark the longest will usually be given priority in case a conflict develops. (See Chapter 11.) No matter how careful your trademark search, there is always the possibility that someone else in the country was using the same mark, or a similar one, before you. It is also possible that someone who started using the mark

after you has also applied to have their mark registered (in such a case your first use would give you some protection).

As stated, the date of first use in commerce that Congress can regulate may be much later in time than the first use anywhere.

EXAMPLE (GOODS): Jon's salad dressing—sold to several local markets—becomes so popular that a gourmet shop with stores in several states decides to buy some to sell in all of its stores. The date the first bottles were shipped to the local markets was the date of first use anywhere. The date the first bottles are shipped from Jon's kitchen for the purpose of distribution to out-of-state stores is the first date his mark is used in commerce.

EXAMPLE (SERVICES): Lori sells watercolor art to order at her local flea market under the mark *Watercolor Wonder*. She does so well that she decides to advertise in a national crafts magazine, using the same mark. The first time Lori sold her art at the flea market is the date of first use anywhere. The date her ad is published in the national magazine is the first date her mark is used in commerce.

Hazy Memory Note: When Did I First Use My Mark Anyway?

Sometimes you will have been using a mark for years before you decide to register it and won't know the exact the date of its first use anywhere or in commerce. Do your best to determine the correct dates. If necessary it is okay to use imprecise dates such as "before March 25, 1990" or "on or about January 16, 1960." You may also give a month or year without a date, such as "in 1966" or "in February 1984." If you are unsure as between two dates, use the earliest possible date that you can reasonably assert as the correct one.

DOCUMENT YOUR USE

If possible, we suggest you document the first use of your mark. This is important not only for the registration process but also in case you become involved in a trademark dispute. (See, for instance, Chapter 11, Sections E3 and I1.) Some examples of documentation include:

- copies of cover letters or invoices sent with product shipments and showing the mark (for goods)
- copies of advertisements offering services under the mark (for services)
- photos of displays, signs or other marketing materials if the business doesn't advertise (services and, in some instances, goods).

Since many advertisements and other marketing materials don't include the date(s) when they appeared, it is helpful to write the date(s) of publication on the back of the ad, photo or display. Even better would be a letter from the publication confirming that your ad will appear on or by a certain date or that your business will attend a trade show on a certain date.

We also suggest you keep examples (or photographs) of the first use of your mark in commerce. See Section B5 where we explain the importance of these examples (called specimens) to the trademark registration process.

5. What Specimens (Examples of Your Mark) Will You Use?

➡️ If you are filing an intent to use application, you will not yet have specimens and need not deal with this information at this time; you should skip to Section B6. However, if and when you put the mark into use and file the proper documents necessary to complete the registration process, you will need this information.

When applying for federal registration on an actual use basis, you must submit three specimens (examples) of how your mark is being used in commerce (as defined in Section A, above). If you plan to apply for registration under more than one trademark class (see Section B6, below), you will need to submit specimens showing use for each class.

All three specimens may—but don't have to—be the same. Even specimens submitted for different classes may be the same. The specimens may not exceed 8 1/2 inches (21.6 cm) wide and 13 inches (33 cm) long, and must be flat. There is no minimum size. As we emphasize later, the specimens must each portray the exact same mark as appears in the drawing that you will be submitting with the application. (See Section D below.)

a. Specimens for Marks on Goods (Trademarks)

Specimens of how the mark is used with goods must show a very close association between the mark and the goods. Acceptable specimens usually include labels, tags or containers showing the mark. Again, specimens must be flat, so if you submit a container such as a box, or a display, it must be flattened. Obviously, there may be many degrees of flatness, depending on the container and materials. Simply do the best you can under the circumstances. If you are dealing with an item that simply won't flatten, like a baseball, take a photograph. (See discussion below on photos.)

DISPLAYS AS SPECIMENS FOR GOODS

Displays such as banners and window displays may also be used, but with caution. The display must be meant to catch the buyer's attention where the sale is made (for instance, at the store), and the mark must be prominent and clearly connected to the goods. For example, if a window sign in a drug store said "See our *All Ears* earrings special!" that would probably qualify as an appropriate specimen. However, the line between displays and advertising can be fuzzy, and advertising is not sufficient for specimens of marks used for goods. (See the discussion below on unacceptable specimens for goods.) If you have a choice, use another type of specimen.

Marks on Goods

If you place your mark on your goods by using a rubber stamp or stencil, you may submit a specimen of an impression of the stamp or stencil on a piece of paper. However, the examiner may ask for proof that the goods themselves are imprinted in that manner. You may save yourself some trouble if you submit a photograph showing the mark imprinted on the goods, along with an impression on paper for the close-up view.

Photographic Specimens

If it's impractical to provide an actual specimen of the mark, three copies of a photograph showing the mark as it is used in commerce are acceptable. (The photo may not exceed 81/2" X 11"). For example, if your *Solve-it Solvent* mark was used in connection with 55-gallon drums of solvent, and printed only on the drums, you would submit a photograph of a drum or drums clearly showing the whole mark. The photograph must show the whole item, or enough of it so the examiner can clearly see what is shown in the picture (a piano, old chair, piece of machinery or whatever), and all writing on the item must be visible. If a photograph of the whole item does not show the mark in enough detail, send one photo of the whole item and another photo close-up of the writing including the mark (the two photos together would constitute one specimen). If there is writing on more than one side, either send more than one photo, or place several items in one photo so they show all sides of the item on which writing appears.

> **EXAMPLE:** Let's continue our example of the 55-gallon drums. Suppose your mark *Solve-it Solvent* appears on the front and back of the drum in large type, surrounded by other writing describing the contents. Your first photo should portray three or four drums, each showing a different part of all the writing (*Solve-it Solvent* and the description). You would then want a few more photos, from a closer range, so that by looking at them the examiner could see all the writing that appears on a typical drum. (Again, all the photos together would constitute one specimen.) If the writing could not be made legible for some reason (maybe too small to photograph well), a separate piece of paper including all text on the drum should also be submitted.

The reason why all the writing has to be visible is that the PTO wants to see the context in which your mark is used to be sure it is consistent with the class under which you are registering the mark (Section B6, below).

Small Specimens

If the specimens are very small (such as clothing tags) put them in an envelope which is labeled "Specimens" with the applicant's name and address, the mark and the date the application was signed. That should prevent their loss from the PTO file.

Movies and Videotapes

Normally, the name of a movie or videotape will appear on the container. But sometimes marks appear only in the film or tape. In this situation, submit a photo of a frame depicting the mark. If your mark includes motion, such as the NBC peacock with tail feathers spreading, submit a videotape of the mark.

World Wide Web Pages

A screen dump of the full Web page should be fine. If the mark is being prominently displayed on the home page, so much the better.

Unacceptable Specimens for Marks on Goods

- Advertising material, including anything that is produced for the sole purpose of telling potential buyers about your product, even if you package it with the goods (such as cards packaged with a new pen telling how wonderful it is and what it's made of)
- Price lists, catalogs, trade directories and publicity releases
- Instruction sheets
- Internal company documents, including invoices and memos sent within an applicant company
- Specimens showing the mark with the ® symbol—it is illegal to use the ® symbol until after your mark is officially registered with the PTO (see Chapter 9, How to Use and Care for Your Mark). However, specimens with a TM next to the mark are okay.
- Any use of the mark merely to identify your business (not in direct connection with particular goods or services), including letterhead stationery, labels carrying only a company name and return address and bags and boxes used at store cash registers to carry sold merchandise.

b. Specimens for Marks Used for Services (Service Marks)

When you are offering a service, you obviously have no product to which you can affix a label. Acceptable specimens for services can include a variety of materials that can't be used for product marks, including advertising and marketing materials such as newspaper and magazine ads, brochures, billboards, direct mail pieces and menus (for restaurants).

Letterhead stationery and business cards showing the mark may be used if the services are plainly reflected on them, since the name or symbol being claimed as a mark would, in that context, be used to identify the services provided—that is, as a mark rather than as a trade name (remember, trade names as such are not registrable).

EXAMPLE 1: Etta's business cards for her personal computer consulting services include her mark *Quick-Bytes* and the text, "consulting services for the PC user."

EXAMPLE 2: Toby's sports trivia 900-line grew and he had stationery printed including the line, "Sports R Us Gives You The Latest Sports Trivia 24 Hours A Day." The stationery would be accepted as a specimen.

A letter on stationery will even be accepted as a specimen for a service mark if the mark appears and the services are described in the letter. Assume Toby's letterhead only said "Gen-X Sports" and gave the address and phone number. He could submit a copy of a letter sent to a national sports magazine asking that his 900-number be listed in their directory, as long as the letter described the services.

Gen-X Sports
555 First Street. West
Sonoma. CA 95476

Dear Sirs:

As you may know, our sports trivia line, 900-555-7777, has been providing customers with sports trivia twenty four hours a day for the past year. We would be honored if you would consider listing our line in your directory of...

Audio Tapes

Most marks appear in writing somewhere. If your mark represents a service, and it appears only on radio ads or in some other audio form, you may submit three audio tapes of the mark being used.

For example, if Etta decides only to advertise her computer consulting service by radio, she would submit as specimens three copies of an audio tape of her ad.

World Wide Web Pages

A screen dump of the full Web page should be fine. If the mark is being prominently displayed on the home page, so much the better.

Unacceptable Specimens for Services:

- News releases or articles based on news releases
- Documents showing trademark rather than service mark usage (use of the mark in connection with goods rather than services)
- Invoices and similar documents such as packing slips
- Specimens showing trade name usage only (use of the mark to identify a company, such as on letterhead). As discussed earlier, one exception to this is if the letterhead or the

text of the letter identifies the services represented by the mark.

TRADE NAMES

Remember from Chapter 1, A Trademark Primer, a trade name is the name of a company and is not registrable as a trademark or service mark unless it is used for more than identification of a company. To be registrable the trade name must also be used to identify goods the company sells (trademark), or to market or promote services (service mark). However, it is very common for a company's trade name and the mark used in providing the company's services to be the same, which makes the trade name registrable in its capacity as a mark. For example, a business known as Reliance Electric Repair almost surely uses that same name to market its services.

---

6. In What Class Does (Or Will) Your Product or Service Mark Belong?

Part of the trademark registration process involves assigning your product or service to one or more international classes. A list of these classes is in the Appendix. We explain this in Chapter 4, How to Tell If Two Marks Are Confusingly Similar, Section B1.

If, after reading the material in Chapter 4, you are in doubt about the proper class or classes for your product or service, you can always call the Applications section of the PTO, describe the product or service and ask them which class or classes may be involved. The clerk will answer your question and normally give you sound advice. Unfortunately, you don't have the legal right to rely on this opinion. If the person who eventually examines your application in the Patent and Trademark Office disagrees with the answer you were given, you will have to assign a different class to the product or service.

 Record the Details of All Advice You Receive From the PTO
Always write down the date you called and the full name of the person who provided you with advice, in case the examiner later disagrees with what you were told. You may not convince the examiner that you are right, but he or she will probably be impressed with your attempts to get correct information, and may consequently treat you with more respect.

It's possible to apply for registration of a mark under more than one class. The reason you would do this is that the class you register under can be an important determinant of the scope of protection you receive.

> **EXAMPLE:** Etta, who both sells computer software and offers consulting services under the mark *Quick-Bytes*, registers the mark under Class 9 (electrical and scientific apparatus). This registration should go far to protect Etta against the same or similar marks used on computer software and other related products. But it may not protect her against uses of the mark in connection with computer services. Only if she also registers the *Quick-Bytes* mark under the appropriate service class (Class 35 or Class 41) will she obtain the maximum possible protection of her mark.

The classification system is designed more for the convenience of the PTO when making registration decisions than as a means for the courts to determine whether infringement exists. Quite simply, courts may find a likelihood of customer confusion (and thus, infringement) where two marks are in different classes, and find no likelihood of customer confusion where two marks are within the same class. Still, the more classes a mark is registered in, the wider the protection the courts are likely to give it.

The number of classes you should include in your initial application depends on your circumstances. The down side of registering under more than one class is that an additional application fee (currently $245) must be paid for each additional class. For this reason, applicants sometimes apply under one class and then wait to see if the mark (and their business) is successful enough to warrant applying under other classes as well.

Applicants who can afford the fees may want to register under several classes in their initial application with the idea that this will block future applicants as much as possible and broaden the scope of protection by the courts. But the classes you can register under are restricted to the goods or services you are already offering, as shown by the specimens you submit, or that you plan to offer (if you are registering on an intent to use basis).

Again, see Chapter 4, Section B1, for how to assign your product or service to the appropriate class.

7. Deciding How Many Marks You Want to Register

So far we have assumed that you have one mark to register—typically a business or product name. However, what may seem like only one mark may in fact be viewed as several different marks. The most common examples of this are marks that combine graphic designs or distinctive typefaces with a business or product name, and marks that combine a business or product name with a slogan. In these situations, the name can be considered as one mark while the combination of a graphic design or a slogan with the name may be viewed as a separate and distinct mark. For in-

stance, on the front cover of several Nolo books the name *Nolo Press* appears. On the spine, the name *Nolo Press* appears with a scales of justice, and on the back cover, the name *Nolo* appears in a stylized script. Each of these manifestations of the word Nolo are really a separate mark, and Nolo has registered all three.

The fact that you may be technically dealing with more than one mark doesn't mean that you have to register more than one mark. After all, the registration fee for each mark is $245 (as of October 1997), and funds may be too scarce to accomplish all possible registrations. Also, if you want to register a mark in more than one class (see Section B6 above), the combination of multiple marks and multiple classes can make it prohibitively expensive to cover all bases. Below we suggest some ways to think about this issue for the most common multiple mark situations.

a. Name Marks Combined With Unusual Typefaces

If your name mark uses an unusual typeface (the Nolo example described above), your mark has two important aspects—the words that constitute the name, and the look and feel of the typeface. If money is no object, register both separately. But if funds are short—as they usually are—you will probably want to choose one or the other. As a general rule you will be better off registering the unadorned name. This gives you the flexibility of using the name in many different configurations in the future without having to effect new registrations, whereas if the only registration for you name is in the unusual typeface, you will need to make new registrations each time your name is used in a different configuration to assure the broadest possible protection for your name.

b. Name Marks Combined With Graphic Designs

If you use your name with a graphic image, you will have several choices when it is time to register:
- register the name alone
- register the combined name/graphic image, or
- register both the name and name/graphic image combination.

Again, if money is no object, the last option is the best. But if money counts, you should probably start with the combination name/graphic image, assuming the graphic image is distinctive. If the graphics are not particularly distinctive, however, then register the name by itself. The idea is to get the most mileage for your initial registration and if you are limited to one mark it is wise to register the mark that has the most distinctive elements.

C. Completing the Registration Application

In this section we tell you how to complete your registration application. As with Section B, some of the parts of the application will be filled in differently, or not at all, depending on whether you are using your mark in commerce or are filing an "intent to use" application.

As you follow our instructions, keep one point firmly in mind: Consistency is key. You will be describing your mark, the goods and services on which the mark is used and the manner or mode of use. You will also be submitting specimens and a drawing of your mark with your application. The descriptions, specimens and drawing must all be internally consistent. For instance, when you are asked to describe the goods or services on which your mark is used, this description must match the specimens you submit. If the description is broad and the specimens seem to show a narrower use you may run into trouble.

Another example: Suppose you apply for registration of the mark *Eatwell* and describe your services as distribution of snack foods to school campuses. If your specimens are fliers directed to preschools, and the fliers all describe one cookie, it may appear as though the proper services description might be "distribution of a particular cookie to preschools." The examiner may ask for specimens proving that you distribute more than this cookie, and to more than preschools.

As we move through the form, we will remind you about this need for consistency, but it is important that you understand this point up front. If you submit an internally inconsistent application (including the specimens and drawing), your application will be delayed while you make the necessary corrections.

1. The Application Form

PTO Form 1478—*Trademark/Service Mark Application, Principal Register, With Declaration*—is the form you will be using. A copy is in the Appendix. The form must be completed in English. It will be accepted if it is neatly handwritten, but the PTO prefers it to be typed. The form does not have numbered blanks, but is divided into several blocks of information. We will address them in the order in which they appear on the form.

PATENT AND TRADEMARK OFFICE FORMS

If you have access to the World Wide Web, you can download PTO Form 1478, as well as virtually every form the PTO publishes, provided you have an Adobe Acrobat reader. You will find this and other forms offered in this book at http://www.uspto.gov.

THE TRADEMARK MANUAL OF EXAMINING PROCEDURE

The Patent and Trademark Office has prepared a manual—*The Trademark Manual of Examining Procedure*—telling its employees what to look for when reviewing applications. A copy of the TMEP is available for downloading on the PTO's site on the World Wide Web (http://www.uspto.gov). It may also be obtained by mail from the Superintendent of Documents, U.S. Government Printing Office, Washington, DC 20402 or by phone at 202-512-1800. It may prove helpful if you find yourself facing issues not covered by this book. The current price for the manual is $19. It takes about two months to receive the manual, so allow plenty of time if you need to order it. The nearest federal publication bookstore may be able to order it more quickly.

2. Mark (Words and/or Design)

This block is where you describe your mark. As we point out in Chapter 10, Evaluating Trademark Strength, marks may be composed of many different elements: words, graphics, colors and combinations of these items. If your mark is made up of words only, the space in Block 1 should be big enough. But if your mark includes a graphic image, your description may be too long for the space. If this occurs, simply begin the identification in the box and state "continued on attachment." Then follow the instructions in the "continuation pages" sidebar set out below to prepare the attachment.

a. Marks Consisting Entirely of Words

The mark should be typed exactly as you want it to appear. Use all capital letters unless you specifically want it to be case sensitive (always appear in specific upper- and lowercase letters. Be sure about your choice for the mark. Only one mark may be used per application, and you may have to start over—and pay a new $245 fee—if you decide to change the mark after you file the application. (See Section G, below, on amending your application.)

As explained in Section A above, some marks can't be registered, for various reasons. If after reading this book you have any questions about whether your mark is registrable, you may wish to consult a trademark attorney (see Chapter 15). But also consider this: It may be cheaper to attempt the registration and lose your $245 filing fee if you fail than to pay a trademark lawyer's hourly rate (often $250 an hour and up for a consultation in advance). (See Chapter 15, Help Beyond the Book.)

b. Marks Consisting of Graphic Images

If all or part of the mark is a design or graphic image, do not draw it in this space (the drawing, described later in this chapter, will show the PTO what the mark looks like). Instead, use words to describe the mark as accurately as you can. Don't agonize about your description; the PTO will suggest a different one if they don't like yours. If you disagree with theirs, discuss the matter with the examiner at that time and an acceptable description will probably emerge.

> **EXAMPLE (TEXT PLUS GRAPHICS):** The mark below, which is owned by The Walt Disney Company, could be described as "Walt Disney World (with a mouse head inside the D)."

EXAMPLE (GRAPHICS ONLY): One of the most famous graphic marks is owned by The Quaker Oats Company. It could be described as "the face of a smiling, white-haired older man wearing a black hat of a type common in America in the early 17th century."

USING CONTINUATION PAGES

You can always use a blank piece of paper as a continuation page if you don't have enough room on the form. (Make plenty of photocopies before using it.) The top of each continuation page should have the following information (in case it gets separated from your application):

Applicant's complete name
Applicant's mailing address
Mark (words or description)
Goods or services with which mark is used
Which answer you are continuing

EXAMPLE:

APPLICANT NAME: Quick-Byte, Inc.
APPLICANT BUSINESS ADDRESS:
1001 Badger Rd., Badger, VT, Zip
MARK: QUICK-BYTES
GOODS OR SERVICES: Computer consulting services
CONTINUATION OF APPLICATION
MARK, Continued: similar thick horizontal stripe, in golden yellow.
APPLICANT BUSINESS ADDRESS, Continued: Address in state of incorporation, 11 Pinkham Square, Denver, CO, Zip

---

c. Marks Consisting of Product Configurations

RULES FOR PRODUCT CONFIGURATIONS

1. If you want to register your product configuration as a trademark, be prepared to furnish the trademark examiner with information about:
   - whether the design is the subject of a design or utility patent
   - similar designs used by competitors, and
   - your advertising and promotional material.

2. If you plan to register a product shape, you must submit a description that clearly defines the configuration. For example, acceptable language would be "The mark consists of the configuration of the blade portion of a fly swatter," or "The mark consists of the configuration of a cologne bottle and cap, both having a 'V' shape as viewed from above." If the configuration comprises a portion of the product, the statement should reflect that. For example, "The mark consists of a red button positioned on the lower front area of a shirt."

3. If your product design is novel then you should research patent law to determine if the design is entitled to a design patent or utility patent.

4. Avoid using product configurations that are unique to competitors (especially competitors who have invested time and money in the promotion of those product shapes or containers).

5. When possible use the product configuration in combination with your name (for example, Levi's distinctive buttons always feature the name "Levi Strauss").

d. Marks That Include Specific Colors

If the mark always appears in one specific color that you intend to be an integral part of the mark, describe the color in this block. For example, the Visa credit card trademark could be described as a white background with the word *Visa* in the middle in royal blue, a thick horizontal stripe over the word *Visa* in the same blue, and a similar thick horizontal stripe below the word *Visa* in golden yellow.

The fact that your mark will appear in color doesn't mean that the color is part of the mark for the purpose of this block. Only if you intend to always use the same color and treat the color as an inseparable part of the mark should you fill in this block.

Consistency Note

Remember, the mark you put here should be consistent with the mark on the specimen you plan to submit.

e. Colors as Trademarks

In Chapter 10 we explain that a color can be used in conjunction with a name mark (the name *Converse* in red), or it can be registered as a separate trademark (pink for insulation material). As a general rule, registering a color as a stand-alone trademark is difficult. There are two requirements. First, the color cannot serve a functional purpose and cannot have some logical relationship to the goods. Examples of colors having a functional purpose are fluorescent yellow for tennis balls or green for camouflage clothing. An example of a color that has a logical relationship to the goods would be red and yellow for fireplace logs or green for environmentally friendly trash bags. Second, you will have to demonstrate that your choice of color distinguishes your product from the competition—that is, it has acquired second-

ary meaning through long use or through marketing and advertising campaigns.

See Chapter 2 for some tips to keep in mind when choosing a color as a trademark that you may later wish to register.

3. Class Number

After reading Chapter 4, Section B1, and the material in Section A, above, assign one or more classes to the product or service for which you are using (or plan to use) the mark. (Remember, each additional class will cost an extra $245.) If you aren't sure which class to use, call the PTO and get their opinion. Or, leave the block blank. The PTO will fill it in for you. The first choice is a little better because you will have more control over what class is ultimately used.

4. Applicant Name

Only the person (including the owner of a sole proprietorship) or legal business entity (such as a partnership or corporation) who owns the mark when the application is filed may file as the applicant. Use the applicant's full legal name here and consistently throughout the application and in the signature to the application.

If the applicant is a limited partnership or general partnership, extra care should be taken to use the correct assumed name. If the general partnership doesn't have an assumed name—that is, it does business using the partners' first and last names—these names should be listed in the order they normally appear.

EXAMPLE:

APPLICANT NAME: Kim Bunch, Gloria Grant & Nancie Valle

Corporations should use the official corporate name, not the name of a division. If the mark is used only by a division, that may be stated in the second part of the last block (Basis for Application) or in a cover letter submitted with the application.

EXAMPLE:

APPLICANT NAME: Quick-Byte, Incorporated

A joint venture is a single business entity and its name should go here.

EXAMPLE:

APPLICANT NAME: The Shacter/Alberts Company

HAS THE OWNERSHIP OF THE MARK CHANGED?

If the mark is owned by a different business entity than previously owned it, extra care should be taken to explain the change in ownership if you are submitting a specimen (see Section B5, above) that includes the name of a former owner—that is, a person other than you, or a company other than yours.

For instance, suppose the specimen is a computer-related newsletter, at the bottom of which is printed "Quick-Bytes is a service mark of Etta Linton." Perhaps after the newsletter was printed Etta was doing so well she formed a corporation, Quick-Bytes, Inc. If the application lists the corporation as the owner of the mark, the examiner will probably notice the discrepancy (newsletter mentions an individual as owner) and want to know which is correct.

More Than One Owner

Usually there is only one owner of a mark, the business that uses it first. This would be the owner of a sole proprietorship, a partnership, a limited partnership, a corporation, an association or a joint venture. If a husband and wife are in-

volved as joint owners, they can be treated as a single entity—a partnership—for the purpose of registering their mark. However, if two separate individuals who are not partners, or two unrelated businesses, agree that both own the mark, joint applicant status may be accepted by the PTO. If you intend to list more than one applicant you should do some research to be sure you actually have a joint owner situation. (See Chapter 15.)

5. Applicant Business Address

Use an address at which mail is received, whether a physical location or a P.O. or private mail box service. (If you need more room, continue on an extra page if needed. See sidebar on continuation pages in Section C2, above.)

For applicants applying as individuals: list either a home or business address.

For joint applicants: list addresses for all parties involved, specifying which address belongs to which applicant.

For corporations, partnerships, joint ventures, associations and sole proprietorships: list the business address. If the corporation also has an address in its state of incorporation (different from its business address), list both.

6. Applicant Entity

Check one appropriate box and fill in the information requested.

- **Individual applicants.** Give your country of citizenship.
- **Partnerships.** Give the state and country under which the partnership was formed. Then list the names and countries of citizenship of the general partners. If a limited partnership is involved, don't list the limited partners.
- **Corporations.** Give the state (or country if outside the U.S.A.) of incorporation.

- **Other.** If the applicant is not an individual, partnership or corporation, check this box. For example, you would check this box if the applicant were a sole proprietorship, an association or a joint venture. The members must be listed by name in the following manner:

"Other: (Specify Nature of Entity and Domicile) Joint Venture domiciled in Ohio, composed of Sabreen Hurt, Marn Reich and Sonja Eriksson."

⚠ Use the precise legal description of your business form. If you're not sure, call the local Small Business Administration office (check in your phone book). They may be able to provide some guidance. Whatever you do, don't use the word "firm" or "company" to describe your legal entity. These words are not specific enough for the PTO and could cause your application to get delayed.

7. Goods and/or Services

Describe the goods or services as clearly and succinctly as possible. Use ordinary English and be as accurate as you can. Here are some important guidelines to use when describing your goods or services:

a. Make Your Description Appropriately Inclusive

Subject to the other hints offered in this section, it is important to make your initial description broad enough to include all the goods or services for which you want your mark to be protected. This is because of a PTO rule that, for the most part, doesn't permit the expansion of a description to include additional products or services once the application has been filed. For example, assume you're a citrus fruit grower and your initial description lists "grapefruit, oranges, lemons,

and limes." If you later realize that you should have included kumquats in this list, the chances are pretty good the examiner won't let you amend your application to list them, or use a more inclusive term such as citrus fruit that would include them. This means that if you offer (or plan to offer) a variety of products or services under your mark, make sure your description is appropriately inclusive. Otherwise you will probably be required to file another application (and pay another application fee) to extend your registration to the additional goods or services.

b. Avoid an Overly Broad Description

Avoid making your description so broad and ambiguous that the examiner will not have a clear idea of the precise goods and services involved. For example, for acrylic paints, you should use the specific phrase "artists' paints" rather than "artists' materials" (which could include many different items in a variety of classes). If the examiner thinks that your description is too broad, he or she will give you an opportunity to amend it. (See sidebar on Calling the Patent and Trademark Office.) Be aware, however, that if you amend your description to reduce the number of goods or services included in it, you won't later be able to add those goods or services back in if you change your mind.

c. Limit Your Description to the Number of Classes You Wish to Register Under

As explained earlier in Section B, you must pay an additional application fee (currently $245) for each additional class you wish to register under. This means that the goods or services in your description should fall within the number of classes you are willing to pay for. For example, assume you produce a desk set that includes pens, pencils and scissors, and your trademark budget dictates that you register under only one class. Since scissors are in a different class from pens and pencils, your description should be "a desk set with pens and pencils" (Class 16), or, "a desk set with scissors" (Class 8), but not "a desk set with pens, pencils and scissors."

d. Be Consistent

Your description of your goods or services must be consistent with your specimens. You will need to use specimens that depict the mark used in a manner that fits the description you have used. After you decide which specimens to use you may have to come back to this section of the form and modify your description accordingly.

e. Avoid Using Open-Ended and Indefinite Terms

Don't use open-ended, indefinite terms such as "and the like," "including," "such as," "for example" and "and so on."

- Unacceptable: Office supplies (pens, pencils *and the like*).
- Acceptable: Office supplies consisting of pens and pencils.
- Unacceptable: Typing paper *including* copy machine paper.
- Acceptable: Paper—namely that suitable for use in offices for typing and copy machines.

The problem with the indefinite phrases is that they are not specific and could lead to the classification inconsistencies mentioned above. Suppose the application only designated Class 16, and then described the goods as "pens, pencils and the like." The examiner would worry that "pens, pencils and the like" could include items in more than one class (Class 16 for pens and pencils, Class 8 for scissors). When descriptions of goods and services are specifically defined or stated, the examiner will feel more certain that the proper class has been designated and the proper filing fee has been paid.

The PTO understands that, in our rapidly changing world, the number of possible goods and services (and descriptions of them) is limitless. Often when a good or service is first created it is difficult to describe it with common language. For example, when Ford first began making cars, the words "motor car" and "automobile" had not yet become common language. Similarly, in the mid-1970s there was no common language for describing consulting services in the field of personal computers (since personal computers had not existed prior to that time).

Fortunately, the PTO will help answer your questions about how to word the description of your goods or services.

CALLING THE PATENT AND TRADEMARK OFFICE

Call the Managing or Senior Attorney who handles the class you plan to register under by calling 703-308-9101 and following the instructions on the recording. For example, if your mark is used in connection with mail box rental services (Class 39, transportation and storage services), follow the instructions to get to the PTO office that handles Class 39 applications. Explain you need help wording a description of your services. The lawyer will give you some suggestions based on your description of the good or service involved. Don't feel bound by the examiner's first suggestion, especially if it would reduce the number of goods and services included in your description or change the class you will register under. It is usually possible to discuss the goods or services and make counter-suggestions until a description that satisfies you and the examiner is found.

Another way you can get help from the PTO is by reading this section, and putting your own description on your application. If the PTO finds your description unacceptable, they will call or write you and suggest another description, sometimes after they get more information about your goods or services. Be aware, however, that this may cause some delay in getting your registration accomplished.

Still another resource is the list of approved descriptions the PTO has prepared for its examiners to use when reviewing applications (termed the U.S. Patent & Trademark Office Acceptable Identification of Goods and Services Manual). The manual is available for searching on the PTO's Web site (http://www.uspto.gov) or can be ordered for $40 plus shipping costs from the International Trademark Association, New York, NY (212-986-5880). This manual has over 13,000 listings and if you are only planning to prepare one application you probably don't need it.

Sample listings from the manual are included in the Appendix; they may give you some ideas.

One final suggestion. If you have access to the federal trademark database (see Chapter 5, Section C1), you can search for marks used by competitors and then examine the goods and services description used for those marks.

This block also mentions an "accompanying drawing" being submitted with the application. Basically, this means a literal representation of the

mark you are registering. But you will need to read the Drawing section of this chapter for details (Section D), as the PTO's definition of "drawing" is unlike any definition you have ever used.

8. Basis for Application

In this block you indicate the basis for your application. Most readers will be basing their application on the fact that their mark is already in use in commerce as defined in Section A above. But some readers will be basing their application on their "bona fide intent to use" the mark within the next six months.

a. Registration Based on Being Used in Commerce

If your mark is already in use in commerce, check the first box and fill in the blanks as we instruct just below.

➡ If you expect your mark to be in use in commerce within the next six months, skip to our instructions in subsection b below (Registration on Basis of Bona Fide Intent to Use the Mark in Commerce).

If you don't know if your mark is in use in interstate commerce see Section A, above. If your application is based on a previous registration or filing in a foreign country, see Chapter 15, Help Beyond the Book, on getting help from a lawyer.

After checking the first box you may notice that the application states "Three specimens showing the mark as used in commerce are submitted with this application." In Section B5, above, we provide precise instructions for completing this important part of the trademark registration process.

The next blanks to complete ask for two dates:
- when your mark was first used anywhere
- when your mark was first used in commerce that Congress may regulate.

The significance of these dates was discussed in Section B4, above.

After you list the two dates, indicate the type of commerce in which the mark was used. This will be one of the following:
- interstate commerce (between one state and one or more other states)
- territorial commerce (between a state and a territory—for instance Florida and Puerto Rico or between two territories—for instance Puerto Rico and the Virgin Islands); name the state and territory
- international commerce (between a state and a foreign country or between a territory and a foreign country); name the state or territory and the foreign country.

If your first use anywhere (as discussed above) was in commerce which the U.S. Congress may regulate, both dates (the first two lines in block 7) will be the same. Even so, you still must fill in both blanks.

Specify Manner or Mode of Use—In Section B5, above, we discuss the different ways a mark may be used with goods and services. In this blank you must describe at least one such way your mark is being used. You need not describe all the ways it is used.

Examples of how marks are used to identify goods:
- If your mark is employed on books, jeans, hats or other goods on which a mark might appear, your manner or mode of use may be: "The mark is placed directly on the goods and used in other ways customary to the trade."
- If your mark is used in connection with window glass, jewelry or other goods on which it is impractical to place the mark directly, try this or similar wording: "The mark is used on labels attached to the goods and on packaging."
- If your mark is used in connection with accounting services, you may state something like: "The mark is used in letters, advertisements and signs used to promote the services."

Consistency Note

The PTO will look to see if the manner or mode of use you describe is consistent with the specimen (sample) you submit. If it isn't, the PTO will ask for clarification. Since you may be using the mark in several different ways, the one you describe here should be consistent with your samples. For instance, suppose you describe the manner or mode of use as follows: "The mark is used in newsletters used to promote the services." If the specimens you submit are copies of phone book advertisements rather than newsletters, the PTO will logically conclude that your specimens are inconsistent with the manner or mode of use you are claiming and send your application back for clarification. For this reason, it is often best to first decide which specimens you plan to use and then fill in this box.

b. Registration on Basis of Bona Fide Intent to Use the Mark in Commerce

If your mark has not been put in use in commerce which the U.S. Congress may regulate, as described in Section A above, but you honestly intend to use it in such commerce within the next six months, you may prepare an Intent to Use (ITU) application. If your mark is approved (the PTO uses the term "allowed"), you will have reserved the right to use the mark in the manner claimed in your application, without having used it at all. Your first period of reservation is for six months. If you can't get the mark into actual use within that period, you may arrange (and pay) for up to five additional six-month extensions, provided you have adequate explanations for each delay. (See Section K1, below.)

If you wish to file your application on an intent to use basis, check the second box, "Applicant has a bona fide intention to use the mark in commerce on or in connection with the above identified goods/services." Bona fide is Latin for good faith.

Specify Manner or Mode of Use—In Section B5, above, we discuss the different ways a mark may be used with goods and services. In this blank you must describe at least one such way your mark will be used in the future. You need not describe all the ways it is to be used.

Examples of how marks are used to identify goods:

- If your mark will be employed on books, jeans, hats or other goods on which a mark might appear, your manner or mode of use may be: "The mark will be placed directly on the goods and used in other ways customary to the trade."
- If your mark is to be used in connection with window glass, jewelry or other goods on which it is impractical to place the mark directly, try this or similar wording: "The mark will be used on labels attached to the goods and on packaging."

- If your mark is to be used in connection with accounting services, you may state something like: "The mark will be used in letters, advertisements and signs used to promote the services."

9. Declaration (on the Back Side of the Application)

The PTO requires that the person signing the application state under oath that he/she:

- understands that willful false statements are punishable by fine, imprisonment or both under federal law, and that such willful false statements may jeopardize the validity of the application or any resulting registration
- is authorized to "execute" (sign) the application on behalf of the applicant (if the applicant is a business entity)
- believes the applicant is either the owner of, or for "intent to use" applications, is entitled to use, the mark for which registration is sought
- believes no other person, firm, corporation or association has the right to use the mark or a mark so similar that consumers could be confused or deceived
- knows all statements in the application are true or is informed and believes that they are true.

This declaration is mostly to warn you that you had better be telling the truth. The PTO rarely, if ever, takes the time to figure out if people are lying, or to prosecute them for making false statements. However, if you ever get into a dispute, any lies you make in your application may come to light and cause you to lose. The bottom line is that you should not file an application if any of the following is true:

- You are not sure whether you are the owner of the mark. (See Section C4, above, regarding who can apply for registration.)

- You know of a clear conflict with a mark used by someone else. (See Chapters 5 and 6.)
- You are making some other statement in the application that you believe is not true.

10. Signature

Consistency Note
Make sure your signature (and title) is consistent with information you entered in Block 3.

Individual: If the applicant is an individual, sign here. If a wife and husband, or any other individuals, are applying together as separate individuals rather than as a partnership, each must sign as joint owners (see below).

Sole Proprietorships: If you are the sole owner of a business you must sign the application. On the line below, print your name and show your position as "sole proprietor."

Partnerships: Any partner of a general (as opposed to a limited) partnership may sign. You need not provide proof that the signer is a general partner with power to make business decisions binding the partnership, but such proof should be available in case the examiner requests it.

Joint Venture: Any principal member of the joint venture may sign.

Corporations (profit and nonprofit) and unincorporated associations (such as labor unions and community groups): The following corporate titles are acceptable without question: president, vice president, secretary, treasurer, CEO, CFO (or controller or comptroller). Clerk is acceptable for mass corporations. Also acceptable

are chairman or chairman of the board of directors (but not a director). Modifications such as VP of Sales or Executive VP are also acceptable. If you decide to use someone with another title not typically considered to be a corporate officer, you must provide proof that the person is in fact an officer. For example, if you decide to have the corporate General Counsel sign the application, you should provide a declaration (statement under penalty of perjury) explaining that the person is an officer, and attach a copy of the corporate minutes in which the person was made a corporate officer. A corporate employee such as an executive director, publisher or managing director may not sign unless she is also a corporate officer.

May 7, 1993	_Ken Andres_
Date	Signature
510-111-1111	Ken Andres, Treasurer
Telephone Number	Print or Type Name and Position

Joint Owners: If there are joint owners (that is, two or more separate persons or entities who have not formed a joint venture, partnership or other entity) then each person must sign and be identified on the line below the signature line.

May 7, 1993	*Kenny Jones* Harriet Rhodes
Date	Signature
510-111-1111	Kenny Jones & Harriet Rhodes
Telephone Number	Print or Type Name and Position

Date: Put the date on the line to the left of the signature line. The application must be filed with the PTO within a reasonable time after it is signed and dated. Eight weeks or less is considered reasonable by the PTO, but we recommend that the application be filed as soon as possible.

Phone Number and Printed Name: Remember to add your phone number and printed name.

D. The Drawing

After completing the declaration it is time to turn your attention to the "drawing," which must be submitted as part of the application. If all goes well, after your application is reviewed your mark will be published in the Official Gazette of the Patent and Trademark Office. (Publication gives others who believe your mark is in conflict with theirs a chance to file papers saying your mark should be denied registration. Publication will be discussed at greater length later in Section I.)

💡 Consistency Note

Your drawing must match—in spelling, style and appearance—the mark as it appears on the specimen you plan to submit. Before you decide on your drawing, make sure you have a specimen that accurately depicts it. See Section B5, above.

1. General Requirements

All drawings must be on white paper of a size from 8 to 8-½ inches (20.3 to 21.6 cm) wide and 11 inches (27.9 cm) long. The drawing itself must be in black either typed or drawn (see below) in ink. There must be a margin on all sides of at least one inch (2.5 cm).

2. Types of Drawings

Drawings fall into two categories: "typed" (marks containing only words, numbers and/or certain typographical symbols in no particular color, type style or size); and "ink" (all other marks). Each type has its own detailed requirements. These are set out in Sections 4 (typed drawings) and 5 (ink drawings), below.

3. The Heading

All drawings require a heading consisting of the following elements taken from your application, each on a separate line:

- Applicant's complete name
- Applicant's mailing address
- Date of first use of the mark (for actual use applications)
- Date of first use of the mark in commerce (for actual use applications)
- The goods or services the mark is (will be) used in connection with.

If your mark is a graphic design or symbol, a description of the essential features of the mark should be added as the last item of the heading. The idea is to depict and describe the mark in enough detail so it can be easily and accurately reproduced. Do your best; if the examiner thinks your description needs revision he or she will contact you.

If any of these items is very long, continue it on a continuation page (see Section C for how to prepare a continuation page), since no heading may extend below the top one quarter of the page (including the 1" margin at the top.)

There must also be at least one inch between the heading and the rest of the drawing.

Applicant: Linton & Company

Applicant Address: 123 Choice Rd., Twinsburg, OH 44087

Date of first use: June 25, 1991

Date of first use in commerce: June 29, 1991

Goods or services: Computerized sign design services

SIGN DESIGNS

1"

1"

4. Typed Drawings

If your mark is made of only words or numbers, and the color, type style and size are not integral factors, simply type (or print out) your mark in all capital letters in the center of the page. You must use all capital letters or your application will be returned.

SIGN DESIGNS

In addition to numbers and letters, the following, but no other, symbols may be used in a typed (printed out) drawing:

. ? " - ; (% $ @ +

, ! ' : /) & # * =

5. Ink Drawings

If your mark includes a graphic design or symbol, your drawing should be an accurate rendering, in ink. If you are not familiar with graphic arts or drafting, consider paying an artist to prepare your drawing. As you will see, there are many requirements the drawing must satisfy.

You must use flexible, smooth, nonshiny white paper. Bond paper may be used but no watermark may be obvious. Use India ink or something similar so the black lines are solid. Ballpoint and felt pens may not be used. No white-out or other correction fluids or tape may be used.

Again, the mark should be placed at least one inch below the heading and should not exceed 4" x 4".

External drawings (such as an artist's rendition) may be pasted to the drawing page, as long as they are flat and well attached.

SPECIAL CONSIDERATIONS FOR INTENT TO USE FILINGS

If you are uncertain about your final choice for a mark, it is possible to file applications for several marks, at $245 each. However, we recommend that you narrow your options to one or at most two marks. Also, if practical, you should settle on a spelling and type style (or design if the mark has graphics) before you file. If this is impractical, file the application using plain block letters and no logo. When you do settle on the final mark, you can file another application showing the mark in its final form (for an extra fee, of course).

EXAMPLE: Suppose Etta couldn't decide whether or not her mark *Quick-Bytes* should always be printed in her favorite color, green. She also thought she wanted to use a drawing of a computer terminal as her logo with the mark, but she wasn't sure. Unless she firmly decides, she should file her application without the logo, and without the green coloring of the mark. That way she can request protection for the most important part of her mark, the words *Quick-Bytes*. If she later decides the color or logo are so important they need federal trademark protection, she can file a new application. And of course there is nothing to stop her from displaying her mark in green against a background featuring a computer terminal in the meantime.

How to Find an Artist

You can find an artist by looking in the phone book of your metropolitan area under "Artists—Commercial." Ask whether they have experience doing trademark application drawings. Hiring a freelance commercial or graphic artist can be expensive; expect to pay from $40 to $80 per hour for the work (which usually takes an hour or less). You could also use a "starving artist" from an art school, but make sure she has the skills you need and that you give clear instructions (based on the information set out below).

 Later, in Section E5, we advise you to mail your application in a large enough envelope to include your drawing without folding it. Typed drawings may be folded if this is absolutely necessary, but the mark on the drawing may not be creased by the fold; the drawing will be rejected if it has crease marks. Ink drawings should never be folded and should be sent with protection (like cardboard) to prevent creasing.

6. Marks With Color as Element

The PTO wants you to identify the colors associated with your mark by following their graphic patterns system under which different patterns represent different colors. See the following examples of these graphic patterns and a sample drawing showing colors.

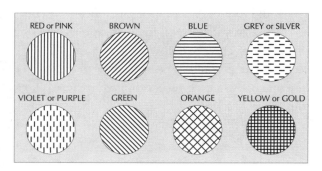

Don't use normal colors in the drawing, only the PTO-approved patterns.

7. Three-Dimensional Marks

If your mark is three-dimensional the drawing must show the mark in perspective in one view.

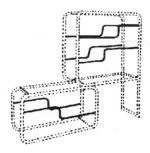

If the mark's position on the goods, or the placement of the label on a container, is an important element of the mark, this should be shown in the drawing. Do this by showing the mark with solid lines and the rest of the drawing with broken lines so the examiner can easily tell the mark from the product.

For example, some athletic goods companies place their marks consisting of stripes on their shoes in particular places. The stripes would be shown in solid lines and the shoe in broken lines.

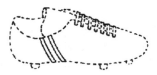

Again, consistency is essential. If your drawing shows one illustration of your mark, and you later use the mark with even a slightly different appearance, your application could be jeopardized. For all intents and purposes you will not be able to amend the drawing. When you start using the mark, make sure the use matches the drawing so the specimens you will eventually submit are consistent with the drawing.

E. Filing Your Application

Here are the steps for filing your trademark registration application and other documents with the PTO. If you haven't set up a good filing system for your trademark application, now is the time to do so. Use at least two manila folders—one for correspondence with the PTO and one for copies of the documents you submit—and, if necessary, an accordion folder.

1. File Promptly

Mail your application as soon as it's completed. If two or more applications for the same mark are received by the PTO, the one filed first will be examined (reviewed by the PTO) and published for opposition first. All conflicting applications will wait in line until the outcome of the first application is known. Also, if you are filing an intent to use application (and you follow up by putting the mark into actual use and getting it placed on the federal trademark register), your date of filing will be the date of first use of your mark, which may prove very important in the event of a later conflict. While it's impossible to say whether a particular filing date will make a difference in your particular situation, yours might be the one case in a thousand where a day's difference in filing date will mean that your rights are senior to another filer's.

If you plan to also register your mark abroad, you can use your U.S. filing date in most countries if you file your international application within six months of your U.S. filing date. (See Chapter 14, International Trademark Protection, Section A.)

2. Compute the Filing Fee

As of the date of this book, the filing fee for your registration application is $245, regardless of the basis for your filing—actual use or intent to use.

You may pay by check or money order made out to the Commissioner, Patent and Trademark Office. Don't send cash. It is always a good idea to call the trademark office (703-308-HELP or 703-557-4636 for the automated trademark information line) to check that the fee set out here is still valid.

3. Prepare a Self-Addressed Stamped Postcard With Your Mark on It

The PTO keeps track of all applications by assigning them serial numbers. Once your application is filed, all your communication with the PTO must include this serial number. The fastest way to be sure your application reached the PTO and to get your serial number is to include with your application a self-addressed, postage-paid postcard with your mark printed clearly on it. The PTO will stamp the card with your serial number and the date your application was received and return it to you. You should receive it within two weeks after you mailed the application. Keep the card in a safe place, as you may need to refer to your serial number frequently during the process.

4. Make Copies

Make photocopies of all the documents you will be sending to the PTO. These are:
- the main application form
- the drawing
- the check for the fees
- three specimens of use (for actual use applications)
- a self-addressed, stamped postcard
- the Express Mail mailing certificate (if you use this method to file your application—see Section 8, below).

Very often you will need to refer to these documents when corresponding with the PTO, as described below.

5. Assemble the Package

Use a large enough envelope to accommodate all your forms without folding them. This is especially crucial for the drawing. As stated, ink drawings can't be folded at all, and typed drawings should not be folded if the fold would put a crease through the drawing.

6. Check Your Application

To make sure you get the filing date you're entitled to, and to cut down on back and forth correspondence with the PTO, check to see that your application is complete. Specifically:

- Has the mark to be registered been entered at the top of the application?
- Has the class number or numbers been entered at the top of the application? (Leave blank if you are leaving this up to the PTO.)
- Has the applicant's name been entered?
- Has the applicant's mailing address been entered?
- Has the type of entity (the applicant's) been entered as well as the additional requested information?
- Have the goods and/or services been described?
- If you are submitting an "actual use" application. have you checked box 7a and entered the requested information?
- If you are submitting an intent-to-use application, have you checked box 7b and provided a brief description of how the mark will be used?
- If you are a foreign applicant, have you checked box 7c or box 7d as appropriate?
- Has the appropriate person signed the Declaration on the back of the application and, if necessary, described his position with the organization?
- Is the drawing appropriately placed on the drawing sheet? (4" by 4" if a graphic; type-

written or printed name marks in the middle of the page)
- For actual use applications, do the three specimens show the same mark as described in the application?
- Does at least one of the specimens reflect a product or service that is consistent with the description of goods and services on the application?
- Are the specimens consistent with what you described as the manner or mode of use of the mark? (If you said labels, do the specimens show labels?)
- Are there three specimens for each class applied for?

7. How to Address Your Trademark Application

Mark the outside of your envelope "Trademark Application."

For both actual use and intent-to-use applications, send it to this address:

Assistant Commissioner for Trademarks
Box New App/Fee
2900 Crystal Drive
Arlington, VA 22202-3513

⚠ If you send documents after your initial application, you'll use a different address. We provide these when we discuss the other documents you may be filing.

8. How to Mail Your Trademark Application

Applications sent by regular mail or private overnight postal services (such as UPS) are considered filed on the day they reach the PTO; those sent by United States Post Office Express Mail with an Express Mail certificate are considered filed on the date they are left with the Express Mail service.

We recommend sending the application via Express Mail (with Express Mail certificate) to get the earliest possible filing date. Send it Express Mail Post Office to Addressee.

⚠ Federal Express, UPS or other overnight mail services, and Express Mail sent via the "Post Office to Post Office" method are not sufficient to qualify as filed when sent. They are only considered filed when received by the PTO.

If you send the application by Express Mail, you must prepare an Express Mail Certificate to be signed by the person who handles the transaction with the post office or prepares the package for shipping. The Express Mail Certificate for Quick-Bytes would look like this:

Mark: Quick-Bytes

Serial No.:

Filing Date:

Applicant: Etta Linton

Paper Being Filed: Trademark Application

Express Mail label No.: 77770

Date of Deposit: January 25, 1992

I hereby certify that this paper and fee is being deposited with the United States Postal Service "Express Mail Post Office to Addressee" service under 37 CFR 1.10 on the date shown above and is addressed to the Assistant Commissioner for Trademarks, Box New App/Fee, 2900 Crystal Dr., Arlington, VA 22202-3513.

Etta Linton (typed or printed)

Etta Linton (signature)

Include the certificate with the rest of the application.

9. Receiving the PTO Filing Receipt

About six to eight weeks after mailing your application, you should receive the PTO's filing receipt. The current form is an 8-½" X 11" white form titled "Filing Receipt for Trademark Application."

The filing receipt includes your application serial number, the date of filing, the mark, the applicant's name and address and other information. The information on the receipt should be checked carefully. If there is a mistake, you should send a correcting letter to the PTO immediately. See Section F below on corresponding with the PTO.

The PTO filing receipt will explain that you should not expect to hear anything about your application for approximately three months. If you have not heard anything in three and a half months, it is wise to call and inquire as to the status of your application. There are two ways to do this:

- TRAM automated system: TRAM stands for trademark reporting and monitoring. From any touch-tone phone, Monday through Friday from 6:30 a.m. to midnight, eastern time, dial 703-305-8747. After the welcome message and tone, enter your mark's eight-digit serial number and the pound symbol. You should immediately hear the computer give you the current status of your mark along with the effective date of the status.
- If you want additional information or would prefer talking with a human, call the Trademark Assistance Center at 703-308-9400 and request a status check.

F. Communicating With the PTO

The chances are great that you will be communicating with the PTO. Few applications sail through completely unscathed.

You are required to be diligent in pursuing your application. If you are expecting some action from the PTO (the ball is in their court) and more than six months have elapsed without your hearing from them, immediately call the PTO Status Line (the TRAM Automated System, described in Section E9 above). If you discover a problem, bring it to the PTO's attention. If your application has been rejected as abandoned due to the problem, you may petition the PTO Commissioner within 60 days to reactivate your application.

1. Form of Communication

After your application is filed, all correspondence with the PTO must include your application's serial number, the date of filing, applicant name and your mark (an actual depiction or a description). If you are responding to an action letter (as described below), also include the mailing date of the action letter, your telephone number and zip code and the PTO examining attorney's name and office number. Always keep copies of your correspondence; if the examiner calls, you will be in a better position to discuss the letter if you are looking at a copy.

If you are corresponding about an ITU application, the letter should be addressed BOX ITU. If you are corresponding about an actual use application, and no fee is involved, the letter should be addressed to Box 5.

For example, letters sent to change information on the filing receipt, as described earlier, should look something like this for an actual use application:

Assistant Commissioner for Trademarks
Attn: OATPA DATA BASE MAINTENANCE STAFF
Box 5
Washington, D.C. 20231
Serial No. 73/123456
Date of Filing: 3/25/73
Applicant: Don Re
Mark: Remarkable

To Whom This May Concern:

Please change the file in this application to reflect my correct mailing address of 9595 Virginia Way, Tulare, California 93274.

Also, please correct the spelling of my last name from Rey to Re.

Feel free to contact me if you have any questions.

Sincerely,
Don Re
Don Re   Phone: 209-555-5555

---

2. Responding to Action Letters

A letter telling you what is wrong with your application is called an action letter, or sometimes, an office action. First, note on it the date you received it, which will probably be a few days after it was sent. The top of the first page shows the mailing date of the action letter and information necessary to identify your application. The remainder of the letter will probably be form paragraphs. Read them carefully.

In order to analyze the action letter and determine the appropriate response, you'll probably need to look at a copy of your application. Most deficiencies are minor, and even if there are several, they can probably be cleared up with one phone call and one letter.

Keep in mind that PTO examiners are people. If you do not understand what they want, call the phone number listed in the action letter and talk with the examiner. They are generally helpful—they prefer to be called by their first name—and will usually cooperate to see that your application succeeds. For example, if they want you to prepare a document, such as your declaration under penalty of perjury that the mark was in use as of the date your application was signed, they will send you a sample.

⚠ Use Express Mail if a Deadline Is Near

When you are responding to a PTO action letter, you will be given a deadline within which to respond, usually six months. Your application will not proceed until you respond, so it is best to do so immediately. If there is any chance that your response may be received after the deadline, send it by U.S. Postal Service Express Mail with Express Mail certificate, as described earlier. You should have the serial number and filing date of the application by then, so that information should be included in the Express Mail certificate.

3. There Is Room for Negotiation

If the examiner wants you to change your application, such as claiming a different description of services or goods, there is usually some room for negotiation. (See sidebar about phone calls to the PTO.)

> **EXAMPLE:** Suppose Frieda claimed her mark was used in connection with buying services for nonprofit institutions and organizations, and submitted specimens showing advertisements of food products aimed at schools.

That description would be found to be too indefinite, and the examiner might suggest "buying services for nonprofit organizations and institutions in the field of food products." If Frieda's services extended beyond food products to include items such as medical and automotive supplies, she probably wouldn't want to agree to the examiner's suggestion. However, after talking with the examiner she should be able to arrive at a description inclusive enough for her, yet definite enough for the examiner. In this instance, perhaps, this would be "buying services for nonprofit institutions and organizations in the fields of food products, medical supplies and automotive parts."

DOCUMENT YOUR PHONE CALLS TO THE PTO

When you call the PTO, keep notes of the date and time of your call, and names of everyone you speak with. Not only are most people easier to talk to if you call them by name, you may need to talk with that person again, or to remind them of an agreement you made about how to prepare or change your application. Keeping notes of your conversations is especially important when you call the examiner and discuss changes she has suggested in your application. To maximize your chances of understanding and being understood, before the call ends, repeat your understanding of any agreements reached. If the agreement is about something significant, you may wish to confirm the agreement in writing, including the date of your call.

4. Examiner's Amendments

If the examiner has a brief question she might call you, and then issue and mail you an examiner's amendment. This is a form on which the examiner records in handwriting a phone conversation or meeting with the applicant. Read the amendment carefully to make sure it matches your understanding of the conversation. If you disagree, or don't understand the amendment, first call the examiner, and then, if necessary, write her a letter with your concerns, explaining your point of view on the communication.

One common example of an examiner's amendment is when you use words as part of your mark that don't qualify for registration. The examiner will ask you to formally disclaim those words. Then, although the mark will be registered in its entirety, you will only have the exclusive right to use the portion not disclaimed.

> **EXAMPLE:** The Exotic Perfume Company manufactures a line of fragrances named for various wildflowers. One of these is called California Snapdragon. If Exotic wants to register this mark, it will have to disclaim the "California" part of it, since California is a geographic term and thus not registrable. If Exotic refuses to disclaim "California," the Patent and Trademark Office will probably refuse registration. If disclaimer is made, however, the entire mark can be registered. But, only the "snapdragon" portion will qualify for protection, and only in relation to perfume or related goods. Then, if a competing fragrance company comes out with California Wild Rose fragrance, there will be no infringement. On the other hand, if the competitor produces Oregon Snapdragon fragrance, it is likely that a court will find infringement.

G. Amending the Application

You may wish to amend your application. The most common reasons for amendments are:

- to correct a mistake the applicant didn't notice until after the application was mailed
- to comply with the examiner's request that different words be used.

1. Correcting Mistakes

Correction are easier to make early in the process, so act right away if you notice an error.

Typical amendments to correct errors might include any of the following:

- **Correction of the applicant's name:** for instance, including "Inc." at the end of a company name, or fixing a misspelling. However, you cannot completely replace a name under the guise of correcting it.

  > **EXAMPLE:** "Please amend the applicant name to spell it correctly and fully; change it from 'Quick-Bite' to 'Quick-Byte, Inc.'"

- **Correction of identification of goods or services:**

  > **EXAMPLE:** "Please amend the identification of goods from 'couches and hairs' to 'couches and chairs.'"

  Generally you may not amend the application to add goods or services. In this situation, you must file a new application. However, you may correct your descriptive language as long as it is for the purpose of making it more specific rather than for adding additional items.

- **Correction of date(s) of first use (for Actual Use applications):** Take special care when correcting a date related to use, as you must be certain the mark, as shown on the specimens submitted with the applications, was in use in commerce before the application was filed. If it wasn't, you may be forced to start all over.

> **EXAMPLE:** Suppose Etta first used the mark *Quik-Bite* for her computer consulting service, but soon stopped using it and changed her mark to *Quick-Bytes*. If she filed an actual use application after she made the decision to change the mark, but before the changed mark was actually in use, the application would be premature. She could not truthfully claim the mark *Quick-Bytes* was in use before the application was filed. She will probably have to file a new application, since the application was filed before the new mark was in use.

To submit corrected information for the application, you must file a document called an Amendment to Application. The amendment must use the heading described in Section F1, above. Below the heading, put the words "Amendment to Application." For information about correcting the application to satisfy the examiner, see Section F, above.

H. If the Examiner Issues a Rejection Letter

An examiner may write three kinds of action letters that constitute trademark application rejections:

- Formal rejections: Usually involve minor matters that can be corrected by amendment as described earlier
- Substantive rejections: Responding to these takes more effort and may well require the help of a trademark lawyer
- "Final" rejections: These are usually written only after you have been given at least one chance to respond to a formal or substantive rejection.

Rejections always specify how much time you have to respond (usually six months). If your response is not received within the time specified, you risk having your application deemed abandoned, so always send the response as early as possible.

1. Formal Rejections

If you followed the instructions earlier in this chapter you probably will not receive a formal rejection, since these are normally based on omissions from your application, such as no drawing or an inadequate specimen. If you do receive a formal objection, however, feel free to call the examiner to make sure you understand what is being requested. You should respond to the rejection in writing, using the same heading as described in Section F1, above. Often a simple amendment (of the description of goods/services, for example) is all that's needed.

2. Substantive Rejections

Substantive rejections tend to be based on the legal requirements for trademark registration, as opposed to the formal requirements for the application itself. They often fall in the following categories:

a. Confusion Rejection

This is the rejection you will receive if the examiner thinks there is a likelihood that consumers will be confused between your mark and a previously registered mark. A copy of the registration certificate for the other mark will be enclosed for your reference.

There are many possible responses to a confusion rejection:

- You could respond to the PTO by mail, explaining why you don't think your mark would create the likelihood of customer confusion. (See Chapter 4, How to Tell If Two Marks Are Confusingly Similar.)
- You could call the owner of the other mark and see if they object to registration of your mark. Considering how fast the marketplace changes, there is always a chance that the owner is no longer using the potentially confusing mark.

b. Descriptive Rejection

This is the rejection an examiner sends if she thinks your mark cannot be registered because it is too descriptive, or because it misdescribes either the goods/services, or their geographic source, or because the mark is primarily a surname. As explained in Section A2, these types of marks may not be registered on the Principal Trademark Register—the one that provides important protection for your mark. If you receive this type of rejection, review the material in Chapter 10, Evaluating Trademark Strength, to try to decide whether the rejection is appropriate.

Occasionally a descriptive rejection can be handled by claiming that the mark has become distinctive under the secondary meaning rule—that is, taken on a meaning of its own in the context of your goods or services. For example, usually the word ivory means a color or animal tusk. However to many people, in the context of soap it has a secondary meaning and identifies a specific product.

To claim distinctiveness under the secondary meaning rule, you usually have to prove you have continuously and exclusively used the mark for five years (before the application was filed), and offer various facts showing that consumers know the mark refers to your goods or services. This kind of showing is complex and you will need the help of a trademark lawyer if you decide to claim secondary meaning as a basis for registration. (See Chapter 15, Section B.)

If this argument doesn't work, you should ask if the examiner will let you amend your publication to apply to the Supplemental Register. See sidebar at the beginning of this chapter, for more about the Supplemental Register.

c. Responding to a Substantive Rejection

Even if you believe the examiner's rejection of your application is wrong, unless you have plenty of money and care a great deal about registering that particular mark, you will probably want to pick another mark. The chances are you can spend thousands of dollars in legal fees responding to a rejection and still not get your mark registered.

If you decide to tough it out and try to get your mark registered, you must respond to the rejection. Consult with a trademark lawyer (see Chapter 15) about how to do this. If you decide to write the response yourself, *Trademark Registration Practice*, by James Hawes (Clark Boardman Callaghan), available in many law libraries, should prove helpful. Chapter 6 of that book discusses confusion rejections and Chapter 7 covers descriptive rejections.

3. If You Receive a "Final" Rejection

A "final" rejection will not arrive until after you have received, and, we hope, responded to, at least one substantive rejection. Your options once the final rejection is received are several. You can:

• write again and ask the examiner to reconsider your application and previous responses

• talk with the examiner by phone or in person to get a better idea of what, if anything, can be done to fix the application

• file an appeal (if the grounds for rejection are appealable) asking the Trademark Trial and Appeal Board to consider your application. (Any substantive dispute is appealable. This includes any judgment made by the examiner (such as when he feels your mark is confusingly similar to another mark, or believes you should disclaim one or more words). Procedural deficiencies, such as your inability to produce an acceptable specimen, are not appealable.)

• file a petition asking the Commissioner of Patents and Trademarks to consider your application (if the grounds for rejection are not appealable)

• request suspension of the application (if allowed this could give you more time to prepare a response or request for reconsideration)

• file an amendment asking for registration on the Supplemental rather than the Principal Register (described earlier)

• abandon (give up) the application.

By the time your application has received a final rejection, the examiner's boss has reviewed the whole file and approved the rejection. It is therefore very unlikely that you will obtain registration after receiving a final rejection.

A discussion of trademark appeals and appealable grounds is beyond the scope of this book. (See Chapter 15, Help Beyond the Book.)

Supplemental Register Note

If the reason your mark was rejected was that it was considered too descriptive, it may qualify for the Federal Supplemental Register. Ask the trademark examiner for details about amending your application, and see Chapter 15 if you need more instructions or help from an attorney.

I. Publication and Opposition

If all goes well, the examiner will "allow" your application and approve the mark for publication in the PTO's Official Gazette. You should receive a notice saying your mark has been approved for publication and will be published on a certain date. The purpose of publication is to allow others an opportunity to tell the PTO that they oppose registration of your mark. Opposers have 30 days to file their oppositions with the PTO. If a potential opposer requests more time in which to decide whether to oppose the mark, the PTO will usually give them another 30 days.

A typical opposer would be a large company that pays a lawyer or trademark monitoring service to review the Official Gazette and bring to their attention any marks that potentially conflict with marks used by the company. Of course, the examiner would have had to determine before approving your mark for publication that there

were no federally registered potentially conflicting marks. Therefore any opposition will probably be based on either an unregistered mark (on the basis of the mark's prior use) or on a registered mark that the examiner did not initially believe was conflicting.

Oppositions are filed against only 3 percent of the published marks. Most likely your mark will be published unopposed and then be approved for registration. For this reason, we do not deal with how to respond to an opposition. But if an opposition is filed, carefully weigh the benefits of sticking with your mark against the high cost of fighting the opposition (usually tens of thousands of dollars). A consultation with a trademark lawyer will help you sort these factors out. (See Chapter 15.)

YOUR MARK IS STILL CHALLENGEABLE IN COURT EVEN IF NO OPPOSITION IS FILED

Even if your mark is published without opposition, someone else might always accuse you later of interfering with (infringing upon) their mark—registered or unregistered—and sue you in court. If that occurs, the fact that no opposition to your mark was filed with the PTO will not strengthen your legal position in the lawsuit. However, if your mark remains on the federal register for five years without challenge and you file the proper form with the PTO, your mark can be made "incontestable," which greatly strengthens it against a later challenge based on infringement. (See Chapter 9.)

J. Receiving Your Certificate of Registration

If your application was based on an intent-to-use the mark, skip this section and go to Section K.

After your mark is published and the time for opposition has expired, your mark will be registered and the certificate will be sent to you—if your application was based on actual use. Depending on the backlog of paperwork at the PTO, it can take as long as three months from the expiration of the opposition date for you to receive the certificate. If you want to know the status of your application before the certificate is received, refer to Section E9, above, where we explain how to keep track of your application (the TRAM system).

CERTIFICATE OF REGISTRATION ON PRINCIPAL REGISTER

The Certificate of Registration reproduces the mark and sets out the date of first use in commerce. In addition, it indicates the particular product or service on which the mark is used, the number and date of registration, the term of registration, the date on which the application for registration was received at the Patent and Trademark Office and any conditions and limitations that may be imposed on the registration, such as disclaimed words.

While you are entitled to hearty congratulations upon receiving your Certificate of Registration, your efforts will be for naught if you forget to file with the PTO some additional paperwork known as a Sections 8/15 Affidavit (which tells the PTO that you are still using the mark). Because this extra paperwork must be filed between the fifth and sixth year after your original registration date, it's easy to let the deadline slip by, especially because the PTO doesn't remind you and very few people have calendars that last beyond the current year. See Chapter 9, Section C for instructions on how to complete the Sections 8/15 Affidavit and some suggestions for a tickler system.

K. Follow-Up Activity Required for ITU Applications

 If you are filing an "actual use" application, skip this section.

An ITU application involves more steps than an actual use application. This is because to complete your registration and own the mark, you must actually get it into use in commerce, tell the PTO about it and pay an additional fee.

To actually get your mark registered, you will use a form called Allegation of Use for Intent-To-Use Application. This form may be filed at any time prior to the date the PTO authorizes the publication of your proposed mark, and any time after the PTO issues a Notice of Allowance. It may not be filed between those two dates.

This form (a copy is in the Appendix) requests some information already set out in your original ITU application as well as some new information. Here we provide instructions for filling in the form in the order in which the blanks appear.

If you are filing the Allegation of Use after the PTO has issued a Notice of Allowance on your intent-to-use application, examine the Notice of Allowance carefully. If there are any mistakes, such as wrong spelling of the mark or wrong date of first use, notify the PTO immediately by phone or letter and request a corrected Notice of Allowance.

a. Identify the Mark

Fill in the mark shown on your ITU application. Use the identical wording.

b. Serial Number

If you followed our recommendation in Section E of this chapter, you got this number when you received your postage-paid postcard back from the PTO a week or two after your application was filed. Otherwise, the serial number should be on the filing receipt you received several weeks after sending out your application.

c. Applicant Name

Put in this blank the exact name that appears in your ITU application.

d. Description of Goods or Services

Check box a if your mark is being used in connection with all of the same product(s) and/or service(s) shown in your original application or on the Notice of Allowance received from the PTO, **Check box b** if you end up using the mark on some but not all of the goods or services identified in your original intent-to-use application and then describe the goods or services that the mark is not being used on.

> **EXAMPLE:** When Etta prepared her ITU application she expected to market computer consulting services and computer programs under the mark *Quick-Bytes* and listed those goods and services in her application. However it took her a year, and more money than she expected, to get her consulting business off the ground. She decides to build that business and delay putting any effort into writing and marketing software. She uses this form to delete the computer programs from her application.

If you are unsure of how to complete this blank, call the PTO and ask an examiner for assistance. As usual, keep records of the examiner's name and what is said. At the worst, the examiner who is reviewing this document will contact you and ask you to fix the goods/services statement at that time.

MR PEANUT
®

e. Date of First Use of Mark in Commerce

First read Section A1. Then fill in the date you first used the mark in commerce.

f. Type of Commerce

Enter the type of commerce (interstate, territorial or international).

g. Date of First Use of Mark Anywhere

First read Section B4. Then fill in the blank with the date you first used the mark anywhere.

⚠️ If you are alleging use for more than one good or service, you need only put the dates of first use and first use in commerce for any one of them (identify the good or service that the date of use pertains to). Remember, however, that you must be using—in commerce—all of the goods or services that you listed earlier unless you described them after checking box b.

h. Specify Manner or Mode of Use of Mark

First read Section B5. Then fill in the requested information.

i. Declaration

First read Section C9. Then date the form, sign it and provide your telephone number and printed name and position.

j. Request to Divide

Check the Request to Divide box if you wish to "divide" your ITU application into two applications. This only applies if:

- your original application designated your mark to apply to more than one good or service
- you have used the mark in connection with one or some, but not all of all those goods or services; and
- you still intend to use the mark in connection with one or more additional good(s) and service(s).

In that event, you should consider dividing your application so that one application now claims usage for one or more of the goods or services while the other application remains on an intent to use (ITU) status in respect to the other goods or services.

EXAMPLE: Suppose Etta's ITU application claimed she was going to use *Quick-Bytes* in connection with computer consulting services and computer programs. If she began offering services two months after her application was filed, she may want to amend her application to claim use of *Quick-Bytes* in connection with the services. When she divides the application she will then have two applications: one, in which use has been alleged, for use of the mark for her services; and one in which she plans to use the mark for computer programs in the future.

The benefit of dividing an application, rather than waiting until the mark is in use for all goods or services originally contemplated, is that the mark in use can be placed on the federal register more quickly.

The downside of dividing the application is that additional paperwork is involved (another Allegation of Use), and you will have to pay an additional $100 filing fee each time you claim usage under an additional classification. If money is scarce, or you soon expect to have the mark in use with all the goods or services you claimed, it's probably best to not divide your application. Just wait until you are using the mark in all the ways you intend and then file one Allegation of Use.

If you do decide to divide your application, we provide a form to be used for this purpose (in the Appendix). However, we recommend that you not file it with the PTO until your work is reviewed by a trademark attorney.

⚠️ Even if you are filing a Request to Divide, you must respond to any office actions on time, or risk giving up your application.

Other Materials to Submit:

- **Specimens:** You must submit three specimens of your use. Read Section B5 for what makes acceptable specimens.

💡 **Consistency Note**
Remember to make your specimens consistent with your description of the goods or services, the manner and mode of the mark's use and the description of your mark.

- **Fees:** A filing fee ($100 for each class) must be submitted with your Allegation of Use.

Filing Your Allegation of Use

See Section F regarding mailing information to the PTO. Your Allegation of Use and fees should be mailed to this address:

Assistant Commissioner For Trademarks
BOX AAU/SOU
2900 Crystal Drive
Arlington, Virginia 22202-3513

⚠️ Once publication of your intent-to-use mark is authorized, you cannot file this form until the PTO issues a Notice of Allowance (assuming no opposition has been filed). Then you can use the Allegation of Use to notify the PTO of the mark's use and get it placed on the federal trademark register.

⚠️ Once you receive a correct Notice of Allowance, you have six months to either prove your mark has been used in commerce—by filing a Statement of Use—or to purchase an extension. (See sidebar.)

REQUEST AN EXTENSION

You may buy another six months to file your Statement of Use by sending in a request for extension and paying a $100 fee. However, your request must be filed before the six-month period has elapsed. If you wait until near the end of the six-month period before filing your statement of use, and the statement is ultimately rejected by the PTO (which occasionally happens), the six-month period for filing an extension will have expired and your basic application will fail. See Section 1, below, for more detail on requesting an extension.

1. Getting a Six-Month Extension to File Your Statement of Use

As long as you still intend to use your mark on at least one of the goods or services mentioned in your application, and are willing to pay $100 per class as a filing fee, you can request an extension and get an extra six months before you have to file your Statement of Use. As stated earlier, the request must be filed before your six months run out.

You can request six-month extensions up to five times, as long as each is filed before the last extension runs out. However, after the first request (for which no reason need be given), you must convince the PTO that there is a good reason why your mark hasn't been used yet, as explained below. No extension of time will be granted beyond 36 months after the Notice of Allowance was issued.

⚠️ Some may be tempted to not seek these extensions but to abandon the application and file a new application when the mark is finally put into use in commerce. While this may save you money, it will lose you the date of first use (your original filing date) that you will be able to claim if you get your mark into actual use within the 36-month period.

The PTO form—Request for Extension of Time in Which to File Statement of Use with Declaration—is in the Appendix. Here we will discuss each blank in that form.

a. Mark

The mark in this block should be exactly the same as the one in your original application.

b. Serial Number

This is the number the PTO stamped on your self-addressed postcard when your application was filed. It also appears on your filing receipt and Notice of Allowance.

c. Applicant Name

Fill in this block exactly as you did for your original application.

d. Notice of Allowance Mailing Date

Get this date from your Notice of Allowance.

e. Request to Divide

This only applies to original applications that listed more than one good or service. If your mark has been used with one but not all of the products and/or services listed in your application, see Section KJ, above, about dividing your application.

f. Continued Bona Fide Intention to Use

If you still intend to use the mark in connection with the same goods and/or services described in your application, check the first box.

If you decide to limit use of your mark to, for example, only two of three products, check the second box. Then list any products or services you want deleted from your application.

In the blank provided, indicate whether it is your first, second, third, fourth or fifth request for an extension. (As mentioned, no extension of time will be granted beyond 36 months after the Notice of Allowance was issued.)

If it is your first request, leave the next two boxes blank. If it is your 2nd, 3rd, 4th or 5th request, you must check one of the next two boxes. Check the first one if you still have not used the mark in commerce. Then explain what you have done to get ready to use the mark in commerce. Your explanation need not be lengthy; a sentence or two will do. Some possible explanations include the following:

- the need for more research or development of your product or service
- the need for more research about your market, including where and how to sell the product or service
- a delay in efforts to arrange for product manufacturing
- the need for more time to develop advertising or promotional activities
- attempts to get government approval are still in progress
- attempts to set up marketing networks are still in progress
- any other reasonable explanation for why you haven't done any of the above. (For instance, a prolonged illness or destruction of vital records of your factory due to fire or other disaster.)

The last box applies if you have used the mark in commerce and are submitting your Statement of Use toward the end of the six-month period.

Finally, the declaration is the same as the one you signed in your application.

See Section F, above, for information about how to mail your extension application and filing fee. You should send your extension request to this address:

Assistant Commissioner For Trademarks
BOX ITU
2900 Crystal Drive
Arlington, Virginia 22202-3513

2. Receiving Your Certificate of Registration

Once you put your mark into use, file the Allegation of Use and pay the additional fees, your mark will be registered as indicated in the Notice of Allowance, and you will receive a Certificate of Registration. If you want to know the status of your application before the certificate is received, refer to Section E9, above, where we explain how to keep track of your application (the TRAM system).

CERTIFICATE OF REGISTRATION ON PRINCIPAL REGISTER

The Certificate of Registration reproduces the mark and sets out the date of first use in commerce. In addition, it indicates the particular product or service on which the mark is used, the number and date of registration, the term of registration, the date on which the application for registration was received at the Patent and Trademark Office and any conditions and limitations that may be imposed on the registration, such as disclaimed words.

While you are entitled to hearty congratulations upon receiving your Certificate of Registration, your efforts will be for naught if you forget to file with the PTO some additional paperwork known as a Sections 8/15 Affidavit (which tells the PTO that you are still using the mark). Because this extra paperwork must be filed between the fifth and sixth year after your original registration date, it's easy to let the deadline slip by, especially because the PTO doesn't remind you and very few people have calendars that last beyond the current year. See Chapter 9, Section C for instructions on how to complete the Sections 8/15 Affidavit and some suggestions for a tickler system. ∎

How to Use and Care for Your Mark

ere we assume that (1) you have chosen and begun to use a mark not already used by others and (2) that those who are entitled to do so have placed their mark on the federal trademark register. Is that the end of the story? No. Ownership of the mark can be lost if you don't use the mark correctly. And your registration may lapse if you fail to take certain required follow-up steps.   This chapter identifies the major pitfalls that owners of marks—registered or nonregistered—can encounter, and suggests some easy steps for keeping your mark strong against all potential copiers.

A. Use of the Trademark Registration ® Symbol

If your mark is federally registered—on either the principal or supplemental register you have the right to use the symbol ® with your mark and should begin doing so immediately. If your mark is not on either of the federal trademark registers, you may not use the ® symbol.

The ® symbol, which lets others know that the mark is federally registered, is usually printed in a very tiny type, to the right of the mark. By placing the ® next to your mark, you improve your chances of collecting damages or defendant's profits if it is ever necessary to take an infringer to court. However, you won't lose ownership of the mark by omitting this notice.

EXAMPLE: While searching for a name for his new word processing program, Phil Programmer sees an advertisement in a trade magazine for a new program called *Sorcerer's Apprentice* that allows the user to construct databases for hobby collections. No "notice of registration" is displayed in the advertisement, so Phil foolishly decides the mark is probably not registered and proceeds to use it as a trademark for his program. The work is in fact registered. While the owners of the mark *Sorcerer's Apprentice* could sue Phil for infringement because the goods are so closely related (they're both software) and can probably force him to stop using the mark, they might have trouble collecting the damages allowed for willful infringement (triple damages, the defendant's profits and possibly attorneys' fees) because they didn't use the ®.

It is enough that the symbol appears at least once on each label, tag or advertisement. You don't need to use the symbol on every occurrence of your mark. Incidentally, instead of using the ® symbol, you may state that "[Your Mark] is a registered trademark of [Your Name]." This has the same legal effect as the ® symbol, but takes up much more space.

Be sure to specify how you want the symbol used when hiring advertising services or printers; it is your responsibility to make sure the world knows your mark is registered.

USE OF ® IF YOUR FEDERAL REGISTRATION IS CANCELED

Federal trademark registrations are canceled by the PTO if the registrants fail to file certain required follow-up documents after the initial registration (see Section C below). Because the PTO doesn't notify the registrant of this cancellation action, it is easy to inadvertently continue using the ® on a mark that is no longer technically registered. Obviously the easiest way to prevent this from happening is to meet the follow-up requirements. But if you slip up—and many do—use your best efforts to stop using the ® unless and until you re-register the mark.

B. Use of the tm or sm symbol for unregistered trademarks

You may use tm (for trademarks) or sm (for service marks) next to an unregistered mark to show that you claim ownership of the mark and intend to assert your rights against copiers. While using the tm or sm symbol provides no statutory legal benefits, in practice it reminds would-be copiers that the name or other device is already being claimed as a mark and in most instances will cause them to stay away from it. As with the ® symbol you want to limit your use of the tm or sm symbol. Nothing can be more distracting than seeing the same word appear over and over again on a page with a little ® or tm mark appearing next to it every time. The main idea about using these symbols is to make sure you get the message across once, or if there are many pages, at least once on every page. There is no rule for how often the symbol should be used; common sense should do fine.

C. File Your Sections 8 and 15 Affidavit

Mark owners who are not federally registering their marks should skip this section and Section D, but read Sections E, F and G, as they contain general principles that apply to all mark owners.

Between the fifth and sixth year after federally registering your mark, you should complete and file with the PTO an important form called the "Sections 8 and 15 Affidavit." By filing this single document, you'll protect your mark in two extremely important ways. The Sections 8 and 15 Affidavit officially advises the PTO that:

- your mark is still in use and that your registration should continue in force, and
- your mark has been in continuous use from the date of registration and therefore deserves extra protection against potential challengers. In PTO jargon, you're requesting "incontestability status" for your mark.

1. How to Qualify for a Sections 8 and 15 Affidavit

You'll need to briefly evaluate the use of your mark to make sure you're eligible to file the important Sections 8 and 15 Affidavit. Here's how.

a. Can You File on Time?

The form must be signed and filed with the PTO between the fifth and sixth years of registration. Your timing is crucial because there are no extensions. For that reason, it should be filed well before the six-year deadline. That way you'll have time to clear up questions or provide the PTO with more information, if needed.

EXAMPLE: If your mark was registered on May 15, 1995, you must sign and file your

Sections 8 and 15 Affidavit between May 15, 2000, and May 14, 2001. It would be best to file it in June or July of 2000 so there is plenty of time to make corrections.

⚠ Failure to file the Sections 8 and 15 Affidavit on time will result in your federal registration being canceled. This means you will have to re-register if you still want the benefit of federal registration. It also means that you will not be able to obtain incontestable status for the mark until an additional five years has passed from your re-registration date. Clearly, it is in your interest to make sure this document is filed on time.

b. Is Your Mark Still in Use?

You must still be using your mark in the manner described in your registration certificate; otherwise your registration for the mark will be canceled. This means that you must still be using it, at a minimum, on the same products or services and in the same way (on packaging, or pamphlets, etc.) as you originally stated, and be able to come up with samples of this continued use.

c. Has Your Mark Been in Continuous Use for Five Years?

As mentioned, you'll qualify for incontestable status if your mark is in continuous use for five years after being placed on the Principal Register. More specifically, your mark can become "incontestable" if all of the following apply:

- Your mark was placed on the Principal Register at least five years ago and you have used the mark continuously—without a lapse—since that registration date in the same manner and on the same goods or services for which it was originally registered. (If you are using the mark for some of those original goods or services but not

for others, it may become incontestable for the goods and services you are still using.)
- No court has rendered a final decision (that is, one that is not on appeal) that affects your ownership claim since the date of registration.
- No court or PTO challenge to your ownership claim is pending.
- You file the Sections 8 and 15 Affidavit on time (see Section C1a, above).
- The mark is not and has not become generic.

Incontestability status makes it more difficult—but not impossible—for anyone to challenge the validity of your mark. The result is that it will be easier for you to protect your mark from infringement. Even though an incontestable mark can still be challenged on a number of grounds (see sidebar), it is safe from attack on the basis that it lacks distinctiveness. This is a key benefit—once a mark is considered distinctive beyond argument, it gets very strong protection.

> **EXAMPLE:** *Park 'N Fly, Inc.,* sued *Dollar Park and Fly, Inc.,* for trademark infringement. *Dollar Park and Fly* defended on the ground that the *Park 'N Fly* mark was too weak to deserve protection. But the U.S. Supreme Court ruled that the *Park 'N Fly* mark had obtained incontestability status and couldn't be challenged on that ground.

Of course, even after the mark attains incontestability status, if you stop using it for a sufficiently long time, the mark may be deemed abandoned and dropped from the federal register. (See Section E, below, on what constitutes abandoning your mark.)

> **EXAMPLE:** In 1996, Frank Brown invents an inexpensive but highly accurate blood pressure testing kit and starts distributing it under the trademark *F/B Stresstest.* After five years have passed, in 2001, the mark will be en-

titled to incontestable status if Frank has kept the mark in continuous use for this five-year period. But if he then stops using it for two years or more, he'll not only possibly give up the incontestable status but may abandon his federal registration altogether.

"INCONTESTABLE" REALLY MEANS "HARDER TO CONTEST"

Paradoxically, you can contest an incontestable trademark in quite a few ways. The up-shot is that "incontestable" really means "harder to contest."

You can challenge a mark that is incontestable on any of the following grounds:

- the registration or its incontestability was obtained fraudulently
- the mark has been abandoned by the registrant
- the mark is being used to misrepresent the source of the goods or services with which it is being used (for instance, use of the mark involves the unfair trade practice known as palming off)
- the infringing mark is an individual's name being used in his own business (that is, a trade name and so not registrable)
- the use of the infringing mark is prohibited or reserved under the Lanham Act
- the infringing mark was used in interstate commerce before the incontestable mark, and before its registration
- the infringing mark was registered before the incontestable mark, or
- the mark is being used to violate the antitrust laws of the United States. (37 USC Sec. 1115(b).)

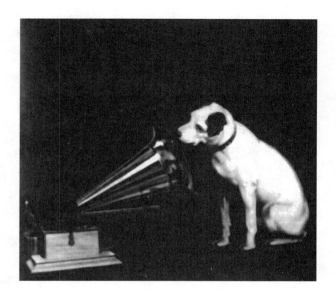

2. How to Complete the Sections 8 and 15 Affidavit

The form for filing a Sections 8 and 15 Affidavit is in the Appendix. The official form name is "Combined 'Affidavit' of Use and Incontestability of a Mark Under Sections 8 and 15, With Declaration." Additional forms may be obtained from the Patent and Trademark Office if needed. (See Chapter 8, Section F, for how to communicate with the PTO.)

a. Mark

Enter the mark exactly as it appears on your trademark registration certificate. If you don't have a copy of your registration, request one from the PTO in plenty of time before it is due.

b. Registration Number

Enter the registration number which also appears on your trademark registration certificate.

c. Registration Date

Enter the registration date for your mark. This will appear on the Certificate of Registration you received from the PTO—usually several months after the mark was published for opposition.

d. Name of Registrant

If you are the current owner of the mark, your name goes here. If you own the mark with another person, both your names go in this blank. If the mark is owned by a corporation, partnership or other business entity, the entity's name goes here. If the names here are not the same as those entered in the registration, use an attachment page to explain why (for instance, ownership changed by assignment or sale of a business). (See Chapter 8, Federal Trademark Registration, Section C4, for more details about how company names must be stated in full.)

e. Registrant's Current Mailing Address

Enter the mailing address for the registrant. If there are more than two registrants, enter the address of the registrant who will be handling communication with the PTO if any is needed.

f. Registration Number

Enter the registration number again.

g. Type of Commerce

Enter the type of commerce the mark has been used in during the previous five years. This will be interstate, territorial, foreign or a combination. If you have any questions about this, or how to describe the type of commerce, see Chapter 8, Federal Trademark Registration, Section A1. The back of the form also gives some suggestions about how to describe the type of commerce.

h. Identify Goods and/or Services

If you are still using the mark on all the goods and services identified on your certificate of registration, enter N.A. in this blank. If there are some goods and services that were listed but which are no longer carrying the registered mark, describe those goods and services here.

i. Specimen

"Specimen" is the word the PTO uses for a sample showing how your mark is being used. The specimen you send must be in use at or near the time you are filing the Sections 8 and 15 Affidavit. (See Chapter 8, Federal Trademark Registration, Section B, for a description of suggested specimens for goods and services.)

In your original registration you listed goods or services in one or more international classes. If you registered in more than one of these classes (and paid an extra application fee) you will need to submit one specimen of goods or services for each class:

1. that you included in your original registration, and
2. that you wish to maintain as part of your registration.

For example, assume you registered your mark under two classes: one class for your products (fanciful shaped wicker baskets) and a separate class for a service that your business provides (basket repair). If you are still using the mark for your products and service, you will need to submit two specimens—one for each use.

If you are continuing registration for less than the total number of classes in your original registration, make sure you specify in your transmittal letter the classes for which the declaration is being submitted.

One specimen needs to be submitted for each class of goods and/or services that will be covered by the Sections 8/15 affidavit.

j. Declaration

Before signing, carefully read the entire declaration. The PTO wants to make sure you still have the right to use the mark, that your right has not been taken away by a court or the PTO and that your right is not being formally challenged. A complete discussion of all this is beyond the scope of this book. The odds are that you have used the mark without fighting about it in court or through the PTO system. If you are not sure whether you can truthfully sign the form, consult a trademark lawyer. (See Chapter 15, Help Beyond the Book.)

If the present owner is an individual, the individual should sign the Declaration. If the present owner is a partnership, the declaration should be signed by a General Partner. If the present owner is a corporation or similar juristic entity, the declaration should be signed by an officer of the corporation/entity. Print or type the officer title of the person signing the declaration. If the registration is owned by two or more parties as joint owners, each owner must sign.

Add the telephone number of one of the persons signing the application and enter the date of signature.

3. How to File the Sections 8 and 15 Affidavit With the PTO

You should send your completed Sections 8 and 15 Affidavit to the PTO within a few days of when it was signed and dated. If you're nearing the six-year deadline, follow the mailing instructions on the back of the form. Your Sections 8/15 Declaration package should be mailed to:

Assistant Commissioner for Trademarks
P.O. Box Reg Fee
2900 Crystal Drive
Arlington, VA 22202-3513

Include the following:
- A transmittal letter
- Original Sections 8 and 15 Affidavit. Keep a copy for your records.
- Specimen.
- Fee. As of October 1997, the PTO charges a $200 fee for each class (for which the mark is being used) for filing a Sections 8 and 15 Affidavit. Call the PTO to confirm the fee if you are filing at a later date. Also, read the box on fees on the back of the form.

- Return postcard. Send a return-receipt postcard as described in Chapter 8, Federal Trademark Registration, Section E3. This allows you to keep track of when your paper was filed.

Don't let the six years expire without being sure your affidavit was filed! The time period within which the form must be filed is rigid, so if you don't receive your postcard within several weeks, contact the PTO. You may have to send a duplicate affidavit if it was lost in the mail or misplaced.

If the PTO finds your affidavit acceptable, you will eventually receive a notice saying they received it and have accepted it.

D. Renew Your Registration

In addition to filing a Sections 8 and 15 Affidavit, you must renew your registration at the end of the registration period if you don't want it to expire. If your registration does expire because of your failure to renew it on a timely basis, your rights to the mark will be based solely on its use unless you re-register it.

1. When to File Your Application for Renewal

If your mark was registered on or after November 16, 1989, it must be renewed within ten years. If it was registered before November 16, 1989, it will last 20 years before renewal is necessary.

The renewal application should be filed within the six-month period directly preceding the ten (or twenty)-year anniversary of your mark's registration. For an additional $100 per class filing fee, however, the renewal may be filed within three months after the ten- (or twenty)-year anniversary date. No renewal application will be accepted after that date. For instance, if your registration expires on May 15, 1999, your renewal application (1) must be dated after November 15, 1998, and (2) may be filed between November 16, 1998, and May 15, 1999 (or between May 16 and August 15, 1999, if you pay the extra fee).

⚠ Small inconsistencies in the information you provide the PTO on this form may cause a delay in getting the renewal filed. For this reason, we strongly recommend that you file your renewal application as soon as you are able, to allow the maximum time possible for curing glitches. If you file early they send back your application but hold onto your money. If you don't make a timely filing, they refund it.

2. How to Complete the Application for Renewal

The renewal form in the Appendix is identical to the Sections 8 and 15 Declaration (Section C above). For that reason, the following instructions direct you to instructions for that form.

a. Mark

Enter the mark exactly as it appears on your trademark registration certificate.

b. Registration Number

Use the registration number that also appears on your certificate.

c. Date of Registration

Follow the directions in Section C2 above.

d. Registrant's Name

Usually the renewal applicant and original registrant are the same person. However, if ownership of the mark has changed since registration, the original registrant will be different from the re-

newal applicant. For example, suppose Roxanne registered her mark *Lollipops* for childrens' toy catalog sales as an individual applicant. If she later formed a corporation to handle her quickly growing business, and transferred ownership of the mark to the corporation by assignment (as discussed in Section H, below), then she is the original registrant, and the corporation is the renewal applicant.

e. Registrant's Current Mailing Address

Follow the instructions in Section C2 above.

f. Registration Number

Enter the registration number again.

g. Type of Commerce

Follow the instructions in Section C2 above.

h. Identify Goods and Services

Follow the instructions in Section C2 above.

i. Specimen

In your original registration you listed goods or services in one or more international classifications. If you registered in more than one of these classifications (and paid an extra registration fee) you will need to submit one specimen of goods or services for each classification:

1. that you included in your original registration, and
2. that you wish to maintain as part of your renewed registration.

For example, suppose Eduardo was renewing the mark *Easy Street* for his massage services (Class 42) and massage oils (Class 3). He would need to submit two specimens (such as a current advertisement for the massage services and a current label for the oils). For general information

APPLICATION FOR RENEWAL OF REGISTRATION OF A MARK, WITH DECLARATION

APPLICATION FOR RENEWAL OF REGISTRATION OF A MARK UNDER **SECTION 9** OF THE TRADEMARK ACT OF 1946, AS AMENDED	MARK (Identify the mark)	
	REGISTRATION NO.	DATE OF REGISTRATION:

TO THE ASSISTANT SECRETARY AND COMMISSIONER OF PATENTS AND TRADEMARKS:

REGISTRANT'S NAME:[1]

REGISTRANT'S CURRENT MAILING ADDRESS: _____

_____

_____

GOODS AND/OR SERVICES AND USE IN COMMERCE STATEMENT:

The mark shown in Registration No. _____ owned by the above-identified registrant is still in use in

_____ commerce on or in connection with all of the goods and/or services identified in the
(type of)[2]

registration, (*except* for the following)[3] _____

_____

as evidenced by the attached specimen(s)[4] showing the mark as currently used.

DECLARATION

The undersigned being hereby warned that willful false statements and the like so made are punishable by fine or imprisonment, or both, under 18 U.S.C. 1001, and that such willful false statements may jeopardize the validity of this document, declares that he/she is properly authorized to execute this document on behalf of the registrant; he/she believes the registrant to be the owner of the above identified registration; the trademark/service mark is in use in commerce; and all statements made of his/her own knowledge are true and all statements made on information and belief are believed to be true.

_____   _____
Date   Signature

_____   _____
Telephone Number   Print or Type Name and Position
                                  [if applicable][5]

PTO Form 4.13a (Rev. 1/93)   U.S. DEPARTMENT OF COMMERCE/Patent and Trademark Office
OMB No. 0651-0009 (Exp. 6/30/95)

about appropriate specimens, see Chapter 8, Federal Trademark Registration, Section B5.

If you are continuing registration for less than the total number of classes in your original registration, make sure you specify in your transmittal letter the classes for which the declaration is being submitted.

j. Declaration

Before signing, carefully read the entire Application for Renewal. The PTO wants to make sure that the registrant is still the owner of the mark, that the mark is still in use and that all other information in the form is true. If the registrant/owner is an individual, the individual should sign the declaration. If the registrant/owner is a partnership, the declaration should be signed by a General Partner. If the registrant/owner is a corporation or similar juristic entity, the declaration should be signed by an officer of the corporation/entity. Print or type the officer title of the person signing the declaration. If the registration is owned by two or more parties as joint owners, each owner must sign.

Add the telephone number of one of the persons signing the application and enter the date of signature.

⚠️ Under no circumstances may the form be dated more than six months before the registration would expire. If it is dated too early, the PTO will send it back and you will have to do a new renewal application.

Fee: As of the November 1997, the PTO charged $300 per class for filing a renewal application. If you are filing in 1998 or later, call the PTO to confirm the fee.

3. How to File the Application for Renewal

You should send your completed Application for Renewal to the USPTO within a few days of when it was signed and dated. If you're nearing the expiration period, follow the mailing instructions on the back of the form. Your renewal package should be mailed to:

> BOX POST REG FEE
> Assistant Commissioner for Trademarks
> 2900 Crystal Drive
> Arlington, Virginia 22202-3513

Include the following in the package:
- a transmittal letter
- Original Application for Renewal (of Registration of a Mark Under Section 9 of the Trademark Act of 1946, as Amended). Keep a copy for your records.
- Specimen(s)
- Fees
- Return postcard. Send a stamped self-addressed receipt postcard as described in Chapter 8, Federal Trademark Registration, Section E3. This allows you to keep track of when your Application for Renewal was filed.

If you don't hear from the PTO within six months as to whether your Application for Renewal has been accepted or rejected, call the Trademark Status Line at 703-305-8747 or the Post Registration Division at 703-308-9500.

4. After the Renewal Application Is Filed

If the PTO thinks something is wrong with your renewal application, it will write you a letter very similar to the action letters discussed in Chapter 8, Federal Trademark Registration, Section F. You must respond within six months; if you don't, the mark will expire without renewal. If you have any questions about their letter, call the PTO and talk with the examiner who sent it. Usually the questions can be cleared up if you write one simple response letter.

Once the PTO is satisfied, the renewal certificate will be sent to you.

Again, don't let the renewal deadline expire, or you will have to re-register your trademark from scratch.

E. Use It or Risk Losing It

Quite apart from federal or state registration, a mark must be in continuous use for the owner to be able to keep others from using it. If the mark falls out of continuous use, it is said to be abandoned. Even a mark that has been registered with the U.S. Patent and Trademark Office, if not used for two years or more, will be presumed abandoned (that is, without evidence to the contrary, the two years of non-use is enough to prove abandonment). In this situation, if the mark's original owner brings a court action against someone who began using it later, the original owner will lose the suit without a good explanation of why the two years of non-use did not constitute an "intent to abandon."

Such contingencies as temporary financial difficulty, bankruptcy proceedings and the need for a product revision may all qualify as satisfactory explanations for non-use of a mark. Although the old adage about maintaining the ownership of a mark counsels "use it or lose it," the law often permits non-use for a considerable amount of time.

For unregistered marks, there is no particular time period that the mark must be out of use to be considered abandoned. Rather, abandonment will be decided on a case by case basis. Of course, the issue usually only arises if another user of the mark claims exclusive rights and challenges your ownership claim on the grounds of your abandonment. If no one else has used the mark between the time you stopped using it and the time you start using it again, then abandonment should not be a problem.

F. Maintain Tight Control of Your Mark

As we explain in other parts of the book, trademarks serve the primary function of identifying a particular product or service in the marketplace. If a mark owner allows others to use the trademark without restricting what product or service it represents, the mark no longer serves as a meaningful indicator of a particular product's or service's origin and will be considered abandoned. For instance, if a fast food hamburger chain allows its franchise operators to have complete discretion as to the food, decor and type of service they offer under the company logo, the logo quickly loses its ability to indicate a particular type of food service. In this situation, the logo is considered abandoned—since it doesn't serve its original function of product or service identification—and anyone will be free to use it.

The way that McDonald's controls its marks exemplifies the type of vigilance over the product or service that is necessary to avoid the possibility of abandonment. This company uses its service mark not only to distinguish its service from its competitors generally, but also to call to a consumer's mind such characteristics as a specific level of service, a specific type of meal at a specific price, and a specific level of cleanliness. It does this by requiring every owner of a *McDonald's* franchise to operate the franchise under tight rules and restrictions, designed to insure that the characteristics associated with the *McDonald's* mark are always present. Without such restrictions, the *McDonald's* service mark soon would stand for nothing, since each *McDonald's* operation would soon cease to provide the consumer with meaningful information about its products and service, and would therefore be considered abandoned, just as if it were no longer used.

Another aspect of controlling your mark is to police its use by others. Even if you don't particularly care whether some others use your mark, your failure to assert your exclusive ownership rights means that the mark may be considered abandoned. Policing your mark might mean annual checks of the trade literature applicable to your business, weekly scrutiny of the *Official Gazette* for new trademark applications or even periodic full trademark searches.

If you do discover other uses of your mark, you could respond in the ways we suggest in Chapter 12, If Someone Infringes Your Mark. Or you could hire a lawyer to sue if this seems necessary. To maintain your rights, you don't immediately have to take an unauthorized user to court, but you should at least write letters to strongly protest the other's use of the mark to assert your claim of ownership and attempt a satisfactory solution. If their use goes on for a long time, your delay may provide them a defense against your legal action, or you may lose your right to obtain an injunction, once you finally do sue.

G. Use the Mark Properly— Avoid Genericide

A few businesses—almost always large ones— have the apparent good fortune of owning a mark that has become a household word. But paradoxically, once the mark becomes so much a household word that it becomes synonymous with any product or service of the sort it originally represented, it ceases to be a mark—it becomes generic. For example, some people refer to all facial paper tissues as Kleenex, and all acetaminophen analgesics as Tylenol. These marks would be in danger of becoming lost through "genericide" if the companies did not protest such improper uses of the marks.

The problem is this: The more well-known a particular mark becomes, the more the public is prone to equate the mark with the underlying product rather than view it as one brand name among many. This is just another way of saying

---

AUTHORIZED USES OF YOUR TRADEMARK

Not all uses of your trademark by others place it in jeopardy. For example, it is common for stores to use marks belonging to other companies to tell their customers that the goods or services identified by the marks can be purchased at that store. When using marks in this way, however, the stores must make it clear that the marks belong to their owners, not to the store. Usually this fact is clear from the context ("Levi's sold here," or, "An authorized distributor of Apple Computer products"). Often you will see on labels of goods that incorporate others' products, like a sofa, a message like "Wear-Dated ® is a trademark of the Monsanto Company," to indicate that the name of the sofa's fabric is a trademark of another company.

Such uses become a problem only when it is not clear that the trademark belongs to the rightful trademark owner. For example, if the trademark does not look like it normally does, that may be a confusing use of the mark.

Generally, use of a trademark that is simply typed is not a problem, but if the advertisement employs special designs, the mark must have the same typeface and logo as used by the original mark owner, or a disclaimer specifying who the owner of the mark is.

that the mark loses its ability to identify a particular brand and becomes generic. Only a tiny number of companies will face this problem—it tends to arise with revolutionary new products that the public comes to associate with the name their first manufacturer gives them, like *Roller Blades* for in-line skates. But because genericide is avoidable, you ought to know how to prevent your mark from going generic if that ever seems to be even a remote possibility.

The best way to keep a mark from becoming generic is to

- accompany every use of the mark with the generic product or service name (for example, *Kleenex* tissues)
- never use the mark as a verb (for instance, you never go "roller blading," you skate on roller blade skates)
- always capitalize your mark (*Tylenol*)
- never use the mark as a general noun (for instance, don't call a photocopy a "Xerox")
- If you become aware that your mark is being used improperly, you must remind the public that it is a mark and not a generic name. For instance, Xerox has spent millions advising the public that *Xerox* is a registered mark that must always be capitalized and used as a proper adjective describing a noun (for instance, a *Xerox* brand photocopier). If later on someone challenges the Xerox Corporation's right to the exclusive use of the word "Xerox," on the ground it

has become generic, Xerox will prevail if it can show that people understood these advertisements and that most use the term "Xerox" as a brand name—not a generic one.

H. Keep Track of the Mark's Ownership

You should consider your registered mark as property with a title, the same as a house or car. The title document is your Certificate of Registration. (See Chapter 8, Federal Trademark Registration, Section J.) If for any reason you sell your business or the rights in products you manufacture or distribute, you will also need to sell the marks used to identify the business and products in the marketplace. The complete transfer of ownership in a mark to another person or entity is called an "assignment." An assignment of a registered mark must be in writing to be valid. It can—and should—be filed with the U.S. Patent and Trademark Office. (Or, if it's a state-registered trademark, it should be recorded like any other title to property. (See Chapter 7, State Trademark Registration.) The new owner can obtain a new Certificate of Registration in his or her name. If you anticipate a sale (assignment) of your mark, see a trademark attorney. A sample assignment form is in the Appendix.

If you are selling a business, the chances are you are also selling any trademarks associated with it. If so, it makes sense to assign your ownership of the marks in a document that is separate from the contract of sale. This enables the new mark owner to record only the transfer of mark ownership with the U.S. Patent and Trademark Office, while keeping private the many details of the deal that do not affect the transfer of trademark rights. ■

Evaluating Trademark Strength

This chapter helps you evaluate a particular mark's legal strength—that is, the degree to which the courts will protect it or something similar against use or misuse by others. You will want to read this chapter if you feel the need for a deeper understanding of the material in Chapter 2, or if you have:

- been accused of violating someone else's mark, or
- think that someone else is treading on your mark.

Assuming you are involved in a conflict situation, once you digest this material you should read Chapter 11, which discusses who has priority in case two marks—or a mark and an Internet domain name—come into conflict. Then you should go to Chapter 12 (if your mark is being infringed) or Chapter 13 (if you are accused of infringement) for suggestions on how to deal with the dispute.

In Chapter 2, How to Choose a Good Name for Your Business, Product or Service, we have already touched on the basics of what makes a mark legally strong—inherent distinctiveness or distinctiveness acquired through secondary meaning. This teaches you how to classify your mark by type (for instance, geographic names and personal names) and explains how far the courts are willing to go to protect that type of mark in case of a dispute.

A. A Brief Review of What Makes a Strong Mark

A legally strong trademark meets two basic tests:

- It successfully identifies your goods or services in the consumer's mind.
- Because of your prior usage (and maybe registration), competitors can't use it or anything like it in any context where customers might 1) be confused about the source of goods or services, or 2) might, because of the similarity of the marks, erroneously conclude your business is associated in

some way with the goods or services being marketed under the conflicting mark.

How your mark measures up to these tests helps determine your mark's strength in relation to any other mark. Below we set out an approach that will help you apply these tests in the real world.

As you have heard repeatedly by now, the tools we give you to evaluate a trademark's strength are guidelines, not guarantees. These rules represent the best guesses that most lawyers could be likely to make based on the relevant court decisions. But we don't promise specific results for a specific mark because that depends on many factors, including use, timing and how the facts strike the judge who decides the particular dispute.

B. The First Step: For Marks Consisting of Words, Identify the Distinctive Part of the Mark

To evaluate the strength of your product or service mark, first separate its distinctive component from the part of the mark that identifies the type of product or service it identifies. For example, the mark *Apple Computers* contains a distinctive element—Apple—and a product/service identifier, Computers. Another example: the distinctive aspect of the name *Guess?* jeans is the word "Guess" followed by a "?".

Sometimes all or most of the individual words of a mark are equally distinctive (or non-distinctive) and it is the combination of the words that is distinctive. Examples: *Trader Joe's* (food market) and *Music Now and Then* (a disk jockey service). Even when there is no specific distinctive part of a word mark, the mark will still have a tail that identifies the underlying product or service. And so, it's still important to understand where the words that give the mark at least some distinctiveness drop off and common identifiers of goods or services kick in. Because the nondistinctive aspect of a word mark can never be protected, we simply disregard it in evaluating the legal strength of the name as a mark.

After you have isolated the word or phrase that forms the distinctive aspect of your mark, match it with one or more of the categories listed in Section C below to understand why your mark does or doesn't have legal strength. If, in addition to your word-based trademark(s), you have a non-word trademark (that is, a symbol, drawing, shape, design or other hard-to-classify feature—the Mickey Mouse silhouette is one), be sure to refer to Chapter 2, Section G.

C. Assess the Legal Strength of the Trademark Aspect of Your Word Mark

Earlier we spoke of the distinctive part of your word mark. That distinctive part is in fact the trademark aspect of your mark. Here we place the different categories of trademarks on a spectrum. We start with the most distinctive marks—the ones with the greatest legal strength. We then move to more ordinary marks which may be easier to promote but harder to protect legally, and finally conclude with generic marks, which can't be protected at all because they utterly lack all distinctiveness. Along the way we provide lists of examples of each category and discuss why various names are classified as they are.

Remember to consider the whole effect of your mark—its sound, its look and all the meanings of the individual elements of the mark—before drawing conclusions about its legal strength. This includes the style of the typeface, as well as its color, shape, size and any other aspect of the overall impression the mark makes. In addition, how the mark is used and the timing of its first use are all relevant in determining relative trademark strengths.

Some of the distinctions that place a mark in one category or another may appear arbitrary and even at times hairsplitting. At first you may feel that it is impossible to tell the difference. If you take your time with this material, however, the better you know it, the more it will make sense.

Do keep in mind that live human beings—with their individual strengths and weaknesses—are the ultimate arbiters of whether a particular mark is to be considered strong or weak. Whether the person is a trademark examiner (employee of the U.S. Patent and Trademark Office), a judge, a juror or an author of this book, his or her analysis of a particular mark is based on a subjective response to mostly visual stimuli, which makes for fuzzy decision making. So, if you find yourself disagreeing with the category a particular mark has been consigned to by the PTO, courts or even the authors of this book (in the many made-up examples they provide), try to understand (if not accept) the rationale we give rather than dissent in the name of some absolute truth.

1. Varieties of Distinctive Marks

Distinctive marks fall into three basic categories—coined, arbitrary and suggestive. All are strong, but coined and arbitrary marks are considered stronger than suggestive marks and therefore receive more protection.

a. Coined Trademarks

These are words that you won't find in any dictionary; they have been made up just to serve as trademarks, so they have no other meaning. Words like *Blistex*, *Kodak*, *Exxon*, *Tylenol* and *Actifed* are the marks lawyers like best. They are inarguably distinctive, and therefore legally strong. Such household words as *Kodak*, *Kleenex* and *Reebok* were all coined specifically as marks. Whether it is registered or not, chances are that a coined mark will automatically entitle you to the strongest protection against copying that courts can provide.

In practice, coined marks can't be used by others in any commercial context. By contrast, most other types of marks can be used by more than one owner as long as:

- the goods and services they are used on are not related and don't compete with each other; and
- it is unlikely that customers will be confused by the multiple use of the mark.

The reason for the special treatment afforded a coined mark is its uniqueness. Since a coined mark's exclusive role is to identify a specific product or service (or product line) in the marketplace, most consumers would expect linkage between all businesses who use the mark, and would therefore be confused as to the origins of the products or services carrying it. So it is highly unwise to borrow a famous coined trademark even for a vastly different product or service.

Not all made-up marks fall into this strongest-of-all category. Marks that are coined wholly new, like *Maalox*, are treated differently and are given more protection than are marks that are composites of recognizable elements of words, like *Accuride*. *Maalox* is automatically strong, because it is not like anything we have heard before. But *Accuride* is too close to "accurate ride" to be considered a purely coined term. Such a mark is therefore usually considered suggestive rather than coined. We discuss suggestive marks below.

b. Fanciful or Arbitrary Marks

Fanciful or arbitrary names, such as *Penguin* books, *Arrow* shirts and *Camel* cigarettes, also make distinctive and legally strong marks. These marks use common words in an unexpected or arbitrary way, so that their normal meanings have nothing to do with the nature of the product or service they identify. They creatively juxtapose unexpected combinations of words and products or services. That's how a skating rink came up with the appealing name *Jellibeans*. Another wonderful example of a fanciful name is *We Be Bop* for a local children's store, and it's difficult to think of a more arbitrary name than *Diesel, A Bookstore*.

These arbitrary or fanciful marks have almost as broad a scope of exclusive use as do coined marks. Most of the time, using an arbitrary or fanciful mark for one type of product or service will prevent the use of the same mark on similar or related services or products. However, unlike a coined mark, arbitrary or fanciful marks may be used if the context of use is entirely different and the original mark is not too well known. If, on the other hand, the arbitrary or fanciful mark has become famous, then—under a principle known as trademark dilution—the mark may be protected against use by others, no matter what the context of use. See Chapter 11, Sorting Out Trademark Disputes, Section D.)

c. Suggestive Marks

A close relative of the arbitrary mark is the suggestive mark. This type of mark uses ordinary words in a clever manner to create a desirable idea or feeling about a product or service, but stays away from literally describing any aspect of the product or service. Examples are *Verbatim* (for computer disks), *Banana Republic* (for a style of clothing), *Greyhound* (for bus service) and *Thistle Dew Inn* (for a bed and breakfast service).

Suggestive marks are considered distinctive and therefore legally strong because they indirectly associate favorable qualities with specific goods and services in a creative way. For example, a *Jaguar* car conveys the idea of aggressiveness, beauty and speed, desirable attributes for a car; *Dove* soap conveys softness and gentleness; *Greyhound* implies speed and sleekness—not adjectives normally associated with bus lines, but desirable ones nonetheless.

Sunkist is an interesting example of a suggestive mark. Although it is just a novel spelling of the adjective "sun-kissed," its creative use on fruit and juices evokes a wonderfully fresh and healthy image. It is the originality of the mark that makes it legally strong.

An excellent example of a suggestive mark is *Thistle Dew Inn* used by a quaint bed and breakfast establishment just off the town square in Sonoma, California. The composite term *Thistle Dew* evokes both a ubiquitous local purple-flowered plant and a feeling of freshness and renewal that people in Northern California seek when they visit Sonoma, the heart of the wine country.

d. More Examples of Distinctive Marks by Category

The line between arbitrary, fanciful and suggestive marks is often a fine one. A mark that might appear to be fanciful or arbitrary may in fact be derived from a little known source and might, therefore, be suggestive to those in the know. For example, some marks employ mythical or fantasy allusions to suggest desirable connotations, like the *Janus* investment fund (Janus = Roman god of beginnings) or *Midas Muffler* (King Midas = the golden touch). A clever mark of this sort is *Prints Valiant* for a copy shop, which combines the name of a cartoon hero with a pun on the kind of shop it is, and implies heroic effort.

Below is a chart showing examples of the different categories of distinctive trademarks. Examine it carefully to see if these distinctions make sense to you.

OVERUSE CAN DIMINISH A MARK'S DISTINCTIVENESS

Sometimes a popular fanciful or suggestive name loses its strength if used too widely. For example, *Mustang* originally was a strong mark when first applied to a particular model of *Ford* automobile. But because *Mustang* evokes an image of energy, speed and stamina, it has also been used for tires, trailers and other products. By now the wide use of the term *Mustang* has diminished its ability to distinguish any single product very well. That means that future users of the word *Mustang* as a mark will receive limited trademark protection, even though existing owners of the *Mustang* mark, like *Ford*, can continue to bar competitors from using the mark on their line of products.

CATEGORIES OF DISTINCTIVE TRADEMARKS

Suggestive

Verbatim computer discs
Suave shampoo
Accuride tires
Glacier ice
Greyhound bus
Coppertone tanning lotion
Roach Motel insect trap
Wearever cookware
Maternally Yours clothes
Esprit clothes
Q-tips
7-Eleven stores
Liquid Paper
Chicken of the Sea tuna

Fanciful/Arbitrary

Jellibeans skating rink
Penguin books
Ajax cleanser
Domino sugar
Apple computers
Nova TV series
Banana Republic clothes
Beefeater gin
Arrow shirts
Hang Ten clothes
Hard Rock Cafe
Camel cigarettes
Ivory soap
Double Rainbow Ice Cream

Coined

Barbasol shaving lotion
Curel hand lotion
Reebok shoes
Exxon
Nyquil
Amtrak
Kodak
Blistex lip balm
Maalox
Tylenol
Actifed

Perplexed? Don't be. Many of these examples can go either way. For example, while some trademark authorities consider *Ivory* soap to be an arbitrary trademark, others argue that it describes the color of the soap, or that it suggests the desirable qualities of ivory—smooth, clean, white, valuable. *Nyquil*, a cold remedy, can be seen either as a coined term, or a composite suggestive mark, combining "night" and "tranquil" to evoke peaceful sleep. *Cachet*, for a women's clothing store, rides the border between suggestive and descriptive, because it means a mark of distinction or individuality, thus promising unique style to the customer. *Banana Republic* could be either arbitrary, because it has nothing to do with clothes, or it could be suggestive of adventure and travel, which is the aura the manufacturer hopes these clothes will create.

As long as your mark is distinctive in the sense of it being unique, clever or just plain memorable, the practical importance of what category it fits in is nil—until you find yourself in a conflict with another mark. Then, to the extent that your mark qualifies as a coined term, it will get the widest scope of protection. We explain more about what this means in Chapter 4, How to Tell If Two Marks Are Confusingly Similar, Section B2. For now it's enough to understand what category your mark falls in and why.

2. Varieties of Non-distinctive (Ordinary) Marks

In Chapter 2 we lumped all the marks that aren't distinctive into a category called ordinary marks. An ordinary mark is one that communicates in a descriptive or otherwise mundane way something about the product or service to which it is attached. It includes five sorts of terms:

- descriptive, describing the nature of the service or product (*Self-Help Divorce Center* for a consulting service helping people file their own divorce forms)
- geographic, describing the geographic area it's in (*Downtown Auto Service*, if it's really downtown)
- laudatory, praising the business or the customer (*Pretty Nails*, for a manicurist; *Fast Feet*, for athletic shoes)
- personal names, consisting primarily of first names, surnames, personal initials, or nicknames (*Maury's Deli, Gooden Chevrolet*)
- business name initials

While these types of word marks ordinarily are considered to be legally weak, they can each become distinctive through long use and customer recognition, via the secondary meaning rule that we discussed in Chapter 2, Section C2. For example, *IBM*, the initials for International Business Machines, originally was a legally weak mark until it became well known over time, thereby acquiring legal strength under the secondary meaning rule.

In the following four subsections we detail the pros and cons of each kind of ordinary mark and give you rules about when a term will be considered strong enough to qualify for protection in the courts.

Generic Name Note

We discuss generic marks—names that have become synonymous with the product itself, such as aspirin and cellophane—in Section C3 below.

a. Descriptive Words and Words of Praise

We lump marks using these kinds of words together because there is little practical difference between them. As long as you know your mark is one or the other, you'd be wasting your time trying to decide which. So let's briefly recap what these marks are before we try distinguishing them from marks that are legally strong.

Descriptive marks are those that literally describe a feature or attribute of a product or service, such as *10-Minute Lube* (auto care), *Hi-Tech Computers, Char-broiler* hamburgers, *FindUHome* (real estate broker) or *Nuts and Bolts* (hardware store).

Laudatory marks (words of praise) hype a product or service's quality or quantity, using common words like *Original Blend* (cat food), *America's Freshest Ice Cream* (ice cream), *Maple Rich* (syrup), *Blue Ribbon* (bakeries) or *Best Foods* (organic food distributors); or they describe the qualities of the product or service the business hopes to deliver, like *Joy* detergent or *Pride* furniture polish.

Descriptive marks make very weak trademarks for two reasons.

- Consumers are so used to commercial hype that descriptive terms don't make the kind of impact on them that would help them to effectively distinguish one product or service from another. For example, the name *Canine Clipping Centers* doesn't by itself clearly differentiate that pet care shop from any other.
- Descriptive terms need to remain freely available for everyone's commercial or everyday use. Trademark law will only protect terms that are unique to a particular product or service brand and that aren't, therefore, necessary for another business to use if it wishes to describe or hype its business in advertising or marketing copy.

You may think that changing the spelling or language—from English to French, for example—makes an otherwise weak mark strong. It usually doesn't work that way. So *La Bread Shoppe*, or *Tastee Kookie* remain weak marks despite the spelling/language variations. But a relatively obscure foreign term, or one that most consumers wouldn't recognize as a foreign language equivalent of a descriptive term, can create a strong mark. So although "xerox" is the ancient Greek word for dry and "dry" describes the photocopying process *Xerox* invented, *Xerox* was a strong mark from the beginning—because only a few Greek scholars knew its meaning. In addition, *La Posada Inns*, directed at English speakers, is considered a distinctive mark although the Spanish translation (The Inn) is descriptive.

XEROX

HOW XEROX ALMOST BECAME A GENERIC MARK

Over a number of years *Xerox* became more and more synonymous with photocopy machines and the photocopying process ("I need a xerox," or "I'm going to xerox that"). This common usage put the *Xerox* mark in danger of becoming generic and therefore not protectible at all. To prevent this, *Xerox* undertook an aggressive and expensive advertising campaign to encourage people to use *Xerox* properly, as a proper adjective, and not as a generic term (a verb or a noun). (See also Section C3, below.)

As we have emphasized in earlier chapters, even descriptive names can become legally strong enough to get full trademark protection, through the secondary meaning rule. That's when a trademark becomes so closely identified with a specific product or service that the public no longer thinks first of the original ordinary meaning of the words. Then the mark is said to have taken on a new "secondary"—and distinctive—meaning, and rivals can no longer use it to identify their products or services.

But even after descriptive marks have acquired secondary meaning, others still can use the ordinary words that make up such marks in non-trademark ways—that is, to legitimately describe their product or service in advertising. This is known as "fair use" of a trademark and it is a valid defense in court if a mark owner challenges the use of your words in their mark.

For example, once *Standard Brands* acquired secondary meaning and became protectible as a trademark, others could not use those words as a trademark on goods, but a store could advertise that they carry "All standard brands" of paint, or tools, or whatever they sell, without fear of infringing. (To understand what the legitimate use of another's trademark in advertising or media is, when it represents that trademark owner's own services or goods, see Chapter 9, Section G.)

Continuous Use for Five Years

If the owner of a weak mark can prove that the mark has been in continuous use for a five-year period, it will be presumed to have acquired a secondary meaning and be eligible for placement on the federal principal trademark register. (See Chapter 8.)

One final point: even without secondary meaning, ordinary trademarks can get limited protection—under unfair competition laws—from a rival with a confusingly similar name in the same area and the same line of business. (See Chapter 11, Section C.)

DECEPTIVE AND MISLEADING MARKS GET NO PROTECTION

Marks that describe a product or service misleadingly get no protection at all. So neither *Neo-Hide* nor *Softhide* can be protected as marks for imitation leather. Most state and federal trademark laws specifically bar these types of marks from registration both to protect consumers from being ripped off, and to protect businesses that accurately describe their products from unfair competition by those who don't.

A second category of marks that are only slightly misleading—called "deceptively misdescriptive"—are viewed as less seriously deceptive. *American Beauty* as a mark for a Japanese sewing machine is one example of this type of mark. When first used, this type of mark does not receive legal protection either. But once it acquires secondary meaning, then it becomes distinctive, and protectible as a mark, on the theory that it is no longer considered misleading. That's because the public no longer thinks of the literal meaning of the words, and instead only associates the words in the mark with the product or service.

b. Geographic Marks

These are marks with a geographic term in them, such as Eastern, Miami, Indiana, English or any other place names, from streets to continents or regions to rivers. There are several subspecies of marks containing geographic terms:

- Literal Geographic Descriptors. Like other ordinary marks, the general rule is that if you use a geographic term descriptively (for example, if the product or service is really connected to the place name), it can't be protected as a mark, absent a showing

of secondary meaning. That's because everyone has a right to use accurate geographic words to describe the origin of their services or products. So marks like *Manhasset Drugs, Central Realty, North Moline Hardware* or *Chestnut Street Pub* (if it's on Chestnut Street) are weak and can't be protected, unless of course, they gain secondary meaning in connection with the particular product or service for which they're used. Examples of geographic marks that got protection by acquiring secondary meaning are *American Airlines, Continental Can Corp.* and *The New Yorker* magazine.

⚠ Although not protectible as marks, these extremely common types of business names may be entitled to some relief in court if a competitor uses the same name in a manner that would be highly likely to confuse customers. For example, *Manhasset Drugs* could stop a competitor from using that exact name in Manhasset. (See Chapter 11, Sorting Out Trademark Disputes, Section C, for a discussion of unfair competition principles.)

- Indirect Geographic Descriptors. Even if your service or product is not factually associated with the place named in your mark, the mark may still be if the public is likely to assume that such a link exists. For example, Chicago is famous for a kind of pizza, so it's descriptive, not distinctive, to call a Dallas pizzeria *Chicago Pizza*. Likewise, *Thai Videos* is weak if it sells videos from Thailand, even though it does so in Los Angeles. So too, *Phnom Penh* is weak for a Cambodian restaurant located in Trenton, New Jersey.
- General Geographical Descriptors. Some words like World, Globe and places in outer space may be far too broad to suggest any specific place of origin, but they are

still weak because they operate like lauda-tory or descriptive marks (see Section C2a above). Thus *American Engineer* on an engineering trade magazine is descriptive and weak because it's aimed at a readership made up of American engineers.

- Ambiguous Geographical Descriptors. Some geographic terms are ambiguous in meaning when used in a trademark. For instance, the term Continental can be interpreted as referring to a literal continental land mass or, more quaintly, to the European continent. National may indicate nationwide scope or patriotism, again depending on how it is used. Whether it's a weak or a strong mark would depend on which meaning applies.

c. Geographic Terms as Strong Marks

As with all marks consisting of ordinary terms, there are times when geographic marks are protectible, apart from acquiring secondary meaning. The best way to make a geographic term distinctive as a mark is to use it in an arbitrary or fanciful way. For example, *American Express* (for travel and credit services) and *California Girl* (for clothes) don't really describe either the service or the product or imply their origins. Instead these words project an image that is fanciful and distinctive for the items on which they are used. So they are protectible as marks.

Likewise, *English Leather* is a distinctive (suggestive) mark, as long as it does not describe a leather product. If it did, it would be either descriptive, if it comes from Britain, or deceptive, if it does not. (See below for more on why deceptive terms can't be marks.) And a fabric store called *Taos Fabrics* has a weak mark if it's in New Mexico, but a strong one if it is in Chattanooga.

In a rather odd way, this makes good sense. The sellers of products or services have a right to truthfully tell where an item came from without infringing another's mark. It would be unfair to all

other New York businesses to give any one company in that city a monopoly on the name. But if an entrepreneur elsewhere wants to evoke the Big Apple in Fargo, North Dakota, that's fair. (If the owner of the Fargo-based *Big Apple* decided later to market its products in New York City, it's possible that its rights would be greater than if the business had started there from the beginning. This would depend on how well known the *Big Apple* mark had become in the meantime, whether the mark had been placed on the federal register, and what competing uses of the mark already existed in New York City at the time of the desired expansion.)

d. Personal Names

Words in this category refer to a person, whether their first name, last name, whole name, nickname or initials. Examples are *Juan's, Houlihan's, Larry Blake's, C.J.'s* and *H&R Block*. As a general rule, anyone can use their personal name as a mark for their service or product, unless the same name is already in use on directly competing products or services.

This means that personal names (at least common ones) make weak marks. But as we discovered in an informal study of the Yellow Pages, more small businesses use a surname or first name as their mark than any other kind of name. Marks using personal initials are also popular. It's understandable why business people are drawn to these types of names; they demonstrate pride of ownership. But using a personal name or initials has potentially serious drawbacks from a trademark point of view.

First, most personal names are legally weak because they are not particularly memorable, especially if they are used in one or more competing businesses. We saw this problem with *Ray's Pizza* in New York (see Chapter 2, How to Choose a Good Name for Your Business, Product or Service). When someone there says "Ray's Pizza," no one can tell which of the 24 Ray's in the city is the right one. Nor does adding an initial make a personal name inherently distinctive enough to become a legally strong trademark. On the other hand, the odder your name, the less likely others will use it on a similar business and the more memorable it will be. Will the real *Orville Redenbacher* please stand up?

Second, as with other ordinary marks, a personal name trademark must usually acquire secondary meaning through being identified with your business to be protected as a strong trademark. However, many personal names have garnered such a large degree of public recognition that the courts permit only very limited other uses of them. *McDonald's* and *Levi's* are two good examples.

Despite the general principles governing personal name marks just described, a few personal name marks do manage to get strong trademark protection without secondary meaning. The general rule is that if the public would not view the mark primarily as a personal name, then it can be protected outright. Put another way, a personal name only works as a trademark if it is so unusual that no one recognizes it as a personal name, like *Garan*. Other personal names that can be distinctive trademarks are ones that have additional meanings like *Bird*, *Kent* or *Fairbanks*, which also of course have common descriptive or geographic significance. The distinctiveness of such marks would depend on how they are used.

Another exception to the general rule that personal names make weak trademarks is well-known historical names, like Da Vinci, Lincoln, Rameses, Robin Hood, which are considered fanciful and distinctive. The use of such marks clearly does not imply that the person named is commercially connected to the product or service

—so their trademark use is not primarily as a personal name. On the other hand, some historical names, like Webster and Longfellow, have been treated as weak marks. What's the difference? Perhaps because the latter names are less mythic—Daniel Webster and Henry Wadsworth Longfellow are less famous by far than Da Vinci or Abraham Lincoln—they carry more of a personal name meaning than do the former. This is another of those gray areas of the law, where the differences are slim.

THE RIGHT OF PUBLICITY

There is a related but separate right that protects famous people's names and personas from the commercial use by others. It's called the right of publicity, and it allows celebrities to prevent others from making money by the unauthorized use of their names. For example, the right of publicity allowed Johnny Carson to prevent the marketing of a line of portable toilets that would have the trademark *Here's Johnny*. And the singer Bette Midler successfully sued a company that used her unique singing style to market its products.

Even using a famous name on unrelated services or products can be a problem. John Walker probably can't operate a motel under the name *Johnny Walker Inn*, but he might be able to use a name that sounds sufficiently different, like *John M. Walker Inn*. And often such potentially confusing uses are permitted with a disclaimer like, "not associated with ..." For example, *Hyatt Corp.* sued *Hyatt Legal Services* over the use of that surname. The suit was eventually settled when the defendant agreed to use the statement: "Hyatt Legal Services is named after its founder, Joel Z. Hyatt."

⚠️ *Hyatt Hotels* sued the Hyatt law firm under a separate provision of the trademark law that prevents "dilution"—the use of a mark similar to a famous one even on a non-competing business. (See Chapter 11, Sorting Out Trademark Disputes, Section D, for more about dilution.)

In practice, there are two likely scenarios when a famous name might be allowed to be copied by a small business. Some names are so famous and applied to such a variety of products that any additional use of them would be confusing to the public, even on a completely unrelated product or service. DuPont or Yves St. Laurent are examples.

YVESSAINTLAURENT

Other names may be equally famous, but are associated so exclusively with specific products or services that even though the public would recognize any use of a similar name, no actual confusion is likely to result where the mark is used on a totally different type of product or service. If such is the case, then you can use your name even if it's also a famous mark. That's why Bob Fanta won a suit by *Coca-Cola* over his use of "Keep Tab with Fanta" to advertise his tax return service: his business is so logically remote from soft drinks that actual confusion is unlikely. It is unlikely that this would be considered a case of trademark dilution, since neither the *Tab* nor the *Fanta* mark enjoys the type of nationally strong reputation for quality or other characteristics that dilution laws are designed to protect. (See Chapter 11, Sorting Out Trademark Disputes, Section D.)

In one famous case detailed by Calvin Trillin in the *New Yorker* magazine (1988), a small bar opened up in Milwaukee under the name of *Mike Houlihan's* (the first name of one of the owners and the last name of the other owner). W.R. Grace, a conglomerate, already owned a chain of

family restaurants called *Houlihan's Old Place*, one of which was in Milwaukee.

The two concerns coexisted peaceably in the same city for a couple of years. It was only when *Mike Houlihan's* opened a second pub in St. Louis, where there was another *Houlihan's Old Place*, that the conglomerate protested the bar's use of a similar mark and threatened to sue. The pub owners were furious and refused to back down: "What do you mean I can't use my surname?" fumed John Houlihan to his lawyer.

The lawyer knew that W.R. Grace appeared to have the law on its side—the Houlihan name was first used and first federally registered in connection with *Houlihan's Old Place*. (How first use and federal registration affects conflicts between marks is discussed in detail in Chapter 11, Sorting Out Trademark Disputes.) But then luck intervened.

It turned out that there really was an old Mr. Houlihan after which *Houlihan's Old Place* was named, and that his written consent for the use of his name had never been obtained—a prerequisite to registering a mark using the name of a living person. For this omission, the court canceled Grace's trademark registration of *Houlihan's Old Place*. And yet the restaurant eventually succeeded in barring the bar's use of the mark in Missouri based on unfair competition, common law trademark rights and state dilution laws. Moral of the story: Using personal names in a mark can be tricky, so always get permission when using the name of a living person.

3. Generic Labels

In Chapter 2, How to Choose a Good Name for Your Business, Product or Service, we introduced you to the concept of generic labels—words that are synonymous with the underlying product or service and which therefore can't distinguish it from others. Examples of generic terms are aspirin, linoleum and lite beer. Here we follow up on that discussion to help you distinguish generic labels from marks that are merely weak. It's an important distinction because while weak marks can gain protection once they acquire secondary meaning, generic labels will never receive any protection at all.

You will see problems with generic words in three different trademark contexts:

1. When you try to protect your weak mark against an infringer and they defend by saying your mark is generic and therefore freely copiable.

2. When you adopt a mark and seek to have it registered under the secondary meaning rule, but it is rejected because the term is generic rather than merely weak.

3. When a mark that was once distinctive (and perhaps even registered) loses all legal protection because it has become synonymous with the product and not just one brand of it. An example of a distinctive mark that is in danger of becoming generic is *Roller Blades*, which many people use for the product itself (more accurately called in-line skates).

We are more concerned with the first circumstance than with the second or third, but most of our examples are drawn from court cases in which a mark was denied protection because it always was or had become synonymous with the product. For example, *Thermos* was once a trademark, but is now seen as a kind of insulated bottle. Although they emerge from a different context, such examples are useful because they illustrate the thinking of a judge or trademark examiner in determining if a mark is protectible at all or simply generic.

Distinguishing generic labels from weak marks may not always be easy to do. Courts ask what a buyer is likely to think of when he or she hears the term—a product or a specific source for that product? Another approach is to try to come up with a generic label for the underlying type of product or service that is different from the mark

itself. As long as a generic label for a product or service can be articulated, a name that is different from the label will qualify for treatment as a mark, no matter how weak it is. Only if the name and the generic label merge over time will the mark suffer genericide.

It usually takes some market research to discover what a term's generally accepted meaning is and some legal advocacy to convince a court of this point of view.

Here's a list of generic labels. Examine them to see if they clarify the concept.

GENERIC LABELS

Lite beer	Cola
Aspirin	copperclad
Baby Oil	dry ice
Bath Oil beads	escalator
Brassiere	Hoagie sandwich
Cellophane	Jujubes candy
Softsoap	Matchbox toys
Superglue	Monopoly game
Thermos	Montessori method
Yo-Yo	Shredded Wheat

Why, you may ask, is matchbox but not *Tinkertoy* on this list? Perhaps the public associates *Tinkertoy* more specifically with one company, whereas matchbox indicates a variety of small toy. Why is copperclad generic, but not *Teflon*? Again, *Teflon* is a material that the public associates with a company, whereas copperclad is more of a process.

Let's take one example a little further. Montessori has been ruled a generic term for a variety of child care centers that share a general philosophy of early childhood education based on the teachings of Maria Montessori. Even though the American Montessori Society certifies certain Montessori schools but not others, any school is free to use the Montessori name to describe the kind of education it provides.

But what makes the name Montessori generic instead of being descriptive of the philosophy of the school? The bottom line is, what does the public think when it hears such a term? It thinks, "Montessori—that's an educational method." Put simply, since the name describes the kind of thing involved, it's generic. By contrast, if the name tells you which thing is involved—even if it does so very descriptively—it has the potential for being a trademark.

Does this mean that no Montessori school can ever have a protectible trademark? Not at all. Many protectible marks have generic terms in them. As long as the trademark contains a non-generic part that distinguishes the service or product from others, in addition to the generic part, then the whole is not generic and may be protected. So to have a protectible name, any Montessori school can simply add a distinguishing modifier to its name, such as Big Trees Montessori School. The modifier, Big Trees, becomes the mark.

4. Composite Terms and Slogans

In this section we discuss composite terms, slogans, designs, shapes and containers. These types of marks also can be distinctive or ordinary, so we discuss them at some length to help you evaluate what makes them weak or strong.

a. Composite Terms

These marks can also be called cross-category marks. They are made up of one or more of the different sorts of words discussed above in Section C2. Examples are: *Shorty's Mean Motorcycles, Gino's New York Pizza, Stormy Weather Home Rehab Services, Kmart.*

Composite marks are not easy to analyze. They usually consist of weak components but still may be considered strong marks. As a general rule, if all the components of a mark are descriptive, the trademark as a whole is also descriptive, and

therefore weak. (See Section C2, above.) But this is by no means always true. In some circumstances, the kind of service or product a mark is attached to, the context of the mark's use and even the public's reaction to the mark can result in weak words combining to form a strong mark.

b. Composites of Whole Words

This type of composite mark consists of individual words with different trademark strengths, like *Gino's Chicago Style Pizza*, which contains a personal name and a geographic term. The first rule about these types of marks is that the whole name is stronger than the sum of its parts. So for example, *Such a Business* is a strong mark for a children's store. It consists of ordinary words, but they are not used descriptively: that is, "Such a Business" tells you nothing about what the business is or what it hopes to purvey. It's the combination of the phrase and the nature of the service that makes it funny, surprising, unique and memorable. The same could be said of *Pea in a Pod* for a maternity store.

Another recent example is a line of books that uses "Don't Know Much About" as a prefix to the subject matter of the book, as in *Don't Know Much About the Civil War*. This prefix is a well-known line from an old Sam Cooke song. The line is sure to grab the attention of most prospective readers over the age of 50 and therefore serves admirably as a trademark, even though it consists entirely of ordinary words. Incidentally, book titles are not, by themselves, entitled to trademark status, but a name that indicates a series of books (*Hardy Boys, Nancy Drew, Dummy*) is entitled to protection.

Other composites of weak elements can also make a stronger whole. For example, *Houlihan's Old Place* is an effective trademark for a restaurant. This composite of two sorts of names is much more suggestive than simply *Houlihan's* (which as a personal name can get no trademark protection without secondary meaning), or the

Old Place (which, although not necessarily descriptive, is vague and not particularly memorable.) Again, taken together, the elements of this mark are more distinctive than either is alone.

On the other hand, *Bette's Oceanview Diner*, in the Oceanview section of Berkeley, California, is a moderately weak composite mark. That's because it combines two ordinary terms, a personal name and a geographic term, and uses them descriptively. As we have learned, this is not a recipe for a strong mark. Unless such a mark can show secondary meaning, the only protection Bette is likely to get is under state unfair competition laws, and then only if a rival restaurant uses a similar mark in the same local area, and if customers are likely to be confused by it. (Chapter 11, Section C, discusses this sort of protection in more detail.)

Now consider the composite mark, *I Can't Believe It's Not Butter!* For the uninitiated, this is a brand of margarine, not just a promotional slogan. It is descriptive because it conveys the information that the product is a close imitation of butter. Furthermore, it's exactly the kind of phrase that a rival margarine producer might want to use in advertising. But the fact that the brand name is a complete sentence with an exclamation point at the end makes it unusual, and even memorable, which means it's distinctive, which gives it legal strength.

Take another example. Colin Moriarity runs a chimney cleaning service called *The Irish Sweep*. The mark is a composite of descriptive terms, because he is in fact an Irish chimney sweeper. But we bet you'd remember the name. Why? Because it plays on a famous horse race, the Irish Sweepstakes. Also, one word, "sweep," is an archaic term for a chimney sweeper, and gives the whole trademark a more evocative feel. To some extent the strength of this trademark depends on whether many people recognize "sweep" as equivalent to chimney cleaner. If they do, it's descriptive. And yet, people can know what it means and still recognize it as archaic. On the

other hand, if the mark's key feature, "sweep," is just a term in common use, then the trademark using it is just descriptive and too ordinary to be a protectible mark, without secondary meaning.

c. Composites of Elements of Words

These are one-word marks, such as *Ultraswim*, *Bushhawk* and *Microsoft*, made up of recognizable separate words. These marks are different from those consisting of coined words discussed in Section C1, above. Coined terms are wholly new words that mean nothing. But because composite marks contain elements of words, they carry meaning, even if it is only to evoke an image. That makes them more akin to suggestive or descriptive marks than to coined terms. (If you are confused, see coined marks and suggestive marks in Section C, above.) What makes this kind of composite mark strong or weak is not what its elements are, but how it is used. For example, *Ultraswim* as a trademark for a piece of swimming equipment would be descriptive and so weak. But as used on a shampoo designed for swimmers, it is suggestive, and so stronger. On the other hand, *Bufferin* is considered an inherently descriptive mark, even though it's a composite that's not in the dictionary. That's because it's simply a contraction of buffered aspirin, and the result is too close to the descriptive word "buffered" and the generic term "aspirin" to be distinctive.

Many businesses have latched on to the idea of creating a mark out of word fragments. Unfortunately they often select terms, at least in computer and technological fields, that are so overused that they have become hackneyed and therefore descriptive. The result is that trademarks using elements like web-, laser-, super-, macro-, -tech, -soft, data- and compu-, even though they are made up, are not unusual, and so not very distinctive or memorable. This is really an instance where the early bird got the worm. Only the first ones to pick such marks, like *Microsoft*, who got in before the genre became so common, had a strong mark even before they built up extensive public recognition.

d. Slogans

Slogans like "Just Do It" (*Nike*), "Life is a Journey: Enjoy the Ride" (*Nissan*), "I Love What You Do For Me" (*Toyota*) and "You're In Good Hands" (*Allstate* insurance) are valuable trademarks because they create indelible consumer impressions. Distinctive (or strong) slogans can be registered as trademarks with the Trademark Office. Some slogans are inherently distinctive—that is, by their very nature they create a memorable association with a particular product or service. For example, "Reach Out and Touch Someone" is inherently distinctive because it does not describe phone services; rather, it cleverly suggests or promotes a quality of life enhanced by phone communication. The same is true of "Just Do It," a slogan that connotes the active life without describing any aspect of Nike or its products. An inherently distinctive slogan is usually a pithy, short phrase that does more than inform or describe—it promotes.

By contrast, a slogan such as "Extra Strength Pain Reliever," is merely informative and does not, by itself, distinguish *Excedrin* from other analgesics. However, even though this particular slogan is not inherently distinctive, it has become distinctive by acquiring a secondary meaning through sales and advertising. This was also the case with "Hair Color So Natural Only Your Hairdresser Knows For Sure" for *Miss Clairol* hair products.

As with other types of marks, slogans that are inherently descriptive or that have become distinctive under the secondary meaning rule may be federally registered and protected nationwide. See Chapter 8, Federal Trademark Registration.

Some slogans, like some generic terms, can never function as marks. For example, the phrases "Why Pay More!" and "Proudly Made in the U.S.A." were both rejected for registration because they were common commercial phrases and failed to distinguish the goods or services to which they were attached.

If your mark is a combination of a business or product name and a slogan, such as *Happy Clown —America's Favorite Ice Cream*, the slogan part must meet the same standards for distinctiveness as if the slogan stood alone. For example, if you attempted to federally register *Happy Clown—America's Favorite Ice Cream* as a mark, the Trademark Examiner would break the mark into two parts—*Happy Clown* and *America's Favorite Ice Cream*. Although Happy Clown would by itself probably qualify as a distinctive mark, America's Favorite Ice Cream would not be considered distinctive, primarily because it uses a common phrase to describe rather than promote the product. For that reason, the Trademark Examiner would require you to disclaim the slogan as a condition of having "Happy Clown" placed on the principal register.

See Chapter 8, Section F4, for more on what it means to disclaim a word or phrase.

TIPS FOR SELECTING A SLOGAN

1. Avoid using common commercial phrases, especially if the phrase is part of the trade language ("Think Green" for recycled paper).
2. Avoid describing the product or service ("Finest Salsa That Money Can Buy.")
3. Keep it short and pithy ("Just Do It.")
4. Use the slogan vigorously on the product, in conjunction with the service and with all advertising.

Sorting Out Trademark Disputes

Most businesses first become aware of trademark principles when:

- the business learns—usually from a customer or trade journal—that a competitor is using a copycat name for a similar product or service in a situation where money may be lost as a result of customer confusion, or
- the business receives a stiff letter from another company's lawyer alleging that the business is improperly using a name or other type of trademark that belongs to the lawyer's client and demanding that the business stop using the mark or suffer the legal consequences, or
- the business's application to use its business name as its Internet domain name is denied because it has already been taken.

Few things disturb a business owner quite as much as a dispute over his or her exclusive right to use the business's chosen name to identify its goods or services. As we discussed in Chapter 1, A Trademark Primer, a business's mark is normally intimately linked with the recognition and good will the business enjoys in the marketplace. So a dispute over that mark sets off alarm bells.

A. How to Think About Trademark Disputes

A trademark dispute may involve the simultaneous use of the same mark (*Elise's-Elise's*) or the simultaneous use of similar marks (*Snapper-Snooper*). When a trademark dispute first surfaces, the question uppermost on the minds of all concerned parties is: Who's in the right? While it is sometimes easy to answer this question, most often it isn't. In essence the answer depends upon the answers to these questions:

- Who was first to use the mark?
- Is the mark famous?
- Was the mark registered with the PTO when the second use occurred?

- Would simultaneous use of the marks create the likelihood of customer confusion?

1. Answers Are Hard to Come By

While it is often possible to determine who used a disputed mark first and whether the mark was registered when the second use began, the other two issues are more problematic. If a mark is famous, the first user can prevent virtually all later uses. For example, McDonald's was able to prevent the use of *McClaim* (for a legal clinic). If the original mark isn't famous, then use of the mark by a different business will only be wrong if it is being used in a context giving rise to the likelihood of customer confusion. No book can give you the definitive answer as to when customer confusion is likely in a given case. Even an attorney can only give you an educated guess. Many trademark cases involve attorneys on opposite sides who are seriously convinced that customers both would and would not be confused by a simultaneous use of the disputed marks. The bottom line is, it is very difficult to tell who is right in any given trademark dispute. This chapter explains the guidelines that the courts use to decide this question if the dispute gets that far. But the operative word is guidelines, not answers.

2. How Most Disputes Are Resolved

If you can't tell for sure who is in the right, then how should you proceed if you are locked in a trademark dispute? The only way to force a resolution is to go to court and find out what a judge has to say. But courts are expensive. (See Chapter 1, Section C5). It may be possible—if both parties agree—to resolve the dispute through mediation or by submitting the issue to arbitration (See Chapter 12). However, most trademark disputes are resolved through negotiation and typically end up with the economically weaker party agreeing to back down, regardless of who was first to use the mark. If, however, the economically weaker party has a strong legal claim to ownership of the mark, the larger company will usually be willing to pay something in exchange for the weaker party's acquiescence. Please understand that the authors aren't endorsing what appears to be a cynical view of how trademark disputes get resolved. It's just the way things are.

3. Changing a Mark May Not Be So Bad

In fact, many marks used by small and medium-size businesses can be modified without significant damage, especially if there is time to plan the change. While some customers may be lost when a new mark is introduced, most will continue patronizing a business or using a product that has served them well. And a name change can even provide a convenient opportunity for a business to draw attention to its goods or services by announcing the change in the media and direct mail pieces. Also, if a big company is challenging a small company's mark, the small company can often get a lot of mileage in the media if they emphasize how they have been bullied into making the change.

4. The Internet Complicates the Decision to Change a Mark

Unfortunately, deciding whether to change a business or product name in response to a trademark conflict has been greatly complicated by the advent of the World Wide Web. If your business is on the Web and is using the name in question to identify its Web site, you will probably have to take the name out of your Web address in order to settle the dispute. To the extent that other sites are already linked to yours under your original address, you will have to rebuild those links, which may take quite an effort. And so, when deciding whether to switch rather than fight, remember that your switch will most likely implicate your Web activities as well as your other marketing actions.

5. Why Trademark Infringement Suits Are Filed

If you decide to hold on to your mark, the other trademark user may decide to sue you to force your hand. If the other user owned the trademark before you started using yours, the decision to sue you may in turn be forced by a fundamental trademark rule: If you don't protect your mark, you'll lose your right of exclusive use. In other words, even if the other trademark user wanted to give you a break, it could only do so at the expense of the value of its own mark, a price that in most instances would be too high. So, if you are sued, don't assume it's because the bad guys want to torture you. As they say in mob movies, "it's just business." (For more information on maintaining a trademark, see Chapter 9.)

6. What Happens in a Trademark Infringement Lawsuit

Even if you are in the right (which this chapter helps you determine), you most likely will have to spend at least $10,000 up front for an attorney in order to hold your own in federal court, which is where most trademark cases are filed. Trademark cases tend to proceed in two phases. In the first phase, a business asks a judge to issue a temporary order (called a Preliminary Injunction) requiring the other user of the mark to stop the use pending further court proceedings. If the judge grants this order, it is because the judge believes that the party bringing the suit (the plaintiff) is likely to win at trial. If the judge denies the order, then he or she has concluded that there is no infringement. Either way, this preliminary finding is often enough to lead the parties to settle the lawsuit out of court. The second phase happens if there is no settlement. In that case, full-bore federal litigation ensues, which can drive the price well into six figures pronto. See Chapter 12 for more about what a federal court trademark suit looks like.

Now that you've been doused with the cold water of legal reality, American style, it's time to turn to the purpose of this chapter; deciding whether existing marks legally conflict and, assuming they do, how to sort out the legal rights of the businesses that claim ownership of the marks. Also, in Section F, we help you resolve the troublesome issue of conflicts between trademarks and Internet domain names.

B. When Do Trademarks Legally Conflict?

Trademarks legally conflict in three situations:

1. There is a likelihood of customer confusion between the goods or services offered by the owners of two marks.

2. There is a likelihood of customer confusion as to the source or origin of the goods or services offered by owners of one mark.

3. There is a likelihood that a nationally well known (famous) mark, such as *Mercedes* (automobiles), *Hyatt* (hotels) or *IBM* (office machines), will have the strength of its name or its reputation for quality degraded by another's use of the mark, even if the context of the second use doesn't necessarily involve customer confusion.

In the first two scenarios, you will seldom be able to use the courts to resolve the conflict unless the marks are in competing or related fields, that is, unless they overlap in market, product or

service category. That's because there must be a likelihood of confusing the consuming public as to the source of the goods, or as to the goods themselves, before you can invoke trademark principles. As a result, it's generally permissible to use the same mark as another if your field is so distinct from the original user's that no confusion will result.

For example, many similar names coexist legally as marks on different goods, like *Cascade*, which separately identifies a whiskey, a baking mix and a dishwashing detergent—all of which are names owned by different companies. *Dunhill* cigarettes and *Dunhill* shoes, and *Sunkist* fruits and *Sunkist* baked goods are other examples of similar names used to identify goods in product categories that are sufficiently different to avoid the likelihood that customers will be confused as to the products or their source.

But the third situation—famous marks—poses an important exception to the rule that trademark disputes require the use of names similar enough to potentially confuse customers. Called the "dilution" doctrine, it operates even in instances where there is no actual likelihood of customer confusion between goods or services. The theory here is that the use of a famous trademark by anyone other than its owner will cause the mark to lose its distinctive character—that is, its legal strength will be diluted or its reputation for denoting the quality of the product or service to which it's attached will be diminished. Also, according to some courts, the public would be confused in any event by the use of a famous mark in that they would necessarily expect the business owning the famous mark to be associated in some way with the second user.

In the next section (Section C), we provide an overview of the laws that govern the way most trademark disputes are resolved. Then in the following sections we give more detail about the dilution doctrine (Section D) and the way the courts resolve disputes between marks that do involve the likelihood of customer confusion (Sections E and H through L). Finally, in Section F, we discuss how disputes between trademarks and Internet domain names are resolved.

C. The Legal Framework for Solving Trademark Conflicts

Four basic sources of law govern the use of trademarks, any of which may apply to you, depending on the facts of your case:

- the federal Lanham Act and its registration provisions
- the federal Lanham Act's unfair competition provision (Section 43(a))
- state statutes governing trademarks
- the common law (based on court decisions, not statutes) of trademark and unfair competition.

The coverage of these laws overlaps frequently —in fact, an infringer may violate all of these at once. In practice, when a trademark dispute ends up in court, the lawyers will claim infringement under every trademark law provision that even remotely applies because you can't be certain which one (or ones) the judge will decide to base a decision on.

1. The Federal Lanham Act's Registration Provisions

The federal statute known as the Lanham Act (37 U.S.C. 1110 et seq.) applies to all trademarks and service marks that are used "in commerce that Congress may regulate." This includes marks that are in use across state, territorial or international boundaries and marks that affect interstate, territorial or international commerce. (See Chapter 8, Federal Trademark Registration, Section A1, for a definition of "commerce.")

The Lanham Act provides for the federal registration of marks that are already in use in commerce, and which the Patent and Trademark Office considers to be distinctive. Although it is

possible to apply to register a mark that isn't being used (called an intent-to-use application), the actual registration won't occur until the applicant files a document showing that mark has been put into actual use in commerce. See Chapter 8.

Marks that are placed on the Principal Federal Trademark Register maintained by the Patent and Trademark Office have the following advantages in case of a dispute:

- The mark's owner is presumed to have the exclusive right to use the mark nationwide.
- Everyone in the country is presumed to know about the mark (even if they haven't actually heard of it).
- Anyone who begins using a confusingly similar mark after your mark has appeared on the federal register will be deemed a willful infringer, assuming a legal conflict exists, which means you can collect large damages and pay for your lawsuit.
- The mark can qualify for "incontestable" status if it stays on the principal register for five years (this status significantly strengthens the mark against legal challenges—see Chapter 9, How to Use and Care for Your Trademark.)

MARKS PLACED ON THE FEDERAL SUPPLEMENTAL REGISTER

Trademarks that are not distinctive do not qualify for the principal federal trademark register, but they do qualify for registration on the federal supplemental register. When we talk about a federally registered mark throughout this chapter, we mean a mark registered on the federal principal register only. This is because the supplemental register doesn't provide the mark owner with the protections that accompany placement on the principal register. Instead it only provides some notice to prospective users of the mark that the mark is already taken.

2. The Lanham Act's Intent to Use Provisions

Over 90% of all applications for federal trademark registration are for marks that have already been placed into use in commerce that Congress may regulate (interstate, international or inter-territorial). However, as outlined in Chapter 8, Federal Trademark Registration, Section B, it is also possible to file a registration application for a mark intended for use within the next six months. Several extensions of this six-month period can be purchased from the trademark office if adequate reasons are given for the delay.

If a dispute arises with another business over who was the first to use the mark described in the "intent to use" application, the application filing date is considered the date the applicant first put the mark into use (called constructive use). The filing date will therefore control ownership of the mark if the mark has not been used previously. If, on the other hand, the mark has been used by another business on similar goods or services prior to the constructive use date, that other business will normally be considered the owner of the mark, assuming it has been kept in use. One court has even ruled that the prior user of a similar mark on dissimilar goods can claim priority. *Eredisar Ltd. v. Virgin Enterprises*, 33 United States Patent Quarterly, 2nd series, Pg. 2020 (Southern District New York 1995).

It's important to understand that a mark described in an intent to use application will not be registered until the applicant files a follow-up document showing that the mark has been placed into actual use in commerce that Congress may regulate (interstate, inter-territorial or international commerce).

3. The Lanham Act's Unfair Competition Provision

In addition to providing for the registration of marks used "in commerce," the Lanham Act allows owners of marks that are used "in com-merce" but that have not been registered to sue infringers in federal court and obtain almost the same relief as if they had registered their marks— although it is harder to get such relief for unregistered marks than it is for registered marks. Under Section 17 U.S.C. §1125(a), also known as 43(a), any person who uses a false designation of origin or a false description of fact on goods or services in commerce, in a way that is likely to confuse or deceive, is liable to another business that suffers damages as a result. This very broad provision prohibits the misleading use of any mark or commercial symbol on goods or services in commerce.

To complain of a violation of Section 43(a) you don't need a registered mark, or a dispute between rival businesses. You do need many of the same facts that must be present for trademark infringement. For example, the likelihood that using a mark (or name or packaging) will confuse the public is an issue in an unfair competition case. As a result, the mark either must be inherently strong or must have attained a secondary meaning through public recognition.

Many cases of trademark infringement also involve violations of unfair competition laws. An example of trademark infringement mixed with broader unfair competition claims occurred between *Big O Tires*, a mid-sized regional tire distributor, and *Goodyear. Big O* began marketing a bias belted tire under the unregistered mark *BigFoot* in early 1974. The tire giant *Goodyear* coincidentally decided to market a radial tire under the *BigFoot* mark in late 1974. The larger company pumped millions of dollars into its advertising effort, which overlapped *Big O's* advertising effort to some extent. As a result, the public began coming to *Big O* asking for *Goodyear's* tire.

Angry and disappointed, consumers suspected *Big O* of stealing the idea from *Goodyear*.

But in fact *Goodyear* had become aware of *Big O's* prior use of the same mark midway into its marketing plans, and had unsuccessfully negotiated to buy the mark from them. Nevertheless, they continued to use the mark. This resulted in a judgment for *Big O* of $4.7 million dollars. That's a clear case of trademark infringement, and it's also a case of unfair competition—*Goodyear* intentionally undertook conduct that deceived the public into thinking badly of a rival.

4. The Lanham Act's Anti-Dilution Provision

In 1996, Congress added a law to the Lanham Act that prohibits activity leading to the dilution of famous marks (42 USC §1125(a)(c), an activity previously only prohibited by state laws. In earlier sections of the book we described dilution as use of a famous mark in a way that would dilute the mark's strength or tarnish its reputation for quality. Although the federal dilution law does not directly prohibit activity that would tarnish a mark's reputation for quality, it is clear that Congress intended it to do so. It is likely that it will be interpreted as such in the future.

While the statute prohibits dilution, it only provides relief if the dilution begins after the mark's fame is achieved and only if use of the mark causes dilution of its distinctive quality. According to the statute, a mark must be distinctive to be famous. (This becomes circular in the extreme, since by definition a famous mark has become distinctive by acquiring a secondary meaning.) When deciding whether a mark is famous, the court is to review the criteria listed below. Because none of the criteria are given specific weight, there is no way to tell for sure what makes a mark famous. But essentially it boils down to the same criteria that make a mark distinctive—the degree to which:

- the mark has inherent distinctiveness
- the mark has acquired distinctiveness through secondary meaning
- the mark has been used, in general, and the length of such use
- the geographical use of the mark is widespread
- the mark is widely recognized in the marketing channels
- the extent to which the mark is used by third parties and
- whether the mark is federally registered.

As we point out in Chapter 10, trying to assess distinctiveness on the basis of so many factors is a difficult task at best. So it is with determining whether or not a mark is famous. Congress has left the question of distinctiveness to the courts and the courts have left it to the lawyers, who can at best make an educated guess. And that's the best we can do too.

Although it is hard to tell what makes a mark famous, it isn't at all hard to tell what activities won't count as dilution of a famous mark under this federal law. The statute tells us that it doesn't apply to the use of a famous mark for noncommercial purposes, such as parodies, advertising (including comparative advertising), consumer product reviews and news coverage.

Although the main relief the courts are authorized to provide under the new Lanham Act provision is injunctive relief against further diluting uses of the famous mark, the new statute also authorizes money damages, including triple damages and attorneys' fees, if the infringer willfully intended to trade on the owner's reputation or to cause dilution of the famous mark. This factor alone provides the new law with considerable punch, since the use of indisputably famous marks such as *McDonald's* (*McClaim, McSleep*) is actually intended in precisely this way. And so, the advice we provide at different points in this book is now precisely on point. Do not get caught trying to pass off your mark as a famous mark belonging to someone else. You may be in for rough sledding that could end up costing you a bundle.

5. State Trademark and Unfair Competition Laws

If neither of the two marks involved in a dispute qualifies for federal protection because neither mark is involved in commerce that Congress may regulate, the conflict will be resolved under state law. States have three types of laws that deal with trademark disputes:

1. A number of states have anti-dilution laws. As we explain in more detail in Section D, these laws allow the owner of a well-known mark to stop the use of a copycat mark without having to establish the likelihood of customer confusion.
2. All states have statutes that govern regular trademark disputes.
3. All states have statutes or a body of court-developed law that prohibits unfair competition.

Both the trademark statutes and the rules against unfair competition almost always dictate that the first to use a name will always have precedence over the second user when the potential for customer confusion exists.

State trademark statutes have provisions that are very much like the federal Lanham Act, but they apply on a statewide basis only. For more about them, see Chapter 7, State Trademark Registration.

STATE TRADEMARK REGISTRATION

Most states have lists of trademarks that are in use in that state. The primary function of these lists is to provide notice to would-be trademark users that the trademark is already taken. When a dispute develops between a mark on a state's trademark list and another mark, state trademark law will usually resolve the dispute in favor of the first user. State registration itself usually has no particular effect on the outcome except as evidence of when the registrant first used the mark. But in a few states, registration makes mark ownership easier to prove in court. (See Chapter 7 for more detail on state trademark registration.)

State rules against unfair competition also mirror the federal unfair competition statute, Lanham Act Section 43(a). They apply to marks that are not registered as well as to situations that don't involve marks—such as disputes over trade dress. (See Chapter 2, Section G, for a discussion of trade dress.) All state unfair competition cases require some evidence that the conflicting use of two marks or of similar trade dress will confuse the consumer before one business will be forced to change, and most demand proof of distinctiveness or secondary meaning.

6. Common Law of Trademarks

Both state and federal courts have developed a body of law over the years that covers trademarks. Much of this law has also been placed in statutes (codified). This court-made law applies to all trademarks, registered or not, and reflects the principles we have been discussing throughout the book. In a nutshell, the common law of trademarks provides that to be protected, a mark must be distinctive or must have developed secondary meaning. And for a legal conflict to exist, there must be a likelihood of customer confusion.

D. Disputes Under State Dilution Laws

In addition to the Lanham Act (see Section C above), over half the states also have statutes that prohibit the copying of a famous mark even in a context where no customer confusion is likely. Before the federal statute, these statutes provided the legal basis for filing a dilution suit. And because most famous marks are famous in every state, these state laws provided an adequate basis for bringing that type of case. Because these state laws are still on the books, dilution suits may still be brought under them.

The states that have these dilution statutes are: Alabama, Arizona, Arkansas, California, Connecticut, Delaware, Florida, Georgia, Hawaii, Idaho, Illinois, Indiana, Iowa, Kansas, Louisiana, Maine, Massachusetts, Minnesota, Missouri, Montana, Nebraska, New Hampshire, New Mexico, New York, Oregon, Pennsylvania, Puerto Rico, Rhode Island, Tennessee, Texas and Washington. An additional five states recognize the dilution doctrine under cases decided by their courts: Kentucky, Maryland, Michigan, New Jersey and Ohio.

⚠ The Following Material Only Applies to State Dilution Statutes

Although in the future most dilution lawsuits will rely primarily on the federal dilution statute, because of its potential for awarding triple damages and attorneys' fees, suits filed in states that have state dilution statutes will also include claims under those state statutes. For that reason, we are setting out some basic principles of state dilution law in this section of Chapter 11. But remember, what we discuss here applies only to the state statutes. Nevertheless, because judges always like to follow what other judges have done, some of the principles discussed here will undoubtedly be adopted by the federal courts when they set out to interpret similar provisions contained in the new federal dilution statute.

1. State Anti-Dilution Statutes Only Apply to Well Known Marks

State Anti-Dilution statues apply only to marks which are identical or very similar to a strong, well-known mark. Thus when the Amstar Corp. sued Domino Pizza for diluting its *Domino* sugar mark, the courts refused to grant the injunction. It said that the *Domino* name had already become weak because many other businesses also use the mark to sell products other than those sold by Amstar.

Even where the original mark is inherently distinctive, dilution may not be found if the mark is not well known. For example, even though the term *Lexis* is well known among attorneys for computerized legal research services, most of the general public has never heard of it. So a judge ruled that it is not a strong enough mark to be damaged (diluted) by the use of *Lexus* as a mark for a luxury car. Further, the courts felt that most of those who are familiar with *Lexis* are sophisticated enough to recognize the spelling difference and market disparity, and so would not be likely to confuse the two marks.

2. What Do State Anti-Dilution Rules Prevent?

As mentioned, there are two basic purposes underlying anti-dilution statutes:

- to prevent a mark's strength from being diluted
- to prevent a mark's reputation for quality from being tarnished.

TIFFANY & CO.

a. Dilution of a Mark's Distinctiveness

Anti-dilution statutes are primarily based on the theory that certain uses of a distinctive mark should be enjoined because they will take away from the mark's distinctiveness or harm its reputation. For example, Polaroid was able to enjoin the use of *Polaraid* as a service mark for installing refrigeration systems, because it would blur the mental image and immediate identification that consumers have between the mark *Polaroid* and quality cameras. On a similar basis, Bacardi Rum stopped a jewelry store from using its mark, and Tiffany & Co., the New York jewelers, prevented a Boston restaurant from using its mark.

In each of these cases, the two marks were identical or very similar, the goods/services did not compete, and no likelihood of confusion existed. Rather the question was whether the distinctive and famous mark in each of those cases was made less distinctive by the second use of the mark.

b. Tarnishment or Injury to Business Reputation

Tarnishment of a mark occurs when the second use creates an unwanted association with the original mark, or detracts from its image for quality goods or services.

> **EXAMPLE:** Mike decides that his plumbing business would gain visibility with the name Gucci's Plumbing. Because plumbing detracts from the fashionable image invoked by the well-known *Gucci* trademark, Mike would probably be prevented from using the *Gucci* name in any state that has dilution laws.

The tarnishment aspect of the dilution rule was also the reason that the owners of *Cabbage Patch Dolls* were able to stop the sale of *Garbage Pail Kids.* Likewise, Anheuser-Busch prevented an insecticide-maker from using the phrase, "Where there's life, there's bugs."

Courts are especially likely to find tarnishment where the offending marks are attached to products that are "unwholesome or unsavory." Examples of marks that have been enjoined under this prong of the dilution theory are the fake American Express card shown with a condom that said, "Never Leave Home Without It," or the use of Dallas Cowboy cheerleader uniforms in a pornographic film, or the "Enjoy Cocaine" poster that used a script and coloring identical to *Coca-Cola's.*

PARODY AND SATIRE ARE NOT DILUTION

Satirical uses or parodies of marks might appear as obvious examples of tarnishment. Nevertheless, our Constitution's First Amendment protects satires and parodies that clearly aren't using a mark to market goods or services commercially. But what about parodies in the form of marks used on commercial products?

Even commercial parodies may not be barred by the dilution doctrine unless all the criteria for dilution are met. For example, when *Jordache* sued *Hogg Wyld, Ltd.,* under a dilution theory for using the mark *Lardache* on wearing apparel, it was not considered dilution. That's because the mark was not identical and the parody tended to increase, not dilute, the public's identification of the *Jordache's* mark with Jordache's products.

---

3. State Dilution Laws Vary Slightly

Most states have based their dilution laws on the provision set out below from the original Model Trademark Act, Section 12. Dilution is now addressed in Section 13 of the amended Model Trademark Act. No state has yet adopted Section 13, which would significantly increase the number of situations in which dilution might be found to occur. But, if history is a guide, Section 13 will be adopted by the same states that adopted the previous Section 12. Section 12 reads:

"Injury to business reputation; dilution

"Likelihood of injury to business reputation or of dilution of the distinctive quality of a mark registered under this Act, or a mark valid at common law, or a trademark valid at common law, shall be a ground for injunctive relief notwithstanding the absence of competition between the parties or the absence of confusion as to the source of goods or services."

Each state interprets those provisions slightly differently. The main differences are whether a mark must be famous or unique in addition to being distinctive, and whether distinctiveness is required to prove tarnishment, as opposed to proving dilution of the distinctive quality of the mark. If you want further information about the peculiarities of your state's dilution statute, see Chapter 15, Help Beyond the Book, for how to use a law library.

E. Disputes That Involve Customer Confusion

Most trademark disputes focus on whether customers are likely to be confused as to which product or service is being purchased, or as to who is behind the product or service. The main idea is to give businesses the benefit of the goodwill they've built up under a mark and prevent unchecked marketplace confusion that would result from overlapping marks.

> **EXAMPLE 1:** Oliver LaRocque of Sedona, Arizona, markets a brand of garlic-stuffed olives to several Sedona markets under the name *Ollie's Stinking Olives*. Pollie Jones, an unfriendly neighbor, decides to compete with Oliver and names her product *Pollie's Garlic Olives*. Because Ollie and Pollie have competing products under marks that could easily be confused by customers (they might mistakenly buy Pollie's olives thinking they are Ollie's olives), the marks legally conflict.

> **EXAMPLE 2:** Sally Lee Humbold sells frozen pizzas under the name *Sally Lee's Italian*. Because customers might think that the pizzas are a *Sara Lee* product, chances are excellent a judge would prevent her from using the name, even though pizzas and baked goods don't directly compete with each other. In addition, because *Sara Lee* is used on such a wide variety of frozen foods that it's reasonable to foresee a *Sara Lee* frozen pizza in the future, *Sally Lee's* use will likely cause confusion.

1. What's the Likelihood of Customer Confusion?

The courts have developed several tests to judge whether customer confusion is likely to result in a given case. We discuss these tests in detail in Chapter 4, How to Tell If Two Marks Are Confusingly Similar. Read that chapter if you need more information on this subject. Generally, however, it's fair to say that potential customer confusion is a factor in your situation if:

- you honestly believe that customers might currently confuse your goods or services with a competitor's because of a physical or perceptive similarity between the two marks, and an overlapping of marketing territories or channels; or
- you purposely selected your mark because of its similarity to another mark and the owner of the other mark is now calling you on it.

2. The Importance of Marketing Territories

Two marks only come into legal conflict if they are used in the same market or marketing territory. In the age of modern communications and the Internet, the definition of what constitutes a marketing territory is rapidly changing. Because of cable TV superstations, the Internet and World Wide Web, online computer services such as *America Online*, national newspapers (*U.S.A. Today*), periodicals and syndicated radio and TV programs, the producers of more and more goods and services are able to claim a national marketing territory.

Still, many businesses in the United States are local in nature, and unless they are doing business on the World Wide Web and reaching out to a wider customer base, they may reasonably claim only a relatively small portion of a city or county as their marketing territory. For instance, two video rental businesses using the same name are likely to have completely different marketing territories if one of them is in Pasadena and the other is in Manhattan Beach, which are separate cities fifty miles apart yet still within the greater Los Angeles area. And even if both businesses have sites on the World Wide Web, their customer bases will almost certainly remain local.

While a marketing territory is impossible to define with precision, it is relatively easy to recognize. It is the rough geographic area from which a business of your type can reasonably expect to attract its customers. If anyone anywhere can order products or services from you through your Web site, or your mail order business is advertised in national periodicals, or your products are regularly reviewed in national trade magazines, your marketing territory is the entire country. If your only marketing is done in your local Yellow Pages, the phone company has, in effect, defined your marketing territory for you.

3. The Crucial Question of When a Mark Is First Used

As a general rule, the first business to use a mark owns it against businesses who try to use it at a later time in a context where a legal conflict exists. Therefore it should not be surprising that most of the rules for resolving trademark disputes that we use in this chapter turn on the question of who used the mark first.

To understand this chapter, therefore, it is necessary to define what we mean by "use." It's simply this:

- actual use in commerce; or
- constructive use through an application to the PTO to register the mark on an intent-to-use basis.

a. Actual Use in Commerce

A mark is in actual use when it is attached to a product that is being sold in the marketplace or is used in a business's marketing materials for the purpose of selling the business's service. Actual use must be a commercial use, not simply a token use to obtain trademark priority. See Chapter 8, Federal Trademark Registration, Section B4, for more on what constitutes actual use for trademark registration purposes and for how to document it.

b. Constructive Use

It is possible to apply to have a mark placed on the federal Principal Trademark Register on the basis of intended use—even though the mark is not yet in actual use. The date an "intended use" application is filed with the Patent and Trademark Office is considered the date the mark was first used, assuming the applicant goes on to actually use the mark at a later time and files the necessary documents to place the mark on the federal Principal Trademark Register. This type of use is termed a constructive use because it is created by the law rather than by real events.

EXAMPLE: In March 1993, Paul begins distributing a line of distinctive jewelry (bracelets and earrings) called *Cleopatra Designs*. Unknown to him, Oscar had previously applied to register *Cleopatra Designs* on the federal Principal Trademark Register in connection with its intended use on a line of women's clothing. Even though Paul actually began using the mark first, and Oscar's application is still pending, Oscar will have priority on the basis of first use if his application is ultimately approved and a legal conflict develops between the two marks.

4. The Crucial Question of Good Faith About an Existing Mark

The rights of a second or junior user of a mark to continue using the mark in the event of a legal conflict depends upon whether the second use was undertaken in good faith. Good faith involves two issues:

- Did the second user know of the existing mark?
- Was the existing mark known in the second user's marketing territory?

If either question can be answered "yes," then good faith is not present and the second user must stop use of the mark upon a challenge by the first user. Let's take a little closer look at these questions.

> **⚠ A Fine Legal Point**
> Technically, the good faith issue only extends to whether the second user knew of the existing mark. The issue of whether the existing mark was known in the second user's marketing territory is usually discussed in terms of remoteness—that is, the second user must qualify as a remote user in order to preserve some rights. We have combined the good faith and remoteness factors under the good faith label for greater simplicity of presentation. It should cause no problem in

understanding your rights as we discuss them in this chapter.

If the second user knew of the first use before adopting the mark, the dispute will be resolved entirely in favor of the first user. However, if the second user didn't know of the first use, the second user may have some rights—although limited—in case of a dispute, unless the mark was known to the customers in the second user's marketing territory. If it was, it won't make any difference that the second user didn't actually know of the mark. The first user will be given priority on the ground that its marketing territory was already established when the second use was initiated. If, on the other hand, neither the second user's customer base nor the second user had knowledge of the existing mark, the second user may continue to use the mark in its current marketing territory, but nowhere else.

As we'll see in the rest of this chapter, the second user will be presumed to know about any mark that is on the federal Principal Trademark Register. This, of course, means that a trademark search is always wise before adopting and using a new business name or other device as a service mark or trademark. Although there is no similar presumption that a second user ought to know of an unregistered mark just because it is well known, we are fast becoming a global village, and more and more marks can be said to have a nationwide exposure. And, as we explained above, if the first user can establish this fact, the first user will prevail over the second user.

F. An Introduction to Trademark Conflicts on the World Wide Web

In Chapter 1, Section D we provide a brief overview of the World Wide Web (the Web) and its impact on trademark law. There we point out that the Web is an electronic community completely devoid of physical location. When you go out into the Web with your browser software you have access to a computer network that crosses state, national and international boundries without so much as a hiccup. Click on a button that says "stamp collecting" and you may be linked with a stamp collector who lives in Athens, Greece; Moscow, Russia; or Patagonia, Argentina. It makes no difference. As long as the stamp collector has a computer that is hooked up to the Internet, the collector might as well be doing business down the street from you.

1. How Customers Find Businesses on the Web

How do customers find businesses on the Web? Every business on the Web has what's called a domain name. The domain name is a unique "address" that computers understand. If you already have been informed about the domain name for a business, you can enter the name in your Web browser and link directly to the business's home page (the introductory page that then typically links to other pages maintained by that business according to topic). For instance, if you watch television you know that many advertisements now include the domain name for the sponsoring company. For example, broadcasts of San Francisco Giants baseball games frequently remind listeners that they can visit the Giants' Web page at http://www.sfgiants.com and get all kinds of fascinating information about the team, its players and its schedule; you can even order tickets.

If you don't have a specific domain name in hand, you can use one of the many freely available search engines—for example, Alta Vista [www.altavista.digital.com] and Excite [www.excite.com]—to find providers of a particular product or service you are looking for. You can do this type of search by key word (enter the words "used" and "automobile" and "dealer" to find used car dealers) or by selecting a predefined category offered by the search engine and then working your way through a series of menus (for example, start with shopping, then to automobiles, then to used automobiles, then to dealers in your state or city). Whichever method you pick, the search will produce a list that the computer thinks is consistent with your search request. Under the brief descriptive text that you see on the list is really a set of domain names for the selected providers. By clicking on a list entry, you are telling your computer to take you to the site identified by the underlying domain name.

2. Understanding Domain Names in More Detail

Most Web business addresses consist of two main sections. Consider this Web address: http://www.nolo.com. The first section (http://www) tells the computer that it is looking for a site on the Web. You will find this section in virtually every Web address, although increasingly the "www" is omitted. The second section (nolo.com) is the domain name. The domain name itself consists of two parts. The ".com" portion is termed a top level domain name (TLD) while the "nolo" section is termed a second level domain name (SLD).

The reason the .com part is called a top level domain is that the Web has been organized, for the purpose of U.S. participants, into five broad categories:

- com (for commercial groups)
- edu (for educational institutions)
- gov (for governmental institutions)
- org (for nonprofit organizations), and
- net (for interactive discussion groups).

The reason the nolo part is called a second level domain is that the name denotes one of the approximately 600,000 unique identifiers that is part of the .com top level domain. (But see the sidebar below where we discuss the plan to add new top level domains.) The fact that all businesses in the U.S. who want to do business on the Web have had to operate under one domain, the .com domain, has given rise to enormous trademark-related problems.

3. What Happens When Domain Names Conflict With Established Business Names and Marks

Because each domain name must be unique—so that all the computers attached to the Internet can find it—it is impossible for two different businesses to have exactly the same domain name. If when Nolo applied for its Web address, another business had already grabbed nolo.com as its domain name, Nolo would have had to come up with something at least a little different. While this may not sound like such a big deal, anyone who entered "Nolo" in their browser with the intent of finding the Nolo Web site would have ended up at the other site, and the fact that Nolo's name is widely recognized would have benefited the other business, at least in terms of commerce on the Web.

Although Nolo was able to register nolo.com without a hitch, many other businesses have experienced difficulty, some well known, like McDonald's, Coke, Fry's Electronics, Hertz, Nasdaq, Viacom, MTV, Avon, Levi Strauss, B. Dalton and Readers Digest, and others not so well known. When these businesses attempted to identify their location on the Web by using their name trademark as their second level domain name, they were told that the name was already being used by another business for that purpose and to pick another name.

In some instances, the conflict was due to an honest mistake while in other instances enterprising souls—popularly termed poachers—had deliberately staked out the territory early with the intent of getting paid off by the legitimate owner of the name when it decided to join the Web. In some cases, payments were made and the companies recaptured the second level domain name for their own use. In other cases, the business that first used the second level domain name refused to give it up—usually because they had launched a business on the Web under that name and felt changing the name (and hence their "location") would harm the business.

When these cases were taken to court, they were usually settled in favor of the original name owner, typically for payments that were kept confidential as part of the settlement. In the few cases that were decided by a judge, the original owner of the name trademark won. (See Section F5 below for more on domain names as trademarks.)

4. The Role of the Domain Name Registration Agency When Conflicts Involving Domain Names Occur

Much of the flak about domain name conflicts has been directed at Nework Solutions, Inc. (NSI), the organization that—under a contract with the National Science Foundation—is responsible for handling domain name registrations.

NSI's DAYS ARE NUMBERED

The contract between NSI and and the National Science Foundation expires later this year (1997). A major reorganization of how domain names get registered is in the works, but details of the changes have not yet emerged. Most likely, however, NSI will no longer be the sole registrar of domain names in the U.S., but rather will be one of many registries. Along with increased registries, there are likely to be many new top level domain names. Also expected is a new administrative procedure under which domain name disputes can be resolved without the need to file a lawsuit.

NSI registers domain names on a first come, first served basis. If and when a business decides to do business on the Web and discovers that it can't because its name is already being used as a domain name, it typically files a complaint with NSI demanding that NSI reassign the domain name to it, the name's rightful owner. The demand is squarely based on two legal theories:

1.   A domain name used by one business that is the same as a name trademark belonging to another business constitutes trademark infringement—either because customer confusion is likely (see Chapter 10) or because the domain name use dilutes the strength of a famous trademark owned by the complaining company (see Section C above).

2.   By assisting another business to use the complaining business's trademark, NSI is itself guilty of trademark infringement.

a. The NSI Domain Name Dispute Policy

In response to these demands, NSI has developed a policy that is periodically updated and that basically works this way (as of August 1997):

- A business may challenge a domain name registration by showing that it (the challenging business) owns a registered U.S. or foreign trademark or service mark in the identical second level domain name and that it notified the domain name registrant of its position that the domain name infringes its registered mark and should no longer be used.

- NSI then gives the domain name registrant 30 days to show either that 1) its domain name registration occurred before the challenging business's first use of the name as a mark, or before the effective date of the challenging business's federal or foreign trademark registration, whichever date is earlier, or 2) the domain name registrant has its own federal or foreign trademark registration for the name as a mark (it's often possible to register the identical name for different goods and services).

- If the registrant can establish the earlier domain name registration date or its own trademark registration, it will be allowed to continue using the disputed domain name, provided it agrees to pay (indemnify) NSI if NSI is sued for letting the registrant continue using the name. If the registrant can't establish the earlier date, it will be given 90 days to come up with a different name. In the meantime, NSI will place the disputed name on "hold," where it is not available to anyone, until the dispute has been settled and NSI is shown either a court order or a settlement agreement.

b. What Issues the NSI Policy Doesn't Deal With

The NSI policy is aimed at situations where the owner of a federally registered name trademark is being prevented from using that identical name as a domain name because of a previous domain name registration by another business. But there are lots of other trademark-related issues that NSI doesn't deal with at all, such as:

- What should happen if a domain name is confusingly similar to a registered trademark—but not identical?

- What should happen if a domain name is identical or confusingly similar to an unregistered trademark or a state registered mark?

- What should happen if a domain name that is identical or confusingly similar to another business's trademark identifies a site offering goods or services that are not related to or competing with the goods or services offered by the trademark owner?

- What should happen if the domain name registrant used the name as a trademark before the challenging business registered it, but never got around to doing its own registration?

We address these issues in the next subsection.

5. When Domain Names Create Trademark Conflicts

Despite the massive changes that the Internet is visiting on trademark law, Congress has not yet passed any statute dealing with them. This means that it's up to the courts to sort out conflicts between trademarks and domain names. While many lawsuits have been filed over various types of conflicts between trademarks and domain names, most of these cases have been settled on terms that remain confidential. The few that have proceeded to judgment have not yet been reviewed by the federal appellate courts, where most federal case law is formulated. The fact is, the courts have not yet given us the answers we would need to confidently tell you, the reader, what is likely to happen if you end up in one of these disputes. However, we are able to draw from existing trademark principles and what little case law there is in this area to make some educated guesses. As with so many other parts of this book, this will have to do, at least for now.

a. When Does Domain Name Usage Qualify the Domain Name as a Trademark?

Solely in its role as a unique address on the Internet, a domain name isn't a trademark because it's not being used to identify goods or services in the marketplace. However, if the domain name also happens to be the name of a company doing business on the Web or a product that is being marketed on the Web, the name is then being used as a commercial identifier—which qualifies it as a trademark.

For instance, assume that Jonah Ishmael creates a personal Web site with the domain name Ahab.com. Jonah uses the site to post pictures of his family, some poems he writes from time to time and a statement of his political philosophy. Since Jonah is not using the term Ahab as a means to identify goods or services or an entity

doing business on the Web, the domain name isn't being used as a trademark. If *Ahab Tours*, a business that offers whale sighting tours, decided to accuse Jonah of trademark infringement, Jonah would respond that since he isn't using the name as a trademark, there is thus no likelihood of customer confusion and thus no infringement.

Assume now that Jonah becomes interested in whale art and decides to open a cyberart gallery featuring contributions by various artists who like to feature whales as part of their art. At this point, there is little question that Jonah is using ahab.com as a trademark, and *Ahab Tours* would have a strong case of trademark infringement.

Finally, assume that instead of whales Jonah decided to market California wildflower art on his Web site. While ahab.com is not, from a marketing standpoint, the best domain name for this sort of business, there is no rule saying that the domain name must reflect the Web site's content. Clearly there is little likelihood that customers would be confused by Jonah's use of the *Ahab Tours* mark on his wildflower site. But if *Ahab Tours* was in fact a well-known national mark used by a chain of whale-watching franchises, the chances are great that Ahab Tours could prevent Jonah from using the domain name under a theory of dilution (see Sections C and D above).

b. What Happens When a Domain Name Is Confusingly Similar to a Registered Trademark—But Not Identical?

As is true with fictitious business name and corporate name registrations (see Chapter 3), no search of the federal and state trademark databases is made when a domain name is registered by NSI. If the exact proposed name has not already been taken by someone else, NSI will assign it to the registration applicant as requested. However, if the proposed domain name is close enough to an already existing trademark (or even another domain name) to create the likelihood of customer confusion, the domain name may be subject to trademark infringement charges—which may well result in a forced change of name. This, of course, means that a domain name registrant uses its new domain name at its peril if it doesn't first conduct its own thorough trademark search. If someone else is already using the proposed domain name as a mark, and the context of the two uses—the other mark and the domain name— would likely lead to customer confusion, the business should pick a different name at the outset. The rules for deciding the likelihood of customer confusion are spelled out in detail in Chapter 4.

c. What Happens When a Domain Name Is Identical or Confusingly Similar to an Unregistered Mark or a State Registered Mark?

Because trademark rights are based on who was first to use the mark rather than on who was first to register it, unregistered marks are just as important as registered marks when deciding what domain name to use. For example, assume that a business decides to register the domain name legaledge.com as a site for a legal newsletter. Some time later, the business receives a complaint from a company that syndicates a TV feature under an unregistered mark called *The Leading Edge*. Although the fact that *The Leading Edge* mark is unregistered will prevent its owner from using the NSI domain name dispute policy (see Section F4 above), the owner still can bring suit for trademark infringement.

d. What Happens When a Domain Name Registrant Used the Same Name as a Trademark Before the Challenging Business Registered It, But Never Got Around to Doing Its Own Federal Registration?

Under the NSI Domain Name Dispute policy, the registrant may be able to hold onto the name if it is willing to agree to reimburse NSI for any liability NSI incurs by letting the registrant continue

using the name. If the dispute ends up in court, it would be resolved the same way as other disputes between registered and unregistered marks. If competing or related goods or services are involved, then the resolution would depend on the scope of the first user's marketing territory at the time of the second user's registration. If the marketing territory was national or widespread in many states, then the domain name registrant would be entitled to priority. If the marketing territory were extremely local, then the owner of the federally registered mark may have priority. For more on these priorities, see Sections I through L below.

NEW TOP LEVEL DOMAIN NAMES (TLDs) ARE COMING

To reduce the pressure placed on existing top level domain names, an International Ad Hoc Committee created by the Internet Society has come up with a plan to add seven new TLDs:

.firm, for businesses or firms;

.store, for businesses selling goods;

.web, for entities emphasizing activities involving the World Wide Web;

.arts, for entities emphasizing cultural and entertainment activities;

.rec, for entities emphasizing recreational entertainment;

.info, for sites offering information services; and

.nom, for sites supported by individuals.

These new top level domain names are expected to be available for assignment by October 1997. They raise a number of new issues, including:

- Can one company register its name under all of these TLDS?
- What happens if the exact same name is used on competing TLDs (for instance, .com, .store, .arts)?
- Who will be registering these new domain names and will all the registration procedures be the same?

6. When Web Page Designs Conflict

An increasingly important part of trademark law has to do with trade dress—the distinctive aspects of packaging, decor, product configuration and labeling that are intended to distinguish a business, product or service in the marketplace from its competitors. Because the Web supports graphic designs, many businesses have put a lot of money into how their Web pages are designed. After all, if a business is willing to spend thousands of dollars on advertising, why not spend some on the look and feel of the place where the business will be visited on the Web?

Most observers believe that the deliberate copying of another business's Web site will constitute trademark infringement if either the Web site as a whole is inherently distinctive (unique, striking, memorable) or over time becomes associated with the host business so that Web customers have come to treat it as a trademark. For more about the basic principles of when trade dress will be protected from copying by the courts, see Chapter 1.

An excellent resource for keeping abreast of the legal developments associated with conflicts between domain names and trademarks is an article prepared by attorneys Sally M. Abel and Marilyn Tiki Dare titled *Trademark Issues in Cyberspace*. The authors have posted this article on the Fenwick and West Web site (http://www.fenwick.com) and periodically update it to account for new developments. Other articles about this issue can be found through the online trademark resources described in Chapter 15, Section A.

G. How the World Wide Web is Affecting the Marketing Territory Factor in Traditional Trademark Conflicts

Trademark law as it exists today developed at a time when geography played an important role in resolving trademark conflicts. If the same trademark was used by different businesses in different parts of the country, there was no likelihood of customer confusion and therefore no need for intervention by a court unless and until one of the users expanded into the other user's territory. This concept of territory is becoming less and less important as more and more businesses buy and sell goods and services on the Web. Although most businesses are still local in the sense that they aren't franchises or chain stores, doing business on the Web automatically extends a business's marketing activity to all parts of the country and world simultaneously.

Even an obviously local business—such as an automobile body shop— reaches out to every point on the globe when it operates a Web page. It is possible for a local potential customer to find our local auto body shop by limiting its search to auto body shops in its city, county or zip code. But it is also possible to search for auto body shops without limits on location. Such a request would produce all the body shops in the U.S. and possibly those in other countries And so, while the mark used by a purely local business on the Web need not necessarily come into conflict with another mark used by another business in another locality, such conflict is possible in a way it never was prior to the advent of Web commerce.

But what if, instead of a body shop, you are operating a business that can deliver goods or services on a mail order basis? The more important information becomes to our society, the greater the chance that you and any other user of the same mark anywhere in the country or world will be offering goods and services that will compete in that new territory we call cyberspace. And this competition will put your marks in conflict, a state of affairs that can only lead to trademark infringement issues.

It should be clear where this discussion is going. The rest of this chapter is heavily based on what happens when conflicting marks are initially used in different marketing territories. Yet, when it comes to commerce, the Web is quickly erasing the boundaries of these territories. Chances are great that if you encounter another mark in conflict with your own, you and the owner of the other mark will likely be sharing the same marketing territory (cyberspace) and will have to pay closer attention to who used the mark first and on what goods and services, and less attention to where the use occurred.

By the year 2000, and assuming the Lanham Act stays pretty much as it is, the resolution of trademark conflicts probably will be based on three primary criteria:

- When was the mark first used?
- Is the mark famous?
- Does the secondary use of the mark create a likelihood of customer confusion?

Such issues as where the mark was first used and where the second mark is being used will no longer be relevant. But until then, the material in this chapter should prove to be helpful in sorting out trademark disputes.

H. How to Use the Rest of This Chapter

Now that you have some general information about trademark disputes under your belt, it's time to get specific. The rest of this chapter will give you a pretty good idea of who has legal priority over the use of a mark in case a legal conflict develops between you and another business. But to apply the discussion to your particular situation, you will need to answer the following questions (except in dilution claims—see Section D above):

- Is the other mark registered on the federal register?
- If the other mark is federally registered, what is the date of registration?
- Was the federal registration based on actual use or intended use?
- When was the other mark first used if the federal registration is based on actual use?

If you don't know the answers to these questions, they can be obtained through a trademark search that should cost about $30–$50. (See Chapter 6, How to Do a Trademark Search.)

To save you from reading information that doesn't apply to your specific situation, we have organized this material into five separate discussions. Normally you will only need to read one or two of them.

WHICH SECTION TO READ

Read Section I if your mark is not on the federal register and the other mark is on the federal register.

Read Section J if neither your mark nor the other mark is on the federal register.

Read Section K if both your mark and the other mark are on the federal register.

Read Section L if your mark is on the federal register and the other mark is not on the federal register.

Go back and read Section D if the other mark is famous and your mark is identical or nearly so (dilution claims).

I. If Your Unregistered Mark Conflicts With a Federally Registered Mark

Here we discuss who has priority in case your mark is not registered on the principal federal register and the other mark is. If your mark is on the principal federal register, skip to Section K or L, below. Note that the information in this section and Section L, while written from opposite points of view, is basically the same. For the best possible understanding of what happens in case one mark is registered and the other mark isn't, read both.

Assume you receive a letter from a lawyer informing you that your unregistered mark conflicts with another mark that is on the federal Principal Trademark Register, and demanding that you cease and desist from any further use of your mark. The fact that the other mark is on the federal Principal Register while yours is not may be pretty scary. And in truth, the other mark's owner holds some high cards. But as you will see from the discussion and examples below, despite the other claimant's federal registration, you may still have some rights, depending on the timing of events.

1. If You Were First to Use the Mark Anywhere

If you used your mark before the other party used its mark and can prove it, you have a right to continue using your mark based on the following rules:

In your existing marketing territory

You may use your mark in the same part of the country where you were using it when the owner of the conflicting mark applied to place that mark on the federal trademark register.

EXAMPLE 1: Assume you opened the *Date Palm* restaurant in Kansas City in 1997. In 1999 a chain of *Date Palm Inns* opens in four southeastern states. The *Date Palm Inn* mark is registered with the PTO in 1999, that same year. In 2002, your existence is discovered by the *Date Palm Inn* chain. A lawyer sends you a cease and desist letter, citing the *Date Palm Inn's* registration of the *Date Palm Inn* mark on the Principal Trademark Register and demanding that you immediately change the name of your restaurant. You may continue operating in Kansas City on an exclusive basis under your existing name because you were the first to use the *Date Palm* mark in that territory.

In all other areas

You may claim the exclusive right to use your mark in all other parts of the country if you can prove that the owner of the registered mark actually knew of your mark's use at the time of the registration application and failed to disclose this fact to the Patent and Trademark Office. The deliberate failure of a registration applicant to disclose the existence of a conflicting mark can lead to cancellation of the trademark registration.

If the owner of the registered mark didn't know of your unregistered mark's use, however, the registered owner will be given priority (that is, the right to exclusive use) in all other parts of the country where a later simultaneous use of the two marks would create the likelihood of customer confusion.

EXAMPLE 2: Continuing the *Date Palm* example, assume you can prove that the *Date Palm Inn* owners actually knew of your use of the *Date Palm* mark prior to 1999, the year it registered the mark with the PTO. This fact would allow you to both continue using the *Date Palm* mark in Kansas City on an exclusive basis and expand your right of exclusive use to the rest of the country, even to the four states in which the *Date Palm Inn* currently operates. That's right. If the *Date Palm Inn* knew of your mark's prior use on a restaurant when it registered its mark and failed to disclose the fact to the PTO, its registration would be to no effect and it would have to change its name if you decided to enter its marketing territory and were prepared to commit the necessary resources to filing a trademark infringement suit in federal court and obtaining a court order, if negotiations failed.

EXAMPLE 3: Continuing the *Date Palm* example, assume you can't show that the *Date Palm Inn* knew of your mark prior to the time it registered its mark. In this situation you can remain in your current marketing territory, but the *Date Palm Inn* will have the exclusive right in the future to use the mark in any other part of the country it chooses to expand into, even if later you have expanded into the area ahead of the *Date Palm Inn*. This is because the *Date Palm Inn's* registration was in good faith (neither it nor the

Trademark Office knew of your mark, and your mark wasn't known in the *Date Palm Inn's* original marketing territory)

TRADEMARK OFFICE SEARCHES

When an application for federal trademark registration is filed, the trademark office conducts its own trademark search to see whether the mark for which registration is being sought is already in use. This search often eliminates the type of conflicts being discussed in this section (between a first user and a first registrant). But if your mark doesn't show up in the major product and service databases available to the PTO, then the PTO may miss your mark and grant the registration.

---

2. If the Registered Owner Was First to Use the Mark

If the owner of the federally registered mark was the first to use the mark (actual use or constructive use through the filing of an "intent to use" application), the following rules apply:

In your marketing territory—without knowledge of the other mark

If neither you nor the customers in your marketing territory had knowledge of the other mark when you first used your mark, and your first use was before the other mark was placed on the federal trademark register, you can continue using the mark in your marketing territory on an exclusive basis.

EXAMPLE: Modifying our *Date Palm* example, after the *Date Palm Inn* chain starts operating in 1999, and, without knowledge of that earlier use, you open the *Date Palm Restaurant* in Shreveport, Louisiana, in 2000, an area in which the *Date Palm Inn* is unknown. The *Date Palm Inn* then places its mark on the federal register in 2001. You may continue using the *Date Palm* mark in Shreveport on an exclusive basis in your marketing territory. This is probably Shreveport, but could be argued to include nearby areas of Louisiana.

In your marketing territory—with knowledge of the other mark

If you knew that the other mark was in use prior to yours, or if the other mark was known in your marketing territory even though you didn't know of it, the other owner may expand into your marketing area and force you to stop using your mark. If you first used your mark after the other mark was registered, knowledge of the other owner's first use will be presumed. This means you may only continue using the mark in your area until the other owner decides to expand its market into your area. Then you will have to stop using the mark altogether. Otherwise, you may be liable for large damages as a willfull infringer.

> **EXAMPLE:** Assume that you know of the *Date Palm Inn's* registered mark when you open your restaurant in 2000 and the *Date Palm Inn* can prove it. (In this situation, all *Date Palm Inn* would have to do to prove your knowledge is to show that their federal registration occurred prior to your first use of the mark.) If and when the *Date Palm Inn* decides to expand into Shreveport, you can be forced to change your restaurant's name. Your name may also be at risk if the *Date Palm Inn* expands into any area that draws its customers from Shreveport, since Shreveport would then be part of its marketing territory and it would have a right to exclude your use of the name. If *Date Palm Inn* launches an advertising campaign designed to draw customers from all over the country—or creates and maintains a site on the World Wide

Web—its marketing territory will be national even if it doesn't move into Shreveport.

In other marketing areas

The registered mark will also have priority where the two marks come into conflict.

> **EXAMPLE 1:** If you start using the *Date Palm* mark before *Date Palm Inn's* registration of the mark, you can use the mark as long it doesn't come into conflict with the *Date Palm Inn's* registered mark. Where conflicts do develop, you will have to withdraw.

If the registered mark is being used nationwide and you started using your mark after the date of registration, you may be subject to heavy damages as a willful infringer.

> **EXAMPLE 2:** A San Francisco Bay Area comedy group puts together a satirical review called *Lawbonics*, a series of skits about lawyers and their bizarre professional speech patterns. The comedy group places Lawbonics on the federal register and seeks national billings. A year later, without actual knowledge of the California group, you start a similar act in Vermont. Because the California *Lawbonics* group federally registered prior to your use of the mark, you have infringed the California group's service mark. And, because that group's registration gave you "constructive notice" of its prior ownership of the mark, you will be considered a deliberate infringer if the matter gets to court, even though you really were unaware of the prior use.

J. Your Unregistered Mark Conflicts With Another Unregistered Mark

Conflicts between unregistered marks are the most common types of business name disputes small businesses are likely to face. These types of disputes are usually between business names that are also being used as service marks. (See Chapter 3, Protecting and Registering Trade Names.) They are usually governed by state trademark and unfair competition principles (see Section C above), which are designed to combat customer confusion in the marketplace and protect the first user of a mark because of fairness considerations. You may also invoke the federal unfair competition provision of the Lanham Act, however, if one of the unregistered marks is used in interstate, inter-territorial or international commerce.

As a general rule, the more distinctive the mark in issue, the more willing the courts are to find the likelihood of customer confusion and protect the first user's right of exclusive use.

EXAMPLE 1: You open a day care center for the elderly in St. Paul, Minnesota, named *The Seniors Club*. Several years later, in the same part of town, another day care center called *The Senior Citizen's Club* opens its doors. You will be able to get the second business to change its name if you can convince a court that customer confusion between the two names is likely—that is, the other center is likely to draw from your customer base and the court believes your name is distinctive enough to protect. In this example, however, the court may find that your name is ordinary and weak rather than distinctive and rule that *The Senior Citizen's Club* is different enough to not risk customer confusion (because customers attach little significance to weak marks). Or, the court may invoke the state's unfair competition laws to order the second user to alter its name in some respect to protect the first user.

EXAMPLE 2: Since 1995, you have sold your ready-to-eat barbecued ribs to a number of Missoula, Montana, supermarkets under the mark *Clarence's L.A. Style Ribs*. They are very popular throughout the Missoula area. In 2000, Steve, based in Coeur d'Alene, Idaho, starts selling *Steve's L.A. Style Ribs* to markets in a three-state area, including Missoula. You can force Steve to adopt another mark for his ribs, since "*L.A. Style*" as applied to ribs has become a distinctive mark over time, and belongs exclusively to you, at least in the Missoula area.

If your mark and another unregistered mark have initially been used in different geographical areas without coming into conflict, but then simultaneously (more or less) come into conflict in a new marketplace, unfair competition principles may resolve the conflict in several ways: dual use may be authorized with certain conditions attached, one of you may prevail on the grounds that the area in question was a natural part of your original marketing territory or one of you may be ordered to change your mark somewhat to distinguish it from the other.

> **EXAMPLE:** You start a sign business in Newport, New Hampshire, that specializes in magnetic signs for trucks (they stick to the truck panel). You call your business *Sign Up* but don't register the name, even though you do a little business across state lines with Massachusetts and Vermont customers. Within the next several years, similar sign businesses are started by other entrepreneurs in San Francisco, Dallas, Chicago and Miami, using the same name. They also don't register the name. Because the name is used in different marketing areas, there is no legal conflict.

What happens, however, if you and one of the other businesses simultaneously decide to operate a national mail order sign business under *Sign Up* by creating a site on the World Wide Web? Since both businesses would be in conflict everywhere in the country, and since both businesses would be in conflict with the other regional users of the name, even if those regional businesses weren't on the Web, clearly something would have to give.

Theoretically, of the two companies that were using the Web to market the sign service, the company that first used the mark in commerce anywhere would have priority and could stop the other Web-based company from using it. As far as the other regional companies, it's possible that they also could be prevented from further use of the mark on the ground that when they adopted their names, they did so at the risk of being forced to stop using them if and when one of the previous users decided to go national.

Traditionally, these regional companies might have been able to continue using the mark in their regions on an exclusive basis, but the way

the World Wide Web works, regional markets are no longer feasible, nor, therefore, are regional marks. (See Section G above.)

The solution ultimately favored by the courts in this type of scenario is an adjustment of one of the marks so that both businesses can continue their operations with a minimum of disruption without creating customer confusion. But if it appears that the second user is deliberately trying to piggyback on the first user's goodwill, the second user may be forced to choose a completely different name and even pay some damages as punishment.

K. Your Federally Registered Mark Conflicts With Another Federally Registered Mark

Here we explain what your rights are if your mark and the other mark are both registered on the federal trademark register. If your mark is not federally registered, see Sections I or J, above.

It occasionally happens that two marks which both have been placed on the federal trademark register come into conflict with each other in the marketplace. This can occur for a variety of reasons. The PTO may approve two identical or very similar marks for registration because:

- the registration applications state that the marks will be used on goods and services in different classes and it appears that the goods or services won't compete in the marketplace and aren't related enough to create the likelihood of customer confusion; or
- an examiner honestly but mistakenly believes the two marks are sufficiently different to eliminate the likelihood of customer confusion.

As stated earlier, once a trademark is placed on the federal register, its owner is presumed to be the rightful nationwide owner of the mark. When you have two presumed rightful nationwide owners claiming title to the same (or very similar mark), the conflict can be difficult to unravel. Sometimes this can be accomplished in proceedings brought in the Patent and Trademark Office itself, while other times court action may be necessary. The result will depend on why and when the conflict developed. (See Chapter 15, Help Beyond the Book, for resources dealing with how the Patent and Trademark Office and courts handle conflicts between two registered marks.)

EXAMPLE 1: You use the mark *TeeTotaler* on a brand of fruit juice while Julie uses this same mark on her chain of vegetable juice bars. Although unlikely, it is possible that you and Julie will both get your respective marks onto the federal trademark register because one is a trademark being used on a juice product sold in supermarkets while the other is a service mark used on a health drink service business. While there is no direct competition between you and Julie, it's easy to see that consumers might think that your product is really being marketed by Julie's business or vice versa. In short, customer confusion is likely if the mark is used in a context where consumers might experience both uses. In this instance, you and Julie might be restricted by a court in the use of your marks to your respective and distinct marketing territories, and whoever can prove first use might be given priority when expanding to areas where the mark is not in use.

EXAMPLE 2: Assume now that you originally applied to register the mark *TeeTotaler* for use on a brand of biodegradable golf tee, but later changed your mind and used the mark on your fruit juice line. Since your use of the mark was vastly different than that described

on your registration application, your registration would not count when resolving the conflict with Julie's mark. In other words, Julie would be treated as a registered owner of the mark and you would be an unregistered owner for purposes of resolving the dispute.

L. Your Federally Registered Mark Conflicts With an Unregistered Mark

You're in a strong position if your mark is registered and the other mark is not. You are presumed to be the nationwide exclusive owner and the other owner is definitely on the defensive. However, the fact of registration doesn't mean you'll win a trademark dispute. It depends, as with other disputes over your mark, on the following principles:

1. If You Were First to Use the Mark Anywhere and Registered the Mark Before the Second Use Began

If you used your mark and federally registered it before the other business used its mark, you have the exclusive nationwide right to use the mark, and can stop the other owner from using the mark in any geographic market that you decide to market your goods or services in. If you maintain a site on the World Wide Web or otherwise nationally market your goods or services, then you can require the other business to stop using the mark immediately. However, if your use is local or regional and the other user's local or regional market is completely separate from yours, you will have to wait until you are on the verge of entering the other market to require your competition to adopt another mark.

EXAMPLE: You are a Rhode Island publisher of travel guides that specialize in the Northeastern states and carry the mark *Yankee Visions*. You successfully obtain a federal registration for the mark. Two years later you learn that a travel guide publisher for the Northwestern states began using the same mark for its publications after the date of your registration, but has not registered it. Because of your registration, the competitor will be deemed to have had knowledge of your mark's previous use, which means you can force the competitor to stop using the mark if and when you decide to market your guides in the Northwest. But if your marketing efforts remain restricted to one portion of the country—say the Northeast and Eastern Seaboard—and the competitor stays in the Northwest, you won't win a trademark infringement case unless you can show that you want to enter the Northwestern market and are prepared to do so.

As we emphasize throughout the book, the World Wide Web and other national marketing techniques make a collision between marketing territories more and more likely.

2. If You Were First to Use the Mark Anywhere, But Registered the Mark After the Second Use Began

It is possible that the other user started to use the mark after your first use but before your mark was placed on the federal register. In this situation, the rights of the second user will turn on the answers to these two questions:

- Did the second user have actual knowledge of your mark's use?
- Was your mark known in the second user's marketing territory?

If the second user had actual knowledge of your mark's previous use (and you can prove it), the second user has no rights and must give way if and when your mark and its mark come into conflict in a marketing territory.

And, regardless of the second user's knowledge, if your mark was known within the marketing territory from which the second user's customer base was being drawn, the second user will have to give way if you decide to use your mark in that territory.

EXAMPLE: Continuing our *Yankee Visions* example, assume you can show that the Northwest competitor knew of your mark before it started using its mark. If you later decide to market your guides in that area, you can force the competitor to drop the name. Similarly, if your guides were being distributed in the Northwest prior to the second use, you can force the competitor to stop using the mark if you now decide to market the guides in the Northwest.

If, however, neither the competitor nor its customer base knew of your *Yankee Visions* mark when the competitor's use of the mark began, and your product wasn't being sold in your competitor's marketing territory, the competitor can continue using the mark in the Northwest and freeze you out of that market. This result stems from the fact that the competitor would be deemed to be a good faith second user (no actual knowledge of your mark) in a remote marketing territory (no marketing or other activity that would make the customers aware of your mark when the second user began using it).

3. If the Other Owner Used the Mark Both Before You Used It and Before You Registered It

If the owner of the unregistered mark was the first to use the mark, you may continue to use your registered mark in the marketing territory where you are currently using it if the following two statements are true:

- You didn't know of the other owner's previous use when your use began.
- The previous use was largely unknown in your marketing territory when your second use began.

EXAMPLE: You invent a digital device that attaches to a tennis racquet handle and keeps track of the score during the game. You attach the trademark *Total Recall* to your invention and register it with the PTO. Test marketing is initiated in California and Arizona. Unknown to you, Felix had earlier been using this same mark on a product designed to keep track of the score of ping pong games he is test marketing in Miami, Florida. Because you had no knowledge of Felix's earlier use when you registered the mark, and because knowledge of Felix's device had not penetrated into your test markets, you may continue using it in your test markets.

> ### BOOK AND MOVIE NAMES CAN'T BE TRADEMARKED
>
> Can the name "Total Recall" be used by anyone, given its wide recognition as the title of a blockbuster Arnold Schwarzenegger movie? As a general rule, the titles of books and movies, as used only on the book or movie, are not considered trademarks, since each title is unique to that particular item and not an indicator of the product's source or a means to distinguish it from competitors. Once a movie title develops secondary meaning, however, there are exceptions to this rule, especially where products emerge following a popular movie ("Little Mermaid Toys") or where customers are likely to become confused. (See Chapter 1, A Trademark Primer, for more on what can't serve as a trademark.)

However, you cannot use the mark in any area of the country where the first user was using it as of the date of your registration.

EXAMPLE: Because Felix was the first user, he has the exclusive right to use the mark in Miami and you would be excluded from marketing your invention in that area.

If you didn't know of the other mark's previous use when you registered your mark, you will have priority over the previous user in all areas of the country that he or she has not yet entered. In other words, you will be rewarded for promptly registering your mark, and the first user will stay frozen in his or her territory.

EXAMPLE: Assuming that you didn't know of Felix's use of the *Total Recall* mark when you registered, Felix's use will be limited to the Miami area and you can market your product nationwide.

If any of the following statements is true, the first user will be given priority in case conflict between the two marks develops:

- You knew of the previous use when you first used your mark.
- Your customer base knew of the previous mark when you first used your mark.
- You knew of the previous use when you registered your mark.

EXAMPLE: If you knew that Felix was using the *Total Recall* mark when you first used yours, or you knew of the use when you registered the mark, or if Felix's test marketing had been going on in the area where you first used your mark, Felix would be given priority in all parts of the country, including your test area. ■

If Someone Infringes Your Mark

Y ou have encountered another business that is using a name for its product or service that is identical or very similar to yours, and you feel you are losing customers and profits as a result. How can you stop them?

Before you pick up the phone to call an attorney, let us take a minute to look at how and whether a lawsuit is likely to solve your problems. If at the end of this chapter you still feel you want to litigate, then grab that phone—after reading Chapter 15, Help Beyond the Book, for suggestions on finding a lawyer—and good luck!

A. What Litigation Costs

Start by reminding yourself that lawsuits usually cost a bundle—a big bundle. Typically, lawyers who handle trademark cases charge $200 per hour and up. It doesn't take a genius to understand that if you hire a lawyer for a month's worth of work (surely a low estimate for a full-blown trademark fight) it will cost you close to $40,000. From start to finish a trademark infringement lawsuit averages about $120,000 in attorney fees for each party.

Perhaps these figures will help you understand why we have great respect for the ancient curse that says, "May you be involved in a lawsuit in which you know you are right."

B. How Much Is Your Mark Really Worth to You?

Given the horrendous costs, it pays to carefully consider whether a particular dispute over a mark is worth litigating. Let's look at this issue a little closer.

1. Can You Recover Attorneys' Fees in State Court?

If your mark is being used in one state only, your infringement suit will most likely be brought in state court and the laws of your state will determine how attorneys' fees will be paid. In most states the courts will not require the loser of a lawsuit to pay the winner's attorneys' fees. Or stated bluntly, even if you win, you'll have to pay your own lawyer and risk ending up in the poorhouse. However, in a few states, such as Colorado, North Carolina, Wisconsin and Puerto Rico, the prevailing party is awarded attorneys' fees as a matter of course, and in a few others (Alaska, Iowa, Maine, Minnesota, Missouri, Oklahoma, Texas and Washington), the court has discretion to award attorneys' fees, usually in exceptional cases only. See Chapter 7, State Trademark Registration, for more specific information on your state.

2. Can You Recover Attorneys' Fees in Federal Court?

If your mark is used across state, territorial or international boundaries, you will probably end up in federal court. Federal law permits an award of attorneys' fees to a victorious plaintiff, but only where the trademark infringement is exceptional—that is, obviously intentional. The bottom line is this: Unless you are dealing with a clear case of bad intentions, don't count on attorneys' fees in federal trademark litigation.

How Treble Damages Can Help Pay Attorneys' Fees

Although courts have discretion to award attorneys' fees in unusual cases, they are required to award treble (or triple) damages—and order the defendant to disgorge any profits caused by the infringement—in cases where willful infringement is proven. Willful infringement cases therefore have the potential to generate a considerable sum of money over and beyond what the true trademark owner actually suffered from the infringement. Since the goal in most cases is to stop the infringing use—which will happen if the court finds that infringement occurred—the trademark owner can use the damages to pay whatever legal fees are incurred. Trademark lawyers understand this and may therefore be willing to represent plaintiffs in willful infringement cases and defer payment of their fees until the case settles or a judgment is obtained. This is not a contingency fee because the fee isn't based on the outcome of the case. It's only a method of deferring fees until the plaintiff is in a better position to pay them.

3. Litigation Short of Trial

A common strategy is to file an infringement lawsuit and ask the court to grant emergency relief until the case can be fully litigated and decided in a trial. This type of relief—termed a preliminary or temporary injunction—typically orders the alleged infringer to stop using the mark in question pending the outcome of the lawsuit. Since, as a practical matter, getting slapped with an order of this type puts the alleged infringer in an untenable position from the outset, the party bringing the suit usually reaches a settlement on very favorable terms.

To obtain a preliminary injunction, you must convince the court of two basic facts:

- If the emergency relief isn't granted your business will suffer irreparable injury.
- Your case is strong enough on the face of things to make it probable that you'll win if and when a trial eventually takes place.

The first fact is very easy to show. The mere existence and use of an infringing mark daily robs the owner of the infringed mark of its customer base and the business good will that the mark represents. Since there is no real way to measure the loss of good will in monetary terms, this type of injury is usually considered irreparable as a matter of course.

The second fact—probable success—is another matter. Here the judge has to be convinced that the plaintiff's infringement claim is strong enough to warrant depriving the infringer of the right to use its mark without first holding a trial. Some judges are more willing to do this than others, and it is impossible to predict whether an attempt to get a preliminary injunction will be successful.

Once the court rules on a request for a preliminary injunction, the losing party has a powerful incentive to settle. If the defendant is enjoined from using the disputed mark pending trial, it means that the judge has found it probable that infringement has occurred. Further, the injunction leaves the defendant little choice but to adopt a new mark to use during the pendency of the case. These facts usually drive the defendant to cave in unless the plaintiff is seeking treble damages and refuses to settle the case (which is unusual). Conversely, if the plaintiff loses, it means that the defendant will be able to continue using the disputed mark during the pendency of the trial, and that the judge has concluded that infringement probably hasn't occurred. Most plaintiffs are willing to settle rather than pursue the case on such facts.

Because the outcome of the preliminary injunction request usually results in an early termination of the case, the legal fees associated with the normal trademark case often are much less than if the case were fully litigated. But they may still be high—routinely at least $10,000—since it takes a lot of preparation to successfully handle the preliminary injunction proceeding.

4. Beware of Being Right

Whether a preliminary injunction and settlement are obtained or the case goes to trial (tack on at least another $50,000), using the courts to resolve an infringement claim clearly can be, and usually is, very costly. But many otherwise reasonable people insist on it. Why? Probably for the same reason many otherwise reasonable people behave like pit bulls in divorce proceedings—emotional attachment to being right. And remember the Gypsy curse we discussed earlier—many lawyers get rich because clients try to vindicate their positions.

Sadly, the question of who has the right to use a mark often affects people in an emotional way that doesn't always serve their long-term economic interest. They get addicted to their mark, and as with any addiction, they may be willing to spend way beyond what common sense would dictate to keep it. And it may be hard to perceive that your litigation is motivated by ego, principle or a sense of outrage when the name of your business (which may even get confused with the existence of the business itself) is threatened.

THE MENTAL STATE OF THE INFRINGER MATTERS IN TRADEMARK LITIGATION

When a mark infringer knew about the infringed mark when the infringement began, he or she will be considered a willful infringer. This knowledge is either something that is proved in a trial (such as continued use by the infringer after having been notified of the infringement), or is presumed to have existed if the mark was on the federal principal register when the infringement began and the owner of the infringed mark properly used the registration notice with the mark (an ® or a statement to the effect that "This is a registered trademark belonging to Rackafrax company"). Once the willful label attaches to an infringer, the infringer can be forced to pay treble damages and surrender its profits made from the goods or services carrying the infringing mark.

On the other hand, if the infringer is considered innocent—the business had no knowledge of the infringed mark—the plaintiff-owner usually cannot collect treble damages or the defendant's profits, and in some cases cannot even prevent the infringer from continuing to use the mark, at least in a limited geographical area.

C. Negotiate—Don't Litigate

Negotiation offers you lots of options that litigation doesn't. For one, it's cheaper; for two it's quicker; and for three, you help fashion the outcome. It gives you a chance to devise a solution both parties can live with rather than wasting time and money trying to allocate fault.

How do you get a purported infringer to the negotiating table? As mentioned, some would advocate a lawsuit to seek a preliminary injunction for that purpose. But that is obviously an expensive method of getting the defendant's attention. And of course whenever litigation is started there is a risk that it will gain too much of its own momentum and escalate.

A better way to start is to send the infringing business a letter, stating the problem and proposing that you negotiate. The fact that both parties must bear the high cost of a lawsuit may even become part of the common ground on which you build a solution, instead of a threatening weapon. But no need to give up all your weapons at once. Even if you don't plan to litigate (or would only do so reluctantly), your opponent need not know that at the start.

On the other hand, negotiation does necessarily imply give and take. So you have to decide what you are willing to give, and what you need in exchange. For example, must the infringer change the mark completely or can you live with it if modifications are made? Do you need the matter resolved right now, or are you able to provide the infringer with some time to make necessary changes? What's the maximum you feel it is worth spending on this dispute? How much would you pay to buy the right to use the name even if you think you already own it?

INSURANCE FOR TRADEMARK LITIGATION

If you are reading this chapter prospectively, and have not yet suffered any harm by another's infringement, check into the option of trademark litigation insurance. This is a rider that can be purchased to augment the coverage of a Comprehensive General Liability policy that all businesses have. The rider offers "advertising injury coverage" which is the coverage that courts have interpreted to extend to trademark and unfair competition claims. This is not yet available in all states, but California, Illinois and Minnesota permit it, among others. Even if you don't have such a rider, there's no harm in asking your agent whether the risk is covered by your regular policy. You may be pleasantly surprised.

You might even consider this: how many dollars would it take for you to change your mark?

Let us add our personal perspective: changing your mark need not be a disaster. In fact, depending on who you are and how you do it, it may cause hardly a ripple.

For example, a very popular Berkeley restaurant had to change from *Fat Albert's* to *Fat Apple's* as a result of an ownership dispute. It never lost a beat in the local restaurant scene and still has 45-minute waits out the door for weekend morning breakfasts.

Even Nolo Press, the publisher of this book, has had to change its marks from time to time. Its computerized will-writing program, now called *WillMaker*, was originally called *WillWriter*. After Nolo had launched the product and established it in the market, they received a series of threatening letters from a New York law firm stating that Will Writer was a federally registered trademark belonging to a small company in New York City that registered wills and printed will forms.

Admittedly, Nolo should have done a more thorough check of the mark before using it, but even if they had, they might have gone ahead and used the mark, because the other company's use was different. It did not make wills or sell computer programs. In addition, the other company's trademark was weak, because it described what the product did—provide a form on which to write a will.

Nolo's first response was to write back to each of these letters, which arrived about six months apart, to say basically, "Don't bother us; you don't have a case." However, the letters kept coming, and the idea of having to defend a suit on the other coast—even one that they might win—loomed as a waste of time and money. So against the almost universal advice of friends and business associates ("You'll lose thousands of sales, confuse your customers and make yourself a commercial laughingstock"), Nolo cast about for a new name, and came up with *WillMaker*, a mark that was similar to the old one, but with a crisper edge to it.

Nolo notified everyone they could, and placed ads that prominently featured the house mark *Nolo* to provide continuity. A few trade journals noted the change, but the upshot was that nobody cared one way or another.

WillMaker flourished, despite the change, perhaps because of Nolo's reputation, perhaps because it was a distinctive product in a narrow field, and perhaps because Nolo's main competitors didn't yet have a comparable product on the market. Still another possibility is that there was nothing all that distinctive about the name *WillWriter* in the first place.

Whether a name change would be similarly trouble-free for another company depends on the business, the product or service and the nature of competition in that field. It may be harder for a fledgling business than for an established one to weather a change in a trademark. A main concern would be how expensive and feasible it would be to notify all the customers, distributors or suppliers who would need to know about the change. And for manufacturers of products, the expense of restamping the products or obtaining new containers may be prohibitive.

Certainly the World Wide Web complicates this issue. If you are using the mark in dispute as your Internet domain name, the cost and hassle associated with changing a domain name (such as getting other Web sites and search engines to change their links to your site) may be so great that changing it may not be a viable option for you.

If you are a small business in a specific market, you can probably contact your client list either through mailings, in-store flyers or targeted advertising. You will be surprised how much interested conversation the name change will generate.

If you are a larger business, perhaps you can make the name change into a news story which industry magazines or newsletters would mention, either as a story or in a column. You might make the name change the basis of a new and different ad campaign. While it does appear a little careless to have adopted someone else's mark, most customers can relate to the misfortune of inadvertently stepping on the toes of some unknown business in a distant city. So it need not ruin your reputation at all. In fact, it may be a shot in the arm. In the metaphor of the self-help therapy industry, you got lemons, so get busy selling lemonade.

D. How to Handle an Infringer

Regardless of how your dispute is finally resolved, you will want to take some or all of the following steps when dealing with infringement of your mark. Obviously, since no two infringement situations are exactly the same, you'll need to adopt and change these steps to fit your needs.

Step 1: Discover the registration and use status of your opponent's mark

Your first step is to discover:
- whether the mark is federally registered and/or registered in your state
- when the other mark was first used anywhere; and
- when the mark was first used in a manner that came into conflict with your mark.

You can find out the registration information by doing a trademark search in the manner described in Chapter 6. If the mark is federally registered, your trademark search can also tell you the date the owner claimed it was first used anywhere. To find out when the mark was first used in a manner that conflicts with your mark, you will need to do a little investigation.

Step 2: Read Chapter 11, Sorting Out Trademark Disputes, to discover who is the infringer

That chapter explains who has priority when two marks conflict in the marketplace. It will teach you which mark owner—you or your opponent—has the strong legal case. This information is vital in the negotiation process, since your negotiating position is likely to be far different if you are clearly the top dog from a legal point of view than if you are just as clearly the infringer.

Step 3: Research as much as you can about the business with which you will be negotiating

You need to know its size, its financial health, its ownership, its market share, its products or services, and, most important, its litigation history. Obviously, this information will help greatly when you have to decide on a negotiating strategy. For example, if the company is on shaky financial ground, you can play harder ball than if they have a robust balance sheet. And if the other business has gone to court before on this or another mark, you should be very cautious in your dealings with them, unless you too are willing to invest a great deal in your favorite law firm. Also you need to know what kind of product they make and how and where it is marketed to properly evaluate their use of the mark in question. If their use is an obvious case of infringement (identical mark, closely related markets) and you have legal priority, you have a much stronger negotiation position than if it is a borderline case.

These pieces of information are not as hard to find as you may think. The computer databases that are available for your use (see information on Dialog in Chapter 6, How to Do a Trademark Search) contain a great deal of information on businesses, in the form of business descriptions and revenue. For example, the Dun and Bradstreet databases should tell you the size of the company, how many employees it has, who owns it, its sales figures and other financial data, and its financial rating.

For either large or small businesses, litigation history is available in state or federal court files, which are public records. They are usually indexed by the names of the parties. In this way you can discover most cases that they have initiated (assuming they filed in the county in which they operate), but not necessarily those in which they have been sued (which is also relevant to their financial health) because that could have happened anywhere.

You can do all this yourself or hire a lawyer, business investigator or information broker to do it for you. Of course you may not need all the pieces of information we've discussed, so just obtain the facts you think are relevant or you can afford.

Step 4. Write a letter

The next step is to write a letter to the infringer. This is what attorneys do and, if you are more comfortable having an attorney write the letter, find one to do it. (See Chapter 15, Help Beyond the Book.) Write to the owner or president or whatever person is the highest level of management for which you can obtain a name, address and phone number.

The letter should be businesslike and firm, but not accusatory, and should state the key facts in a clear and concise way. "It has come to our attention that your business is using x trademark or trade name in x manner" is an acceptable way to start. State your claim that your mark has legal priority—including the nature of your business, how you use the mark, when and where you began using it, when you registered it (if you registered it) and whatever else you think is relevant. Then state that you believe the use of the mark by the other business infringes on your rights, and firmly ask the business to cease and desist its use of the mark.

⚠ Let Sleeping Dogs Lie

If the material in Chapter 11, Sorting Out Trademark Disputes, indicates that you and not your opponent clearly are in the wrong, the worst thing you can do is bring the conflict to the opponent's attention. Here the old adage of "let sleeping dogs lie" is very appropriate.

Make sure you provide the other business with enough information, including, for example, a copy of your registration certificate, so they can independently verify the basic facts that you allege and respond appropriately. But there is no need to exhaustively recount your business history or give extraneous information. Whatever you put in this letter must be accurate because it can be used later in court as evidence of some sort of inconsistency or misdescription.

⚠️ **Don't Set Deadlines or Make Threats**

Don't set deadlines or make threats in this first letter. If you do, you will feel compelled to take some action if the business doesn't comply with your demand, in order to show that you are serious. And it is likely that your action will be premature. Better to give yourself room and expect to write a second or even a third letter before giving your opponent an ultimatum.

SAMPLE LETTER

Dear [Name of Infringer},

It has recently come to our attention that your business is using x trademark or trade name on x [service or product]. We believe that this use infringes on our ownership rights in x trademark. We first became aware of your mark [state the circumstances—e.g., at the 1997 Weaving Trade Show in Albuquerque.]

We have the exclusive right to use this trademark based on the following facts: [now list the bases of your rights—federal or state registration numbers, date of first use, date of registration, on what products or services you use it, and in what geographical areas. Attach copies of your registration papers and samples of how you use the mark.]

We believe that your use of this mark is likely to confuse our customers [and suppliers] and will damage the good reputation that our [goods, services] have enjoyed until now. Therefore we request that you cease any further use of this mark.

Please reply with an acknowledgment of the ownership right that we claim in this mark and a proposed timetable for halting its continued use.

Sincerely,

(Your name)
(Your title)

THE FOUR SEASONS

IF THERE IS NO ACTUAL CONFLICT

Sometimes the use of a mark that—on its face—overlaps with another mark does not result in a conflict in the marketplace. For instance, if you own the national right to a mark but are only using it in the Southwest, an infringing use in the Northeast won't affect you. However, if you later decide to move into that region, the dual use of the marks would be very confusing. Also, as we indicated in Chapter 9, How to Use and Care for Your Mark, it is important for you to police the use of your mark so it won't be weakened by overuse or considered abandoned.

If you discover an infringer whose use of the mark isn't in conflict with yours, consider writing a letter pointing out that you own the exclusive national right to the mark and intend to enforce your right when you start using your mark in that part of the country. You need not demand that their use cease immediately. If you never expand in that direction, no harm is done. But if you do want to start using your mark in that part of the country, you've at least preserved your right to force the other user to adopt a different mark at that time.

Step 5: Negotiate

This process can be as flexible as you wish it to be. The outcome is only limited by the creativity of the negotiators. But once you reach an agreement, it makes sense to be aware of all its ramifications. For instance, if you agree to let the defendant continue using the mark in exchange for a license fee, your pocketbook may be in better shape, but you may lose control of the mark (it will be considered abandoned) if it no longer serves its function of uniquely identifying the source of goods or products in the marketplace. On the other hand, if the mark is being used on entirely different goods and services and no customer confusion is likely, it may not hurt to assign the defendant all rights to the mark for that other purpose in exchange for cash. The bottom line is, have a trademark attorney read over the agreement before you commit to it.

Here are five possible negotiation strategies.

1. You can bluff your opponent into thinking you are on the verge of filing a lawsuit. This strategy works best when your mark is federally registered and theirs is not, and it appears that they began to use their mark after your mark's registration date. The reason for this is that under these facts, your opponent is legally liable to you for treble (triple) damages, the profits they realized from the sale of the goods or services carrying the mark and possibly your attorney's fees. You might scare your opponent into stopping use of their mark entirely. Or you might just get them to agree to modify the mark. Of course, you must be prepared to spend a fair amount of energy (and attorney's fees if you use an attorney as part of your bluff) to convince them that you're not bluffing. And you ought to be prepared to go to court if the bluff fails.

2. A good fallback position is to suggest an agreement on territory or manner of usage—such as, "you can have the name in Nebraska and Kansas, and I'll use it in Oklahoma and Texas," or "you use it only as a trade name for your crockery manufacturing business, and I'll use it only as a mark on my line of stuffed animals."

3. Perhaps you and the other party can make a few modifications to the way your marks appear to distinguish each more clearly from the other. For instance, you change your mark from the *Homemade Cafe* to *Homemade Diner*, and the other party changes from *HomeMade Cafe* to the *Home Cooking Cafe*.

4. You may offer to buy your opponent's rights in the trademark. It may seem unfair to have to pay the other party to change their name, but that might solve your problem in an economical way, considering that you are saving yourselves and them the cost of litigating over the trademark.

5. You might even sell your rights to the mark to the other party for a handsome sum in exchange for adopting a new mark. The money could serve as a much needed capital infusion, as well as the means to afford an advertising campaign around your new name.

Step 6: Consider other dispute resolution options

Traditionally, trademark-related disputes have been settled by negotiation or ended up in court before a judge or jury. However, in recent years several alternative, informal and private ways to handle these and other types of disputes have become popular. They are faster and cheaper than traditional court processes, they often produce superior solutions, and, because of their informality, they don't necessarily require representation by an attorney.

Unless a written contract provides that a particular approach to dispute resolution must be followed in case a dispute under the contract arises, these alternative approaches are usually voluntary, which means all parties have to agree to use them. However, some courts are beginning to require litigants to first attempt one of these alternative approaches before the case is allowed to proceed to a trial.

The two best known alternative ways to resolve disputes are arbitration and mediation. Although arbitration and mediation are often mentioned in the same breath and frequently confused with each other, they are actually quite distinct in the way they approach disputes. The most striking difference between them is that in arbitration you still present your case to a third party—called an arbitrator—for a decision, while in mediation you enlist the aid of a third party to help you and the other parties reach your own solution, without any particular resolution being imposed on you. Think of it as structured negotiation. Let's take a closer look at how each approach works.

a. Arbitration

In arbitration, the parties agree to select and pay one arbitrator—or a panel of three arbitrators—to hear the dispute. If three arbitrators are desired, the usual selection method is for each party to select its own arbitrator and then leave it to these arbitrators to pick the third.

As a general rule, arbitrators are selected from panels put together by such large national organizations as the American Arbitration Association and JAMS (Judicial Arbitration and Mediation Services). However, smaller, more specialized groups of arbitrators may also be available in your locality (see the Yellow Pages). The American Arbitration Association may be contacted at:

American Arbitration Association
140 West 51st St.
New York, NY 10020-1203
201-484-4100

Although many of the arbitrators offered by the larger organizations are attorneys or retired judges, many are not. It is up to the parties to decide whether their particular dispute should be decided by someone with a legal background or someone who perhaps has a more appropriate expertise—such as a contractor in a construction

dispute or an insurance broker if the dispute involves the interpretation of an insurance contract. In the case of a trademark dispute, it is likely that you will in fact want at least one experienced trademark lawyer to arbitrate the dispute.

The rules used to choose the arbitrator(s) and conduct the arbitration are also usually provided by the organization to which the parties turn to provide the arbitrators. For instance, it is common to agree to have the arbitration conducted under the "rules of the American Arbitration Association."

Unlike court, arbitration can proceed very rapidly and be finished in a matter of weeks, although several months is more common. Obviously, the length of time a particular arbitration will take depends on the complexity of the dispute and the eagerness of the parties to push the matter. Even if one party to an arbitration is in a hurry, it is usually possible for the other party to slow things down.

As a general rule, the arbitrator's fees are paid equally by the parties, by agreement. These fees can be considerable. For instance, an arbitrator supplied by JAMS typically charges between $250 and $300 an hour. If the arbitration only takes an hour or two of the arbitrator's time, this can be very cheap. However, if the arbitration takes days, then the expense will mount accordingly. The arbitrator's fees are in addition to what each side is paying their attorney, if they decide to use one.

Probably the biggest issue in any arbitration is whether the decision of the arbitrator(s) is to be final or will the loser be permitted to go to court for a regular trial?

This issue is typically addressed by the parties when they decide to arbitrate unless the matter has already been addressed in a contract. Since a decision to arbitrate usually is based on a wish to resolve the dispute quickly and cheaply, most parties opt to make the arbitrator's decision final, meaning that it can be entered in a court with competent jurisdiction as a final non-appealable judgment, which makes it enforceable.

⚠ **Beware of Binding Arbitration.**
The finality of an arbitration can be troublesome if the arbitrator strays far from established legal principles in arriving at the decision. Under most court rules dealing with binding arbitration, an arbitrator's departure from the law cannot be challenged in an appeal. For that reason, businesses who believe they are legally in the right are often reluctant to turn their fate over to a decision maker who is, in essence, unconstrained by the law. Better the costs of litigation, these businesses believe, than creating the risk of a runaway and crippling arbitration result.

b. Mediation

The central idea underlying mediation is simple. Most disputes can be settled in a manner that is at least minimally satisfactory to each of the disputing parties—the colloquial win-win scenario. Mediators use a number of techniques designed to identify potential points of agreement and help the parties understand and move towards these points on a voluntary basis.

If the mediation does not produce a settlement, the parties are free to pursue other avenues, including litigation. While they will have spent the money used to pay the mediator (typically $150–$200 an hour split between the parties), they will at least have gained a better understanding of the other party's point of view, which may help them settle the case down the road.

The same organizations that provide arbitrators usually also furnish mediators. Also, a number of individual business attorneys and law firms are beginning to offer mediation services to people engaged in business disputes—including disputes over trademarks. The best way to locate these services is to use the Yellow Pages and look for announcements that emphasize business mediation.

If this produces no results, contact one of the following organizations for a possible referral:

Conflict Resolution Center, Inc.
2205 E. Carson St.
Pittsburgh, PA 15203-2107
412-481-5559

Society of Professionals in Dispute Resolution
815 15th St. NW
Suite 530
Washington, DC 20005
202-783-7277

A list of business mediators in your area may also be obtained from the Mediation Information and Resource Center at http:// www.mediate.com.

Because mediation is about reaching agreement rather than trying to convince a decision maker—as is the case with arbitration—there is no need to involve an attorney. However, attorneys often can help you find an appropriate mediator. They also can be helpful as advisors during the course of the mediation, and, assuming an agreement is reached, can reduce a general oral agreement to a detailed written agreement that both you and the other party will feel comfortable signing.

Step 7: Consult an attorney

If none of the above gets you anywhere, by all means call a trademark lawyer. They might have a better letter-writing technique, or they might tell you to forget about the conflict. They probably will be able to help you find a mediator or arbitrator, if you want to pursue one of these options, or they might advise that your best shot is to go to court. If you've tried everything else first, they might be right. (See Chapter 15, Help Beyond the Book.) ∎

CHAPTER

13

If Someone Claims That You Infringed Their Trademark

You have gotten an irate letter from Ms. Blowhard in North Noluk demanding not only that you immediately cease using your new mark for clothing designs, *Nines*, but also that you account for all your profits derived from the use of that name and pay them treble (triple) damages for the insult, or they will see you in court. What to do?

Stay calm.

First, you need to know that no matter how threatening the letter, the world won't fall on your head today, tomorrow or even next week. However, legal steps may eventually follow. So first we'll tell you what those are. Next we will help you decide what your options are in response. Finally, before you actually adopt a strategy, you'll need to think about your version of the big name picture—how valuable is your name and given the legal realities, how much energy and money are you willing to spend to protect it?

Much of this discussion is very similar to the information in Chapter 12, If Someone Infringes Your Mark. It's a good idea to read that whole chapter (it's short) to get an idea of the other guy's point of view.

Start by understanding the same key point we emphasize in Chapter 12, that trademark lawsuits are extremely expensive (the median cost for each party is $10,000 and up, win or lose). You have to be very rich, or your name must be a very, very valuable asset to think that going to court is the most reasonable option.

From the point of view of either the infringer or the infringee, negotiation is a more pragmatic, cost-effective and often more fruitful way to resolve a trademark dispute. With that guiding principle, let us help you respond to someone's claim that you infringed on their mark.

A. What the Complaining Party Can Do to You

Right away you should know that your opponent can only stop your use of your mark with a court order (that is, a temporary injunction). To get this, they must leap two legal hurdles:

1. They must convince a judge that they have suffered, or will suffer, irreparable immediate damage without an immediate court order barring your continued use of the mark.

2. They must convince a judge that they are likely to eventually win in court (that is, they must show that they have superior rights to the mark and that you infringed on those rights).

In cases where the two names compete in the marketplace, the first hurdle will often be assumed, since trademark infringements siphon off goodwill in a way that cannot easily be measured and repaired in a later action for damages (which is why the injury is called irreparable).

The second hurdle is much more difficult to overcome, since the judge, without the benefit of a full trial, is being asked to make an important finding about the primary issue in the case—has infringement really occurred? To develop and prove the facts that the judge will need to arrive at this conclusion normally involves quite a bit of (always expensive) legal time. So unless your opponent is both solvent and determined, he or she will not likely leap into court without first: (1) finding out as much about you and your use of the mark as they can, and (2) testing your reac-

Buster Brown®

tion to their infringement claims. The upshot is, you probably have a little time to figure out what to do.

B. Steps You Should Take

We don't, however, mean to imply that you should ignore the letter. On the contrary, you should get busy with the following steps, lest you end up with a process server at your door.

Step 1: Find out what you can about the complaining firm and their use and registration of the mark at issue

Here we echo the discussion in Chapter 12, Section D, on the same issue from the opposite perspective. Please read that material. In essence, the more you know about the other party, the better you can evaluate how to respond to their allegations. In addition, it's essential to the development of your case that you know exactly how they use their mark, and where and how long they have used it.

Once you get all that information, you should reread Chapter 11, Sorting Out Trademark Disputes, to help you make up your mind if your opponent has a case against you.

Step 2: Get advice

After you have gathered as much information as possible, consult a trademark attorney to confirm or correct your understanding of the situation as well as to get the point of view of a disinterested experienced party. Although you may understandably want to avoid attorneys and their attendant costs, paying several hundred dollars for a reasoned legal opinion about your situation is cheap given the probable cost of ending up on the losing side of a lawsuit or even retooling your stationery and marketing materials if your decision is to switch rather than fight. You may also want to get the advice of friends or business associates whom

you trust. They may have had comparable experiences, or they may simply have reliable common sense and good tactical reactions.

Once you fully inform yourself of the legal and practical implications of the trademark dispute, trust your gut. It's almost always a mistake to follow a course of action you don't feel comfortable about. Fortunately, since the complaining business is likely to write you several letters before taking legal action, you probably have enough time to consider your next step carefully.

Step 3: Chose your tactical responses

Here now are some common responses and at least some of the possible consequences of each.

1. **The Ostrich Technique.** You can ignore the infringement claim and hope it goes away. In fact, if you are convinced that the other business doesn't have a case and knows it, this may work. Otherwise, it's probably a mistake as it risks your being sued just to get your attention.

2. **The German Shepherd Response.** You can send back a letter full of sound and fury, informing them that under no circumstances will you ever stop using your mark and the mere suggestion that you are infringing is a shocking insult. Remember, however, that this is a typical lawyerly tactic, and lawyers often profit most when they fan the flames of small disputes into true conflagrations.

3. **The Elephantine Response.** You reply in a calm and polite letter, stating the facts as you see them, and explaining why you disagree with the infringement claim. Your tone makes it clear that you are reasonable and flexible, perfectly willing to engage in further discussion and to hear more information on the subject. This sort of letter does not predispose you to any particular strategy, because you can always dig in your heels later, but in our view it's most

likely to put you further along the road to fruitful discussion than does either of the other two responses.

Step 4: Plan your negotiation strategy

Now let's assume that negotiation by letter, fax or phone has begun. What sort of strategies should you consider? These are identical to the ones discussed in Chapter 12, If Someone Infringes Your Mark, and we suggest you read (or reread) that material. Also, once again let us make the

point that changing your name need not be a disaster and may even be a marketing opportunity.

Step 5: Seek mediation

One approach that may help you reach agreement without being dragged into court is to seek arbitration or mediation. These alternative approaches to dispute resolution are described in more detail in Chapter 12, If Someone Infringes Your Mark, Section D6, Step 6. ■

CHAPTER

14

International Trademark Protection

Perhaps you are wondering if you should consider filing for an international trademark. Yes, by all means if you expect to use your trademark abroad at any point in the future.

The important thing to know is that in almost every country trademark ownership is based entirely on who registered the mark first, not on who used it first. This means that anyone can get a registration on your mark in another country without having used it there first. This presents a serious problem for marks that appear to be headed for international use after becoming well known in this country. Some businesses have made money by spotting these types of marks, preemptively registering them in key countries and then demanding large fees to transfer (assign) the names back to their original U.S. owners. Also, in some countries you may not be able to import your goods without first registering the mark you attach to them.

As your mark becomes well known, consider if you'll ever want to protect it in another country or import your product into that country. If so, you should take some steps to do that now, even if you are not likely to begin using it there right away.

Our basic advice about international trademarks is this: get an experienced trademark attorney who has done international registrations to help you register your trademarks in any country other than the U.S. While it is increasingly possible for a lay person to accomplish international registrations, the difficulty of finding all the information you will need to do it right makes it risky. In addition, giving you all the information you would need to do it yourself is beyond the scope of this book. This is one area where the expertise you are buying is well worth the cost.

Make sure the attorney you hire has experience with international registrations—you don't want to pay for their training. (See Chapter 15, Help Beyond the Book.)

A. A General Approach to International Trademark Protection

Here are some basic steps you can take if you want to get started on international protection, even assuming that you hire a trademark lawyer to finish the job or consult with along the way.

If you have applied for federal registration, you can use your U.S. application date as your international application date if you file your international application within the following six months of the U.S. application date.

Step 1: Pick the country(ies) in which you intend to register

This depends, obviously, on where you plan to market your services or products. All countries require you to use the mark within a period of time after registration or it will lapse, so only register in those countries where it is reasonable to foresee sales in the next several years. However, you may not yet know into which countries you will be expanding. If so, consider registering your trademark in Canada and Mexico, which are natural choices, following the signing of the North American Free Trade Agreement (NAFTA) in 1993.

Additional candidates for international registration will depend on the nature of your product and how it might fit into the international market. Perhaps you should consider Japan and the Pacific Rim countries, or the European Common Market countries, or maybe your goods will find a perfect niche in the developing markets of Eastern Europe or Latin America. The point is for you to do some thinking and research about what your business's future international position might be so you can secure the trademark registrations you will need later.

The possibility always exists that your service or product will be so unique and timely for a particular use that it creates a booming demand in an unexpected country for unexpected reasons. Since you can't foresee all contingencies, your basic business philosophy will dictate this decision: either cover as many possibilities as you can by registering in many countries (the expensive choice), or restrict your international registrations to your one or two best choices and hope your choice pays off.

THE COMMUNITY TRADEMARK

Effective April 1, 1996, the European Union has begun accepting applications for a community trademark that would be good in fifteen EU countries. In order to qualify for community trademark status, the proposed mark must be acceptable in all 15 countries. If it is rejected by even one country, separate national applications for trademark registration must be made in all the countries. An application for a community trademark may be made to the Office for Harmonization of the Internal Market in Alicante, Spain.

Step 2: Check your mark for conflicts with existing marks in the country(ies) you have chosen

For this, you must arrange for or conduct an international trademark search. Note that in those countries in which registration alone forms a basis for ownership rights, such searches are much simpler to do than in "use" countries, because all potential conflicts will be found on the national register of trademarks, without the need to search for unregistered trademarks. But in the "use" countries (the United Kingdom, Canada, Australia, New Zealand, and other current and former British Commonwealth members), the same sorts of common law and register searches that we describe in Chapters 5 and 6 will be required. (See Chapter 5, Preparing for a Trademark Search and Chapter 6, How to Do a Trademark Search.)

USE Sc[i]3 FOR INTERNATIONAL TRADEMARK SEARCHING

In Chapter 6 we point out that the Sunnyvale Center for Innovation, Invention and Ideas (Sc[i]3) offers a reasonably priced trademark search service. This service also includes international searching. Unlike their domestic searches, the fees charged for international searches vary according to the time spent. For more information, call 408-730-7290.

Step 3: Decide how distinctive your mark is and if it poses a problem in the language of that country

It may have unintended translations or connotations. For example, *Pschitt* was a French mark that could not be marketed as a soft drink in the U.S. This even applies to English-speaking countries—in Australia, a "Whopper" (a U.S. trademark for a hamburger) is slang for male genitalia, and so not advisable as a trademark there. To get an opinion on this, consult a native speaker of that country, or contact the foreign language department of a major university for a professor of that language.

Step 4: Discover what the registration process is for that country, and comply with it

You will find helpful in this regard the Clark Boardman Callaghan publication, *Trademarks Throughout the World*, a useful guide for securing an international trademark, available in most law libraries. You can also use Chapter 15, Help Beyond the Book, for assistance in using a law library to find the statutes of the foreign country (if you can read that language) or to find another secondary source that might cover what you can't find elsewhere. Research into the laws of other nations almost certainly requires the assistance of a law librarian and the use of a major law school library.

Step 5: Make sure you discover and comply with use time limits and renewal requirements

These include how soon you must begin to use your mark after registration. In addition, other countries may have laws regarding licensing and taxes that may apply to your service or product and its mark. This is another reason to consult an experienced international trademark attorney—to make sure you find out about and comply with all applicable laws.

B. Reciprocal Rights

If you do choose to protect your trademark abroad, with the exception of the Community Mark (see sidebar above) you must register in each country separately, and each country has slightly different laws about what makes an acceptable trademark. This maze of legalities is made slightly easier by the fact that many coun-

tries—including the U.S.—have signed an international treaty on trademarks, the International Convention for the Protection of Industrial Property (known as the Paris Convention).

This law has standardized a few things. One of the most important is that a trademark owner from one Paris Convention country who registers their trademark in another Paris Convention country is entitled to the same rights as are native trademark owners of that country. Because each country's laws are different, this may not be the same as the rights accorded to U.S. trademark owners in the U.S., but it does put all trademark owners in any one Paris Convention country on the same legal footing.

Another important benefit is that once a U.S. citizen applies to register a federal trademark in the U.S., the date of that application serves as the effective date of application in all other Paris Convention countries in which you apply, if you do so within six months of the U.S. application. This is important because in most of those countries rights are based on registration, and the effective date of application (or priority date) is an important method of determining rights. Thus it is imperative to file an international registration soon after filing one in the U.S., if you plan to do so at all.

THE MADRID AGREEMENT

Twenty-two countries (but not the U.S., Canada or Mexico) have signed another agreement, the Madrid Agreement Concerning the International Registration of Trademarks, which allows an international application to be filed automatically in any of those countries upon registration in the home country. But each country still has the right to refuse an individual registration if it chooses. Whether the U.S. will sign this treaty continues to be a matter of speculation.

C. Deciding to Register Abroad

Again, who needs to register abroad is a very subjective decision depending on all the facts of your situation. To put your decision in context, listen to this cautionary tale, and then see what you think.

In 1971 a young, recently divorced mother and her friend started a unique low-profile company that:

- sold pure and simple cosmetics, lotions and perfumes
- offered its products in small-size recyclable bottles with no extraneous ingredients, and
- didn't test its products on animals.

The business was named *The Body Shop* (because its first place of business was in a former auto repair shop). The owners had the foresight to register the name with the PTO not long after business started to blossom. It was a timely enterprise, and a great success, eventually opening several outlets within its region. It was the kind of business that made people who moved out of the area beg friends traveling back there to bring them some *Body Shop* products. Soon it also had a booming catalog business.

Years passed. Meanwhile, in London, another entrepreneur had the same idea for similar products and the same name. The second *Body Shop* also took off, even faster and on a wider basis than the original had in the U.S. Eventually, the *Body Shop* (U.K.) had over 500 flourishing franchises throughout Europe. It was confusing to travelers, but since the U.S. company had obtained only the exclusive rights to the name in the U.S., they could not stop the British *Body Shop's* use.

Then came the day when the British store owners sought to enter the U.S. market. The U.S. corporation had the legal right to the name and therefore potent weapons at its disposal. But the British firm had many times the capital of its U.S. counterpart. Like reasonable business people, the U.S.-based *Body Shop* heeded the bottom line, settling the dispute amicably. It sold its U.S. rights to its name to the British company, agreeing to change its name within 18 months, in exchange for an undisclosed (but sizable) sum of money. Everybody's happy, more or less.

The point of this story depends on your perspective. Some might say: Don't fetter yourself with needless chains—trademark your name everywhere you can at once! Others could reflect that the protagonists in our story, by federally registering their trademark, showed foresight that was unusual at the time for a small "new age" concern. That act gave them the leverage they needed to extract a price from the English company for use of the trademark in the U.S.

In the end, the U.S. company suffered the inconvenience of changing their name, but that's something that many companies do willingly when their circumstances change. Further, they weren't, as a practical matter, deprived of expansion opportunities. They hadn't expanded much before the conflict arose and even now, they are still a relatively small—but profitable—concern with a few regional outlets and a catalog. And that's fine with the owners. They bargained for enough time to reach all their regular customers and notify them of the new name, and they received a handy infusion of capital from the sale of their trademark. ■

15

Help Beyond the Book

We hope that this book provides all the information you will need to choose and protect your trademark, service mark or trade name. But you may need additional help, either in the form of more advanced legal resources or a trademark attorney's assistance.

In Section A, we introduce you to several comprehensive sources containing more information on trademark law. Written for law students and lawyers, these books discuss recent legal trends and developments and provide citations to substantive trademark law including statutes, court decisions and trademark office rules. Finally, in Section B, we provide some tips for finding a good trademark lawyer.

DON'T BE AFRAID OF LEGAL RESEARCH

Looking up the law for yourself needn't be scary. By reading this book you will have already learned the basic trademark vocabulary necessary to understand the more technical legal materials we discuss in Section A. In addition, Nolo publishes a basic legal research guide, *Legal Research: How to Find and Understand the Law*, by Stephen Elias and Susan Levinkind, and an excellent 2-hour video, *Legal Research Made Easy*, by law librarian Robert Berring, both of which teach you how to efficiently do basic legal research. You will also find most law librarians to be of great help.

A. Doing Your Own Research

When seeking answers in a law library, you will find useful the three-step approach that we describe below:

1. Read one or more discussions by experts in the field to get a background and overview of the topic being researched. In this case, you will already have a basic background from this book and will be looking for additional details on a particular topic.
2. Read the law itself (cases and statutes) upon which the experts base their opinions. Reading primary materials such as these can be confusing without first digesting an expert's analysis (Step 1).
3. Make sure the law you read is completely up-to-date.

1. Read One or More Discussions by Experts

The following are some recommended publications written by trademark law experts. You can find others via your law library's card catalog.

Federal Trademark Law. The most authoritative book on trademark law is the two-volume set entitled *McCarthy on Trademarks and Unfair Competition*, by J. Thomas McCarthy, published by Clark Boardman Callaghan. McCarthy, a law professor at the University of San Francisco, is the most widely respected trademark law expert in the United States. His book is so comprehensive and well respected that judges often consult it and refer to it in their decisions. You can find this treatise, with its annual supplements, in most public and academic law libraries.

Trademarks and Unfair Competition includes discussions of virtually every issue that has arisen with respect to the trademark and unfair competition areas of law. Each point that McCarthy makes is supported by footnote references to court cases and statutes—the primary sources that you may want to consult next as part of your overall legal research plan.

You can find your topic of interest in *Trademarks and Unfair Competition* by consulting the detailed table of contents, the extensive index or the headings that precede each chapter.

Don't overlook the handy appendices in Volume 2, which include the complete text of the Lanham Act (the federal trademark statute), other statutes related to trademark law, and the Trademark Rules of Practice of the U.S. Patent and Trademark Office.

Although very comprehensive, McCarthy's material may not give you enough detail on how to apply trademark law to real-life situations, such as rules on using the ®, or filing and prosecuting a trademark action in the U.S. Patent and Trademark Office (PTO). Probably the best resource for questions of this type is the *Manual of Trademark Examining Procedures* (MTEP), published by the PTO and available for purchase from the Superintendent of Documents, U.S. Government Printing Office, Washington, DC, or, usually, from whatever source in your area sells U.S. government publications. Also, there are two respected resources that provide how-to information. They are:

- *Trademark Law—A Practitioner's Guide*, by Siegrun D. Kane, published by the Practicing Law Institute
- *Trademark Registration Practice*, by James E. Hawes, published by Clark Boardman Callaghan.

The first of these resources provides practical advice for lawyers about the practice and litigation of trademark cases, which may prove helpful if you end up in court or you want a better idea of what lies ahead should a lawsuit loom.

The second resource provides detailed advice and forms about dealing with the U.S. Patent and Trademark Office. Although Chapters 8 and 9 of this book should suffice for most transactions with the PTO, you will need to consult *Trademark Registration Practice* if:

- your federal trademark registration is opposed
- you wish to oppose someone else's federal trademark registration, or
- someone files an action in the PTO to cancel your mark.

State Trademark Law. A good source of information on state trademark law is *State Trademark and Unfair Competition Law*, a publication of the International Trademark Association (see sidebar below). It has chapters discussing trademark and unfair competition laws of every state. At the end it has a chart listing the registration requirements for each state. Clark Boardman Callaghan publishes it for the INTA, with updates one or more times a year. You can find this resource in most major law libraries.

Law Review Articles. If you have a very unusual trademark problem that is not covered by the resources already mentioned (for example, how to register a distinctive sound as a trademark), or a problem in an area in which the law has changed very recently (perhaps because of a new Supreme Court case), the best sources of available information may be articles appearing in scholarly journals called "law reviews." You can find citations (references) to all the law review articles on a particular topic by looking under "trademark" or "unfair competition" in the *Index to Legal Periodicals*, the *Current Law Index* or one of the cumulative electronic indexes that are (with increasing frequency) found in law libraries. A key to the abbreviations used in these indexes is located at the front of each index volume. Substantial collections of law reviews are usually located in large public law libraries or university libraries.

TRADEMARK ASSOCIATIONS AND LEGAL PUBLISHERS

Two associations of trademark lawyers and one general legal publisher offer other materials that you might find helpful. You can get a list of their publications by writing or calling them.

International Trademark Association (INTA)
1133 Avenue of the Americas
New York, NY 10036
212-768-9887
http://www.inta.org/

Among other materials, the INTA publishes an annual paperback, *Trademark Law Handbook*, which analyzes current trademark issues, and *The Trademark Reporter*, a bi-monthly law review that discusses recent trademark cases and issues. Only members can subscribe to it, but law libraries carry it for the public's use.

American Intellectual Property Law
   Association (AIPLA)
Suite 203, 2001 Jefferson Davis Highway
Arlington, VA 22202
703-415-0780
http://www.aipla.oag/aipla

The AIPLA is an association of lawyers that conducts scholarly studies and publishes articles by its members. Materials by AIPLA are available only in libraries or through members of the association.

Clark Boardman Callaghan
155 Pfingsten Road
Deerfield, IL 60015-4998
800-323-1336

Clark Boardman Callaghan is the principal publisher of trademark materials for lawyers. You can get a list of their publications or order them by calling the 800 phone number.

2. Read the Law Itself (Cases and Statutes)

Statutes. The main law governing trademarks in the United States is the Lanham Act, also known as the Federal Trademark Act of 1946 (as amended in 1988). It is codified at Title 15, Chapters 1051 through 1127, of the *United States Code*. You can find it in either of two series of books, *United States Code Annotated* (U.S.C.A.) or *United States Code Service*, Lawyers Edition (U.S.C.S.). All law libraries carry at least one of these series. To find a specific section of the Lanham Act, consult either the index at the end of Title 15, or the index at the end of the entire code.

Regulations. The regulations implementing the Lanham Act consist of the specific rules that govern registration of a trademark. They are found in Title 37, Chapter 1, of the *Code of Federal Regulations* (C.F.R.). It comes in a paperback form, which you can purchase from the Superintendent of Documents, U.S. Government Printing Office, Washington, DC 20402, and is available in most law libraries.

Court Decisions. There are several ways to find the pertinent court decisions on a particular trademark issue. As we discussed, an excellent way to get started is to consult *Trademarks and Unfair Competition*, by J. Thomas McCarthy, a law review or one of the other secondary sources we mentioned above. These will list ("cite" in legal parlance) and usually discuss all the significant pertinent cases. In addition, the *U.S. Code Annotated* and *U.S. Code Service* both refer to and briefly summarize all the decisions relevant to each section of the Lanham Act. These "case notes" are located just after each section of the act.

You can also get cites to cases from a series of books by West Publishing Company called *Federal Practice Digest*. If you look under the term "trademark," in the detailed table of contents, or under a more specific topic in the very detailed subject matter index, you will find short summaries of trademark law decisions.

CASE CITATIONS

Throughout the secondary sources we have described you will find citations to trademark cases of four sorts:

1. Citations to cases decided by federal district courts. Each state is divided into different regions over which individual federal district courts have jurisdiction.

2. Citations to decisions by federal appellate courts, which review decisions of the federal district courts. The nation is geographically divided into 12 federal Courts of Appeals plus the Court of Appeals for the Federal Circuit.

3. Citations to the U.S. Supreme Court, which is the last level of review possible for any federal or state case.

4. Citations to decisions by state appellate courts. These are more rare because most trademark cases occur in federal court.

Opinions by federal district court judges are cited this way: *Pedi-Care v. Pedi-A-Care Nursing, Inc.*, 656 F.Supp. 449 (DC NJ 1987). This identifies a particular court decision and tells you where to find it. Any case decided by a federal district court is published in a series of books called the *Federal Supplement*. The cite above tells you that the *Pedi-Care* case is located in the *Federal Supplement* (F.Supp.) in volume 656 at page 449. The cite also tells us that the *Pedi-Care* case was decided by a district court for the central district of New Jersey (DC NJ) in 1987.

Federal court of appeals citations look like this: *Accuride International, Inc. v. Accuride Corp.*, 871 F.2d 1531 (9th Cir. 1989). This tells you to look in the second series of the *Federal Reporter* (F.2d.) in volume 871 at page 1531. It also tells you that the court was the Ninth Circuit Court of Appeals and that the decision was issued in 1989.

Trademark cases from both the district and appeals courts are also often published in the first and second series of the *U.S. Patent Quarterly*, (USPQ), which you will find cited in this way: 10 USPQ2d 1589. For example, *Accuride* can also be found in the second series of the USPQ, volume 10, at page 1589. Most major law libraries carry the *Federal Reporter*, the *Federal Supplement*, and the *U.S. Patent Quarterly*.

Cases decided by the U.S. Supreme Court are located in three publications, any of which is fine to use: *United States Reports* (identified as "U.S."); the *Supreme Court Reporter* (identified as S.Ct.); and the *Supreme Court Reports*, Lawyers Edition (identified as L.Ed.). Supreme Court case cites may refer to all three or to only one, for example, *Park 'N Fly, Inc. v. Dollar Park & Fly, Inc.*, 469 U.S. 189, 83 L.Ed.2d. 582, 105 S.Ct. 658, 224 U.S.P.Q. 327 (1985).

State cases are reported in such a wide variety of ways that we can't describe them all here. Instead we suggest that if you find a cite that does not look like the above, and that has a state abbreviation in it, you may assume it is a state appellate court decision. Ask the librarian for help in finding those cites.

3. Finding Trademark Laws and Information on the World Wide Web

The World Wide Web offers convenient access to an enormous amount of trademark materials, including:

- the federal trademark statutes and regulations
- informative articles by trademark experts
- the federal trademark database (for a reasonable fee), and
- recent changes in PTO trademark examination procedures.

Here is a brief list of sites that will either have the information you are looking for or will provide you with links to other sites that do.

http://www.uspto.gov The U.S. Patent and Trademark Office is the place to go for recent policy and statutory changes and transcripts of hearings on various trademark law issues. This site also links to other useful trademark-related sites.

http://www.findlaw.com This search engine offers an excellent collection of trademark-related materials on the Web, including trademark statutes, regulations, classification manuals and articles of general interest. Click the intellectual property link in the topics section on the Findlaw home page, and then click trademark in the subcategory section on the intellectual property page.

http://www.ggmark.com/ This site, maintained by a trademark lawyer, provides basic trademark information and a fine collection of links to other trademark resources.

http://www.sci3.com This site, maintained by the Sunnyvale Center for Innovation, Invention and Ideas (a Patent and Depository Library), provides information about their excellent, low-cost trademark search service conducted by the Center's librarians.

http://www.micropat.com/ trademarkwebindex.html This site maintained by Micropatent lets you do your own search of the federal trademark register for $20 a day (text) and $30 a day (text and images). You can get a lot of searching done within a 24-hour period if you're adequately prepared.

http: //www.kuesterlaw.com/ This site, maintained by an Atlanta, Georgia intellectual property law firm, also is an excellent springboard for finding trademark statutes, regulations, court cases and articles on such recent trademark law developments as domain name disputes.

4. Make Sure the Law You Read Is Completely Up-to-Date

Once you have found a statute or case that seems to address your research question, you will need to check that it is still good law. For statutes this usually means checking the back of the volume you are using for an insert called a "pocket part." Pocket parts are published annually and include any recent changes in the statute. Updating the status of rules announced in cases means using a tool that is known throughout the legal research world as *Shepard's Case Citations*.

Explaining how to use this valuable tool is beyond the scope of this book. We recommend *Legal Research: How to Find and Understand the Law*, by Elias and Levinkind (Nolo Press) for a crash course on the subject.

If you intend to do legal research yourself, be aware that interpreting statutes and cases can be difficult even for those with legal training and a specific background in the area you are researching. Before you act in reliance on anything you find in the law library, it usually makes sense to double check with a knowledgeable attorney. (Section B below.)

B. Finding a Lawyer

If you become involved in a trademark dispute, are having trouble getting your mark registered or simply want some advice from a professional about a trademark issue, you will want to consult a trademark lawyer—but not just any trademark lawyer. Start by understanding that if you have read substantial portions of this book you already know more about trademarks than most lawyers. This puts you in the difficult position of finding someone who knows more than you do and yet is willing to acknowledge the considerable competence that you've now gained in this area. You want a trademark lawyer who:

- knows the trademark field well
- is willing to acknowledge your competence gained from using this book, and
- is honest and conscientious.

Fortunately, by arming yourself with the information in this book, you have a good shot at finding a lawyer with all of these characteristics. Unfortunately, we know of no sure-fire way to do so, but here are some suggestions.

1. Find a Lawyer Who Knows the Trademark Field Well

Trademark lawyers usually advertise in the Yellow Pages and legal journals as intellectual property specialists, able to handle patent, trademark, copyright and trade secret cases. Because each of these fields is increasingly becoming a complicated legal world all to itself, in fact the ads lie—most intellectual property law specialists tend to be very knowledgeable in one or two of these areas, and only passingly familiar with the others.

For instance, it is common for patent lawyers to be far more knowledgeable in that area than in trademark law, even though both patents and trademarks involve practice before the U.S. Patent and Trademark Office. Similarly, some lawyers specialize in trademarks and do little or no patent work.

The point of knowing this, of course, is that you want a trademark lawyer who really knows trademarks, not someone willing to brush up on trademarks at your expense.

When you call on the intellectual property specialist, ask these questions:

- What percentage of your practice involves trademark work?
- Are you a member of the International Trademark Association or the American Intellectual Property Law Association?

The first inquiry will help you find a true specialist in this area, while the second will help you find a lawyer who is curious enough about the subject of trademarks to join this association of trademark specialists.

2. Find a Lawyer Who Is Willing to Acknowledge Your Competence

In addition to satisfying yourself that a lawyer is competent, you want to find someone who is reasonably congenial to work with. You don't need us to tell you that lawyers tend to look down on laypersons when it comes to the lawyer's area of expertise. Which means that many of the lawyers you initially encounter are likely to be turned off by your expertise. Fortunately, however, some lawyers are willing to respect their clients' knowledge and know how to work with it rather than against it. It is this type of lawyer you should be looking for.

You can find a lawyer who isn't intimidated by a competent client if you:

- explain over the phone that you have been using this book
- articulate exactly what you want the lawyer to do; and
- carefully monitor the lawyer's reaction.

If the lawyer scoffs at the idea of a self-help law book or you get a whiff of, "Don't tell me what you need, I'm the lawyer," go on to the next name on the list. If the response appears to respect your self-help efforts and admits of the possibility that you are a competent human being, make an appointment.

3. Find a Lawyer Who Is Honest and Conscientious

If you are just seeking advice, then you needn't worry much about the lawyer's character. But if you are looking for someone to represent you, the human being you are dealing with becomes paramount. The best analytical trademark lawyer in the world can bring you to financial and emotional ruin, if he or she lacks the ability to understand your needs and to represent you with your best interests in mind.

a. Honesty

While some would argue that there's no such thing as an honest lawyer, we maintain that it is possible to have honest dealings with your lawyer. Start by clearly understanding that the lawyer's financial interest—to run up lots of billable hours over a period of time—is the opposite of yours—which is to arrive at a fast, cost-efficient and reasonably livable resolution of the problem.

Once you understand this you'll also understand that it is essential that you and your lawyer agree up front about what the lawyer is to do and the amount of control you are to have over the lawyer's activities. Rule one is that the lawyer is working for you, not vice versa; and rule two is that you have a right to understand the reason for every minute of the lawyer's time that will be billed to you.

b. Conscientiousness

Your lawyer must be willing to agree to have you regularly consulted on all phases of the case and to promptly return your phone calls. Although nothing leads to a ruinous relationship faster than bad communication, too few lawyers keep their clients well posted. Lawyers faced with complaints about their lousy client contact habits often reply that many clients call or expect too much. But since the client is paying for the lawyer's time, this seems like a pretty weak excuse. Our experience tells us that the usual reason lawyers don't return phone calls is that they have neglected some facet of the case and simply don't want to face the client.

Your lawyer must also be willing to follow through on your case to its completion. This one is tricky to monitor, since it involves predicting the future. However, as long as good communication is established at the outset, there's an improved chance that your lawyer will give you good service.

4. Find a Lawyer Who is Open to Dispute Resolution Alternatives

In recent years many lawyers have discovered that there often are better ways to resolve disputes than the old "haul 'em into court" technique. The two most common of these alternative approaches are arbitration and mediation. When you search for an attorney, make sure that the attorney is fully up to speed on these private, fast, inexpensive and often successful techniques and is willing to help you explore them as a potential way to solve your problem. Arbitration and mediation are discussed in Chapter 12, If Someone Infringes Your Mark, Section D, Step 6. ■

Appendix

International Schedule of Classes of Goods and Services

U.S. Schedule of Classes of Goods and Services

Descriptions of Goods and Services (From USTA—International Classes)

State Trademark Agencies and Statutes

Patent and Trademark Depository Libraries

Trademark/Service Mark Application, Principal Register, With Declaration

Allegation of Use for Intent-to-Use Application, With Declaration

Request for Extension of Time Under 37 CFR 2.89, to File a Statement of Use, With Declaration

Combined Declaration of Use and Incontestability Under Sections 8 & 15 of the Trademark Act of 1946, as Amended

Application for Renewal of Registration of a Mark Under Section 9 of the Trademark Act of 1946, as Amended

Sample Request to Divide Application

Sample Assignment

International Schedule of Classes of Goods and Services

Goods

1. Chemical products used in industry, science, photography, agriculture, horticulture, forestry; artificial and synthetic resins; plastics in the form of powders, liquids or pastes, for industrial use; manures (natural and artificial); fire extinguishing compositions; tempering substances and chemical preparations for soldering; chemical substances for preserving foodstuffs; tanning substances; adhesive substances used in industry.

2. Paints, varnishes, lacquers; preservatives against rust and against deterioration of wood; colouring matters, dyestuffs; mordants; natural resins; metals in foil and powder form for painters and decorators.

3. Bleaching preparations and other substances for laundry use; cleaning, polishing, scouring and abrasive preparations; soaps; perfumery, essential oils, cosmetics, hair lotions; dentifrices.

4. Industrial oils and greases (other than oils and fats and essential oils); lubricants; dust laying and absorbing compositions; fuels (including motor spirit) and illuminants; candles, tapers, night lights and wicks.

5. Pharmaceutical, veterinary, and sanitary substances; infants' and invalids' foods; plasters, material for bandaging; material for stopping teeth, dental wax, disinfectants; preparations for killing weeds and destroying vermin.

6. Unwrought and partly wrought common metals and their alloys; anchors, anvils, bells, rolled and cast building materials; rails and other metallic materials for railway tracks; chains (except driving chains for vehicles); cables and wires (nonelectric); locksmiths' work; metallic pipes and tubes; safes and cash boxes; steel balls; horseshoes; nails and screws; other goods in nonprecious metal not included in other classes; ores.

7. Machines and machine tools; motors (except for land vehicles); machine couplings and belting (except for land vehicles); large size agricultural implements; incubators.

8. Hand tools and instruments; cutlery, forks and spoons; side arms.

9. Scientific, nautical, surveying and electrical apparatus and instruments (including wireless), photographic, cinematographic, optical, weighing, measuring, signalling, checking (supervision), life-saving and teaching apparatus and instruments; coin or counterfreed apparatus; talking machines; cash registers; calculating machines; fire extinguishing apparatus.

10. Surgical, medical, dental, and veterinary instruments and apparatus (including artificial limbs, eyes and teeth).

11. Installations for lighting, heating, steam generating, cooking, refrigerating, drying, ventilating, water supply, and sanitary purposes.

12. Vehicles; apparatus for locomotion by land, air or water.

13. Firearms; ammunition and projectiles; explosive substances; fireworks.

14. Precious metals and their alloys and goods in precious metals or coated therewith (except cutlery forks and spoons); jewelry, precious stones, horological and other chronometric instruments.

15. Musical instruments (other than talking machines and wireless apparatus).

16. Paper and paper articles, cardboard and cardboard articles; printed matter, newspaper and periodicals, books; bookbinding material; photographs; stationery, adhesive materials (stationery): artists' materials; paint brushes; typewriters and office requisites (other than furniture); instructional and teaching material

(other than apparatus); playing cards; printers' type and cliches (stereotype).

17. Gutta percha, india rubber, balata and substitutes, articles made from these substances and not included in other classes; plastics in the form of sheets, blocks and rods, being for use in manufacture; materials for packing. stopping or insulating; asbestos, mica and their products; hose pipes (nonmetallic).

18. Leather and imitations of leather, and articles made from these materials and not included in other classes; skins, hides; trunks and travelling bags; umbrellas, parasols and walking sticks; whips, harness and saddlery.

19. Building materials, natural and artificial stone, cement, lime, mortar, plaster and gravel; pipes or earthenware or cement; roadmaking materials; asphalt, pitch and bitumen; portable buildings; stone monuments; chimney pots.

20. Furniture, mirrors, picture frames; articles (not included in other classes) of wood, cork, reeds, cane, wicker, horn, bone, ivory, whalebone, shell, amber, mother-of-pearl, meerschaum, celluloid, substitutes for all these materials, or of plastics.

21. Small domestic utensils and containers (not of precious metals, or coated therewith); combs and sponges; brushes (other than paint brushes); brushmaking materials; instruments and material for cleaning purposes, steel wool; unworked or semi-worked glass (excluding glass used in building); glassware, porcelain and earthenware, not included in other classes.

22. Ropes, string, nets, tents, awnings, tarpaulins, sails, sacks; padding and stuffing materials (hair, kapok, feathers, seaweed, etc.); raw fibrous textile materials.

23. Yarns, threads.

24. Tissues (piece goods); bed and table covers; textile articles not included in other classes.

25. Clothing, including boots, shoes and slippers.

26. Lace and embroidery, ribbons and braid; buttons, press buttons, hooks and eyes, pins and needles; artificial flowers.

27. Carpets, rugs, mats and matting; linoleums and other materials for covering existing floors; wall hangings (nontextile).

28. Games and playthings; gymnastic and sporting articles (except clothing); ornaments and decorations for Christmas trees.

29. Meats, fish, poultry and game; meat extracts; preserved, dried and cooked fruits and vegetables; jellies, jams; eggs, milk and other dairy products; edible oils and fats; preserves, pickles.

30. Coffee, tea, cocoa, sugar, rice, tapioca, sago, coffee substitutes; flour, and preparations made from cereals; bread, biscuits, cakes, pastry and confectionery, ices; honey, treacle; yeast, baking powder; salt, mustard, pepper, vinegar, sauces, spices; ice.

31. Agricultural, horticultural and forestry products and grains not included in other classes; living animals; fresh fruits and vegetables; seeds; live plants and flowers; foodstuffs for animals, malt.

32. Beer, ale and porter; mineral and aerated waters and other nonalcoholic drinks; syrups and other preparations for making beverages.

33. Wines, spirits and liqueurs.

34. Tobacco, raw or manufactured; smokers' articles; machines.

Services

35. Advertising and business.

36. Insurance and financial.

37. Construction and repair.

38. Communication.

39. Transportation and Storage.

40. Material treatment.

41. Education and entertainment.

42. Miscellaneous.

U.S. Schedule of Classes of Goods and Services

(a) Goods:

1. Raw or partly prepared materials
2. Receptacles
3. Baggage, animal equipments, portfolios, and pocketbooks
4. Abrasives and polishing materials
5. Adhesives
6. Chemicals and chemical compositions
7. Cordage
8. Smokers' articles, not including tobacco products
9. Explosives, firearms, equipments, and projectiles
10. Fertilizers
11. Inks and inking materials
12. Construction materials
13. Hardware and plumbing and steam-fitting supplies
14. Metals and metal castings and forgings
15. Oils and greases
16. Paints and painters' materials
17. Tobacco products
18. Medicines and pharmaceutical preparations
19. Vehicles
20. Linoleum and oiled cloth
21. Electrical apparatus, machines, and supplies
22. Games, toys, and sporting goods
23. Cutlery, machinery, and tools and parts thereof
24. Laundry appliances and machines
25. Locks and safes
26. Measuring and scientific appliances
27. Horological instruments
28. Jewelry and precious metalware
29. Brooms, brushes, and dusters
30. Crockery, earthenware, and porcelain
31. Filters and refrigerators
32. Furniture and upholstery
33. Glassware
34. Heating, lighting, and ventilating apparatus
35. Belting, hose, machinery packing, and non-metallic tires
36. Musical instruments and supplies
37. Paper and stationery
38. Prints and publications
39. Clothing
40. Fancy goods, furnishings, and notions
41. Canes, parasols, and umbrellas
42. Knitted, netted, and textile fabrics, and substitutes therefore
43. Thread and yarn
44. Dental, medical, and surgical appliances
45. Soft drinks and carbonated waters
46. Foods and ingredients of foods
47. Wines
48. Malt beverages and liquors
49. Distilled alcoholic liquors
50. Merchandise not otherwise classified
51. Cosmetics and toilet preparations
52. Detergents and soaps

(b) Services:

100. Miscellaneous
101. Advertising and business
102. Insurance and financial
103. Construction and repair
104. Communications
105. Transportation and storage
106. Material treatment
107. Education and entertainment

Descriptions of Goods and Services (From USTA—International Classes)*

Goods

Class 1: Chemicals

Chemicals used in industry, science and photography as well as in agriculture, horticulture and forestry; unprocessed artificial resins, unprocessed plastics; manures; fire extinguishing compositions; tempering and soldering preparations; chemical substances for preserving foodstuffs; tanning substances; adhesives used in industry.

This class includes mainly chemical products used in industry, science and agriculture, including those which go to the making of products belonging to other classes.

Includes, in particular: compost; salt for preserving other than for foodstuffs.

Does not include, in particular: chemical products for use in medical science (Cl. 5); fungicides, herbicides and preparations for destroying vermin (Cl. 5); raw natural resins (Cl. 2); salt for preserving foodstuffs (Cl. 30); adhesives for stationery purposes (Cl. 16); straw mulch (Cl. 31).

Class 2: Paints

Paints, varnishes, lacquers; preservatives against rust and against deterioration of wood; colourants; mordants; raw natural resins; metals in foil and powder form for painters, decorators, printers and artist.

This class includes mainly paints, colourants and preparations used for the protection against corrosion.

Includes, in particular: paints, varnishes and lacquers for industry, handicrafts and arts; dyestuffs for clothing; colourants for foodstuffs and beverages.

Does not include, in particular: laundry blueing (Cl. 3); cosmetic dyes (Cl. 3); insulating paints and varnishes (Cl. 17); paint boxes (articles for use in school) (Cl. 16); unprocessed artificial resins (Cl. 1); mordants for seed (Cl. 5).

Class 3: Cosmetics and cleaning preparations

Bleaching preparations and other substances for laundry use; cleaning, polishing, scouring and abrasive preparations; soaps; perfumery, essential oils, cosmetics, hair lotions; dentifrices.

This class includes mainly cleaning preparations and toilet preparations.

Includes, in particular: deodorants for personal use; sanitary preparations being toiletries.

Does not include, in particular: chemical chimney cleaners (Cl. 1); de-greasing preparations for use in manufacturing processes (Cl. 1); sharpening stones and grindstones (handtools) (Cl. 8); deodorants other than for personal use (Cl. 5).

Class 4: Lubricants and fuels

Industrial oils and greases; lubricants; dust absorbing, wetting and binding compositions; fuels (including motor spirit) and illuminants; candles, wicks.

This class includes mainly industrial oils and greases, fuels and illuminants.

Does not include, in particular: certain special industrial oils and greases (consult the Alphabetical List of Goods).

Class 5: Pharmaceuticals

Pharmaceutical, veterinary and sanitary preparations; dietetic substances adapted for medical use, food for babies; plasters, materials for dressings; material for stopping teeth, dental wax; disinfectants; preparations for destroying vermin; fungicides, herbicides.

* Adapted from *The Trademark Manual of Examining Procedure,* published by the U.S. Trademark and Patent Office.

This class includes mainly pharmaceuticals and other preparations for medical purposes.

Includes, in particular: sanitary preparations for medical purposes and for personal hygiene; deodorants other than for personal use; cigarettes without tobacco, for medical purposes.

Does not include, in particular: sanitary preparations being toiletries (Cl. 3); deodorants for personal use (Cl. 3); supportive bandages (Cl. 10).

Class 6: Metal goods

Common metals and their alloys; metal building materials; transportable buildings of metal; materials of metal for railway tracks; non-electric cables and wires of common metal; ironmongery, small items of metal hardware; pipes and tubes of metal; safes; goods of common metal not included in other classes; ores.

This class includes mainly unwrought and partly wrought common metals as well as simple products made of them.

Does not include, in particular: mercury, antimony, alkaline and alkaline-earth metals (Cl. 1); metals in foil and powder form for painters, decorators, printers and artists (Cl. 2); bauxite (Cl. 1).

Class 7: Machinery

Machines and machine tools; motors (except for land vehicles); machine coupling and belting (except for land vehicles); agricultural implements; incubators for eggs.

This class includes mainly machines, machine tools, engines and motors.

Does not include, in particular: certain special machines and machine tools (consult the Alphabetical List of Goods); motors for land vehicles and their parts (Cl. 12); hand tools and implements, hand operated (Cl. 8).

Class 8: Hand tools

Hand tools and implements (hand operated); cutlery, forks and spoons; side arms; razors.

This class includes mainly hand operated implements used as tools in the respective professions.

Includes, in particular: cutlery of precious metals; electric razors and clippers (hand instruments).

Does not include, in particular: certain special instruments (consult the Alphabetical List of Goods); machine tools and implements driven by a motor (Cl. 7); surgical cutlery (Cl. 10); paperknives (Cl. 16); fencing weapons (Cl. 28).

Class 9: Electrical and scientific apparatus

Scientific, nautical, surveying, electric, photographic, cinematographic, optical, weighing, measuring, signalling, checking (supervision), life-saving and teaching apparatus and instruments; apparatus for recording, transmission or reproduction of sound or images; magnetic data carriers, recording discs; automatic vending machines and mechanisms for coin-operated apparatus; cash registers, calculating machines and data processing equipment; fire-extinguishing apparatus.

Includes, in particular: apparatus and instruments for scientific research in laboratories; apparatus and instruments for controlling ships, such as apparatus and instruments, for measuring and for transmitting orders; the following electrical apparatus and instruments:

a. certain electrothermic tools and apparatus, such as electric soldering irons, electric flat irons which, if they were not electric, would belong to Class 8;

b. apparatus and devices which, if not electrical, would be listed in various classes, i.e., electrically heated cushions (not for medical purposes), electric kettles, electrically heated clothing and other articles worn on the body, cigarlighters for automobiles;

c. electrical apparatus for the household, used for cleaning (electric suction-cleaners and floor polishers for domestic use) which, if not electrical, would belong to Class 21

protractors; punched card office machines; amusement apparatus adapted for use with television receivers only.

Does not include, in particular: the following electrical apparatus and instruments:

a. electromechanical apparatus for the kitchen (grinders and mixers for foodstuffs, fruitpresses, electrical coffee mills, etc.), and certain other apparatus and instruments driven by an electrical motor, all coming under Class 7;

b. electric razors and clippers (hand instruments) (Cl. 8); electric toothbrushes and combs (Cl. 21);

c. electrically heated blankets (Cl. 10); electrical apparatus for space heating or for the heating of liquids, for cooking, ventilating, etc. (Cl. 11);

clocks and watches and other chronometric instruments (Cl. 14); control clocks (Cl. 14).

Class 10: Medical apparatus

Surgical, medical, dental and veterinary apparatus and instruments, artificial limbs, eyes and teeth; orthopedic articles; suture materials.

This class includes mainly medical apparatus, instruments and articles.

Includes, in particular: special furniture for medical use; hygienic rubber articles (consult the Alphabetical List of Goods); supportive bandages.

Class 11: Environmental control apparatus

Apparatus for lighting, heating, steam generating, cooking, refrigerating, drying, ventilating, water supply and sanitary purposes.

Includes, in particular: air conditioning apparatus; electric foot-warmers; electric cooking utensils.

Does not include, in particular: steam producing apparatus (parts of machines) (Cl. 7); electric kettles (Cl. 9).

Class 12: Vehicles

Vehicles; apparatus for locomotion by land, air or water.

Includes, in particular: engines for land vehicles; transmission couplings and belting for land vehicles; air cushion vehicles.

Does not include, in particular: certain parts of vehicles (consult the Alphabetical List of Goods); railway material of metal (Cl. 6); engines, transmission couplings and belting other than for land vehicles (Cl. 7).

Class 13: Firearms

Firearms; ammunition and projectiles; explosives; fireworks.

This class includes mainly firearms and pyrotechnical products.

Does not include, in particular: matches (Cl. 34).

Class 14: Jewelry

Precious metals and their alloys and goods in precious metals or coated therewith, not included in other classes; jewelry, precious stones; horological and chronometric instruments.

This class includes mainly precious metals, goods in precious metals and, in general jewelry, clocks and watches.

Includes, in particular: jewelry (i.e., imitation jewelry and jewelry of precious metal and stones); cuff links, tie pins; objects of art fashioned in bronze.

Does not include, in particular: certain goods in precious metals (classified according to their function or purpose), for example: metals in foil and powder form for painters, decorators. printers and artists (Cl. 2); amalgam of gold for dentists (Cl. 5); cutlery (Cl. 8); electric contacts (Cl. 9); writing pens of gold (Cl. 16); objects of art not in precious metal nor in bronze are classified according to the material of which they consist.

Class 15: Musical Instruments

Musical instruments.

Includes, in particular: mechanical pianos and their accessories; musical boxes; electrical and electronical musical instruments.

Does not include, in particular: apparatus for the recording, transmission, amplification and reproduction of sound (Cl. 9).

Class 16: Paper goods and printed matter

Paper, cardboard and goods made from these materials, not included in other classes; printed matter; bookbinding material, photographs; stationery; adhesives for stationery or household purposes; artists' materials; paint brushes; type-writers and office requisites (except furniture); instructional and teaching material (except apparatus); plastic materials for packaging (not included in other classes); playing cards; printers' type; printing blocks.

This class includes mainly paper, goods made from that material and office requisites.

Includes, in particular: paper knives; duplicators; plastic sheets, sacks and bags for wrapping and packaging.

Does not include, in particular: certain goods made of paper and cardboard (consult the Alphabetical List of Goods); colours (Cl. 2); hand tools for artists (for example: spatulas, sculptors' chisels) (Cl. 8).

Class 17: Rubber goods

Rubber, gutta-percha, gum, asbestos, mica and goods made from these materials and not included in other classes; plastics in extruded form for use in manufacture; packing, stopping and insulating materials; flexible pipes, not of metal.

This class includes mainly electrical, thermal and acoustic insulating materials and plastics, being for use in manufacture in the form of sheets, blocks and rods.

Includes, in particular: rubber material for re-capping tyres; padding and stuffing materials of rubber or plastics; floating anti-pollution barriers.

Class 18: Leather goods

Leather and imitations of leather, and goods made of these materials and not included in other classes; animal skins, hides; trunks and travelling bags; umbrellas, parasols and walking sticks; whips; harness and saddlery.

This class includes mainly leather, leather imitations, travel goods not included in other classes and saddlery.

Does not include, in particular: clothing, footwear, headgear (consult the Alphabetical List of Goods).

Class 19: Non-metallic building materials

Building materials (non-metallic); non-metallic rigid pipes for building; asphalt, pitch and bitumen; non-metallic transportable buildings; monuments, not of metal.

This class includes mainly non-metallic building materials.

Includes, in particular: semi-worked woods (for example: beams, planks, panels); veneers; building glass (for example: floor slabs, glass tiles); glass granules for marking out roads; letter boxes of masonry.

Does not include, in particular: cement preservatives and cement-waterproofing preparations (Cl. 1); fireproofing preparations (Cl. 1).

Class 20: Furniture and articles not otherwise classified

Furniture, mirrors, picture frames; goods (not included in other classes) of wood, cork, reed, cane, wicker, horn, bone, ivory, whalebone, shell, amber, mother-of-pearl, meerschaum and substitutes for all these materials, or of plastics.

This class includes mainly furniture and its parts and plastic goods, not included in other classes.

Includes, in particular: metal furniture and furniture for camping; bedding (for example: mattresses, spring mattresses, pillows); looking glasses and furnishing or toilet mirrors; registration number plates not of metal; letter boxes not of metal or masonry.

Does not include, in particular: certain special types of mirrors, classified according to their function or purpose (consult the Alphabetical List of Goods); special furniture for laboratories (Cl. 9); special furniture for medical use (Cl. 10); bedding linen (Cl. 24); eiderdowns (Cl. 24).

Class 21: Housewares and glass

Household or kitchen utensils and containers (not of precious metal or coated therewith); combs and sponges; brushes (except paint brushes); brush-making materials; articles for cleaning purposes; steelwool; unworked or semi-worked glass (except glass used in building); glassware, porcelain and earthenware not included in other classes.

This class includes mainly small, hand-operated, utensils and apparatus for household and kitchen use as well as toilet utensils, glassware and articles in porcelain.

Includes, in particular: utensils and containers for household and kitchen use, for example: kitchen utensils, pails, and pans of iron, aluminum, plastics and other materials, small hand-operated apparatus for mincing, grinding, pressing, etc.; candle extinguishers, not of precious metal; electric combs; electric toothbrushes; dish stands and decanter stands.

Does not include, in particular: small apparatus for mincing, grinding, pressing, etc., driven by electricity (Cl. 7); cooking utensils, electric (Cl. 11); razors and shaving apparatus, clippers (hand instruments), metal implements and utensils for manicure and pedicure (Cl. 8); cleaning preparations, soaps, etc. (Cl. 3); certain goods made of glass, porcelain and earthenware (consult the Alphabetical List of Goods); toilet mirrors (Cl. 20).

Class 22: Cordage and fibers

Ropes, string, nets, tents, awnings, tarpaulins, sails, sacks and bags (not included in other classes); padding and stuffing materials (except of rubber or plastics); raw fibrous textile materials.

This class includes mainly rope and sail manufacture products, padding and stuffing materials and raw fibrous textile materials.

Includes, in particular: cords and twines in natural or artificial textile fibres, paper or plastics.

Does not include, in particular: strings for musical instruments (Cl. 15); certain nets, sacs and bags (consult the Alphabetical List of Goods).

Class 23: Yarns and threads

Yarns and threads, for textile use.

Class 24: Fabrics

Textiles and textile goods, not included in other classes; bed and table covers.

This class includes mainly textiles (piece goods) and textile covers for household use.

Includes, in particular: bedding linen of paper.

Does not include, in particular: certain special textiles (consult the Alphabetical List of Goods); electrically heated blankets (Cl. 10); table linen of paper (Cl. 16); horse blankets (Cl. 18).

Class 25: Clothing

Clothing, footwear, headgear.

Does not include, in particular: certain clothing and footwear for special use (consult the Alphabetical List of Goods).

Class 26: Fancy goods

Lace and embroidery, ribbons and braid; buttons, hooks and eyes, pins and needles; artificial flowers.

This class includes mainly dressmakers' articles.

Includes, in particular: slide fasteners.

Does not include, in particular: certain special types of hooks (consult the Alphabetical List of Goods); certain special types of needles (consult the Alphabetical List of Goods); yarns and threads for textile use (Cl. 23).

Class 27: Floor coverings

Carpets, rugs, mats and matting, linoleum and other materials for covering existing floors; wall hangings (non-textile).

This class includes mainly products intended to be added as furnishings to previously constructed floors and walls.

Class 28: Toys and sporting goods

Games and playthings; gymnastic and sporting articles not included in other classes; decorations for Christmas trees.

Includes, in particular: fishing tackle; equipment for various sports and games.

Does not include, in particular: playing cards (Cl. 16); diving equipment (Cl. 9); clothing for gymnastics and sports (Cl. 25); fishing nets (Cl.

22); Christmas tree candles (Cl. 4); electrical lamps (garlands) for Christmas trees (Cl. 11); confectionery and chocolate decorations for Christmas trees (Cl. 30); amusement apparatus adapted for use with television receivers only (Cl. 9).

Class 29: Meat and processed foods

Meat, fish, poultry and game; meat extracts; preserved, dried and cooked fruits and vegetables; jellies, jams; eggs, milk and milk products; edible oils and fats; salad dressings; preserves.

This class includes mainly foodstuffs of animal origin as well as vegetables and other horticultural comestible products which are prepared for consumption or conservation.

Includes, in particular: mollusca and crustacea (living as well as not living); milk beverages (milk predominating).

Does not include, in particular: living animals (Cl. 31); certain foodstuffs of plant origin (consult the Alphabetical List of Goods); baby food (Cl. 5); dietetic substances adapted for medical use (Cl. 5); fertilized eggs for hatching (Cl. 31); foodstuffs for animals (Cl. 31).

Class 30: Staple foods

Coffee, tea, cocoa, sugar, rice, tapioca, sago, artificial coffee; flour and preparations made from cereals, bread, pastry and confectionery, ices; honey, treacle; yeast, baking-powder; salt, mustard; vinegar, sauces (except salad dressings); spices; ice.

This class includes mainly foodstuffs of plant origin prepared for consumption or conservation as well as auxiliaries intended for the improvement of the flavour of food.

Includes, in particular: beverages with coffee, cocoa or chocolate base, cereals prepared for human consumption (for example: oat flakes and those made of other cereals).

Does not include, in particular: certain foodstuffs of plant origin (consult the Alphabetical List of Goods); salt for preserving other than for foodstuffs (Cl. 1); medicinal teas and dietetic substances adapted for medical use (Cl. 5); baby food (Cl. 5); raw cereals (Cl. 31); foodstuffs for animals (Cl. 31).

Class 31: Natural agricultural products

Agricultural, horticultural and forestry products and grains not included in other classes; living animals; fresh fruits and vegetables; seeds, natural plants and flowers; foodstuffs for animals, malt.

This class includes mainly land products not having been subjected to any form of preparation for consumption, living animals and plants as well as foodstuffs for animals.

Includes, in particular: raw woods; raw cereals; fertilized eggs for hatching.

Does not include, in particular: semi-worked woods (Cl. 19); rice (Cl. 30); tobacco (Cl. 34); cultures of micro-organisms and leeches for medical purposes (Cl. 5); fishing bait (Cl. 28); mollusca and crustacea (living as well as not living) (Cl. 29).

Class 32: Light beverages

Beers; mineral and aerated waters and other non-alcoholic drinks; fruit drinks and fruit juices; syrups and other preparations for making beverages.

This class includes mainly non-alcoholic beverages, as well as beer.

Includes, in particular: de-alcoholised drinks.

Does not include, in particular: beverages for medical purposes (Cl. 5); milk beverages (milk predominating) (Cl. 29); beverages with coffee, cocoa or chocolate base (Cl. 30).

Class 33: Wine and spirits

Alcoholic beverages (except beers).

Does not include, in particular: medicinal drinks (Cl. 5); de-alcoholised drinks (Cl. 32).

Class 34: Smokers' articles

Tobacco; smokers' articles; matches.

Includes, in particular: tobacco substitutes (not for medical purposes).

Does not include, in particular: certain smokers' articles in precious metal (Cl. 14) (consult the Alphabetical List of Goods); cigarettes without tobacco, for medical purposes (Cl.5).

Services

Class 35: Advertising and business

This class includes mainly services rendered by persons or organizations principally with the object of:

1. help in the working or management of a commercial undertaking, or
2. help in the management of the business affairs or commercial functions of an industrial or commercial enterprise, as well as services rendered by advertising establishments primarily undertaking communications to the public, declarations or announcements by all means of diffusion and concerning all kinds of goods or services.

Includes, in particular: services consisting of the registration, transcription, composition, compilation, transmission or systematization of written communications and registrations, and also the exploitation or compilation of mathematical or statistical data; services of advertising agencies and services such as the distribution of prospectuses, directly or through the post, or the distribution of samples. This class may refer to advertising in connection with other services, such as, those concerning bank loans or advertising by radio.

Does not include, in particular: activity of an enterprise the primary function of which is the sale of goods, i.e., of a so-called commercial enterprise; services such as evaluations and reports of engineers which do not directly refer to the working or management of affairs in a commercial or industrial enterprise (consult the Alphabetical List of Services); professional consultations and the drawing up of plans not connected with the conduct of business (Cl. 42).

Class 36: Insurance and financial

This class includes mainly services rendered in financial and monetary affairs and services rendered in relation to insurance contracts of all kinds.

Includes, in particular: services relating to financial or monetary affairs comprise the following:

a. services of all the banking establishments, or institutions connected with them such as exchange brokers or clearing services;
b. services of credit institutions other than banks such as co-operative credit associations, individual financial companies, lenders, etc.;
c. services of "investment trusts," of holding companies;
d. services of brokers dealing in shares and property;
e. services connected with monetary affairs vouched for by trustees;
f. services rendered in connection with the issue of travelers' cheques and letters of credit; services of realty administrators of buildings, i.e., services of letting or valuation, or financing; services dealing with insurance such as services rendered by agents or brokers engaged in insurance, services rendered to insurers and insured, and insurance underwriting services.

Class 37: Construction and repair

This class includes mainly services rendered by contractors or subcontractors in the construction or making of permanent buildings, as well as services rendered by persons or organisations engaged in the restoration of objects to their original condition or in their preservation without altering their physical or chemical properties.

Includes, in particular: services relating to the construction of buildings, roads, bridges, dams or transmission lines and services of undertakings specializing in the field of construction such as those of painters, plumbers, heating installers or roofers; services auxiliary to construction services like inspections of construction plans; services consisting of hiring of tools or building materials; repair services, i.e. services which undertake to put any object into good condition after wear, damage, deterioration or partial destruction (restoration of an existing building or another object that has become imperfect and is to be restored to its original condition); various repair services such as those in the fields of electricity, furniture, instruments, tools, etc.; services of maintenance for preserving an object in its original condition without changing any of its properties (for the difference between this class and Class 40 see the explanatory note of Class 40).

Does not include, in particular: services consisting of storage of goods such as clothes or vehicles (Cl. 39); services connected with dyeing of cloth or clothes (Cl. 40).

Class 38: Communication

This class includes mainly services allowing at least one person to communicate with another by a sensory means. Such services include those which:

1. allow a person to talk to another,
2. transmit messages from one person to another, and
3. place a person in oral or visual communication with another (radio and television).

Includes, in particular: services which consist essentially of the diffusion of radio or television programmes.

Does not include, in particular: radio advertising services (Cl. 35).

Class 39: Transportation and storage

This class includes mainly services rendered in transporting people or goods from one place to another (by rail, road, water, air or pipeline) and services necessarily connected with such transport, as well as services relating to the storing of goods in a warehouse or other building for their preservation or guarding.

Includes, in particular: services rendered by companies exploiting stations, bridges, railroad ferries, etc., used by the transporter; services connected with the hiring of transport vehicles; services connected with maritime tugs, unloading, the functioning of ports and docks and the salvaging of wrecked ships and their cargoes; services connected with the functioning of airports; services connected with the packaging and parcelling of goods before dispatch; services consisting of information about journeys or the transport of goods by brokers and tourist agencies, information relating to tariffs, timetables and methods of transport; services relating to the inspection of vehicles or goods before transport.

Does not include, in particular: services relating to advertising transport undertakings such as the distribution of prospectuses or advertising on the radio (Cl. 35); services relating to the issuing of travelers' cheques or letters of credit by brokers or travel agents (Cl. 36); services relating to insurances (commercial, fire or life) during the transport of persons or goods (Cl. 36); services rendered by the maintenance and repair of vehicles, nor the maintenance or repair of objects connected with the transport of persons or goods (Cl. 37); services relating to reservation of rooms in a hotel by travel agents or brokers (Cl. 42).

Class 40: Material treatment

This class includes mainly services not included in other classes, rendered by the mechanical or chemical processing or transformation of objects or inorganic or organic substances.

For the purposes of classification, the mark is considered a service mark only in cases where processing or transformation is effected for the account of another person. A mark is considered a trademark in all cases where the substance or object is marketed by the person who processed or transformed it.

Includes, in particular: services relating to transformation of an object or substance and any process involving a change in its essential properties (for example, dyeing a garment); consequently, a maintenance service, although usually in Class 37, is included in Class 40 if it entails such a change (for example, the chroming of motor vehicle bumpers); services of material treatment which may be present during production of any substance or object other than a building; for example, services which involve shaping, polishing by abrasion or metal coating.

Does not include, in particular: repair services (Cl. 37).

Class 41: Education and entertainment

This class contains mainly services rendered by persons or institutions in the development of the mental faculties of persons or animals, as well as services intended to entertain or to engage the attention.

Includes, in particular: services consisting of all forms of education of persons or training of animals; services having the basic aim of the entertainment, amusement or recreation of people.

Class 42: Miscellaneous

This class contains all services which could not be placed in other classes.

Includes, in particular: services rendered in procuring lodgings, rooms and meals, by hotels, boarding houses, tourist camps, tourist houses, dude ranches, sanatoria, rest homes and convalescence homes; services rendered by establishments essentially engaged in procuring food or drink prepared for consumption; such services can be rendered by restaurants, self-service restaurants, canteens, etc.; personal services rendered by establishments to meet individual needs; such services may include social escorts, beauty salons, hairdressing salons, funeral establishments or crematoria; services rendered by persons, individually or collectively, as a member of an organisation, requiring a high degree of mental activity and relating to theoretical or practical aspects of complex branches of human effort; the services rendered by these persons demand of them a deep and extensive university education or equivalent experience; such services rendered

by representatives of professions such as engineers, chemists, physicists, etc., are included in this class; services of travel agents or brokers ensuring hotel accommodation for travelers; services of engineers engaged in valuing, estimates, research and reports; services (not included in other classes) rendered by associations to their own members.

Does not include, in particular: professional services giving direct aid in the operations or functions of a commercial undertaking (Cl. 35); services for travelers rendered by travel agencies (Cl. 39); performances of singers or dancers in orchestras or operas (Cl. 41).

1401.02(b) Short Titles for International Trademark Classes [R-6]

The United States Patent and Trademark Office associates the following word titles with the respective international trademark class numbers:

Goods

1. Chemicals
2. Paints
3. Cosmetics and cleaning preparations
4. Lubricants and fuels
5. Pharmaceuticals
6. Metal goods
7. Machinery
8. Hand tools
9. Electrical and scientific apparatus
10. Medical apparatus
11. Environmental control apparatus
12. Vehicles
13. Firearms
14. Jewelry
15. Musical instruments
16. Paper goods and printed matter
17. Rubber goods
18. Leather goods
19. Non-metallic building materials
20. Furniture and articles not otherwise classified

21. Housewares and glass
22. Cordage and fibers
23. Yarns and threads
24. Fabrics
25. Clothing
26. Fancy goods
27. Floor coverings
28. Toys and sporting goods
29. Meats and processed foods
30. Staple foods
31. Natural agricultural products
32. Light beverages
33. Wine and spirits
34. Smokers' articles

Services

35. Advertising and business
36. Insurance and financial
37. Construction and repair
38. Communication
39. Transportation and storage
40. Material treatment
41. Education and entertainment
42. Miscellaneous

These short titles are not an official part of the international classification. Their purpose is to provide a means by which the general content of numbered international classes can be quickly identified. Therefore the titles selected consist of short terms which generally correspond to the major content of each class but which are not intended to be more than merely suggestive of the content. Because of their nature these titles will not necessarily disclose the classification of specific items. The titles are not designed to be used for classification but only as information to assist in the identification of numbered classes. For determining classification of particular goods and services and for full disclosure of the contents of international classes, it is necessary to refer to the Alphabetical List of Goods and Services and to the names of international classes and the

Explanatory Notes in the volume entitled "International Classification of Goods and Services for the Purposes of the Registration of Marks" (4th ed. 1983), published by the World Intellectual Property Organization (WIPO). The full names of international classes appear in Section 6.1 of the Trademark Rules of Practice. 37 CFR § 6.1.

The short titles are printed in the OFFICIAL GAZETTE in association with the international class numbers under MARKS PUBLISHED FOR OPPOSITION, Sections 1 and 2, under TRADEMARK REGISTRATIONS ISSUED, PRINCIPAL REGISTER, Section 1, and under SUPPLEMENTAL REGISTER, Sections 1 and 2.

The international trademark classification was adopted by the United States as its system of classification as of September 1, 1973 (*see* TMEP section 1401.02 and 911 O.G. TM 210, June 26, 1973).

The use of short titles was announced in the Official Gazette of July 16, 1974 (924 O.G. TM 155).

1401.03 Marking Classification on Copies in Search Library (R-5]

Beginning September 1, 1973 all published marks, registrations and renewals will be assigned not only an international class number but also a class number according to prior United States classification.

By placing a prior United States class number, as well as an international class number, on copies of registrations which are placed in the Trademark Search Library after the international classification becomes official, searching may continue to be conducted on the basis of the prior United States classification. Registration copies placed in the Search Library prior to September 1, 1973 bear prior United States class numbers, so that placing prior United States class numbers on registration copies on and after September 1, 1973 will provide continuity in the identification of classes on copies of registrations.

State Trademark Agencies and Statutes

Alabama

Ala. Code § 8-12-1 to 8-12-44
Secretary of State
Lands & Trademark Division
Room 528, State Office Building
Montgomery, AL 36130-7701
205-242-5325

Alaska

Alaska Stat. 45.50.101 et seq.
Department of Commerce and Economic Development
   Corporations Section
P.O. Box D
Juneau, AK 99811
907-465-2530

Arizona

Ariz. Rev. Stat. 44-1441 et seq.
Office of Secretary of State
1700 W. Washington St.
Phoenix, AZ 85007
602-542-6187

Arkansas

Ark. Code A. §§ 4-71-101 through 4-71-114
Secretary of State
State Capitol
Little Rock, AR 72201-1094
501-682-3405
FAX 501-682-3481

California

Cal. Bus. & Prof. Code §§ 14200 et seq.
Secretary of State
Attn: Trademark Unit
State of California
1230 "J" Street
Sacramento, CA 95814
916-445-9872

Colorado

Colo. Rev. Stat. §§ 7-70-102 to 7-70-113
Colorado Secretary of State
Corporations Office
1560 Broadway, Suite 200
Denver, CO 80202
303-894-2251

Connecticut

Conn. Gen. Stats, 621a §§ 35-11a et seq.
   and 622a §§ 35-18a et seq.
Secretary of State
Division of Corporations, UCC & Trademarks
Attn: Trademarks
State of Connecticut
30 Trinity St.
Hartford, CT 06106
203-566-1721

Delaware

6 Del. C. §§ 3301 et seq.
State of Delaware
Department of State
Division of Corporations
Attn: Trademark Filings
Townsend Building
P.O. Box 898
Dover, DE 19903
302-739-3073

Florida

Fla. Stat. ch. 495.011 et seq.
Corporation Records Bureau Division of Corporations
Department of State
P.O. Box 6327
Tallahassee, FL 32301
904-487-6051

Georgia

O.C.G.A. §§ 10-1-440 et seq.
Office of Secretary of State
State of Georgia
306 W. Floyd Towers
2 MLK Drive
Atlanta, GA 30334
404-656-2861

Hawaii

Hawaii Revised Stats. §§ 482 et seq.
Department of Commerce and Consumer Affairs
Business Registration Division
1010 Richards St.
Honolulu, HA 96813
808-586-2730

Idaho

Idaho Code §§ 48-501 et seq. (1979)
Secretary of State
Room 203
Statehouse
Boise, ID 83720
208-334-2300
FAX 208-334-2282

Illinois

Ill. Rev. Stat. 1987, ch. 140, §§ 8-22
Illinois Secretary of State
The Index Dept., Trademark Division
111 E. Monroe
Springfield, IL 62756
217-782-7017

Indiana

Indiana Code §§ 24-2-1-1 et seq.
Secretary of State of Indiana
Trademark Division
Rm 155, State House
Indianapolis, IN 46204
317-232-6540

Iowa

Iowa Code ch. 548
Secretary of State
Corporate Division
Hoover Bldg.
Des Moines, IA 50319
515-281-5204

Kansas

K.S.A. §§ 81-111 et seq.
Secretary of State
Statehouse Bldg., Room 235N
Topeka, KS 66612
913-296-2034

Kentucky

K.R.S. 365.560 to 365.625
Office of Kentucky Secretary of State
Frankfort, KY 40601
502-564-2848

Louisiana

La. Rev. Stat. Ann. 51:211 et seq.
Secretary of State
Corporation Division
P.O. Box 94125
Baton Rouge, LA 70804-9125
504-925-4704

Maine

10 M.R.S.A. §§ 1521-1532
State of Maine
Department of State
Division of Public Administration
State House Station 101
Augusta, ME 04333
207-287-4195

Maryland

Md. Ann. Code Art. 41, §§ 3-101 through 3-114
Secretary of State
State House
Annapolis, MD 21404
301-974-5521

Massachusetts

Mass. Laws Ann., Ch. 110 B, § 1-16.
Office of Secretary of State
Trademark Division
Rm. 1711
One Ashburton Place
Boston, MA 02108
617-727-8329

Michigan

MSA §§ 18.638(21) through 18.638 (36)
Michigan Department of Commerce
Corporations and Securities Bureau
Corporation Division
P.O. Box 30054
Lansing, MI 48909
517-334-6302

Minnesota

M.S.A. §§ 333.001-333.54
Secretary of State of Minnesota
Corporations Division
180 State Office Bldg.
St. Paul, MN 55155
612-296-3266

Mississippi

Miss. Code Ann., § 75-25-1 through 75-25-27
Office of Secretary of State
P.O. Box 1350
Jackson, MS 39215
601-359-1350
FAX 601-359-6344

Missouri

Missouri Rev. Stat. 1978 §§ 417.005 et seq.
Office of Secretary of State
Attn: Trademark Division
P.O. Box 778
Jefferson City, MO 65101
314-751-4756

Montana

Mont. Code Ann., §§ 30-13-301 et seq. (1985)
Office of Secretary of State
Montana State Capitol
Helena, MT 59620
406-444-3665
FAX 406-444-3976

Nebraska

R.R.S. 1943, ch. 87 §§ 87.101 et seq.
Secretary of State
State Capitol Bldg.
Lincoln, NE 68509
402-471-4079

Nevada

Nev. Rev. Stat. 600.040 et seq.
Secretary of State of Nevada
Capitol Complex
Carson City, NV 89710
702-687-5203

New Hampshire

RSA 350-A
Corporation Division
Office of Secretary of State
State House Annex
Concord, NH 03301
603-271-3244

New Jersey

N. J. Stat. § 56:3-13.1 through 56:3-13-19
Secretary of State
State House
CN-300
West State Street
Trenton, NJ 08625
609-984-1900

New Mexico

N.M.S.A. 57-3-1 through 57-3-14
Secretary of State
Capitol Bldg. Rm. 400
Santa Fe, NM 87503
505-827-3600

New York

N. Y. Gen. Bus. Law §§ 360 et seq.
Secretary of State
Department of State
Miscellaneous Records
162 Washington Avenue
Albany, NY 12231
518-473-2492

North Carolina

N.C.G.S. §§ 80-1 et seq.
Trademark Division
Office of Secretary of State
300 N. Salisbury Street
Raleigh, NC 27611
919-733-4161

North Dakota

N.D.C.C., ch. 47-22 through 47-22-13
Secretary of State
State Capitol
Bismark, ND 58505
701-328-4284
FAX 701-328-2992

Ohio

ORC, ch. 1329.54 through 1329.68
Secretary of State
Corporations Department
30 E. Broad St., 14th Floor
Columbus, OH 43215-0418
614-466-3910

Oklahoma

78 Okla. St. Ann. §§ 21 through 34
Office of the Secretary of State
State of Oklahoma
101 State Capitol Bldg.
Oklahoma City, OK 73105
405-521-3911

Oregon

ORS 647.005 through 647.105(i) and 647.115
Director, Corporation Division
Office of Secretary of State
158 12th Street N.E.
Salem, OR 97310-0210
503-986-2200

Pennsylvania

54 Pa. Cons. Stat. Ann. §§ 1101-1126
(Purdon 1987 Supp.)
Department of State
Corporation Bureau
308 North Office Bldg.
Harrisburg, PA 17120
717-787-1057

Puerto Rico

Title 10, Laws of P. R. Ann. §§ 191 through 215
Secretary of State of Puerto Rico
P.O. Box 3271
San Juan, PR 00904
809-722-2121, Ext. 337

Rhode Island

R. I. Gen. Laws §§ 6-2-1 through 6-2-18
Secretary of State
The Trademarks Division
100 No. Main St.
Providence, RI 02903
401-277-2340

South Carolina

S. C. Code Ann. §§ 39-15-1105 et seq.
Office of Secretary of State
P.O. Box 11350
Columbia, SC 29211
803-734-2158

South Dakota

SDCL ch 37-6-1 through 37-6-32
Secretary of State
State Capitol Bldg.
500 East Capitol
Pierre, SD 57501
605-773-3537

Tennessee

Tenn. Code Ann. §§ 47-25-501 et seq.
Secretary of State
Suite 500
James K. Polk Bldg.
Nashville, TN 37219
615-741-0531

Texas

Tex. Bus. & Com. Code § 16.01 through 16.28
Secretary of State
Corporations Section, Trademark Office
Box 13697, Capitol Station
Austin, TX 78711-3697
512-463-5576

Utah

U.C.A. 70-3-1 et seq.
Division of Corporations & Commercial Code
Heber M. Wells Bldg.
160 E. 300 South St
Salt Lake City, UT 84111
801-530-4849

Vermont

§ 9 V.S.A. §§ 2521 through 2532
Vermont Secretary of State
Corporations Division
Redstone Bldg, 26 Terrace St.
Mail: State Office Bldg.
Montpelier, VT 05602-2199
802-828-2386

Virginia

Va. Code §§ 59.1-77 et seq.
State Corp. Commission
Division of Securities and Retail Franchises
1220 Bank Street
Richmond, VA 23209
804-271-9051

Washington

R.C.W. 19.77.010 et seq.
Corporations Division
Office of Secretary of State
Republic Building—2nd Floor
505 E. Union St
Olympia, WA 98504
206-753-7120

West Virginia

W. Va. Code §§ 47-2-1- et seq. and §§ 47-3-1 et seq.
Secretary of State
Corporations Division
State Capitol
Charleston, WV 25305
304-558-8000

Wisconsin

Wisconsin Stat. §§ 132.01 et seq.
Secretary of State
Trademark Records
P.O. Box 7848
Madison, WI 53707
608-266-5653

Wyoming

W.S. §§ 40-1-101 et seq.
Office of Secretary of State
Corporation Division
Capitol Bldg.
Cheyenne, WY 82002
307-777-7311

Patent and Trademark Depository Libraries

Alabama	Auburn University Libraries	205-844-1747
	Birmingham Public Library	205-226-3620
Alaska	Anchorage: Z.J. Loussac Public Library	907-562-7323
Arizona	Tempe: Noble Library, Arizona State University	602-965-7010
Arkansas	Little Rock: Arkansas State Library	501-682-2053
California	Los Angeles Public Library	213-228-7220
	Sacramento: California State Library	916-654-0069
	San Diego Public Library	619-236-5813
	San Francisco Public Library	415-557-4488
	Santa Rosa: Bruce Sawyer Center (not a PTDL, but useful)	707-524-1773
	Sunnyvale Center for Innovation	408-730-7290
Colorado	Denver Public Library	303-640-6249
Connecticut	New Haven: Science Park Library	203-786-5447
Delaware	Newark: University of Delaware Library	302-831-2965
District of Columbia	Washington: Howard University Libraries	202-806-7252
Florida	Fort Lauderdale: Broward County Main Library	305-357-7444
	Miami: Dade Public Library	305-375-2665
	Orlando: Univ. of Central Florida Libraries	407-823-2562
	Tampa: Tampa Campus Library, University of South Florida	813-974-2726
Georgia	Atlanta: Price Gilbert Memorial Library, Georgia Institute of Technology	404-894-4508
Hawaii	Honolulu: Hawaii State Public Library System	808-586-3477
Idaho	Moscow: University of Idaho Library	208-885-6235
Illinois	Chicago Public Library	312-747-4450
	Springfield: Illinois State Library	217-782-5659
Indiana	Indianapolis: Marion County Public Library	317-269-1741
	West Lafayette: Purdue University Libraries	317-494-2872
Iowa	Des Moines: State Library of Iowa	515-281-4118
Kansas	Wichita: Ablah Library, Wichita State University	316-689-3155
Kentucky	Louisville Free Public Library	502-574-1611
Louisiana	Baton Rouge: Troy H. Middleton Library, Louisiana State University	504-388-2570
Maine	Orono: Raymond H. Fogler Library, University of Maine	207-581-1678
Maryland	College Park: Engineering and Physical Sciences Library, University of Maryland	301-405-9157
Massachusetts	Amherst: Physical Sciences Library, University of Massachusetts	413-545-1370
	Boston Public Library	617-536-5400, Ext. 265
Michigan	Ann Arbor: Engineering Transportation Library, University of Michigan	313-764-5298
	Big Rapids: Abigail S. Timme Library, Ferris State University	616-592-3602
	Detroit Public Library	313-833-1450
Minnesota	Minneapolis Public Library and Information Center	612-372-6570
Mississippi	Jackson: Mississippi Library Commission	601-359-1036

Reprinted with permission, from *Patent It Yourself*, by David Pressman (Nolo Press).

Missouri	Kansas City: Linda Hall Library	816-363-4600		Pennsylvania	Philadelphia, The Free Library of	215-686-5331
	St. Louis Public Library	314-241-2288, Ext. 390			Pittsburgh, Carnegie Library of	412-622-3138
Montana	Butte: Montana College of Mineral Science & Technology Library	406-496-4281			University Park: Pattee Library, Pennsylvania State University	814-865 4861
				Puerto Rico	Mayaguez General Library, University of Puerto Rico	not yet operational
Nebraska	Lincoln: Engineering Library, University of Nebraska	402-472-3411		Rhode Island	Providence Public Library	401-455-8027
Nevada	Reno: University of Nevada-Reno Library	702-784-6579		South Carolina	Clemson University Libraries	803-656-3024
New Hampshire	Durham: University of New Hampshire Library	603-862-1777		South Dakota	Rapid City: Devereaux Library, South Dakota School of Mines and Technology	605-394-6822
New Jersey	Newark Public Library	201-733-7782		Tennessee	Memphis & Shelby County Public Library and Information Center	901-725-8877
	Piscataway: Library of Science & Medicine, Rutgers University	908-445-2895			Nashville: Stevenson Science Library, Vanderbilt University	615-322-2775
New Mexico	Albuquerque: University of New Mexico General Library	505-277-4412		Texas	Austin: McKinney Engineering Library, University of Texas at Austin	512-495-4500
New York	Albany: New York State Library	518-474-5355				
	Buffalo and Erie County Public Library	716-858-7101			College Station: Sterling C. Evans Library, Texas A & M University	409-845-3826
	New York Public Library (The Research Libraries)	212-930-0917			Dallas Public Library	214-670-1468
					Houston: The Fondren Library, Rice University	713-527-8101, Ext. 2587
North Carolina	Raleigh: D.H. Hill Library, North Carolina State University	919-515-3280		Utah	Salt Lake City: Marriott Library, University of Utah	801-581-8394
North Dakota	Grand Forks: Chester Fritz Library, University of North Dakota	701-777-4888		Virginia	Richmond: James Branch Cabell Library, Virginia Commonwealth University	804-828-1104
Ohio	Cincinnati and Hamilton County, Public Library of	513-369-6936				
	Cleveland Public Library	216-623-2870		Washington	Seattle: Engineering Library, University of Washington	206-543-0740
	Columbus: Ohio State University Libraries	614-292-6175		West Virginia	Morgantown: Evansdale Library, West Virginia University	304-293-2510
	Toledo/Lucas County Public Library	419-259-5212		Wisconsin	Madison: Kurt F. Wendt Library, University of Wisconsin	608-262-6845
Oklahoma	Stillwater: Oklahoma State University Library	405-744-7086			Milwaukee Public Library	414-286-3051
Oregon	Salem: Oregon State Library	503-378-4239		Wyoming	Casper: National County Public Library	307-237-4935

TRADEMARK/SERVICE MARK APPLICATION, PRINCIPAL REGISTER, WITH DECLARATION	MARK (Word(s) and/or Design)	CLASS NO. (If known)

TO THE ASSISTANT COMMISSIONER FOR TRADEMARKS:

APPLICANT'S NAME:

APPLICANT'S MAILING ADDRESS:

(Display address exactly as it should appear on registration)

APPLICANT'S ENTITY TYPE: (**Check one** and supply requested information)

Individual - Citizen of (Country):

Partnership - State where organized (Country, if appropriate): _____
Names and Citizenship (Country) of General Partners: _____

Corporation - State (Country, if appropriate) of Incorporation:

Other (Specify Nature of Entity and Domicile):

GOODS AND/OR SERVICES:

Applicant requests registration of the trademark/service mark shown in the accompanying drawing in the United States Patent and Trademark Office on the Principal Register established by the Act of July 5, 1946 (15 U.S.C. 1051 et. seq., as amended) for the following goods/services (**SPECIFIC GOODS AND/OR SERVICES MUST BE INSERTED HERE**):

_____
_____
_____
_____
_____

BASIS FOR APPLICATION: (Check boxes which apply, **but never both the first AND second boxes,** and supply requested information related to each box checked.)

[ ] Applicant is using the mark in commerce on or in connection with the above identified goods/services. (15 U.S.C. 1051(a), as amended.) Three specimens showing the mark as used in commerce are submitted with this application.
- Date of first use of the mark in commerce which the U.S. Congress may regulate (for example, interstate or between the U.S. and a foreign country): _____
- Specify the type of commerce: _____
  (for example, interstate or between the U.S. and a specified foreign country)
- Date of first use anywhere (the same as or before use in commerce date): _____
- Specify manner or mode of use of mark on or in connection with the goods/services: _____
  (for example, trademark is applied to labels, service mark is used in advertisements)

[ ] Applicant has a bona fide intention to use the mark in commerce on or in connection with the above identified goods/services. (15 U.S.C. 1051(b), as amended.)
- Specify intended manner or mode of use of mark on or in connection with the goods/services: _____
  (for example, trademark will be applied to labels, service mark will be used in advertisements)

[ ] Applicant has a bona fide intention to use the mark in commerce on or in connection with the above identified goods/services, and asserts a claim of priority based upon a foreign application in accordance with 15 U.S.C. 1126(d), as amended.
- Country of foreign filing: _____ • Date of foreign filing: _____

[ ] Applicant has a bona fide intention to use the mark in commerce on or in connection with the above identified goods/services and, accompanying this application, submits a certification or certified copy of a foreign registration in accordance with 15 U.S.C 1126(e), as amended.
- Country of registration: _____ • Registration number: _____

NOTE: Declaration, on Reverse Side, MUST be Signed

PTO Form 1478 (REV 6/96)
OMB No. 0651-0009 (Exp. 06/30/98) There is no requirement to respond to this collection of information unless a currently valid OMB Number is displayed.

U.S. DEPARTMENT OF COMMERCE/Patent and Trademark Office

DECLARATION

The undersigned being hereby warned that willful false statements and the like so made are punishable by fine or imprisonment, or both, under 18 U.S.C. 1001, and that such willful false statements may jeopardize the validity of the application or any resulting registration, declares that he/she is properly authorized to execute this application on behalf of the applicant; he/she believes the applicant to be the owner of the trademark/service mark sought to be registered, or if the application is being filed under 15 U.S.C. 1051(b), he/she believes the applicant to be entitled to use such mark in commerce; to the best of his/her knowledge and belief no other person, firm, corporation, or association has the right to use the above identified mark in commerce, either in the identical form thereof or in such near resemblance thereto as to be likely, when used on or in connection with the goods/services of such other person, to cause confusion, or to cause mistake, or to deceive; and that all statements made of his/her own knowledge are true and that all statements made on information and belief are believed to be true.

_____   _____
DATE   SIGNATURE

_____   _____
TELEPHONE NUMBER   PRINT OR TYPE NAME AND POSITION

INSTRUCTIONS AND INFORMATION FOR APPLICANT

TO RECEIVE A FILING DATE, THE APPLICATION MUST BE COMPLETED AND SIGNED BY THE APPLICANT AND SUBMITTED ALONG WITH:

1. The prescribed **FEE ($245.00)** for each class of goods/services listed in the application;
2. A **DRAWING PAGE** displaying the mark in conformance with 37 CFR 2.52;
3. If the application is based on use of the mark in commerce, **THREE (3) SPECIMENS** (evidence) of the mark as used in commerce for each class of goods/services listed in the application. All three specimens may be the same. Examples of good specimens include: (a) labels showing the mark which are placed on the goods; (b) photographs of the mark as it appears on the goods, (c) brochures or advertisements showing the mark as used in connection with the services.
4. An **APPLICATION WITH DECLARATION** (this form) - The application must be signed in order for the application to receive a filing date. Only the following persons may sign the declaration, depending on the applicant's legal entity: (a) the individual applicant; (b) an officer of the corporate applicant; (c) one general partner of a partnership applicant; (d) all joint applicants.

SEND APPLICATION FORM, DRAWING PAGE, FEE, AND SPECIMENS (IF APPROPRIATE) TO:

Assistant Commissioner for Trademarks
Box New App/Fee
2900 Crystal Drive
Arlington, VA 22202-3513

Additional information concerning the requirements for filing an application is available in a booklet entitled **Basic Facts About Registering a Trademark,** which may be obtained by writing to the above address or by calling: (703) 308-HELP.

This form is estimated to take an average of 1 hour to complete, including time required for reading and understanding instructons, gathering necessary information, recordkeeping, and actually providing the information. Any comments on this form, including the amount of time required to complete this form, should be sent to the Office of Management and Organization, U.S. Patent and Trademark Office, U.S. Department of Commerce, Washington, D.C. 20231. Do NOT send completed forms to this address.

ALLEGATION OF USE FOR INTENT-TO-USE APPLICATION, WITH DECLARATION (Amendment To Allege Use/Statement Use)	MARK (Identify the mark)
	SERIAL NO.

TO THE ASSISTANT COMMISSIONER FOR TRADEMARKS:

APPLICANT NAME:

Applicant requests registration of the above-identified trademark/service mark in the United States Patent and Trademark Office on the Principal Register established by the Act of July 5, 1946 (15 U.S.C. §1051 *et seq.*, as amended). Three specimens per class showing the mark as used in commerce and the prescribed fees are submitted with this statement.

Applicant is using the mark in commerce on or in connection with the following goods/services (CHECK ONLY ONE):

☐ (a) those in the application or Notice of Allowance; **OR**

☐ (b) those in the application or Notice of Allowance **except** (if goods/services are to be deleted, list the goods/services to be **deleted**): _____

_____

_____

Date of first use in commerce which the U.S. Congress may regulate:_____
Specify type of commerce: _____
                    (for example, interstate and/or commerce between the U.S. and a foreign country)
Date of first use anywhere:_____

Specify manner or mode of use of mark on or in connection with the goods/services: (for example, trademark is applied to labels, service mark is used in advertisements):_____

_____

_____

The undersigned, being hereby warned that willful false statements and the like so made are punishable by fine or imprisonment, or both, under 18 U.S.C. §1001, and that such willful false statements may jeopardize the validity of the application or any resulting registration, declares that he/she is properly authorized to execute this Amendment to Allege Use or Statement of Use on behalf of the applicant; he/she believes the applicant to be the owner of the trademark/service mark sought to be registered; the trademark /service mark is now in use in commerce; and all statements made of his/her own knowledge are true and all statements made on information and belief are believed to be true.

_____   _____
Date   Signature

_____   _____
Telephone Number   Type or Print Name and Position

Check here if Request to Divide is being submitted with this statement (if Applicant wishes to proceed to publication or registration with certain goods/services on or in connection with which it has used the mark in commerce and retain an active application for any remaining goods/services, a divisional application and fee are required. 37 C.F.R. §2.87)

PLEASE SEE REVERSE FOR MORE INFORMATION

INSTRUCTIONS AND INFORMATION FOR APPLICANT

In an application based upon a bona fide intention to use a mark in commerce, **the Applicant must use its mark in commerce before a registration will be issued.** After use begins, the applicant must file the Allegation of Use. If the Allegation of Use is filed before the mark is approved for publication in the *Official Gazette* it is treated under the statute as **an Amendment to Allege Use (AAU).** If it is filed after the Notice of Allowance is issued, it is treated under the statute as **a Statement of Use (SOU).** The Allegation of Use cannot be filed during the time period between approval of the mark for publication in the *Official Gazette* and the issuance of the Notice of Allowance. The difference between the AAU and SOU is the time at which each is filed during the process.

Additional requirements for filing this Allegation of Use:

1) the fee of $100.00 per class of goods/services **(please note that fees are subject to change, usually on October 1 of each year)**; and
2) three (3) specimens of the mark as used in commerce for each class of goods/services (for example, photographs of the mark as it appears on the goods, labels for affixation on goods, advertisements showing the mark as used in connection with services).

• The Applicant may list dates of use for one item in each class of goods/services identified in the Allegation of Use. The Applicant must have used the mark in commerce on all the goods/services in the class, however, it is only necessary to list the dates of use for one item in each class.

• Only the following persons may sign the verification on this form: (a) the individual applicant; (b) an officer of a corporate applicant; (c) one general partner of a partnership applicant; (d) all joint applicants.

• The goods/services in the Allegation of Use must be the same as those specified in the application or Notice of Allowance. The Applicant may limit or clarify the goods/services, but cannot add to or otherwise expand the identification specified in the application or Notice of Allowance. If goods/services are deleted, they may **not** be reinserted at a later time.

• Amendments to Allege Use are governed by Trademark Act §1(c), 15 U.S.C. §1051(c) and Trademark Rule 2.76, 37 C.F.R. §2.76. Statements of Use are governed by Trademark Act §1(d), 15 U.S.C. §1051(d) and Trademark Rule 2.88, 37 C.F.R. §2.88.

> **MAIL COMPLETED FORM TO:**
>
> **ASSISTANT COMMISSIONER FOR TRADEMARKS**
> **BOX AAU/SOU**
> **2900 CRYSTAL DRIVE**
> **ARLINGTON, VIRGINIA 22202-3513**

Please note that the filing date of a document in the Patent and Trademarks Office is the date of receipt in the Office, not the date of deposit of the mail. 37 C.F.R. §1.6. To avoid lateness due to mail delay, use of the certificate of mailing set forth below, is encouraged.

COMBINED CERTIFICATE OF MAILING/CHECKLIST

Before filing this form, please make sure to complete the following:

☐ three specimens, per class have been enclosed;
☐ the filing fee of $100 (subject to change as noted above), per class has been enclosed; and
☐ the declaration has been signed by the appropriate party

CERTIFICATE OF MAILING

I do hereby certify that the foregoing are being **deposited** with the United States Postal Service as first class mail, postage prepaid, in an envelope addressed to the Assistant Commissioner for Trademarks, 2900 Crystal Drive, Arlington, VA 22202-3513, on _____ (date).

_____
Signature

_____
Print or Type Name of Person Signing Certificate

_____
Date of Deposit

This form is estimated to take 15 minutes to complete including time required for reading and understanding instructions, gathering necessary information, record keeping and actually providing the information. Any comments on the amount of time you require to complete this form should be sent to the Office of Management and Organization, U.S. Patent and Trademark Office. U.S. Department of Commerce, Washington, D.C. 20231. Do not send forms to this address.

REQUEST FOR EXTENSION OF TIME TO FILE A STATEMENT OF USE, WITH DECLARATION	MARK (Identify the mark)
	SERIAL NO.

TO THE ASSISTANT SECRETARY AND COMMISSIONER OF PATENTS AND TRADEMARKS:

APPLICANT NAME:

NOTICE OF ALLOWANCE MAILING DATE:

Applicant requests a six-month extension of time to file the Statement of Use under 37 CFR 2.89 in this application.

Applicant has a continued bona fide intention to use the mark in commerce on or in connection with the following goods/ services: (Check One below)

☐ Those goods/services identified in the Notice of Allowance.

☐ Those goods/services identified in the Notice of Allowance except: (Identify goods/services to be **deleted** from application)

_____

_____

_____

This is the_____ request for an Extension of Time following mailing of the Notice of Allowance.
　　　　　(Specify: First - Fifth)

If this is not the first request for an Extension of Time, check one box below. If the first box is checked explain the circumstance(s) of the non-use in the space provided:

☐　　Applicant has not used the mark in commerce yet on all goods/services specified in the Notice of Allowance; however, applicant has made the following ongoing efforts to use the mark in commerce on or in connection with each of the goods/services specified above:

_____

_____

If additional space is needed, please attach a separate sheet to this form

☐　　Applicant believes that it has made valid use of the mark in commerce, as evidenced by the Statement of Use submitted with this request; however, if the Statement of Use does not meet minimum requirements under 37 CFR 2.88(e), applicant will need additional time in which to file a new statement.

The undersigned being hereby warned that willful false statements and the like so made are punishable by fine or imprisonment, or both, under 18 U.S.C. 1001, and that such willful false statements may jeopardize the validity of the application or any resulting registration, declares that he/she is properly authorized to execute this Request for an Extension of Time to File a Statement of Use on behalf of the applicant; and that all statements made of his/her own knowledge are true and all statements made on information and belief are believed to be true.

_____
Date

_____
Signature

_____
Telephone Number

_____
Type or Print Name and Position

Check here if Request to Divide is being submitted with this statement (if Applicant wishes to proceed to publication or registration with certain goods/services on or in connection with which it has used the mark in commerce and retain an active application for any remaining goods/services, a divisional application and fee are required. 37 C.F.R. §2.87)

PTO Form 1581 (REV. 6-96)
OMB No. 0651-0009
Exp. (06/30/98)　　There is no requirement to respond to this collection of information unless a currently valid OMB Number is displayed.

U.S. Department of Commerce/Patent and Trademark Office

INSTRUCTIONS AND INFORMATION FOR APPLICANT

Applicant must file a Statement of Use within six months after the mailing of the Notice of Allowance based upon a bona fide intention to use a mark in commerce, UNLESS, within that same period, applicant submits a request for a six-month extension of time to file the Statement of Use. The written request **must**:

(1)   be received in the PTO within six months after the issue date of the Notice of Allowance,

(2)   include applicant's verified statement of continued bona fide intention to use the mark in commerce,

(3)   specify the goods/services to which the request pertains as they are identified in the Notice of Allowance, and

(4)   include a fee of $100 for each class of goods/services **(please note that fees are subject to change, usually on October 1 of each year).**

Applicant may request four further six-month extensions of time. No extensions may extend beyond 36 months from the issue date of the Notice of Allowance. Each further request must be received in the PTO within the previously granted six-month extension period and must include, in addition to the above requirements, a showing of **GOOD CAUSE**. This good cause showing must include:

(1)   applicant's statement that the mark has not been used in commerce yet on all the goods or services specified in the Notice of Allowance with which applicant has a continued bona fide intention to use the mark in commerce, **and**

(2)   applicant's statement of ongoing efforts to make such use, which may include the following: (a) product or service research or development, (b) market research, (c) promotional activities, (d) steps to acquire distributors, (e) steps to obtain required governmental approval, or (f) similar specified activity.

Applicant may submit one additional six-month extension request during the existing period in which applicant files the Statement of Use, unless the granting of this request would extend the period beyond 36 months from the issue date of the Notice of Allowance. As a showing of good cause for such a request, applicant should state its belief that applicant has made valid use of the mark in commerce, as evidenced by the submitted Statement of Use, but that if the Statement is found by the PTO to be defective, applicant will need additional time in which to file a new statement of use.

Only the following person may sign the declaration of the Request for Extension of Time: (a) the individual applicant; (b) an officer of corporate applicant: (c) one general partner of partnership applicant; (d) all joint applicants.

MAILING INSTRUCTIONS

MAIL COMPLETED FORM TO:

ASSISTANT COMMISSIONER FOR TRADEMARKS
BOX ITU
2900 CRYSTAL DRIVE
ARLINGTON, VIRGINIA 22202-3513

Please note that the filing date of a document in the Patent and Trademarks Office is the date of receipt in the Office, not the date of deposit of the mail. 37 C.F. R. §1.6. To avoid lateness due to mail delay, use of the certificate of mailing set forth below is encouraged.

CERTIFICATE OF MAILING

I do hereby certify that this correspondence is being **deposited** with the United States Postal Service as first class mail, postage prepaid, in an envelope addressed to the Assistant Commissioner for Trademarks, 2900 Crystal Drive, Arlington, VA 22202-3513, on _____ (date).

_____
Signature

_____
Print or Type Name of Person Signing Certificate

_____
Date of Deposit

This form is estimated to take 15 minutes to complete including time required for reading and understanding instructions, gathering necessary information, record keeping and actually providing the information. Any comments on the amount of time you require to complete this form should be sent to the Office of Management and Organization, U.S. Patent and Trademark Office, U.S. Department of Commerce, Washington, D.C. 20231. Do not send forms to this address.

<table>
<tr><td>

COMBINED DECLARATION OF USE AND INCONTESTABILITY UNDER SECTIONS 8 & 15[1] OF THE TRADEMARK ACT OF 1946, AS AMENDED

</td><td colspan="2">

MARK (Identify the mark)

</td></tr>
<tr><td></td><td>

REGISTRATION NO.

</td><td>

DATE OF REGISTRATION:

</td></tr>
</table>

TO THE ASSISTANT SECRETARY AND COMMISSIONER OF PATENTS AND TRADEMARKS:

REGISTRANT'S NAME:[2]

REGISTRANT'S CURRENT MAILING ADDRESS: _____

_____

_____

GOODS AND/OR SERVICES AND USE IN COMMERCE STATEMENT:

The mark shown in Registration No. _____ , owned by the above-identified registrant, has been in

continuous use in _____ commerce for five consecutive years from the date of registration or the
(type of)[3]

date of publication under §12(c)[4] to the present, on or in connection with all of the goods and/or services

identified in the registration, (*except* for the following)[5]_____

_____ ;

as evidenced by the attached specimen(s)[6] showing the mark as currently used. There has been no final

decision adverse to registrant's claim of ownership of such mark for such goods or services, or to registrant's

right to register the same or to keep the same on the register; and there is no proceeding involving said

rights pending and not disposed of either in the Patent and Trademark Office or in the courts.

DECLARATION

The undersigned being hereby warned that willful false statements and the like so made are punishable by fine or imprisonment, or both, under 18 U.S.C. 1001, and that such willful false statements may jeopardize the validity of this document, declares that he/she is properly authorized to execute this document on behalf of the registrant; he/she believes the registrant to be the owner of the above identified registration; the trademark/service mark is in use in commerce; and all statements made of his/her own knowledge are true and all statements made on information and belief are believed to be true.

_____   _____
Date   Signature

_____   _____
Telephone Number   Print or Type Name and Position
                                                       [if applicable][7]

FOOTNOTES

1. If you do not have five years of continuous use, you should file a Section 8 affidavit only. Please see PTO Form #1583.

2. The present owner of the registration must file this form between the 5th and 6th year after registration. If ownership of the registration has changed since the registration date, provide supporting documentation if available or a verified explanation. The present owner should refer to itself as the registrant.

3. "Type of Commerce" must be specified as "interstate," "territorial," "foreign," or such other commerce as may lawfully be regulated by Congress. Foreign registrants must specify commerce which Congress may regulate, using wording such as "foreign commerce between the U.S. and a foreign country."

4. Use this combined form only when the five year period of continuous use, required for Section 15, (1) occurs between the 5th and 6th year after registration on the Principal Register, or (2) after publication under §12(c) as is required for Section 8.

5. List only those goods and/or services for which registrant is no longer using the mark. You should fill in this blank only if you are no longer using the mark on all the goods or services in the registration.

6. A specimen showing current use of the registered mark for at least one product or service in each class of the registration must be submitted with this form. Examples of specimens are tags or labels for goods, and advertisements for services. The registration number should be printed directly on the specimen.

7. If the present owner is an individual, the individual should sign the declaration.

8. If the present owner is a partnership, the declaration should be signed by a General Partner.

9. If the present owner is a corporation or similar juristic entity, the declaration should be signed by an officer of the corporation/entity. Please print or type the officer title of the person signing the declaration.

NOTE: If the registration is owned by more than one party, as joint owners, each owner must sign this declaration.

PTO Notification

You should receive written notification from the PTO of either the acceptance or rejection of this post registration document. If you do not receive written notification from the PTO within six months after filing, you may wish to telephone the Trademark Status Line at (703) 305-8747 or the Post Registration Division at (703) 308-9500.

FEES

For each declaration under Sections 8 & 15, the required fee is $200.00 per international class. Please be aware that our fees may change. Changes, if any, are normally effective October 1 of each year. If this declaration is intended to cover less than the total number of classes in the registration, please specify the classes for which the declaration is submitted. The declaration, with appropriate fee(s), should be sent to:

BOX POST REG
FEE
Assistant Commissioner for Trademarks
2900 Crystal Drive
Arlington, Virginia 22202-3513

MAILING INSTRUCTION BOX

You can ensure timely filing of this form by following the procedure described in 37 CFR 1.10 as follows: (1) on or before the due date for filing this form, deposit the completed form with the U.S. Post Office using the "Express Mail Post Office to Addressee" Service; (2) include a certificate of "Express Mail" under 37 CFR 1.10. Papers properly mailed under 37 CFR 1.10 are considered received by the PTO on the date that they are deposited with the Post Office.

When placing the certificate directly on the correspondence, use the following language:

Certificate of Express Mail Under 37 CFR 1.10

"Express Mail" mailing label number: _____

Date of Deposit: _____

I hereby certify that this paper and fee is being deposited with the United States Postal Service "Express Mail Post Office to Addressee" service under 37 CFR 1.10 on the date indicated above and is addressed to the Assistant Commissioner for Trademarks, 2900 Crystal Drive, Arlington, Virginia 22202-3513.

_____   _____
(Typed or printed name of person mailing paper & fee)   (Signature of person mailing paper & fee)

This form is estimated to take 15 minutes to complete. Time will vary depending upon the needs of the individual case. Any comments on the amount of time you require to complete this form should be sent to the Office of Management and Organization, U.S. Patent and Trademark Office, U.S. Department of Commerce, Washington, D.C. 20231, and to the Office of Information and Regulatory Affairs, Office of Management and Budget, Washington, D.C. 20503. DO NOT SEND FORMS TO EITHER OF THESE ADDRESSES.

APPLICATION FOR RENEWAL OF REGISTRATION OF A MARK UNDER **SECTION 9** OF THE TRADEMARK ACT OF 1946, AS AMENDED	MARK (Identify the mark)	
	REGISTRATION NO.	DATE OF REGISTRATION:

TO THE ASSISTANT SECRETARY AND COMMISSIONER OF PATENTS AND TRADEMARKS:

REGISTRANT'S NAME:[1]

REGISTRANT'S CURRENT MAILING ADDRESS: _____

_____

_____

GOODS AND/OR SERVICES AND USE IN COMMERCE STATEMENT:

The mark shown in Registration No. _____ owned by the above-identified registrant is still in use in

_____ commerce on or in connection with all of the goods and/or services identified in the
(type of)[2]

registration, (***except*** for the following)[3] _____

_____

as evidenced by the attached specimen(s)[4] showing the mark as currently used.

DECLARATION

The undersigned being hereby warned that willful false statements and the like so made are punishable by fine or imprisonment, or both, under 18 U.S.C. 1001, and that such willful false statements may jeopardize the validity of this document, declares that he/she is properly authorized to execute this document on behalf of the registrant; he/she believes the registrant to be the owner of the above identified registration; the trademark/service mark is in use in commerce; and all statements made of his/her own knowledge are true and all statements made on information and belief are believed to be true.

_____

Date

_____

Telephone Number

_____

Signature

_____

Print or Type Name and Position
[if applicable][5]

FOOTNOTES

1. The present owner of the registration must file this form within 6 months prior to the expiration of the registration term. The form may also be filed within a 3 month grace period following the expiration of the registration term upon payment of the late fee. If ownership of the registration has changed since the registration date, provide supporting documentation if available or a verified explanation. The present owner should refer to itself as the registrant.

2. "Type of Commerce" must be specified as "interstate," "territorial," "foreign," or such other commerce as may lawfully be regulated by Congress. Foreign registrants must specify commerce which Congress may regulate, using wording such as "foreign commerce between the U.S. and a foreign country."

3. List only those goods and/or services for which registrant is no longer using the mark. You should fill in this blank only if you are no longer using the mark on all the goods or services in the registration.

4. A specimen showing current use of the registered mark for at least one product or service in each class of the registration must be submitted with this form. Examples of specimens are tags or labels for goods, and advertisements for services. The registration number should be printed directly on the specimen.

5. If the present owner is an individual, the individual should sign the declaration.

6. If the present owner is a partnership, the declaration should be signed by a General Partner.

7. If the present owner is a corporation or similar juristic entity, the declaration should be signed by an officer of the corporation/entity. Please print or type the officer title of the person signing the declaration.

NOTE: If the registration is owned by more than one party, as joint owners, each owner must sign this declaration.

PTO Notification

You should receive written notification from the PTO of either the acceptance or rejection of this post registration document. If you do not receive written notification from the PTO within six months after filing, you may wish to telephone the Trademark Status Line at (703) 305-8747 or the Post Registration Division at (703) 308-9500.

FEES

For each renewal application under Section 9, the required fee is $300.00 per class. Please be aware that our fees may change. Changes, if any, are normally effective October 1 of each year. If filed during the three month grace period a late fee of $100.00 per class must also be submitted. If this renewal application is intended to cover less than the total number of classes in the registration, please specify the classes for which the renewal application is submitted. The renewal application, with appropriate fee(s), should be sent to:

BOX POST REG
FEE
Assistant Commissioner for Trademarks
2900 Crystal Drive
Arlington, Virginia 22202-3513

MAILING INSTRUCTION BOX

You can ensure timely filing of this form by following the procedure described in 37 CFR 1.10 as follows: (1) on or before the due date for filing this form, deposit the completed form with the U.S. Post Office using the "Express Mail Post Office to Addressee" Service; (2) include a certificate of "Express Mail" under 37 CFR 1.10. Papers properly mailed under 37 CFR 1.10 are considered received by the PTO on the date that they are deposited with the Post Office.

When placing the certificate directly on the correspondence, use the following language:

Certificate of Express Mail Under 37 CFR 1.10

"Express Mail" mailing label number: _____
Date of Deposit: _____
I hereby certify that this paper and fee is being deposited with the United States Postal Service "Express Mail Post Office to Addressee" service under 37 CFR 1.10 on the date indicated above and is addressed to the Assistant Commissioner for Trademarks, 2900 Crystal Drive, Arlington, Virginia 22202-3513.

_____   _____
(Typed or printed name of person mailing paper & fee)   (Signature of person mailing paper & fee)

This form is estimated to take 15 minutes to complete. Time will vary depending upon the needs of the individual case. Any comments on the amount of time you require to complete this form should be sent to the Office of Management and Organization, U.S. Patent and Trademark Office, U.S. Department of Commerce, Washington, D.C. 20231, and to the Office of Information and Regulatory Affairs, Office of Management and Budget, Washington, D.C. 20503. **DO NOT SEND FORMS TO EITHER OF THESE ADDRESSES.**

United States Department of Commerce
Patent and Trademark Office

Applicant

Mark   Trademark Law Office _____

Serial Number   Trademark Attorney _____

Filed _____

Assistant Commissioner for Trademarks
Box ITV
2900 Crystal Drive
Arlington, VA 22202-3513

Request to Divide Application

The applicant hereby requests that the application identified above be divided as follows:

Please retain in the original application the following goods/services—(use the language of the original application insofar as possible).

Please include in the new, divided application the following goods/services—(they should be different from and should not overlap, those remaining in the original application).

(Check one)

☐ Enclosed is a check in payment of the filing fee for the divided application.

☐ The divided application includes all goods or services in a single class presented in the original, parent application; therefore the applicant submits that no filing fee is due or required.

DATED: Respectfully,

                                            _____

Telephone Number:

Address:

Assignment

_____ (Assignor),
name of registrant

of _____ ,
mailing address

has adopted, used and is using a mark which is registered in the United States Patent and

Trademark Office, Registration No._____ [get number from registration certificate],

dated_____ [get date from registration certificate].

_____ (Assignee)
name of person or company which will be the new owner of the mark

of _____ ,
mailing address

wants to acquire the mark and the registration thereof.

    For good and valuable consideration, receipt of which is hereby acknowledged, Assignor hereby

assigns to Assignee all right, title and interest in and to the mark, together with the goodwill of the

business symbolized by the mark, and the above identified registration.

_____
Signature of Assignor

_____
Title [if assignor is a business, list official title of person signing]

State of _____)

County of _____) ss.

)

On this _____ day of _____ , _____ before me appeared
month   year

_____ , the person who signed this instrument,
Assignor's name

who acknowledged that he/she signed it as a free act on his/her own behalf (or on behalf of the

identified entity with authority to do so).

_____
Signature of notary public

NOTE: This form is only valid when the assignee is a United States resident or company.

Index

CATALOG

...more from Nolo Press

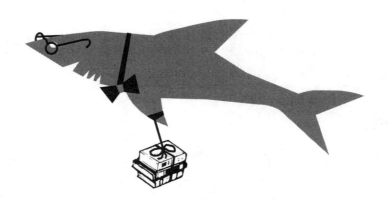

		PRICE	CODE

BUSINESS

		PRICE	CODE
	The California Nonprofit Corporation Handbook	$29.95	NON
	The California Professional Corporation Handbook	$34.95	PROF
	The Employer's Legal Handbook	$29.95	EMPL
	Form Your Own Limited Liability Company	$34.95	LIAB
☐	Hiring Independent Contractors: The Employer's Legal Guide, (Book w/Disk—PC)	$29.95	HICI
☐	How to Form a CA Nonprofit Corp.—w/Corp. Records Binder & PC Disk	$49.95	CNP
☐	How to Form a Nonprofit Corp., Book w/Disk (PC)—National Edition	$39.95	NNP
☐	How to Form Your Own Calif. Corp.—w/Corp. Records Binder & Disk—PC	$39.95	CACI
	How to Form Your Own California Corporation	$29.95	CCOR
☐	How to Form Your Own Florida Corporation, (Book w/Disk—PC)	$39.95	FLCO
☐	How to Form Your Own New York Corporation, (Book w/Disk—PC)	$39.95	NYCO
☐	How to Form Your Own Texas Corporation, (Book w/Disk—PC)	$39.95	TCOR
	How to Handle Your Workers' Compensation Claim (California Edition)	$29.95	WORK
	How to Market a Product for Under $500	$29.95	UN500
	How to Mediate Your Dispute	$18.95	MEDI
	How to Write a Business Plan	$21.95	SBS
	The Independent Paralegal's Handbook	$29.95	PARA
	Legal Guide for Starting & Running a Small Business, Vol. 1	$24.95	RUNS
☐	Legal Guide for Starting & Running a Small Business, Vol. 2: Legal Forms	$29.95	RUNS2
	Marketing Without Advertising	$19.00	MWAD

☐ Book with disk
● Book with CD-ROM

		PRICE	CODE

□ The Partnership Book: How to Write a Partnership Agreement, (Book w/Disk—PC) ...... $34.95 PART

  Sexual Harassment on the Job .... $18.95 HARS

  Starting and Running a Successful Newsletter or Magazine .... $24.95 MAG

□ Taking Care of Your Corporation, Vol. 1, (Book w/Disk—PC) .... $29.95 CORK

□ Taking Care of Your Corporation, Vol. 2, (Book w/Disk—PC) $39.95 CORK2

  Tax Savvy for Small Business .... $28.95 SAVVY

  Trademark: Legal Care for Your Business and Product Name .... $29.95 TRD

  Wage Slave No More: The Independent Contractor's Legal Guide .... $34.95 WAGE

  Your Rights in the Workplace .... $19.95 YRW

CONSUMER

Fed Up With the Legal System: What's Wrong & How to Fix It .... $9.95 LEG

How to Win Your Personal Injury Claim .... $24.95 PICL

Nolo's Everyday Law Book .... $21.95 EVL

Nolo's Pocket Guide to California Law .... $11.95 CLAW

Trouble-Free Travel...And What to Do When Things Go Wrong .... $14.95 TRAV

ESTATE PLANNING & PROBATE

8 Ways to Avoid Probate (Quick & Legal Series) $15.95 PRO8

How to Probate an Estate (California Edition) .... $34.95 PAE

Make Your Own Living Trust .... $21.95 LITR

□ Nolo's Will Book, (Book w/Disk—PC) .... $29.95 SWIL

Plan Your Estate .... $24.95 NEST

The Quick and Legal Will Book .... $15.95 QUIC

Nolo's Law Form Kit: Wills .... $14.95 KWL

FAMILY MATTERS

A Legal Guide for Lesbian and Gay Couples .... $24.95 LG

California Marriage Law .... $19.95 MARR

Child Custody: Building Parenting Agreements that Work .... $24.95 CUST

Divorce & Money: How to Make the Best Financial Decisions During Divorce .... $26.95 DIMO

Get A Life: You Don't Need a Million to Retire Well .... $18.95 LIFE

The Guardianship Book (California Edition) .... $24.95 GB

□ Book with disk
● Book with CD-ROM

	PRICE	CODE
How to Adopt Your Stepchild in California	$22.95	ADOP
How to Do Your Own Divorce in California	$24.95	CDIV
How to Do Your Own Divorce in Texas	$19.95	TDIV
How to Raise or Lower Child Support in California	$18.95	CHLD
The Living Together Kit	$24.95	LTK
Nolo's Law Form Kit: Hiring Childcare & Household Help	$14.95	KCHLO
Nolo's Pocket Guide to Family Law	$14.95	FLD
Practical Divorce Solutions	$14.95	PDS
Smart Ways to Save Money During and After Divorce	$14.95	SAVMO

GOING TO COURT

	PRICE	CODE
Collect Your Court Judgment (California Edition)	$24.95	JUDG
How to Seal Your Juvenile & Criminal Records (California Edition)	$24.95	CRIM
How to Sue For Up to 25,000...and Win!	$29.95	MUNI
Everybody's Guide to Small Claims Court in California	$18.95	CSCC
Everybody's Guide to Small Claims Court (National Edition)	$18.95	NSCC
Fight Your Ticket ... and Win! (California Edition)	$19.95	FYT
How to Change Your Name (California Edition)	$24.95	NAME
Mad at Your Lawyer	$21.95	MAD
Represent Yourself in Court: How to Prepare & Try a Winning Case	$29.95	RYC
The Criminal Law Handbook: Know Your Rights, Survive the System	$24.95	KYR

HOMEOWNERS, LANDLORDS & TENANTS

	PRICE	CODE
The Deeds Book (California Edition)	$16.95	DEED
Dog Law	$14.95	DOG
⌨ Every Landlord's Legal Guide (National Edition)	$34.95	ELLI
Every Tenant's Legal Guide	$24.95	EVTEN
For Sale by Owner (California Edition)	$24.95	FSBO
Homestead Your House (California Edition)	$9.95	HOME
How to Buy a House in California	$24.95	BHCA
The Landlord's Law Book, Vol. 1: Rights & Responsibilities (California Edition)	$34.95	LBRT
The Landlord's Law Book, Vol. 2: Evictions (California Edition)	$34.95	LBEV
Leases & Rental Agreements (Quick & Legal Series)	$18.95	LEAR
Neighbor Law: Fences, Trees, Boundaries & Noise	$18.95	NEI
Safe Homes, Safe Neighborhoods: Stopping Crime Where You Live	$14.95	SAFE
Tenants' Rights (California Edition)	$19.95	CTEN
Stop Foreclosure Now in California	$29.95	CLOS

⌨ Book with disk

● Book with CD-ROM

	PRICE	CODE

HUMOR

	PRICE	CODE
29 Reasons Not to Go to Law School	$9.95	29R
Poetic Justice	$9.95	PJ

IMMIGRATION

	PRICE	CODE
How to Get a Green Card: Legal Ways to Stay in the U.S.A.	$24.95	GRN
U.S. Immigration Made Easy	$39.95	IMEZ

MONEY MATTERS

	PRICE	CODE
101 Law Forms for Personal Use: Quick and Legal Series (Book w/disk)	$24.95	101LAW
Chapter 13 Bankruptcy: Repay Your Debts	$29.95	CH13
Credit Repair (Quick & Legal Series)	$15.95	CREP
The Financial Power of Attorney Workbook	$24.95	FINPOA
How to File for Bankruptcy	$26.95	HFB
Money Troubles: Legal Strategies to Cope With Your Debts	$19.95	MT
Nolo's Law Form Kit: Personal Bankruptcy	$14.95	KBNK
Stand Up to the IRS	$24.95	SIRS

PATENTS AND COPYRIGHTS

	PRICE	CODE
The Copyright Handbook: How to Protect and Use Written Works	$29.95	COHA
Copyright Your Software	$39.95	CYS
▣ License Your Invention (Book w/Disk)	$39.95	LICE
The Patent Drawing Book	$29.95	DRAW
Patent, Copyright & Trademark: A Desk Reference to Intellectual Property Law	$24.95	PCTM
Patent It Yourself	$44.95	PAT
▣ Software Development: A Legal Guide (Book with disk—PC)	$44.95	SFT
The Inventor's Notebook	$19.95	INOT

RESEARCH & REFERENCE

	PRICE	CODE
● Government on the Net, (Book w/CD-ROM—Windows/Macintosh)	$39.95	GONE
● Law on the Net, (Book w/CD-ROM—Windows/Macintosh)	$39.95	LAWN
Legal Research: How to Find & Understand the Law	$19.95	LRES
Legal Research Made Easy (Video)	$89.95	LRME

▣ Book with disk
● Book with CD-ROM

Special Upgrade Offer
Get 25% off the latest edition off your Nolo book

It's important to have the most current legal information. Because laws and legal procedures change often, we update our books regularly. To help keep you up-to-date we are extending this special upgrade offer. Cut out and mail the title portion of the cover of your old Nolo book and we'll give you 25% off the retail price of the NEW EDITION of that book when you purchase directly from us. For more information call us at 1-800-992-6656. This offer is to individuals only.

▣ Book with disk
● Book with CD-ROM

ORDER FORM

Code	Quantity	Title	Unit price	Total
		Subtotal		
		California residents add Sales Tax		
		Basic Shipping ($6.00 for 1 item; $7.00 for 2 or more)		
		UPS RUSH delivery $7.50–any size order*		
		TOTAL		

Name

Address

(UPS to street address, Priority Mail to P.O. boxes)

* Delivered in 3 business days from receipt of order.
S.F. Bay Area use regular shipping.

FOR FASTER SERVICE, USE YOUR CREDIT CARD AND OUR TOLL-FREE NUMBERS

Order 24 hours a day	1-800-992-6656
Fax your order	1-800-645-0895
e-mail	cs@nolo.com
General Information	1-510-549-1976
Customer Service	1-800-728-3555, Mon.-Fri. 9am-5pm, PST

METHOD OF PAYMENT

☐ Check enclosed
☐ VISA ☐ MasterCard ☐ Discover Card ☐ American Express

Account #   Expiration Date

Authorizing Signature

Daytime Phone

PRICES SUBJECT TO CHANGE.

VISIT OUR OUTLET STORES!

VISIT US ONLINE!

You'll find our complete line of books and software, all at a discount.

BERKELEY
950 Parker Street
Berkeley, CA 94710
1-510-704-2248

SAN JOSE
111 N. Market Street, #115
San Jose, CA 95113
1-408-271-7240

on the Internet
www.nolo.com

NOLO PRESS 950 PARKER ST., BERKELEY, CA 94710

"Nolo's home page is worth bookmarking."
—WALL STREET JOURNAL

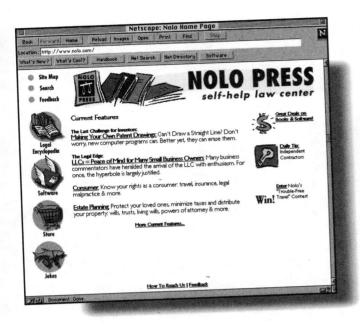

LEGAL INFORMATION ONLINE
www.nolo.com

24 HOURS A DAY

AT THE NOLO PRESS SELF-HELP LAW CENTER ON THE WEB, YOU'LL FIND:

○ Nolo's comprehensive Legal Encyclopedia, with links to other online resources

○ Downloadable demos of Nolo software and sample chapters of many Nolo books

○ An online law store with a secure online ordering system

○ Our ever-popular lawyer jokes

○ Discounts and other good deals,
our hilarious SHARK TALK game

THE NOLO NEWS

Stay on top of important legal changes with Nolo's quarterly magazine, *The Nolo News*. Start your free one-year subscription by filling out and mailing the response card in the back of this book. With each issue, you'll get legal news about topics that affect you every day, reviews of legal books by other publishers, the latest Nolo catalog, scintillating advice from Auntie Nolo and a fresh batch of our famous lawyer jokes.